D1001549

The United Nations Trusteeship System

The United Nations Trusteeship System

JAMES N. MURRAY, JR.

ILLINOIS STUDIES IN THE SOCIAL SCIENCES: *Volume 40*

THE UNIVERSITY OF ILLINOIS PRESS
URBANA, 1957

Second Printing

 LIBRARY OF CONGRESS CATALOG CARD NO. 57-6954.

To My Father

Contents

Introduction

This study has three purposes.

The first part describes the process by which the trusteeship system of the United Nations came into being. Starting with the League of Nations mandates system as a background, the development of trusteeship before and during the San Francisco Conference of 1945, decisions made by the Preparatory Commission at London in the same year, and the process of drafting the various trusteeship agreements are traced. The trust territory of Somaliland has been singled out for special consideration, in this connection, because the trusteeship agreement for the area differs radically from the others, and because the negotiations surrounding the decision to place that territory under trusteeship provide an excellent example of how the problem of the disposition of African territories can become enmeshed in the greater issues of world power politics.

Part II of the study is concerned with the regular functioning of the Trusteeship Council. The word "regular" is used, because no attempt has been made here to describe special problems with which the Council has been faced. That is, such questions as the drafting of a statute for Jerusalem and the problems raised by the refusal of the Union of South Africa to place the mandated area of South West Africa under trusteeship, while considered by the Council, are not part of the normal activities which the Council was designed to perform. The regular activities of the Council are centered around the supervision of the administration of each of the trust territories. To carry out this function the Council has been empowered to consider annual reports on the territories, submitted by each of the administering authorities, to send visiting missions to the territories, and to receive and consider petitions concerning the territories. Each of these devices of supervision is described following a brief survey of the general organization and procedure of the Council. Finally, since the Council is but one of six major bodies of the United Nations, the relationship of the Council to the other major organs is discussed.

In connection with the functioning of the trusteeship system it should be noted that it is possible to examine the question from at least two different points of view. That is, it is perfectly possible to be concerned primarily with the effects on a territory resulting from a status of trusteeship, and only secondarily on the process of how the Council reaches any substantive decision affecting the territory. But, from another point of view, the effect on the territories may be considered of secondary importance, while the central theme is the actual functioning of the international supervisory machinery involved. This study follows the latter course. In doing this, however, the actual conditions in the trust territories cannot be ignored, if only because one measure of the successful functioning of the trusteeship system is the degree to which the territories are being advanced along the lines indicated in the Charter. Consequently one chapter deals with the evolution of the system in terms of the political developments within some of the trust territories. But it should be emphasized that this is essentially a study of international organization, and it is the process of Council functioning which is considered of utmost importance.

From what has just been said, it can be seen that the primary emphasis of the study is one of description. Together with description, however, is the attempt to suggest, in passing, tentative conclusions as to the nature of the decision-making process in international organization. These conclusions are valid, of course, only for matters relating to trusteeship, but they are offered as possible hypotheses for broader studies of international organizations generally, and of the United Nations specifically. This constitutes the third purpose of the study.

The sources used have been almost exclusively documentary material on the League of Nations and especially on the United Nations. In addition, standard works on the mandates system such as Quincy Wright's *Mandates Under the League*, contemporary sources such as James F. Byrnes' *Speaking Frankly* and Cordell Hull's *Memoirs*, as well as newspaper accounts of various negotiations, have been consulted. The writer was also fortunate in being able to interview several people who have had direct access to information about the trusteeship system. These included Mr. Jack Harris, former member of the Trusteeship Division of the United Nations Secretariat, Mr. Benjamin Gerig, Director of the Office of Dependent Areas of the United States Department of State, and Mr. Henry Fosbrooke, a former District Commissioner in Tanganyika, among others. In the main, however, the goal has been to obtain the story of trusteeship from the official documents, and to rely on secondary sources and interviews only for background material or for information not revealed by the documents.

One of the difficulties connected with describing a going system is that in a sense any study is perpetually out of date. With this in mind, the writer arbitrarily stopped his research with the sixteenth session of the Council in the fall of 1955. The only exceptions to this concern some recent developments in Somaliland and the final disposition of

British Togoland which, because of its importance to the entire trusteeship system, has been traced through the summer of 1956.

In the pages that follow it is hoped that the reader will find, in addition to the formal description of the trusteeship system, the answers to these questions: What are the significant differences between the mandates and trusteeship systems? To what extent are the administrative duties of the Trusteeship Council influenced by the vicissitudes of the world political situation? What modifications in the functioning of the trusteeship system are observable, and what do these modifications portend for the future? What does the evolution of the system reveal concerning the attainment of self-government or independence for the trust territories? Finally, what does a study of the formation and functioning of the trusteeship system indicate concerning the nature of the general international decision-making process?

The study of trusteeship is valuable not only for the intrinsic importance of the subject itself, but also because it provides a microcosm of the general process of international politics. The clash and resolution of the various national policies, albeit over comparatively undramatic questions, is nowhere better illustrated nor more fully documented. It was with the twofold importance of the subject in mind that this study was written.

The writer is indebted to a number of people for numerous and helpful comments and suggestions. They include Mrs. Elaine Nierenberg, who gave freely of her time in typing the manuscript; Mr. Ben Imoh of Nigeria, who helped bring Africa a bit closer to the writer; and the writer's wife, who both helped to type the manuscript and acted as "the critical reader." Professor Clarence A. Berdahl, of the University of Illinois, supervised the writing of the study in its original form as a doctoral dissertation. For his thoughtful, precise, but always benevolent criticism, as well as for his constant encouragement, the writer expresses his heartfelt gratitude. It goes without saying that all deficiencies in the work are, however, the author's.

J. N. M., Jr.
State University of Iowa

Part I

Formation

CHAPTER ONE

The Mandates System[1]

It is obvious to even the casual student of the history of international affairs that the mandates system of the League of Nations was the precursor of, and to some extent served as a pattern for, the trusteeship system of the United Nations. While there are certain fundamental differences between the two systems, the essential feature of the mandates system—the administration of a dependent area by a state responsible in some way to an international organization for that administration—has remained in the provisions concerning trusteeship of the United Nations Charter. The question arises, then, what were the origins of the mandates system?

Formation. Too commonly mandates appear to be regarded as the outgrowth of humanitarian ideas which have been put into practice by government leaders.[2] Thus, in the words of one authority, there exists "the popular myth" that the mandates system was due "to the sudden welling up in the barren desert of European diplomacy of transatlantic idealism, bearing with it the new gospel of 'no annexation' and the welfare of native peoples." [3] Of course there had existed, prior to the mandates system, certain organizations whose aims could be designated humanitarian insofar as they espoused the amelioration of conditions among dependent peoples. And undoubtedly such terms as "sacred trust" and "self-government" had been used in relation to dependent peoples before these same phrases found their way into the Covenant of the League of Nations. But it is one thing to note that there were certain ideas and institutions pre-existent to the mandates system which were incorporated in it, and quite another to conclude from this that these precedents in and of themselves explain the origin of that system.

[1] This chapter is designed merely to explain the main elements of the formation and functioning of the League of Nations counterpart to the United Nations trusteeship system. The purpose is twofold: (1) to provide a description of the historical basis for trusteeship, and (2) to provide a basis for comparison between the two systems. For a detailed examination of the mandates system, see Quincy Wright, *Mandates Under the League*, and H. Duncan Hall, *Mandates, Dependencies and Trusteeship*.

[2] For examples of this approach see F. D. Lugard, *The Dual Mandate in British Tropical Africa*, pp. 17-18, and A. M. Margalith, *The International Mandates*, pp. 22, 52.

[3] Hall, p. 92.

The important thing about such precedents is not that they explain why or how the mandates system evolved, but rather that because of their existence, the framers of Article 22 of the Covenant could use them in the solution of a particular problem with which they were confronted in connection with the general question of the post-World War I settlement.

Broadly, there are two ideas which underlay the mandates system and which have been carried over into the trusteeship system: (1) accountability for administration of a dependent area, and (2) international supervision of the administration. In both aspects the mandates system had been anticipated. For example, in the Berlin Act of 1865 the principal powers concerned in Africa entrusted the administration of the Congo Basin to Belgium, subject to the limitations laid down in the convention.[4] Earlier, the Congress of Vienna had authorized the protection of the Ionian Islands by Great Britain, making the latter accountable for its administration.[5] Another important antecedent of the mandates system was to be found within the British Empire. Both the Commonwealth of Australia and the Dominion of South Africa were entrusted with the administration of other British territories by England, subject to limitations laid down by the mother country.[6] In each of these cases, both the principle of accountability and, to a degree at least, the idea of international supervision were apparent. But the supervisory powers of the Congresses of Vienna and Berlin, while of an international character, were somewhat less than effective; and the supervision of England over Australia and South Africa, no doubt as effective as the mother country desired, was not really international. So it remained for the mandates system to combine accountability with international supervision of a reasonably definite character.

A fundamental fact to be kept in mind with regard to the formation of the mandates system is that it was the solution to a specific question faced by the negotiators at the Paris Peace Conference of 1919. The League of Nations, of which the mandates system formed but one part, was envisaged primarily as a peace-keeping agency rather than one having

[4] N. W. V. Temperley, *A History of the Peace Conference at Paris*, Vol. VI, p. 502. The relevant portion of the Act reads: "All the Powers bind themselves to watch over the preservation of native tribes and to care for the improvement of the conditions of their moral and material well-being. . . ." Article VI, par. 1. E. Hertslet, *The Map of Africa By Treaty*, Vol. II, p. 473. Succeeding paragraphs provided for the suppression of slavery and the slave trade, and the protection of freedom of conscience and religion.

[5] Wright, p. 18. In this connection Professor Wright also cites the responsibility of France to protect Christians in the Lebanon with an authorization to land troops for same, deputed by Protocol I of the Paris Conference, August 3, 1860.

[6] Norman Bentwich, *The Mandates System*, p. 6. The territories were Papua, under Australia, and Basutoland and Bechuanaland, under South Africa.

positive functions with regard to beneficent actions along economic and and social lines.[7] Thus the problem of colonies at the Conference was not one of a general nature regarding all dependent areas, but a specific question of to whom, and how, should the territories formerly belonging to Germany and Turkey be disposed?

There seemed to be three possible answers to this: restoration, independence, or annexation. None of these, however, was satisfactory. Restoration found favor in no quarter. Not only did the peoples living in the territories in question, insofar as their opinions were ascertained,[8] oppose such a solution, but the Allied and Associated Powers seemed fully agreed that restoration would not be considered. In December, 1918, President Wilson declared his opposition to the return of German colonies to the mother country,[9] and since Japan, Great Britain, and France were each entitled to various territorial claims on the basis of secret treaties made during the war,[10] this meant that at least four of the Big Five were in agreement on this point before the Conference met. Independence likewise found little support at the Conference. It is true that some of the leaders of the Allied and Associated Powers apparently favored the application of the principle of self-determination to the enemy colonies,[11] and some of the native peoples, specifically the Arabs, indicated a desire for independence.[12] But such a solution was ruled out primarily because the occupying powers in many of the territories were adamant in their position that they should exercise some degree of control over those territories as a matter of national security. This, plus the fact that in many of the areas under consideration independence was a practical impossibility in view of the obvious incapacity of the natives to govern

[7] A good example of this attitude occurred at a meeting of the Big Five (Wilson, Lloyd George, Clemenceau, Orlando, and Makino) on January 30, 1919, when Clemenceau's remarks on the subject were summarized as follows: "The League of Nations, he [that is, Clemenceau] thought, was to ensure the peace of the world . . . and not a League of Nations with governmental functions to interfere in internal affairs, with trustees in various places sending reports to — he did not know whom." "Secretary's Notes of a Conversation Held at M. Pichon's Room at the Quai d'Orsay, Paris, on Thursday, January 30, 1919." in David Hunter Miller, *My Diary at the Paris Peace Conference,* Vol. XIV, p. 49.

[8] See below, p. 12.

[9] David Hunter Miller, *The Drafting of the Covenant*, Vol. I, p. 41.

[10] Wright, pp. 26, 27, 35.

[11] *Ibid.*, pp. 24-25.

[12] Feisal, second son of King Hussein of the Hedjaz, appeared at the Conference with Lawrence of Arabia to recall pledges of the English government granting the interior of Syria to the Arabs, and to ask for independence for all Arab countries. Temperley, Vol. VI, pp. 144-45. The pledges referred to an exchange of notes between Sir Henry MacMahon representing the British Government and King Hussein, October, 1915. Wright, p. 27, n. 11.

themselves, effectively precluded the consideration of independence for the former colonies.[13]

The possibility of annexation, however, was more immediate; in fact, it is essentially correct to look upon the negotiations at Paris concerning former enemy colonies as the battle between the proponents of outright annexation and those opposed to it. Of all the delegations evincing a real interest in the question, only that of the United States was actively opposed to annexation, while the delegates from Italy and Great Britain were at best neutral.[14] France, Belgium, Japan, the Union of South Africa, Australia, and New Zealand all put forward claims to various territories to be detached from Germany and Turkey. The fact that undiluted annexation did not win out at the Conference, and that the mandates system was adopted can be ascribed to two main factors. First, each of the proponents of annexation was committed in principle to "no annexation" as part of the pre-Armistice agreement,[15] so that any annexation proposals of necessity had to be in the form of exceptions to that principle. Thus for New Zealand, Australia, and Japan some other form of control was satisfactory for the Middle Eastern and African lands, but the Pacific Islands should be annexed; for France, the exceptions would be the Cameroons and Togoland; and the Union of South Africa, which through General Smuts officially espoused a mandates system, wanted this system to exclude German South West Africa. In such a situation President Wilson pointed out that the discussion on colonies disclosed "a negation in detail—one case at a time—of the whole principle of mandatories." [16] Thus the fact that the mandates system was accepted "in principle" considerably weakened contentions with regard to exceptions in specific cases. But perhaps more important was the fact that as the negotiations proceeded various states secured—or at least thought they secured—enough of the substance of annexation within the mechanism of the mandates system to make further opposition to that plan unnecessary. This point is nicely illustrated by the negotiations surrounding the introduction of class "C" mandates. At first, as conceived in the British modifications of the Smuts plan for mandates—which served as the basis for discussion at the Conference—two types of mandates were envisaged: " 'vested territories' which . . . are to be transferred to states and shall be held by such states upon trust to afford to their inhabitants peace,

[13] There were exceptions to this in the form of the creation of semi-nomadic, independent states in parts of Arabia. See Wright, p. 46.

[14] On Italy's position see Miller, *My Diary at the Paris Peace Conference*, Vol. XIV, p. 47, where Orlando is cited as having formally agreed to abide by whatever the rest of the Big Five decided on the matter. Great Britain confined her activity on this point to supporting the claims of Australia and New Zealand.

[15] *Ibid.*, pp. 24-25.

[16] Miller, *The Drafting of the Covenant*, Vol. XIV, p. 42.

order, and good government;" and "'assisted states' which . . . are to attain their independence, and shall be entitled to such assistance as they may desire for the purpose of securing peace, order, and good government."[17] These corresponded to what proved to be the "B" and "A" mandates, respectively, and France, with some reservations, was willing to accept former enemy colonies as "B" mandates.[18] Australia, New Zealand, and South Africa, however, insisted on making the islands in the Pacific south of the Equator, and German West Africa, exceptions to the system. Since, to use President Wilson's own words, the United States was steadfastly determined to keep those states from negating in detail what they had agreed to in principle, either the discussion of the colonial question would break down on this point, or some middle road would have to be found.

It was General Smuts who fathered the compromise solution of the dilemma.[19] The problem as far as the Dominions were concerned, was to arrive at a formula by which the Pacific Islands and South West Africa could be brought under the system, thus satisfying President Wilson, while at the same time giving the administering states sufficient control over the territories to ensure the protection of what they conceived to be their vital interests. The answer lay in the introduction of a third class of territories within the mandates system—territories which could "be best administered under the laws of the mandatory state as integral portions thereof," subject to protection for the indigenous populations.[20] This class specifically included South West Africa and the Pacific Islands south of the Equator, and was accepted by New Zealand and Australia only reluctantly as the utmost they were willing to concede.[21]

Thus the mandates system as it emerged from the conference represented a complete victory for neither the annexationists nor President Wilson. Rather it was a compromise solution to a specific problem, and as such contained both the good and bad elements of any compromise: a decision, but a decision which completely satisfied nobody. Annexation was not used to resolve the question, but the mandates system had to be modified to the extent of pacifying the more violent opposition to it by the incorporation of the "C" mandates.

Another important fact about the negotiations concerning mandates was that the proceedings were *ex parte*, insofar as representatives of de-

[17] British "Draft Convention regarding Mandates," in *ibid.*, Vol. I, pp. 106-7.

[18] *Ibid.*, pp. 216-220. Wright, pp. 38-39.

[19] Miller, *The Drafting of the Covenant*, Vol. I, p. 105.

[20] *Ibid.*, pp. 109-10, contains a copy of the Smuts compromise in the form of a resolution presented at the Conference.

[21] *Ibid.*, pp. 205-6.

pendent peoples were concerned. The key decisions were made in the Council of Ten [22] by powers which did not directly represent the views of dependent peoples. The closest thing to a concerted effort to ascertain the opinion of the native peoples was an agreement by France and Great Britain "in principle" to send an investigatory commission to the Middle East, as desired by President Wilson. When these two states showed reluctance to implement this plan, Wilson sent an American commission under Henry Churchill King and Charles R. Crane. This commission, however, did its investigating after the mandates system had been decided upon, and thus concerned itself not with native opinion on the structure of the mandates system, but only with how the native felt about independence as against being placed under mandate. The commission's report [23] showed a marked preference for independence, and if a mandated status was necessary, the United States and Great Britain, in that order, were preferred as mandatories. There was a strong feeling against French administration in any form.

It is of interest to note that the natives actually evinced vigorous antipathy toward the mandates system because, according to the commission's report, they considered it merely disguised annexation. Independence was very clearly their desire and if this was impossible *assistance* from the United States and Great Britain was acceptable. The fact that "assistance" was hard to distinguish from the position of an "A" mandate apparently was not clear to the natives. If a little more had been done to permit the views of the native peoples to be heard while the mandates system was being created, those peoples would doubtless have felt much less repugnance for it. It is unlikely that the report had any effect on the allotment of mandates, since the United States did not take official part in the discussion on this point with regard to former Turkish colonies.[24]

Even though the viewpoint of the natives was not ascertained it is logical to suppose that some of the states at the Conference who had once been colonies might espouse the cause of the dependent peoples. Far from representing what might be called native viewpoint, however, such states at Australia, New Zealand, and the Union of South Africa

[22] The Council of Ten refers to meetings of the Big Five, each represented by two delegates. These meetings proceeded throughout the Conference and were in addition to the meetings of the Commission on the League of Nations appointed to draft the Covenant. *Ibid.*, p. 77, n. 3.

[23] *Editor and Publisher*, Vol. LV (December 2, 1922), pp. 4-26, contains the "Report of the King-Crane Commission." The Commission did its investigating during the summer of 1919, the text of the Covenant having been approved by the Peace Conference the previous February.

[24] Wright, pp. 45-46.

were leaders in the demand for annexation.[25] At the United Nations Conference, as will be seen, states which had felt the effect of colonial rule comparatively recently, and could therefore speak with authority about the rights of dependent peoples, were given a chance to propose modifications to the trusteeship system—and did so with marked effect. Such was not the case in 1919. Once the decisions were made by the Council of Ten, there were no modifications of Article 22 of the Covenant made at the Conference in the direction of giving more rights, protections, or benefits to the dependent peoples concerned.

The mandates system as envisaged in Article 22 can be summarized under three general headings: (1) application of the idea of trust, (2) classification of territories to be mandated, and (3) provision for the international supervision of the mandates.

The first two paragraphs of the article state that the "well-being and development" of the peoples in former enemy territories form "a sacred trust of civilization," that "securities for the performance of this trust should be embodied in" the Covenant, and that the best way of giving effect to these ideas was to entrust the tutelage of these peoples to advanced nations acting as "Mandatories on behalf of the League." Thus while the mandated areas were to be administered directly by an "advanced" nation, this would only be on behalf of the League, and these administering states would be responsible to the League for their mandates.

The territories were to be classified on the basis of their "stage of development," into one of three types:

A. Former Turkish colonies whose "existence as independent nations" could be provisionally recognized with the mandatory state rendering only temporary "administrative advice and assistance." A principal consideration in the selection of mandatory states for these territories was to be "the wishes of these communities" themselves.

B. Former German colonies in Africa, except South West Africa, wherein the administering state was to be responsible for the territory under the following conditions:
   1. Provision for freedom of conscience and religion.
   2. Prohibition of the slave trade, and of the arms and liquor traffic.
   3. Prevention of the establishment of fortifications or military and naval bases, and of military training of the natives for "other than police purposes and the defence of the territory."
   4. Security of the "open door" in the territory for all members of the League.

[25] The United States is not considered an exception to this statement, since its colonial period occurred a comparatively long time ago. The writer has in mind such states as the Dominions. Cf. the role of Egypt at the San Francisco Conference, below, pp. 38-40.

C. Former German colonies in the Pacific and South West Africa, which could "best be administered under the laws of the Mandatory as integral portions of its territory," subject to the above mentioned safeguards.

The functions of the League were laid down in the final three paragraphs. The actual arrangements governing the administration of a mandate were left to a decision of the Council, if the "Members of the League" had not previously acted. Each mandatory state was to render to the Council an annual report on the conditions in any territory committed to its charge. Finally a permanent commission was envisaged to "examine the annual reports of the Mandatories and to advise the Council on matters relating to the observance of the mandates."

That, in essence, summarizes the provisions of Article 22 as they concern this study. Obviously it is of little value to establish our own standards of what *should* have been written into the mandates provisions of the Covenant, but it is worth while to note some of the actual suggestions made at the Conference which, for one reason or another, were not adopted. The important relevant proposals, so far as they are recorded, are all found in the drafts of the Covenant made by President Wilson at Paris. This is not surprising when it is remembered that the President was really the only effective spokesman for the dependent peoples at the Conference. Viewing the three drafts of the Covenant made by Wilson at Paris [26] as a whole, there are five proposals which, had they been adopted, would have materially modified the mandates system with respect to the rights of the indigenous populations and the protection of those rights by the League.

The first of these appears in the first two drafts and provides that the former enemy colonies should revert to the League of Nations. While in one sense it is true that the League was the reversionary of these colonies in that it had ultimate supervisory control of their administration, in the strictest sense it was not, for by the treaties of peace with Germany and Turkey their colonies were turned over to the Allied and Associated Powers, and the disposal was made not by the League, but by the Supreme Council representing those powers.

The second proposal was that "whenever or wherever possible . . . the mandatory shall be nominated or approved" by the indigenous population. The clause closest to this in the Covenant refers only to the "A" mandates: the "wishes of which must be a principal consideration in the selection of the mandatory." And, outside of the King-Crane Commission, there is little evidence to show that an attempt was made to ascertain those wishes.

A third proposal of Wilson's that did not find its way into the

[26] The texts of these drafts are contained in Miller, *The Drafting of the Covenant*, Vol. II, pp. 65-93, 98-105, 145-54.

Covenant concerned a statement of the purpose of the mandates system. In his second Paris draft the President argued that the object of the tutelary oversight by the League was to enable the dependent peoples to attain self-government in as short a time as possible. Article 22 did look to the eventual independence of the "A" mandates, but the nearest it comes to this for "B" and "C" mandates is the "well-being and development" clause. In other words, the general objective of Wilson was particularized to apply definitely only to the "A" mandates, while eventual self-government for the other two classes remained indefinite at best. This point is particularly interesting in view of the similar question raised at San Francisco.

Closely connected with the third proposal was a fourth: that the League could release an area from mandate and consent to its independence. On this point Article 22 was completely silent, although this by no means meant that independence was precluded. As a matter of record, all the "A" mandates achieved independence, and all save Palestine in a comparatively orderly and peaceful manner.[27]

Finally, in both the second and third drafts of President Wilson, provision was made for the right of indigenous inhabitants of mandated territories to petition the League. No such right is found in Article 22, although this practice, subject to certain limitations, evolved in the course of the functioning of the mandates system. But it might well have become a much more important device if it had been written into the original mandates provisions. Certainly the value of formally providing for petitioning by the natives is indicated by the increased importance the practice has attained under the trusteeship system.

Before the mandates system could begin to function the areas to be mandated had to be alloted to the various mandatory powers, the terms of the mandates had to be agreed upon, and a permanent commission to advise the Council on matters pertaining to mandates had to be created.

By the treaties of peace with Germany and Turkey, those states renounced their colonies in favor of the Allied and Associated Powers. The former German colonies were allotted by the Supreme Council representing those powers, on May 7, 1919,[28] while mandatories for the former Turkish colonies were designated on April 25, 1920,[29] as follows:

[27] For a summary of the process by which each of the mandates achieved independence see Hall, pp. 149, 263-70.

[28] This meeting of the Supreme Council was made up of representatives of the governments of the United States, France, Great Britain, and Italy. *The Treaty of Versailles and After, Annotations of the Text of the Treaty* (State Department Publication No. 2724, Conference Series 92, p. 97).

[29] This meeting was made up of representatives of the same governments with the exception of the United States, which was represented unofficially by an observer. *Ibid.*, p. 94.

Mandated Area	*Mandatory Power*
Syria (including Lebanon)	France
Mesopotamia (Iraq)	Great Britain
Palestine [30]	Great Britain
Togoland and Cameroons	France and Great Britain to make a joint recommendation to the League [31]
German South West Africa	Union of South Africa
German Samoan Islands (Western Samoa)	New Zealand
Other German Pacific Possessions South of the Equator excluding Nauru	New Zealand
Nauru	British Empire [32]
German East Africa (Tanganyika)	Great Britain [33]
German Islands North of the Equator	Japan

The terms of the mandates were drawn up by the principal Allied Powers and submitted to the Council of the League for approval. There was some delay in negotiating these instruments owing mainly to the fact that the United States manifested simultaneously a lively interest in the fate of the areas and a reluctance to take part in the Council's discussion concerning mandates.[34] Eventually the terms of the mandates were approved by the Council, while the United States position with regard to the mandated areas was defined in a series of treaties with some, though not all, of the mandatory powers.[35]

The basic issue which had to be resolved in connection with the Permanent Mandates Commission concerned the position of the mandatory states on the Commission. If, on the one hand, the mandatories

[30] The separate administration of Trans-Jordan was approved by the League of Nations Council on September 16, 1922. *League of Nations Official Journal,* Vol. 3 (July-December, 1922), pp. 1188-89, 1390. This had been envisaged in the draft mandate for Palestine. Cf. Wright, pp. 605-6.

[31] *The Mandates System, Origin—Principles—Application* (League of Nations Publication 1945, VI. A. 1), p. 19, n. 1, cites an agreement delimiting the portions of the Cameroons and Togoland under British and French mandates reached by the two governments on July 10, 1919.

[32] Great Britain, Australia, and New Zealand reached a tripartite agreement, on July 2, 1919, entrusting the administration of Nauru to Australia for five years. This arrangement continued throughout the duration of the mandates system. *Ibid.* See also Hall, p. 174.

[33] On August 21, 1919, the Supreme Council approved an agreement between Belgium and Great Britain by which the territories of Ruanda and Urundi were detached from Tanganyika and mandated to Belgium. Wright, p. 44.

[34] *Ibid.,* pp. 48-62.

[35] The United States, despite repeated efforts, was not able to negotiate treaties with Australia, New Zealand, or the Union of South Africa with regard to their mandates. It did, however, conclude treaties with the other mandatory powers. Hall, p. 140, n. 5.

were members of the Commission they would in effect be judges in their own cause, and thus give substance to the charge that mandates were but a convenient fiction, a disguise, for annexation. On the other hand, there would be manifest disadvantages should the mandatory states not be represented on the Commission. It would be necessary to have nationals of those states on the Commission if only to put them in a position to present the necessary facts about the mandates.[36]

After a good deal of discussion in the Council the matter was resolved by a decision providing that the Permanent Mandates Commission should consist of nine members, all acting in their private capacities, the majority to be from non-mandatory states.[37] The only drawback to this plan was that in discussing any particular mandate, it would be necessary for the Commission to have access to official information. This had been one of the arguments for members of the Commission being government representatives. The introduction of a new expedient solved this problem. It was agreed that as each mandate was brought up for discussion in the Commission, an Accredited Representative of the mandatory state would appear before the Commission to furnish information and answer any questions which the Commission might put to him.[38] On this basis the Council approved the Commission's Constitution on November 29, 1920.[39]

Functioning. The primary responsibility for supervision of the mandates devolved upon the Council and the Permanent Mandates Commission. In addition, however, the Assembly and the Secretariat had parts to play. Since the Assembly, under Article 3 of the Covenant, could "deal . . . with any matter within the sphere of action of the League," it obviously could consider questions concerning mandates which might arise. In practice, it became customary for some member to draw the attention of the Assembly to some point in the chapter concerning mandates in the Secretary-General's annual report on the

[36] *Proces-Verbal of the Eighth Session of the Council of the League of Nations* (July-August, 1920), pp. 39-43.

[37] *Proces-Verbal of the Eleventh Session of the Council, Held at Geneva* (November-December, 1920), p. 14. At the same time the Council decided to permit the International Labour Office to appoint an expert who "would have the right to be present in an advisory capacity at all meetings of the Commission at which labour questions in mandated territories were discussed." On December 11, 1924, the Council added, as an extraordinary member, M. Rappard, the latter to assume his duties on the Commission upon his retirement as Director of the Mandates Section of the League Secretariat. *League of Nations Official Journal*, Vol. 6 (January-June, 1925), pp. 143, 233. On September 9, 1927, the regular membership of the Commission was increased to ten by the appointment of a German member. *League of Nations Official Journal*, Vol. 8 (July-December, 1927), pp. 1120, 1132.

[38] *Proces-Verbal of the Eleventh Session of the Council, Held at Geneva* (November-December, 1920), p. 13.

[39] *Ibid*., p. 15. Annex 133 (a) of this session contains a copy of the Constitution. *Ibid*., pp. 90-91.

work of the League, whereupon the Assembly would refer it to a committee—the Sixth Committee, on political questions—and eventually adopt a resolution stressing some particular phase of mandatory administration. In this way the Assembly came to act as a sort of "Keeper of the Council's Conscience" on matters affecting mandates.[40] The Mandates Section of the League Secretariat, in addition to its formally prescribed duties,[41] had the important function of serving as the main link between the Commission, the Council, and the Assembly, as well as, in some instances, the mandatory governments, since all important correspondence, petitions and publications, passed through that office.[42]

The decision-making agency on mandates questions was the Council. It was to the Council that the mandatory states rendered their annual reports, and it was to the Council that the Permanent Mandates Commission gave advice and assistance on matters relating to mandates. It was the Council which approved the terms of the mandates, and which had to approve any changes in those terms. Finally, the Commission itself was established by the Council, its members selected by the Council, and its rules subject to Council approval. But if the Council was the ultimate authority concerned with League supervision of mandates, the routine activities of the League concerning that supervision were left in the capable hands of the experts on the Permanent Mandates Commission. And, indeed, the Council seldom acted without the advice of the Commission, and usually accepted such advice as was rendered to it by the Commission. Thus it was the Commission on which was placed the responsibility for the immediate supervision of mandates.

At the outset the Council was faced with the question of how broadly to construe its functions regarding mandates. On the one hand it could be argued that the Council should "content itself with ascertaining that the mandatory Power has remained within the limits of the powers which were conferred upon it." But on the other hand should not the Council also "ascertain . . . whether the mandatory Powers has made a good use of these powers and whether its administration had conformed to the

[40] *The Mandates System, Origin—Principles—Application* (League of Nations Publication 1945, VI, A. 1), p. 35. See also Wright, pp. 89-91, 133.

[41] The League Budget Statement for 1926 outlined the duties of the Mandates Section as follows:

(a) To prepare the work of the Council and of the Assembly on this question [mandates];
(b) To correspond with the governments of the Mandatory Powers;
(c) To serve as a permanent secretariat for the Mandates Commission . . .
(d) To collect and classify . . . data in public and private documents on the mandated areas, the policy of the Mandatory Powers with regard to these areas, and general questions of colonial administration.

Cited in Hall, pp. 165-66.

[42] Wright, pp. 136-37.

interests of the native population?" [43] The Council, without much hesitation, accepted the latter view and in a report presented to the Assembly on December 6, 1920, stated that: "With regard to the responsibility of the League for securing the observance of the terms of the mandates, the Council interprets its duties in this connection in the widest manner." [44] The Permanent Mandates Commission, accordingly, did not confine itself to consideration of whether or not a mandatory state stayed "in bounds," but endeavored to discover in each case whether or not the administration of a mandated territory was being conducted with an eye to the interest of the native populations. To carry out this task the Commission instituted a number of devices with which to secure information about, and conduct investigations concerning, the administration of mandates.

The chief source of information was the annual report submitted to the Council, via the Commission, by each of the mandatories. To facilitate the preparation of these reports, the Commission drew up three sets of questionnaires corresponding to each of the three types of mandates. These questionnaires were extremely comprehensive and were designed to cover the entire range of administration of the mandates. Moreover, in 1924, the Council passed a resolution providing that attached to these annual reports should be the texts of all legislative or administrative decisions adopted in the mandated territories.[45]

Closely connected with the reception and examination of reports was the practice of hearing an accredited representative of the mandatory at the time each report was considered. The Rules of Procedure of the Permanent Mandates Commission, approved by the Council on January 10, 1922,[46] provided that the "examination and discussion of the reports shall take place, in each case, in the presence of the accredited representative;" but the observations which were submitted to the Council were agreed upon after the representative had withdrawn. This questioning of the accredited representative of the mandatory state served a two-fold purpose. The Commission was able to obtain elucidation on any points which might not have been clear in the report or to ask questions of a general nature not covered in the report, while the mandatory state was given the opportunity to explain or defend anything which on its surface might have given an unfavorable impression. The procedure has been said to have resembled "partly that of a University examination, and partly that of a Parliamentary debate." [47]

[43] *Proces-Verbal of the Eighth Session of the Council of the League of Nations* (July-August, 1920), Annex 90, p. 13.

[44] Quoted in *The Mandates System, Origin—Principles—Application* (League of Nations Publication 1945, VI. A. 1), p. 34.

[45] *League of Nations Official Journal*, Vol. 5 (July-December, 1924), p. 1287.

[46] *Ibid.*, Vol. 3 (January-June, 1922), p. 89.

[47] Bentwich, p. 115.

There was nothing in Article 22, the Constitution of the Permanent Mandates Commission, or the Rules of Procedure for that body concerning the right of the native inhabitants of mandated territories to petition the Commission. Nevertheless the natives proceeded to assume such a right, and in January, 1923, the Council, acting on the basis of proposals made by the British, approved a series of rules governing the procedure for handling petitions.[48] Under these rules petitions could emanate from either the indigenous inhabitants, or from any other source. If a petition came from the natives, it had to be sent to the Secretariat, via the mandatory state concerned, which in turn could make such comments as it desired before sending it on to the League. If a petition originated from some other source it was sent directly to the Chairman of the Permanent Mandates Commission for decision as to whether or not it was worthy of consideration. If so, it was then sent to the mandatory state for comment. The Chairman submitted a report on all unacceptable petitions to the Commission. If the Commission considered a petition it was usually in the presence of the accredited representative, and the Commission's observations together with the petition were submitted to the Council. In practice this right of petition was used primarily by the inhabitants of "A" mandates, and only very little by the natives in the "B" and "C" mandated territories.[49] Most of the petitions considered by the Commission never got as far as the Council, either because they were regarded as too trivial or as not receivable.[50] Petitions also served a twofold purpose; they provided the native inhabitants a chance to air their grievances, and they constituted an important source of information and supervision for the Permanent Mandates Commission. They are of particular significance to this study because they represented the most direct form of relationship between the League and the dependent peoples, and the comparison between the League and the United Nations on this point is striking.

The question of whether or not there should be oral hearings of petitioners arose early in the meetings of the Commission. At the ninth

[48] *League of Nations Official Journal*, Vol. 4 (January-June, 1923), pp. 200-201; 211, 298-300.

[49] Hall, p. 198. Cf. Wright, pp. 177-78.

[50] Hall, p. 202. Wright, p. 178. Petitions were unacceptable:

(a) If they contained complaints which were incompatible with the provisions of the Covenant or the terms of the mandates;
(b) If they emanated from an anonymous source;
(c) If they covered the same ground as was covered by a petition recently communicated to the mandatory power and did not contain any new information of importance.

Secretariat memorandum summarizing The Procedure to be Followed in the Matter of Petitions Concerning Mandated Territories. Permanent Mandates Commission, *Minutes of the Twelfth Session* (1927), pp. 176-78.

session it was decided that: "Experience having shown that sometimes the Commission has been unable to form a definite opinion as to whether certain petitions are well founded or not, the Commission is of the opinion that in those cases it might appear indispensable to allow the petitioners to be heard by it. The Commission, however, would not desire to formulate a definite recommendation on this subject before being informed of the view of the Council." [51] Following this the Council called upon the mandatory states to express their views on the matter, and the replies of those states all opposed hearing the petitioners in person.[52] The main reasons given in opposition were (1) such a procedure would transform the Commission into a court of law hearing controversies, which would be inconsistent with the mandates system, (2) it would weaken the authority of the mandatory in the territory concerned, and (3) there was no such right of a hearing in countries where the right of petition was recognized, hence any argument for the practice on grounds of analogy was unsupported. The Council, accepting these views, held that there was no reason to modify the procedure then being followed by the Commission with reference to petitions (which did not include oral hearings), although the Rapporteur pointed out in his report that exceptional circumstances might arise necessitating oral hearings in particular cases.[53] The members of the Commission, however, did regard themselves as "entitled to hear persons who applied to them for an interview," but only on an unofficial basis.[54]

One other possible device for supervision was suggested but not adopted as a regular procedure. At the first session of the Assembly the Haitian delegate, Mr. Doret, suggested that each mandatory state send an annual mission to its mandated territories, the results of whose inquiry would be communicated to the Council.[55] Neither the Permanent Mandates Commission nor the Council came to a definite decision on this suggestion, although the Council, in a few cases, sent special commissions to mandated territories.[56] In none of these cases, however, was the general administration of the mandate examined—only the facts concerning some particular litigious questions; so that it cannot be concluded that the

[51] Permanent Mandates Commission, *Minutes of the Ninth Session* (June, 1926), Annex 9, p. 215.

[52] *League of Nations Official Journal*, Vol. 7 (July-December, 1926), p. 1239; Vol. 8 (January-June, 1927), pp. 348, 438.

[53] *Ibid.*, Vol. 8 (January-June, 1927), pp. 348, 438.

[54] Permanent Mandates Commission, *Minutes of the Seventh Session* (October, 1925), p. 34.

[55] *The Records of the First Assembly, Plenary Meetings* (November-December, 1920), pp. 715-16.

[56] *The Mandates System, Origin—Principles—Application* (League of Nations Publication 1945. VI. A. 1), pp. 44-45.

visiting missions of the trusteeship system were in any real sense anticipated by the practice under the mandates system.[57]

To summarize, the most important supervisory device of the Permanent Mandates Commission—and the only one formally provided for in the Covenant—was the report of the mandatories, later with the supplementary practice of oral questioning of the special representatives. Neither petitions nor visiting missions were used to a significant extent and it seems fair to say, therefore, that even though the League interpreted its powers broadly, direct contact between the dependent peoples in mandated areas and the Permanent Mandates Commission was almost nil. And this, in turn, obviously placed an important limitation on the League's capacity to oversee effectively the administration of mandated areas. Nevertheless, as compared to any previous attempt at international supervision of dependent areas—and especially as compared to the historic practice of unilateral domination of backward areas by "advanced" states—the League of Nations mandates system definitely demonstrated the possibilities for an international organization not only to supervise the administration of dependent areas, but also to provide an orderly process by which these areas could attain the status of independent states in the family of nations.

[57] In almost every case of these special missions the matter was not even referred to the Permanent Mandates Commission. *Ibid.*, p. 45.

CHAPTER TWO

The San Francisco Conference

Pre-Conference Developments. When the United Nations Conference on International Organization convened in San Francisco on April 25, 1945, the Big Five [1] had not as yet reached agreement as to the main provisions concerning trusteeship which were to be included in the Charter. The Dumbarton Oaks Conversations of the previous year had laid down the main outlines of the new international organization, but these included no reference to trusteeship.[2] This did not mean, however, any lack of discussion on either the governmental or private level in the years immediately preceding the writing of the Charter. Indeed, in both this country and abroad, the problem of dependent areas was the subject of a good deal of speculation.

On the unofficial plane interest in this country did not become noticeably aroused until the war years, when such groups as the Universities Committee on Post-War International Problems and the Commission to Study the Organization of Peace published various pamphlets and articles calling for some sort of international control of dependent areas.[3] In Europe, and especially England, discussion of the question had been occasioned somewhat earlier by Germany's desire to regain her position as a colonial power. An article published in 1944, in the British *Round Table*, distinguished schools of thought on the subject ranging all the way from the mere employment of supplementary expedients in the mandates system, such as creating international corporations for colonial development, to putting all colonies under an international body having broad supervisory powers.[4] The significant point about this

[1] "The Big Five" refers to those states given permanent seats on the Security Council. Four of these, China, the United Kingdom, the United States, and the Soviet Union, were the Sponsoring Powers of the Conference. The fifth, France, was invited to take part in discussions concerning the Conference after the Yalta Conference. *State Department Bulletin,* Vol. XII (1945), pp. 214, 394.

[2] *United Nations Conference on International Organization, Documents,* Vol. 3, pp. 2-23. Hereinafter cited as *UNCIO, Documents.*

[3] See, for example, W. E. Hocking, *Colonies and Dependent Areas,* Problem IX, written under the auspices of the Universities Committee on Post-War International Problems, and the Commission to Study the Organization of Peace, "Colonial Aspects of Post-War Settlement," by Benjamin Gerig and others, for *International Conciliation,* No. 379 (April, 1943), pp. 195-217.

[4] "The International Interest in Colonies," *Round Table,* Vol. 35, December, 1944, pp. 26-27. For an extensive list of organizations on both sides of the Atlantic, which published suggestions on the subject, see *The Times* (London), January 25, 1945.

unofficial discussion is that, with negligible exceptions,[5] the direction of argument pointed to increasing international supervision of dependent areas, either by a single body or regional commissions, over that of the League system. In general, then, the climate of private opinion seemed favorable to an extension of the devices of the mandates system.

On the official level the key decisions concerning trusteeship provisions in the Charter were made by the Big Five, as will be explained shortly. Their respective attitudes toward the subject are perhaps best summarized by the draft plans for a trusteeship system which each submitted at the Conference. The United States proposals provided, in effect, the basis for discussion at the Conference, and consequently their formation is of considerable importance, especially for those aspects of the trusteeship system which derive directly from the United States plan.

The development of these United States proposals concerning trusteeship may be divided into two stages: (1) their evolution within the State Department, and (2) the important modification made during the course of interdepartmental discussions among the departments of State, War, and Navy. In general, the evolution in the first stage is marked by a transition from sweeping proposals including all colonial territories, and providing for the ultimate independence for all, to a much more confined plan, limited both as to scope and objectives, though still representing a real change from the mandates system in the direction of increased international supervision, broadened areas of application, and a more specific statement of self-government as a goal for all territories brought within the system. This transition in the first stage of development, covering roughly the year and a half from January, 1943, to July, 1944, can be illustrated by comparing the first draft formulated for the Secretary of State with the draft made in preparation for the Dumbarton Oaks Conversations.

Official consideration of a possible trusteeship plan began in this country in August, 1942, when a Special Subcommittee on International Organization, under the Political Subcommittee of the Advisory Committee on Post-War Foreign Policy, undertook the drafting of specific proposals on the subject.[6] These proposals, submitted to the Political

[5] For an exception see F. D. Lugard, "A World Colonial Charter," *The Times* (London), January 10, 1945. Lord Lugard, while favoring a declaration of "fundamental freedoms" for the dependent peoples, did not want these freedoms "safeguarded by a permanent body collecting data and making reports."

[6] *Post-War Foreign Policy Preparation* (Department of State Publication 3580, General Foreign Policy Series 15), pp. 108-9. The Advisory Committee on Post-War Foreign Policy was established after Pearl Harbor by direction of President Roosevelt. Under the chairmanship of the Secretary of State, it was composed of "members drawn from private life, the Congress, the Department of State, and other departments and agencies of government and was assisted by a specially constituted research staff." *Ibid.*, p. 3.

Subcommittee on December 5, envisaged a system covering all dependent territories. But this all-embracing plan, at least in undiluted form, was not accepted by either the Political Subcommittee nor Secretary of State Hull, and the first draft given serious consideration at the policy making level was drawn up by a special group of State Department officers working under Mr. Hull.[7] This first draft,[8] of March 17, 1943, is interesting in that although it distinguished between colonies on the one hand, and mandates and territories to be detached from the enemy states at the end of the war on the other, nevertheless it would have brought all dependent territories under some sort of international supervision. Colonies were to be overseen by regional commissions composed of the representatives of states which "are directly responsible for their future" and representatives of such other states as "have substantial interests in the regions." Mandates and ex-enemy territories were to be placed under an International Trusteeship Administration, which would operate through regional councils, composed of members with major interests in the area—such councils to administer the territories concerned. For both types of dependent areas, in addition to protections for the well-being of the natives and an undertaking to promote self-government within each territory, the proposals called for the fixing "at the earliest possible moments," of dates upon which the areas would be accorded a "status of full independence within a system of general security. . . ." Thus under this system the difference between colonies and other dependent areas was only in the form of their administration—through the mother country in collaboration with other states on a regional basis, or by regional councils. Whether in the latter case these councils would in turn mandate the area to a single state was not mentioned. The tenor of the proposals suggests that an aura of cooperation rather than international supervision should surround the administration of colonies, while the other territories were to be more directly overseen by the United Nations.

By July, 1944, the United States position on a possible trusteeship system had undergone considerable modification. In preparation for the forthcoming Dumbarton Oaks Conversations, a series of "Tentative Proposals for a General International Organization"[9] was prepared by the State Department, and a section on "Arrangements for Territorial Trusteeships"[10] was included. These Arrangements differed from the original

[7] *Ibid.*, p. 110. Cf. Cordell Hull, *Memoirs*, Vol. II, pp. 1234-35.

[8] This draft, in the form of a "Declaration by the United Nations on National Independence," is reprinted in *Post-War Foreign Policy Preparation*, Appendix 12, pp. 470-72.

[9] *Ibid.*, Appendix 38, pp. 596-606.

[10] *Ibid.*, Appendix 39, pp. 606-7.

proposals in three fundamental respects—differed to the extent, indeed, that they constituted almost a change in kind rather than merely in degree. First, the scope of the system was now confined to ex-enemy territories and areas under mandate. Other territories were envisaged as possibly coming under the system by "action of the general assembly," but only "if requested by member states having control over such territories."[11] Second, the objectives of the system, while otherwise about the same as originally, now did not include independence as a goal for the territories. This question of independence as an objective was to crop up again at San Francisco and provide one of the most difficult obstacles to the drafting of the chapters on trusteeship in the Charter. Finally, the organizational framework was considerably modified. Where the original proposals had provided for a decentralized administration operating through regional councils, the responsibilities of trusteeship were now to be placed in the General Assembly operating through a Trusteeship Council composed of representatives of states administering trust territories and representatives of an equal number of other states designated periodically by the General Assembly. Regionalism within the system was provided for only to the extent that the General Assembly was empowered to "establish advisory commissions of a regional . . . character with respect to trust territories situated in a given region. . . ." In addition to these changes the functions of the General Assembly and Trusteeship Council were spelled out in some detail. These remained to all intents and purposes unchanged in the final United States proposals which will be summarized below.

The precise reasons for this modification of United States policy will not be fully known until the relevant documentary materials are made public. It is possible, however, to account for the general change in the direction of limiting the scope and objectives of the system in terms of the known policies of other interested states. The first proposals were rather in the the form of a proposed United Nations declaration than a specific plan for a trusteeship system, and it was only natural that when such a declaration was implemented with specific proposals some limiting modification would occur.[12]

Just as President Wilson's and Prime Minister Lloyd George's general pre-Paris Conference statements regarding the inhabitants of territories to be detached from enemy states at the end of the first World War were not completely carried out when it actually came to setting up

[11] The idea of expressing international concern for all dependent territories had not been completely given up, since a paper on minimum standards for all nonself-governing areas was eventually added as a supplement to United States policy on international organization. *Ibid.*, p. 388.

[12] *The Times* (London) referred to the first United States proposals on trusteeship as "of the Kingdom-of-Heaven-or-nothing order." April 4, 1945.

a mandates system, so a declaration of a general nature as to the future of dependent peoples could not be entirely fulfilled when it came to transforming expressions of general aims into an actual international system. This is not to be cynical about declarations of ideals made by allies while fighting a war; the point is rather that such declarations must be taken as goals to be strived for and not pledges of specific action.

Two of the leading colonial powers, Great Britain and France, consistently made it known throughout the pre-San Francisco Conference period that they would be opposed to any system which included all dependent territories. The Prime Minister of Great Britain, who (in his own words) did not "become the King's First Minister" in order to watch over the liquidation of the British Empire, made his views public both in Parliament and at the Yalta Conference in discussion with Marshal Stalin and President Roosevelt.[13] Moreover, the British Colonial Secretary, Mr. Stanley, in an address at Oxford in March, 1943, stated that "the administration of British colonies must continue to be the sole responsibility of Great Britain." [14] Neither was independence acceptable as a goal for dependent territories, at least in all cases. When Secretary Hull first discussed the original State Department proposals with the British Foreign Secretary, Anthony Eden, the latter was bothered by the word "independence;" and later, at the Moscow Conference in the fall of 1943, Eden "could state that his Government was not in agreement" with the American position on dependent areas.[15] The British view was that self-government within the Empire, rather than independence, was the desirable goal for territories committed to her care.[16]

The French, too, were by no means ready to accept any such broad system as originally planned by the United States Department of State. As a matter of fact, they were reluctant to see any change in the mandates system which "would upset the existing balance of national and international control . . . to the disadvantage of the mandatory." [17] In view of this attitude on the part of the two major colonial powers among the Big Five, it is not surprising that when the United States came to formulate specific proposals for the Dumbarton Oaks Conversations, the original proposed declaration was considerably watered down, particularly since discussions between this government and the British were

[13] Edward R. Stettinius Jr., *Roosevelt and the Russians*, pp. 236-38.

[14] *The Times* (London), March 6, 1943. Mr. Churchill stated in Parliament that this represented the Government's position. *Ibid.*, March 18, 1943.

[15] Hull, Vol. II, pp. 1237, 1305.

[16] *The Times* (London), January 20, 1945, reporting a talk by Mr. Stanley, British Colonial Secretary, to the Foreign Policy Association of New York. Cf. Hull, Vol. II, p. 1599.

[17] *The Times* (London), April 4, 1945.

being carried on periodically during the formulation of the "Arrangements for Territorial Trusteeship" to be presented at Dumbarton Oaks.[18] With respect to the third major modification of the American proposals for trusteeship, the limiting of the regional concept, the change can be accounted for in terms of the growing desire on the part of the State Department to carry out two ideas: (1) insure direct international control of territories brought within the system, with nonadministering states taking part in that control, and (2) not deviate too much from the mandates system, in which a centralized body rather than regional ones had operated satisfactorily.[19] Regionalism was not totally discarded, however, as an additional paper was prepared on the subject in case the United Kingdom or some other state should bring up the matter.[20]

The United States proposals at the Dumbarton Oaks Conferences, however, omitted these trusteeship arrangments, and, largely in deference to American wishes, trusteeship was not discussed at the time. The American position was the result of a decision made on July 18, 1944, at the request of the Joint Chiefs of Staff, to avoid questions "directly or indirectly related to the subject of post-war territorial settlements. . . ."[21] Trusteeship was discussed at the Yalta Conference, in February, 1945, but the only decision reached there was that concerning the types of territories to be brought under the system. These were to include: (1) former mandated areas, (2) territories which might be detached from enemy states at the end of World War II, and (3) other territories voluntarily placed under the system. It was decided at that time, however, that a consultation among the Big Five on the subject should take place prior to the San Francisco Conference to bridge the gap in the Dumbarton Oaks Proposals.[22] To effect this consultation the United States Department of State sent out invitations to the other Sponsoring Powers and France for a meeting scheduled for "around" April 8, 1945, and received word, by the first of April, that the governments of China, France, and the United Kingdom agreed to send representatives to the meeting.[23] But this prior consultation had been of necessity delayed, because of difficulties within the United States government which arose in

[18] *Post-War Foreign Policy Preparation*, pp. 254, 389.

[19] This information was obtained by the writer in conversation with Mr. Benjamin Gerig, Director of the Office of Dependent Areas, Department of State, who took part in the formulation of American policy.

[20] *Post-War Foreign Policy Preparation*, p. 388. The British, early in the postwar planning period, seemed to favor a system formed on a regional basis. See, for example, *The Times* (London), July 14, 1942, in which Colonial Secretary Stanley is reported to have favored this idea in debate before the House of Commons.

[21] *Post-War Foreign Policy Preparation*, pp. 295-96.

[22] Stettinius, pp. 232, 343.

[23] *Post-War Foreign Policy Preparation*, p. 431.

connection with the question of this country's precise position on the issue of trusteeship.[24] The solution of these difficulties constitutes stage two of the development of United States policy on the subject.

On April 2, at a meeting of the Secretaries of State, War, and the Navy, it appeared that further consideration given to trusteeship by our government would have to be undertaken by the President.[25] This was necessitated by the divergence of opinion which had developed between the State Department, on the one hand, and the War and Navy Departments, on the other, over the latter's desire to have at least some of the former Japanese mandates, because of their strategic importance to this country, exempted from the proposed system and placed directly under the control of the United States. Their position was summed up in a "Memorandum for the Secretary of State" from Mr. Henry L. Stimson, the Secretary of War, dated January 23, 1945: "They [the Pacific islands] do not really belong in such a classification [colonial areas]. Acquisition of them by the United States does not represent an attempt at colonization or exploitation. Instead it is merely the acquisition by the United States of the necessary bases for the defense of the security of the Pacific for the future world. To serve such a purpose they must belong to the United States with absolute power to rule and fortify them. They are not colonies; they are outposts, and their acquisition is appropriate under the general doctrine of self-defense by the power which guarantees the safety of that area of the world." [26] Against this reasoning, advocates of the State Department plan for trusteeship, which would include former mandated territories within the system, argued that adoption of the position of the military would lead to "reservations of other territory by other nations until the non-aggrandizement plan of the Atlantic Charter would become a mockery. . . ." [27] On April 10, the Secretary of State, in response to a request for a prompt determination of our government's position after a conference of the President and the three departments concerned, received word from the President that the State Department's views on international trusteeship were "approved in principle," and that the President would see representatives of the three departments on April 19.[28]

Before this conference could take place, however, President Roosevelt

[24] Further reason for delay was the fact that no information concerning a Soviet representative had been received.

[25] *Post-War Foreign Policy Preparation*, p. 431.

[26] Quoted in Henry L. Stimson and McGeorge Bundy, *On Active Service in Peace and War*, p. 600.

[27] Article by Arthur Krock, in The New York *Times*, April 3, 1945. The similarity between this cleavage within the American government and that between President Wilson and the Dominions and France at Paris in 1919 is striking.

[28] *Post-War Foreign Policy Preparation*, p. 431.

died, on April 12, and it was necessary to brief the new President on the status of our policy on trusteeship. Following this, further interdepartmental discussions were held and resulted in a general statement of proposed American policy for submission to the President. This statement was considered by the United States Delegation to the San Francisco Conference on April 17, with Secretaries Stimson and Forrestal present, together with military and naval advisers. On the basis of this meeting, the proposed statement was revised, and as such was approved by all concerned, including President Truman, on April 18.[29]

A comparison of the United States proposals with regard to trusteeship before and after the War and Navy Department had been brought into the discussion [30] shows that the modification of these proposals designed to protect our interests in the Pacific consisted of a provision for strategic areas removed from the purview of the General Assembly and placed under the aegis of the Security Council, where the United States would have the veto power and where somewhat less international supervision was contemplated. This represented a compromise between making no distinction between strategic and nonstrategic areas, as in the "Arrangements" prepared for Dumbarton Oaks, and removing strategic areas entirely from the proposed system, as some of the military leaders desired. This compromise, however, did not quiet all the proponents of outright annexation. Representative Wadsworth, Republican, of New York, speaking on the floor of the House of Representatives, declared that the United States must retain unhampered control of "Japanese mandated islands recovered by our blood and treasure. . . ." [31] And Admiral King publicly asserted that "American possession of the bases in the Pacific islands, which have been taken from Japan, was essential to the United States and world security after the war." [32] But, apparently, even though there existed some division in American ranks after the formulation of the strategic-area concept, most of the leaders of the military regarded that concept as an adequate protection of American security interests. Thus the basic distinction between strategic and nonstrategic areas as written into the Charter originated in United States policy, and it seems obvious that this was one point on which our delegation could not, as indeed it did not, change its position in the negotiations at San Francisco.

---

[29] *Ibid.*, p. 443.

[30] The two documents in question are: "Arrangements for Territorial Trusteeships" as prepared for the Dumbarton Oaks Conversations (cited above, p. 25, n. 10), and "Arrangements for International Trusteeship," Additional Chapter Proposed by the United States. *UNCIO. Documents*, Vol. 3, pp. 607-8 (Doc. 2, G/26 (c)).

[31] Quoted in The New York *Times*, April 19, 1945.

[32] *Ibid.*

The position of the United States on the question on trusteeship as it emerged by the opening of the Conference, then, was in summary: (1) that a system of international trusteeship should be established under the authority of the United Nations; (2) that the basic objectives of the system should be to (a) further international peace and security; (b) promote the political, economic, and social advancement of the trust territories and their inhabitants and their progressive development toward self-government; and (c) provide for nondiscriminatory treatment in trust territories with respect to the economic and other appropriate activities of the nationals of all member states; (3) that the system should apply to the three types of territories defined in the Yalta agreement; (4) that the trusteeship arrangement for each territory to be placed under the system should be agreed upon by the states directly concerned; (5) that a distinction should be made between strategic and nonstrategic areas; all functions of the organization relating to each to be handled by the Security Council and General Assembly respectively; (6) that a Trusteeship Council should be established to help carry out the functions of the General Assembly, consisting of persons of special competence designated (a) one each by the states administering trust territories; (b) one each by an equal number of other states named periodically by the General Assembly; (7) that the General Assembly, and under it the Trusteeship Council, should be empowered to consider reports by the administering state, accept petitions, and institute investigations.[33]

Big Five Consultation at the Conference. At the San Francisco Conference itself the task of preparing "draft provisions on principles and mechanism of a system of international trusteeship for such dependent territories as may by subsequent agreement be placed thereunder," [34] was assigned to a technical committee, II/4, working under Commission II which itself had charge of provisions relating to the General Assembly. The committee, under the chairmanship of Mr. Peter Fraser, then Prime Minister of New Zealand, met sixteen times from May 5 to June 20, 1945, and was composed, as were all other committees, of representatives of all states participating in the Conference.

Since the Dumbarton Oaks Proposals had omitted any reference to a trusteeship system and the "prior consultation" among the Big Five on the subject had not as yet taken place, it was necessary for the committee to start from scratch, as it were, in the formulation of its draft provi-

[33] "Arrangements for International Trusteeship," Additional Chapter Proposed by the United States. *UNCIO, Documents,* Vol. 3, pp. 607-8 (Dec. 2, G/26 (c)).

[34] The quotation is from the terms of reference of Committee II/4 from the memoranda on the organization of the Conference, which had been adopted in plenary session. See *UNCIO, Documents,* Vol. 10, p. 423, "Summary Report of the First Meeting" of Committee II/4.

sions. At the fifth meeting of the committee, however, the delegate from the United States, Mr. Harold Stassen, presented a "Proposed Working Paper For Chapter on Dependent Territories and Arrangement For International Trusteeship" [35] which was used by the committee as a basis for discussion in its work. While technically the committee did the actual work of formulating the provisions for trusteeship as they appear in the Charter of the United Nations, it would be a serious error to view these provisions as solely the product of "open covenants openly arrived at" by representatives of all the United Nations assembled at the committee meetings. This is true to the extent that all the provisions as they appear in the Charter were approved by the committee, but it must be kept in mind that fundamental decisions as to the trusteeship provisions in the Charter were first made by the sponsoring powers and France in private consultation. And the Proposed Working Paper mentioned above was itself the product of this private, or informal, negotiation among the Big Five. Moreover, there was general agreement among the Big Five that on any question resolved by the time of the introduction of the working paper they would present a united front in Committee II/4, while continuing informal consultation on those questions not as yet settled. To get a correct picture of the writing of trusteeship provisions at San Francisco, then, one must keep in mind that while Committee II/4 did the actual drafting of the trusteeship provisions, this was done on the basis of the working paper previously agreed to by the major powers. Furthermore, as questions arose during the considerations of the working paper by the committee, informal consultation among the Big Five and other interested states relative to various points at issue continued.

The "informal consultation" alluded to in the preceding paragraph was carried on at San Francisco during the Conference because for various reasons already mentioned, the "prior consultation" among the Big Five had never occurred. The United States position at the outset of these meetings has been explained in some detail for the simple reason that it was the American proposals which served as the basis for discussion at the Big Five informal meetings. This is not to say, however, that the other major powers came to those meeting without ideas of their own for while the United States had been achieving unity of policy on trusteeship, the other sponsoring powers and France had been giving attention to the question, and each presented, in the form of comments on and amendments to the Dumbarton Oaks Proposals, individual plans for trusteeship.[36] In general, the Chinese and French proposals followed the

[35] *UNCIO, Documents,* Vol. 10, pp. 660-83 (Document 323, II/4/12).

[36] "Draft Proposals of the Chinese Delegation on International Territorial Trusteeship," *UNCIO, Documents,* Vol. 3, pp. 615-17 (Doc. 2 G/26 (e)). "International Trusteeship System," French Preliminary Draft, *UNCIO, Documents,* Vol. 3, pp.

same pattern, as noted below. The Soviet Union confined itself to offering amendments to the United States draft, but accepted the main outlines of it in principle. The United Kingdom desired to follow the lines of the mandates system to the extent of providing for an expert commission to examine annual reports, but both the United States and the Soviet Union agreed that a new system should be devised with a Trusteeship Council composed of national delegations, and this view prevailed. The Big Five consultation, when it finally did occur (beginning April 30), was held in the Fairmont Hotel and was at the Delegate,[37] not the Foreign Minister level. In addition to proposals by each of the Big Five, Australia submitted a proposed "Chapter on Dependent Peoples,"[38] and other states, notably Mexico, Ecuador, Panama, and Venezuela, made comments on all the proposals.[39] Based on these, the Big Five produced, on May 15, the Proposed Working Paper used by Committee II/4.

This working paper consisted basically of the American proposals as amended to take into account the other proposals, but it did not mean, as one might suppose, that the Big Five had reached agreement on all points regarding trusteeship. There were still issues which had to be thrashed out, but the committee could at least get started with consideration of the provisions which were acceptable to all the sponsoring powers and France as of that time. Those questions still not settled were bypassed by the committee, usually at the suggestion of Mr. Stassen, until such time as informal discussion had produced agreement.

The working paper was divided into two parts: (A) a statement of general policy regarding dependent territories, and (B) arrangements for a Territorial Trusteeship System. Part A, drawn largely from language used in the British proposals, eventually found its way into the Charter, in a modified form, as Chapter XI, "Declaration Regarding Non-Self-Governing-Territories," and since it is not part of the trusteeship system proper it is not germane to the present study. Discussion of the working paper will therefore be confined to Part B, the provisions relating to the trusteeship system and the formation of a Trusteeship Council.

This working paper, as presented by Mr. Stassen to Committee II/4,

604-6 (Doc. 2 G/26 (a)). "Amendments of the Soviet Delegation to the United States Draft on Trusteeship System," *UNCIO, Documents,* Vol. 3, pp. 616-19 (Doc. 2 G/26 (f)). "United Kingdom Draft of Chapter for Inclusion in United Nations Charter," *UNCIO, Documents,* Vol. 3, pp. 609-14 (Doc. 2 G/26 (d)).

[37] The Delegates were: Mr. Stassen, United States, Chairman; Viscount Granborne, United Kingdom; Mr. Sobolev, Soviet Union; Dr. Koo, China; M. Naggiar and later M. Pleven, France. *Post-War Foreign Policy Preparation,* pp. 445-46.

[38] *UNCIO, Documents,* Vol. 3, pp. 548-49 (Doc. 2 G/14 (1)). This followed the English plan of carrying on the expert commission of the mandates system.

[39] The comments and suggestions of these states are summarized in "Analysis of Papers Presented by Australia, China, France, United Kingdom, and United States," *UNCIO, Documents,* Vol. 10, pp. 641-55 (Doc. 230, II/4/5).

represented seven substantive changes in the original American proposals. These modifications were, first, that the promotion of progressive development toward self-government be in forms appropriate to the varying circumstances of each territory. This addition came from the British proposals and was designed to take into account the fact that the trust territories would differ widely in culture, degree of civilization, and capacity for self-government, and therefore the particular form or degree of self-government must vary from area to area.

The second change concerned the clause providing for nondiscriminatory treatment in trust territories with regard to economic activities of member nations. An "open door" clause of this type was significantly absent from the British Proposals,[40] and in early discussion in Committee II/4 the South African delegate, supporting the original British proposals, pointedly stated that such a principle had not applied to "C" mandates and that "his government could not contemplate its application to their mandated territory."[41] Moreover, the proposals of France revealed concern that the "open door" principle might work to the disadvantage of the trust territory itself.[42] These anxieties were allayed by adding to the clause in question the words "without prejudice to the attainment of (a) and (b) above [promotion of peace and security and the welfare of the trust peoples], and subject to provisions of paragraph 5 below [a 'conservatory' clause preserving existing rights in all territories unless and until changed by a trusteeship agreement]."

This conservatory clause just referred to, appearing as a completely new paragraph, was the third modification of the American proposals. There is no similar paragraph in any of the proposals submitted to the Conference, but it seems reasonable to assume that it was inserted to assure the mandatory powers that their existing relationships with mandated territories would not be changed without their consent. This interpretation is in a measure confirmed by the fact that in subsequent discussion of this paragraph in Committee II/4 Egypt and Syria, and to a lesser extent the Soviet Union, attacked its provisions, while some of the mandatory states defended it.[43]

[40] The British delegate to Committee II/4 commented unfavorably on the clause. "Summary Report of the Fourth Meeting of Committee II/4," May 14, 1945. *UNCIO, Documents*, Vol. 10, p. 440.

[41] "Summary Report of the Third Meeting of Committee II/4," May 11, 1945. *Ibid.*, p. 434.

[42] This concern manifested itself in a provision that the trust territories should, reciprocally, be equitably treated. "International Trusteeship System," French Preliminary Draft, *Ibid.*, Vol. 3, p. 605. The British expressed anxiety on this point in the fourth meeting of the committee, cited above, this page, n. 41.

[43] Summary Reports of the Ninth and Tenth Meetings of Committee II/4. *UNCIO, Documents*, Vol. 10, pp. 447, 488. Cf. The New York *Times*, May 31, 1945. The fact that the Soviet Union's attack on this clause was mild can be traced to the acceptance by the colonial powers among the Big Five of permanent representation of all the Big Five on the Trusteeship Council.

The fourth change in the American proposals pertained to the scope of application of the trusteeship system. Where the United States plan had stated that it would be a matter of subsequent agreement as to which territories would be brought under the system, the Soviet amendments to that plan added that it would also be a matter of subsequent agreement as to "which states would be authorized to take over a trusteeship." [44] This would have the effect of permitting the Soviet Union to have a voice in the determination of the administering state as well as the trust territory provided it was "directly concerned." [45] This modification, accepted by the other members of the Big Five, apparently with little opposition, has not proved important so far. All but one of the present trust territories were former mandates, and in the exceptional case, Italian Somaliland, the administering state, Italy, was chosen over the opposition of the Soviet Union.[46]

The fifth and sixth alterations were based on British dissatisfaction with the American plan of differentiating between strategic and non-strategic areas. In the British view this differentiation was unsatisfactory on three grounds: (1) supervision of the indigenous inhabitants is a paramount consideration, and this supervision is just as necessary in strategic areas as in other areas; (2) it is impossible, particularly in large territories, to draw a hard and fast line separating the two types of areas, and consequently it might often be necessary to designate the whole of a large area as strategic and so remove it from close international supervision; and (3) it is most desirable to permit an administering state to mobilize the war potential of trust territories as part of its contribution to the maintenance of international peace and security. "The United Kingdom draft, by avoiding any distinction between 'strategic' and other areas, but differentiating between civil and security functions, not only meets any possible charge of annexation . . . but states in more positive form than does the United States proposal that territories under the 'Trusteeship' System will be called upon to contribute from their resources toward international peace and security." [47]

Remembering that the device of recognizing some areas as strategic in the American proposal represented a compromise between the State Department and military leaders in this country, it is not difficult to see

[44] "Amendments of the Soviet Delegation to the United States Draft on Trusteeship System," *UNCIO, Documents,* Vol. 3, pp. 618-19. (Dec. 2 G/26 (f)). See also article by James Reston in The New York *Times,* May 12, 1945.

[45] That it was the desire of the Russians to be able to have a voice in the matter is corroborated by the fact that in their "Amendments . . ." they replaced the American phraseology "directly concerned" with "which were or are concerned in this matter."

[46] See below, pp. 85-102.

[47] "An explanatory note on the draft Chapter submitted by the United Kingdom Delegation," *UNCIO, Documents,* Vol. 3, pp. 612-13 (Doc. 2 G/26 (d)).

why, despite British objections, if the former Japanese mandates in the Pacific were to be brought under the trusteeship system, the concept of strategic areas had to remain in the revised proposals. And lest the American delegation might waver on this point, a subcommittee of the Senate Naval Affairs Committee, composed of Senators Byrd of Virginia, Eastland of Mississippi, Democrats, and Tobey of New Hampshire, and Capehart of Indiana, Republicans, arrived in San Francisco during the first week in May "to make sure of U.S. interests in Japan-Mandated Pacific Isles." [48] To take into account the objections of the British, however, the American proposals were changed to the extent of making the basic objectives of the system specifically applicable to the people of strategic areas, and an entirely new paragraph was added stating that it shall be the duty of an administering state to insure that the territory play its part in the maintenance of international peace and security, and empowering the administering state to make use of "volunteer forces, facilities, and assistance from the territory in carrying out the obligations undertaken by the state for the Security Council."

The last change in the American proposals can be viewed as clarifying rather than as introducing anything particularly new or different. Following the language used in the Soviet amendments to the American plan, in the paragraph dealing with the powers of the General Assembly, and under it the Trusteeship Council, the words "to institute investigations" were changed to read "to make periodic visits to the respective territories at times agreed upon with the administering state." There were apparently no serious objections to this wording, although the British and French preferred to leave the powers of the Trusteeship Council rather vague following the precedent of the Covenant with regard to the Mandates Commission.[49] The original phraseology did not include the provision that the visits would be at times agreed to by the administering state, and it is reasonable to assume that this was added to satisfy states such as the United Kingdom and France who would undoubtedly be administering trust territories under the new system.

One important subject discussed privately by the Big Five which is not manifested by the differences between the United States draft and the working paper was the question of "self-determination." In the Soviet amendments to the American draft those words were used in the para-

[48] The New York *Times*, May 4, 1945.

[49] "United Kingdom Draft of Chapter for Inclusion in United Nations Charter," *UNCIO, Documents*, Vol. 3, pp. 609-14 (Doc. 2 G/26 (d)). "International Trusteeship System," French Preliminary Draft, *UNCIO, Documents*, Vol. 3, pp. 604-6 (Doc. 2 G/26 (a)). Neither of these proposals specifically empowered the Trusteeship Council to do anything more than examine annual reports of the administering state.

graph dealing with the objectives and purposes of the trusteeship system. When the Russian delegate brought up this matter orally, he was met by rather pronounced opposition from the French and, more especially, the British. The latter pointed to the pitfalls which would inevitably develop were the phrase to be incorporated in the Charter. In Palestine, for example, strict adherence to "self-determination" would mean the complete political ascendancy of the Arabs at the expense of the Jews—obviously an unthinkable arrangement if peace were to be preserved in that area. A similar situation, the British argued further, obtained in parts of Africa where it would be impossible in many cases to distinguish between the various tribes, especially where various groups of one tribe lived in different territories.[50] The Soviet delegate's answer to this was that his position could not be changed without authorization from his home government. As this was not immediately forthcoming the matter was left in abeyance for a time, and was finally resolved by the inclusion of the sense of the phrase (the actual words "self-determination" are not used), but in a manner so as to render the precise meaning obscure, to say the least.[51]

Committee II/4. With this extensive basis of agreement among the sponsoring powers and France, it was possible for Committee II/4 to begin definite action, following the method of considering the Proposed Working Paper point by point. Despite the fact that widespread accord existed, there were still two or three important changes to be made in the proposals in order that the Big Five might reach complete agreement. Furthermore, states such as Egypt and Syria, representing the point of view of dependent peoples, had not as yet had much to say about the proposals.

The first four meetings of the committee, May 5 to May 14, were confined to general discussion and comments on the American and British proposals for a trusteeship system. At the fifth meeting, May 15, the United States delegate, Mr. Stassen, submitted the working paper, and beginning with the seventh meeting, on May 16, the committee turned its attention to Part B of the document.[52] At the outset one of the few important remaining points of contention among the Big Five became

[50] To the writer, this argument about the African tribes seems weak, since the problem of "who's who in Africa" would have to be faced in any event if the territories were to achieve "self-government or independence."

[51] Article 76, section (b) reads: "to promote the political, economic, social and educational advancement of the inhabitants of the trust territories, and their progressive development towards self-government or independence as may be appropriate to the particular circumstances of each territory and its peoples *and the freely expressed wishes of the peoples concerned*, and as may be provided by the terms of each trusteeship agreement." Italics, the writer's, indicate the phrase in point.

[52] The sixth meeting, on May 17, was devoted to part A of the proposals.

apparent when the committee decided to postpone consideration of paragraph B2, relating to the basic objectives of the system, pending the completion of informal discussion between "certain delegations." [53] This concerned the proposed addition of independence as a goal for people living in territories brought under the trusteeship system. Both the Chinese and Soviet proposals had included reference to independence, and the Russians especially were adamant in their position that "full national independence" should be a goal for all territories brought under the system.

The debate on this issue extended throughout most of the period during which Committee II/4 met and proved to be one of the knottiest problems in connection with the drafting of trusteeship provisions. The chief opposition to the Russians came from the British delegation, with the Americans trying to reconcile the opposing points of view, but on the whole siding with the British.[54] Originally, the Russians pressed for their aim to be included in Part A of the working paper, the declaration of principles regarding dependent areas generally, as well as in the objectives for territories coming under the trusteeship system. But the compromise which was eventually worked out provided that "independence" would not be mentioned in Part A, although it would be included in Part B with the qualifying phrase "as may be appropriate to the particular circumstances of each territory and its peoples and the freely expressed wishes of the peoples concerned, and as may be provided by the trusteeship arrangement." [55] Throughout the informal discussions on this point, the delegates from some of the former mandated territories, such as Syria, in addition to such states as the Philippines and Egypt, put up a real fight for the inclusion of independence at least in Part B of the proposals, and this undoubtedly had some effect on the Big Five's eventual agreement to include the term.

While these informal discussions were proceeding the committee soon ran into further difficulty with regard to the conservatory clause,[56] about which the delegate from Egypt argued that it was not clear just whose rights the paragraph was designed to protect. He desired to amend the wording to make it clear that it was the rights of the peoples of the mandated territories, not the rights of the mandatory states, which were being safeguarded. This, as one might suppose, produced some reaction on the part of the mandatory powers, and action on the matter was

[53] "Summary Report of the Seventh Meeting of Committee II/4," May 19, 1945. *UNCIO, Documents,* Vol. 10, p. 459.

[54] The New York *Times,* May 19, 1945. On the informal negotiations on this point generally, see The New York *Times,* May 19 to June 2, 1945.

[55] "Summary Report of the Thirteenth Meeting of Committee II/4," June 8, 1945. *UNCIO, Documents,* Vol. 10, p. 514.

[56] See above, p. 34.

postponed in order to give the delegates from Egypt and the United States, the latter acting as moderator, a chance to harmonize the different points of view.[57] The question was settled, finally, at the thirteenth meeting of the committee, by the acceptance of the following substitute paragraph proposed by the United States representative:

> 5. Except as may be agreed upon in individual trusteeship arrangements, made under paragraphs 3, 4, and 6, placing each territory under the trusteeship system, and until such agreements have been concluded, nothing in this Chapter shall be construed in or of itself to alter in any manner the rights whatsoever of any states or any peoples or the terms of existing international instruments to which member states may respectively be parties. This paragraph should not be interpreted as giving grounds for delay or postponement of the negotiation and conclusion of the agreements for placing mandated and other territories, as provided for in paragraph 3, under the trusteeship system.[58]

This was agreed to unanimously with the understanding that among the "rights whatsoever of any states or any peoples" there were included any rights set forth in paragraph 4 of Article 22 of the League of Nations Covenant.[59]

Another important modification of the working paper made in Committee II/4 concerned representation on the Trusteeship Council. At the thirteenth meeting the United States delegate proposed that the Trusteeship Council be composed of an equal number of administering and non-administering states, but included in this would be representatives from each of the Big Five. This was doubtless in deference to Soviet wishes, as the Soviet Union alone had originally provided for such composition of the Trusteeship Council. In the discussion which followed, the delegate from Egypt argued that each of the Big Five should be considered as an administering state in that they were interested parties. Thus at least half the seats on the Trusteeship Council should, and would, following Egypt's contention, be taken by elected members. This view, however, was not accepted and the United States amendment was adopted in unaltered form.[60]

The fourth important change made by the committee referred to the relationship of the Security Council to the Trusteeship Council with regard to strategic areas. The working paper provided that the former "may" avail itself of the assistance of the latter, and the Egyptian dele-

[57] "Summary Report of the Ninth Meeting of Committee II/4," May 23, 1945. *UNCIO, Documents*, Vol. 10, p. 477.

[58] "Summary Report of the Thirteenth Meeting of Committee II/4," June 8, 1945. *Ibid.*, pp. 516-17.

[59] *Ibid.*, p. 515.

[60] "Summary Report of the Thirteenth Meeting of Committee II/4," June 8, 1945. *UNCIO, Documents*, Vol. 10, p. 516.

gate proposed that this be changed to "should" since the humanitarian function went beyond the competence of the Security Council and should be exercised by the Trusteeship Council. Against this it was argued that it was not always possible "to separate 'political, economic, and social matters' from security matters and that it was essential to avoid laying a basis for future jurisdictional conflicts between the Security and Trusteeship Councils."[61] The matter was left unsettled until the next meeting of the committee when, apparently after informal discussions among the interested states, Egypt and the United States jointly offered a substitute phrase reading "shall, without prejudice to security considerations. . . ." This satisfied all the members of the committee, and was adopted unanimously.[62]

Finally, the objectives of the system were expanded to include the encouragement of "respect for human rights and for fundamental freedoms for all without distinction as to race, language, religion, or sex," as well as a clause providing for equal treatment for the nationals of all members of the United Nations "in the administration of justice." The origins of these additions are not disclosed in the records of the meetings of Committee II/4, except that in proposing them the United States delegate stated that they, together with the incorporation of independence as a goal, took into account "ideas expressed by China, Mexico, Iraq, Egypt, and others on the Committee, and adjusted language to meet certain French suggestions."[63]

In addition to the modifications just noted there were other minor changes, but these were of a clarifying rather than substantive nature. In the fourteenth and fifteenth meetings of Committee II/4[64] it was decided, in each case unanimously, (1) that the committee recommend to Committee I/2 (dealing with membership, amendments, and the Secretariat) that the Trusteeship Council be included among the principal organs of the organization as set forth in the Charter; (2) that the Trusteeship Council should adopt its own rules of procedure, including required meetings, such rules to include provision for the calling of a meeting on the request of a majority of the members of the Council; and (3) that the committee recommend that voting in the Trusteeship Council be by simple majority. Each of these was included in the final draft of Chapter XIII of the Charter. The first undoubtedly stemmed from the recognition of the importance of dependent areas in the postwar

[61] "Summary Report of the Ninth Meeting of Committee II/4," May 23, 1945. *Ibid.*, p. 478.

[62] "Summary Report of the Tenth Meeting of Committee II/4," May 24, 1945. *Ibid.*, p. 486.

[63] "Summary Report of the Thirteenth Meeting of Committee II/4," June 8, 1945. *Ibid.*, pp. 513-14.

[64] *Ibid.*, pp. 543-44, 564. These meetings were held on June 15 and 16, 1945.

world—an importance further recognized by the provision for permanent representation of the Big Five on the Council.

In general the Summary Records of the meetings of Committee II/4 reveal that most of the discussion involved criticisms and suggested modifications of the working paper by those members who took it upon themselves to represent the interests of dependent peoples. The delegates were successful in broadening the rights and protections afforded the inhabitants of trust territories to a substantial degree. The fact that the committee was able to effect these changes is ample evidence that the trusteeship provisions of the Charter were not "crammed down the throats" of the smaller powers, as it were, by the Big Five.[65] The specific inclusion of independence as a goal for territories brought within the system, while representing a compromise, nevertheless is alone a significant enough modification of the working paper to illustrate the important part played by the small states—particularly those of a former dependent status. It is possible, however, to overemphasize the role of the small states in the formation of the trusteeship system, for it must be kept in mind that what was being created was a *voluntary* system, one which would in the last analysis depend for its success on the cooperation of the administering states—so that always in the background lurked the possibility that these latter states might be pushed too far. This possibility undoubtedly had an effect on the small states as well as on China and the Soviet Union and induced them to compromise on many issues.

In this connection it is worth while to note at least three proposals directed toward further benefiting the dependent peoples, which were not included in the Charter. Two of these were suggested simultaneously, and referred to the termination of a trust and the transfer of a trust to another administering authority if a trusteeship agreement were broken or the administering authority ceased to be a member of the United Nations.[66] These, it was argued, would fill obvious gaps in the trusteeship provisions as they then stood. Furthermore, the experience of the League when Japan withdrew, yet retained her mandates, disregarding obligations in respect to those mandates, should be a lesson. Against this reasoning, it was pointed out that provision for the termination or transfer of a

[65] The phrase "smaller powers" is used advisedly. Despite the fact that China and the Soviet Union sided with them in many instances in Committee II/4, these two major powers had agreed to the Proposed Working Paper submitted to the committee, and had agreed to present a solid front with the other members of the Big Five on questions agreed to in private consultation. Further, there must have been some incentive, although this is difficult to substantiate, for them to avoid the creation of irreconcilable divergencies among the Big Five on trusteeship if only to reinforce their solidarity on other issues such as the veto.

[66] "Summary Report of the Twelfth Meeting of Committee II/4," June 1, 1945. *UNCIO, Documents*, Vol. 10, p. 506.

trust without the consent of the administering authority would be contrary to the voluntary basis upon which the trusteeship proposals had been built, and there would be obvious difficulties if the organization should attempt to take away a trust from a reluctant state. Moreover, League experience had shown that there was no necessity for a specific formula in order that a trust territory attain independence.[67] At the end of the discussion, Egypt, which had sponsored the proposals, agreed not to press a motion for amendment when the chairman asked the representatives of the United States and the United Kingdom to answer the following questions:

(1) If a state withdraws from the United Nations Organization and continues to hold a trust territory under the Charter, how is the Organization to continue to exercise its responsibilities with respect to the administration of that trust territory?

(2) If a state administering a trust territory commits an act of aggression, what consequences will follow in relation to its trust?

These questions were answered at the next meeting of the committee to the effect that in the case of (1) if the state withdraws "in good standing" there should be no reason for transferring the trust territory; if it leaves under other circumstances the General Assembly or Security Council must decide on appropriate actions; (2) the administering state will be treated just as any other aggressor, and specific action will depend on decisions of the Security Council.[68] These answers satisfied the interested states, and specific provision in the Charter for the determination and/or transfer of a trust was therefore omitted.[69]

The third unaccepted suggestion, backed strongly by the delegates from Egypt, India, and Iraq, was that in the selection of the administering authority due regard should be given "to the wishes of the population." [70] For the proposal it was argued that the Covenant had done this in certain cases (with regard to "A" mandates), and that much trouble in the mandates would have been saved had the idea been extended to the other types. Moreover, it was unfair to assign peoples to an administering authority without consulting their wishes. The opponents of the amendment pointed out that the wishes of the dependent peoples were already provided for in the paragraph on objectives of the system, but then proceeded to weaken their contention somewhat by asserting that there

[67] "Summary Report of the Fourteenth Meeting of Committee II/4," June 15, 1945. *Ibid.*, pp. 547-48.

[68] The specific replies are contained in Annex C of the Report of the Rapporteur of Committee II/4, (Doc. 1115, II/4/44 (1) (a)), in *ibid.*, pp. 620-21.

[69] "Summary Report of the Fifteenth Meeting of Committee II/4" June 20, 1945. *Ibid.*, pp. 601-2.

[70] "Summary Report of the Fourteenth Meeting of Committee II/4" June 15, 1945. *Ibid.*, p. 545.

were practical difficulties in determining the wishes of the people, and that other considerations, strategic for example, had to be taken into account. At any rate, all attempts to include the proposal or even to postpone further discussion failed.[71] The three proposed modifications were mentioned by Mr. Al-Jamali of Iraq in Commission II when the proposals of Committee II/4 were discussed, but only as possibilities for future action,[72] and no attempt was made at the commission stage to reintroduce them.

With the completion of the work of Committee II/4, the trusteeship provisions in the Charter were in final substantive form. The Coordinating Committee of the conference made several changes in these provisions, but those were only changes in style or in the position of some of the clauses. As they appear in the Charter the trusteeship provisions are contained in two chapters: XII, outlining the general system, and XIII, providing for the Trusteeship Council.[73] A Declaration Regarding Non-Self-Governing Territories, based on Section A of the Proposed Working Paper, which refers to all dependent territories both within and without the trusteeship system, appears as Chapter XI of the Charter. The Charter itself was signed on June 26, 1945, and went into effect on October 24 of the same year.

Undoubtedly the most striking differences, and those most germane to this study, between Article 22 of the Covenant and Chapters XII and XIII of the Charter, pertain to the scope and objectives of the two systems, and to the devices for international supervision in each. The mandates system, as part of the treaties of peace ending the First World War, was logically confined to ex-enemy territories, while the trusteeship system embraces potentially any and all dependent areas, including the former mandates. The Covenant classification of mandates into "A," "B," and "C" types was not followed in the Charter. Instead, each trusteeship agreement is to be drawn up by the states directly concerned, and approved by the General Assembly or Security Council, depending upon whether the area is nonstrategic or strategic. This is a much more flexible arrangement than that of the League, since each agreement may vary according to the territory concerned without the rigidifying effect of prior classification.[74] For those territories brought within the trusteeship system self-government or independence, depending on the particular circumstances of each territory, is specifically laid down as an objective.

[71] *Ibid.*, pp. 546-47.

[72] "Verbatim Minutes of the Third Meeting of Commission II," June 21, 1945. *Ibid.*, Vol. 8, p. 133.

[73] These two chapters are contained in Appendix, Part I, B.

[74] *Cf.* Ralph Bunche, "The Trusteeship System and Non-Self-Governing Territories in the Charter of the United Nations," *State Department Bulletin*, Vol. XIII (July-December, 1945), p. 1041.

The Covenant had provisionally recognized the independence of "A" mandates only, although the possibility that other territories might become independent was not ruled out. Under Chapter XIII of the Charter the devices for international supervision include, in addition to reports by the administering authority as had been required under the League, the acceptance of petitions by the Trusteeship Council, and provision for periodic visits to the trust territories at times agreed upon by the administering authorities. Both the latter two devices were considered by the Permanent Mandates Commission, but were never given any real application, at least as a regular method of supervision.

In more general terms, Chapters XII and XIII of the Charter are much more specific in laying down the lines of international control of dependent areas than were the Covenant's provisions. This is perhaps best illustrated by the body set up in each case to exercise international supervision. The Permanent Mandates Commission was provided for in Article 22 only in so far as "it shall be constituted," nothing being said about its composition or status, except that it was to receive and examine the reports of the mandatories and advise the Council. The Trusteeship Council, on the other hand, is the subject of a separate chapter in the Charter, and rather detailed provisions are made for its composition, functions, and to a certain extent its procedure. The commission of private experts under the League has been changed to a council of government representatives under the United Nations—a council which, while exercising its functions under the authority of the General Assembly and Security Council, nevertheless is a principal organ of the United Nations in its own right with considerably increased powers of supervision over those of its predecessor.

Much can be said both for and against this change from a commission of private experts to a council of government officials. Against the change it can be argued that the League body could and did keep aloof from the vicissitudes of the power politics which were so manifest in the Council and Assembly. Further, this meant that the supervision of mandatory administration could be, and was undertaken in an objective manner by which the rights of both the mandatory states and the dependent peoples were protected, rather than having the mandated territories become the subject of accusation and counter-accusation were government officials involved. Finally, it can be maintained that since the mandates (or trusteeship) system is primarily a matter of administration, colonial experts are much more qualified to sit in the international supervisory agency than are government representatives who may have little experience in the field.

For the change, however, it can be asserted that governmental representatives can speak with more authority than private experts. The

Commission could only advise—the Trusteeship Council can act.[75] Further, there is no use blinding one's self to the fact that dependent areas are very much a part of the power factor in world politics and putting the supervision of trust territories in the hands of an expert commission would not change the essential strategic importance of those territories nor diminish the interest various states have in them. And, finally, although theoretically a representative on the Trusteeship Council might know nothing of colonial administration, in practice it behooves a government to appoint a well-qualified man to the position; and the history of the Trusteeship Council to date shows that this has, in the main, been the case.

In sum, then, it can be said that if the rights, particularly political rights, of the dependent peoples within the system, and the mechanism of international guarantee of those rights are taken as criteria, the trusteeship system as formulated in the Charter represents a decided advance over the mandates system. Yet the Charter itself is nothing more than a piece of paper—and if that advance is to mean anything more than a potentiality the provisions of the Charter must be carried out in practice.

[75] This point can be illustrated by the power of the Trusteeship Council to send visiting missions to the trust territories, a practice which the Permanent Mandates Commission felt constrained to avoid.

CHAPTER THREE

Setting Up the Trusteeship System

By its constitutional design the Trusteeship Council, and hence the general trusteeship system, could not begin to function until agreements putting territories under trusteeship had been reached. The Charter provides that the Trusteeship Council should be composed of an equal number of administering and nonadministering states, always including the Big Five. Thus the Council could not be established until there were a sufficient number of states administering territories under the system to provide this equality.[1]

The central problem in organizing the new system was how to proceed as quickly as possible in the negotiation of trusteeship agreements. Of the three types of dependent areas envisaged by the Charter as potentially coming under the trusteeship system, the first—mandates—offered the most immediate possibilities of implementing the Charter's terms. Territories to be detached from World War II enemy states could not be considered until peace treaties with those states had been signed; and while there was nothing to prevent various colonial powers from offering to put "other areas" under the system, proposals of this nature were not forthcoming so that mandated territories were naturally the first to be put under trusteeship.

The Preparatory Commission. In so far as it dealt with problems of trusteeship the Preparatory Commission was primarily concerned with exploring the problems of the transfer of mandates to the trusteeship system. This Commission, set up under the Interim Arrangements signed at San Francisco at the close of the Conference on International Organization, did not meet until the latter part of November, 1945, some five months after the close of the Conference. In the meantime, however, an Executive Committee made up of representatives from fourteen states[2] was set up to give preliminary consideration to the actual formation of the United Nations and to make recommendations to the full Commission. This Executive Committee met in the period August to October, 1945, and it was on the basis of its recommendations that the Preparatory

[1] The smallest number of administering authorities needed to effect this was 3; and this only if at least 2 of the administering authorities were among the Big Five.

[2] Australia, Brazil, Canada, Chile, China, Czechoslovakia, France, Iran, Mexico, the Netherlands, the Soviet Union, the United Kingdom, the United States, and Yugoslavia.

Commission itself based its work. The Committee divided itself into ten subcommittees, one of which was charged with the task of formulating recommendations concerning trusteeship.[3]

Subcommittee Four, which dealt with trusteeship arrangements, faced a procedural dilemma in connection with inaugurating the system. On the one hand, the Trusteeship Council could not be organized until territories had been placed under the trusteeship system. But on the other hand, the Charter provides that one of the duties of the Trusteeship Council is to advise the General Assembly or the Security Council, as the case may be, on the terms of the trusteeship agreements which bring the territories within the system.[4] The British representative suggested three alternatives to meet this problem: (1) the Trusteeship Council could be composed of the Big Five alone until agreements with other powers had been reached; (2) the organization of the Council could be deferred until agreements had been reached by the states directly concerned; or (3) the need for interim arrangements could be recognized and a Temporary Trusteeship Council could be set up composed of the Big Five and those powers who within a given time (the British delegate suggested two weeks) before the opening of the first General Assembly indicated their intention of putting one or more territories under the trusteeship system. The British delegate argued that of these, the first was undesirable because those mandatory powers not among the Big Five would naturally desire full voting rights on the Trusteeship Council while the agreements were being considered. The second left the Council in too vague a position, especially since there was as yet no accepted definition of the "states directly concerned." He therefore preferred the third alternative, and after further discussion and modification the subcommittee, acting on the basis of Article 22 of the Charter,[5] adopted this plan.[6]

As the proposal for a Temporary Trusteeship Council developed in Subcommittee Four, it provided for a membership composed of the Big Five, of mandatory states, and of sufficient other states elected by the General Assembly to maintain equality between administering and nonadministering states. Relevant to this was an apparent understanding that the Netherlands should be included in the last category.[7] The

[3] *Report of the Executive Committee to the Preparatory Commission of the United Nations*, p. 5.

[4] "Summary Report of the First Meeting of Subcommittee Four" of *Executive Committee of the Preparatory Commission*, September 14, 1945.

[5] Article 22 provides: "The General Assembly may establish such subsidiary organs as it deems necessary for the performance of its functions."

[6] "Summary Report of the Fourth Meeting of Subcommittee Four" of *Executive Committee of the Preparatory Commission*, September 21, 1945.

[7] "Summary Report of the Second Meeting," *ibid.*, September 18, 1945.

Council's duties were to include assisting the General Assembly "in expediting the constitution of the trusteeship system and, pending the establishment of the Trusteeship Council, in taking such other action in connection with the trusteeship system as may be found necessary. . . ." [8] There was no apparent disagreement on this proposal in the subcommittee, and it therefore surprised many of the delegates that in the Executive Committee the Soviet representative came out strongly against the formation of a Temporary Trusteeship Council on the grounds that it was not only unconstitutional (there being no provision for it in the Charter), but also that it "would merely cause confusion particularly since no territories under trusteeship were in existence at the moment." [9] Despite this objection from a crucial quarter, the Executive Committee by a vote of seven to three, with four abstentions, approved the proposal for the Temporary Council. Even so, in view of the newly arisen opposition on the part of the Soviet Union, it was obvious that the proposal would have a difficult time in the Preparatory Commission.

The latter convened in London in November, 1945, and organized itself into a number of committees, each responsible, on the basis of the recommendations of the Executive Committee, for formulating proposals designed to carry out the provisions of the Charter setting up the actual machinery of the United Nations. In the period between the adoption of the recommendations of the Executive Committee and the first meeting of Committee IV (Trusteeship) of the Preparatory Commission, those states opposed to the creation of the Temporary Trusteeship Council had time to formulate specific alternative proposals of their own, and at the third meeting of Committee IV, Mr. Franic, the delegate from Yugoslavia, submitted a plan which, in the opinion of its supporters, would obviate the necessity of creating the temporary organ and insure the early formation of the Trusteeship Council.[10]

This plan called for the General Assembly, at its first session, to invite the submission of declarations by the mandatory powers of their intention to place their mandates under the trusteeship system. The mandatory states would then, in the period between the first and second parts of the first session of the Assembly, negotiate agreements with the members

[8] The quotation is from "Recommendations Concerning Trusteeship," *Report of the Executive Committee to the Preparatory Commission of the United Nations*, p. 7.

[9] "Summary Report of the Twenty-seventh Meeting" of *Executive Committee of the Preparatory Commission*, September 19, 1945. Subsequently the Soviet Union added the argument that the creation of the Temporary Trusteeship Council would permit the mandatory powers to delay the transfer of mandates to the new system. *Preparatory Commission, Committee IV: Trusteeship, Summary Record of Meetings* (November-December, 1945), p. 3. The obvious implication behind this argument was, of course, that the mandatory powers were "stalling."

[10] *Preparatory Commission, Committee IV: Trusteeship*, Third Meeting, (November 30, 1945), p. 6.

of the Big Five not holding mandates, as well as those states bordering the proposed trust territories. It was hoped that the second part of the first session of the Assembly could then approve the draft agreements and on that basis proceed to organize the Trusteeship Council.[11]

It will be noticed that in making this proposal Mr. Franic, in addition to raising again the question of whether or not a temporary body should be created, brought up a second issue—every bit as important as the first—of what states were "directly concerned" in the negotiations of the trusteeship agreements, at least those regarding mandates. The Charter provides that all trusteeship agreements "shall be agreed upon by the states directly concerned, including the mandatory power," in the case of mandates. The Charter does not, however, contain a specific definition of "states directly concerned," and this was apparently the first of many unsuccessful attempts to reach agreement on a definition.

There was some discussion of the Yugoslav plan during the third and fourth meetings of Committee IV, during the course of which it was pointed out that while the proposal was constructive there were certain attendant difficulties, among which was the possibility that the agreements might not be reached by the end of the first session of the General Assembly; if this proved true, there would be no organ to deal with trusteeship matters until the next General Assembly. The main purpose of the Temporary Trusteeship Council was to provide a continuously functioning agency until such time as the permanent Trusteeship Council could be organized.[12] Extended discussion was delayed, however, until such time as various delegations, notably the British and American, could get instructions from their home governments.[13] There is little available evidence to support any conclusion as to why the Soviet Union and its satellites changed their minds about the temporary organ other than their known dislike of the mandates system, and the consequent dislike of any plan which might permit delay in establishing the new arrangements. The question of the definition of the states directly concerned, however, is a different matter. If the Yugoslav plan had been adopted it would have meant not only that the Soviet Union—as a member of the Trusteeship Council, permanent or temporary—would have a voice in approving the trusteeship agreements, but also that, as a state directly concerned, it would be one of the negotiating states in drawing up the agreements. This is reported to have worried both Great Britain, with

[11] The New York *Times*, December 1, 1945. At the time of the Preparatory Commission it was generally agreed that the first part of the first session of the General Assembly was to be devoted to problems of organization; these resolved, the second part could begin work on substantive questions.

[12] *Preparatory Commission, Committee IV: Trusteeship*, Fourth Meeting, (December 1, 1945), p. 10.

[13] The New York *Times*, December 2, 1945.

reference to Italian possessions on her Mediterranean "life-line," and the United States, concerning the Japanese islands in the Pacific.[14]

At the tenth meeting of the committee a subcommittee composed of Belgium, the United Kingdom, the United States, the Soviet Union, and Yugoslavia, was appointed to consider the various proposals and to recommend to the full committee a new draft based on these proposals.[15] While documentary records of the meetings of this subcommittee are not available, secondhand reports, based on interviews with some of the delegates involved, indicate that the Soviet Union maintained uncompromising opposition to any form of a temporary trusteeship body.[16] In effect, what the subcommittee finally agreed upon was a postponement of the decision on the issues involved by turning over the entire question to the General Assembly. The proposal, as ultimately adopted by the Commission, after approval by Committee IV, recommended:

> that the General Assembly adopt the following resolution:
>
> The General Assembly of the United Nations calls on states administering territories under League of Nations mandate to undertake practical steps, in concert with the other states directly concerned, for the implementation of Article 79 of the Charter (which provides for the conclusion of agreements on the terms of trusteeship for each territory to be placed under the trusteeship system), in order to submit these agreements for approval preferably not later than during the Second Part of the First Session of the General Assembly.
>
> Those trusteeship matters which will be taken up by the General Assembly at the First Part of its First Session for the purpose of expediting the establishment of the trusteeship system, will be considered by the Trusteeship Committee of the General Assembly, using the methods which the General Assembly considers most appropriate for the further consideration of these matters.[17]

From one point of view this represented a victory for the Soviet Union and its supporters since the proposal to create some form of temporary organ was not accepted. Actually, however, the General Assembly could still set up an *ad hoc* committee if it so desired, and perhaps more important, the thorny issue of just what countries constituted "states directly concerned" with respect to any given territory to be brought under the trusteeship system remained undecided. In the General Assembly itself a *modus vivendi* was reached with regard to the states directly concerned, a *modus vivendi* which did not include the Soviet Union as a participating power in the initial stages of drafting the trusteeship agreements, and which that power opposed to the point of

[14] *Ibid.*, December 11, 1945.

[15] *Preparatory Commission, Committee IV: Trusteeship*, Tenth Meeting, (December 10, 1945), p. 27.

[16] The New York *Times*, December 12, 1945.

[17] *Report of the Preparatory Commission of the United Nations*, p. 49.

boycotting the early meetings of the Trusteeship Council, ostensibly on this issue.

The First Session of the General Assembly, Part I. When the General Assembly met in January, 1946, the general discussion included the subject of trusteeship. In the course of this discussion the Assembly unanimously expressed its desire that the Trusteeship Council should be set up at the earliest possible date, and in response to this the delegates from the United Kingdom, Australia, New Zealand, and Belgium all indicated that they were willing to place their mandated territories under the trusteeship system.[18] This left the mandated areas under the control of France, the Union of South Africa, and the United States in doubt. France indicated that it would study arrangements for placing her mandated territories under trusteeship, South Africa stated that it would consult the indigenous population of South West Africa (its mandate), while the United States remained silent about the Pacific islands formerly mandated to Japan and now under American military control.

The hesitancy of the United States was officially explained in terms of the legal ambiguities involved if the United States were to assume responsibilities as an administering authority for the islands before a peace treaty had been negotiated with Japan by which the latter surrendered all relevant rights.[19] While this might serve as a topic of discussion concerning the question of sovereignty in the mandates, it is irrelevant because it was in no sense the real reason for American silence. Actually the matter became involved with the question of United States security interests in the Pacific and a re-emergence of the old battle between the State Department, on the one hand, and the military, with support from Congress, on the other, which had supposedly been settled by the concept of strategic territories. The issue now concerned the fact that strategic areas would be under the aegis of the Security Council, and it was feared that defense plans of the United States in the area would be subject to the veto.[20] It does not seem to have occurred to those who demanded annexation of the islands that the United States could, as it did, insure our security interests in the trust agreement; for without American acceptance of the agreement there would be no trusteeship. At any rate, the matter simmered some time, and the United States Pacific Trust did not come into existence until well after other mandated areas had been transferred to the new system.

After the plenary discussion in the General Assembly, Chapter IV of the *Report of the Preparatory Commission* was referred, on January 19,

[18] *Yearbook of the United Nations, 1946-47*, pp. 575-76.

[19] The New York *Times*, January 10, 1946.

[20] *Ibid.*, January 15-18, 25, February 17, 1946.

to the Fourth Committee (Trusteeship) for consideration and report.[21] The Fourth Committee, after some discussion concerning the position of France and South Africa with regard to the mandated areas under their respective jurisdictions, turned its attention to the question of "states directly concerned." The issue arose in connection with a proposed United States amendment of the *Report of the Preparatory Commission*. This proposal, among other things, called upon the General Assembly to urge "that all practical steps . . . be taken by the states directly concerned so as to permit the establishment of the Trusteeship Council." [22] The Syrian delegate, while in general agreeing with the proposal, argued that the phrase in question had to be defined so that the General Assembly would know upon whom to call. This precipitated an extended discussion of the issue.

During the course of the ensuing debate two general positions, in opposition to each other, became defined. On the one hand the mandatory powers, the United States, and Canada, favored in one form or another the postponement of a decision. It was argued that (1) the decision was beyond the competence of the committee, (2) the General Assembly by its approval or disapproval of the trusteeship agreements would indicate whether it felt that all the states directly concerned had been consulted, (3) it was up to the Trusteeship Council to make the decision, and (4) the state placing a territory under the system could so declare and the states considering themselves directly concerned could thereupon enter negotiations through diplomatic channels.[23] On the other hand the Syrian delegate, backed in general by the Arab delegates, argued that it was necessary to establish some criteria, for guidance if nothing more. He proposed the following as a general guide for determining whether or not a state was directly concerned:

1. Mandatories in the case of mandates
2. States submitting colonies to the system
3. States which were concerned, by virtue of geographical proximity, or cultural, linguistic, economic, social and continued historical ties, with the territories to be placed under trusteeship.[24]

The attempt to establish specific criteria strikingly points up the difficulties involved in defining the troublesome phrase. Leaving aside the obvious questions raised concerning the definition of such words as "cultural" and "social," the question arises: who is to decide whether a

[21] *Official Records of the First Part of the First Session of the General Assembly, Plenary Meetings* (January-February, 1946), pp. 241, 572.

[22] United Nations Document A/C.4/3.

[23] *Official Record of the First Part of the First Session of the General Assembly, Fourth Committee, Trusteeship* (January-February, 1946), pp. 19-21.

[24] *Ibid.*, p. 20.

given state meets the requirements? In the first instance it was bound to be the mandatory (or, generally, the state desiring to place a territory under trusteeship). Then, if the General Assembly or Security Council is to approve or disapprove that decision, as they must under the Charter, the matter reverts to the basic fact that the decision in any case must await General Assembly or Security Council action. Further, by attempting to lay down specific criteria there is a danger of ruling out some state that for other reasons might be vitally concerned in the area. As was wisely pointed out by the Chinese delegate, the adoption of a specific definition of the phrase might well have delayed, rather than have facilitated, the early establishment of the trusteeship system, if only because of the opportunities for bickering during the process of negotiating the agreements.[25]

After further discussion, a subcommittee was appointed to draft a complete proposal after consideration of all the amendments submitted.[26] When the subcommittee reported its draft,[27] it was noticeable that there was no attempt to define "states directly concerned." Commenting on this, the Philippine delegate asked the reason for the omission and was told that, following extensive but inconclusive discussion, the subcommittee had decided to leave the matter in abeyance, and that the Arab delegates had consented not to press for a final determination of the question at that time.[28] The draft resolution was then passed unanimously. Actually, while the "states directly concerned" issue came up several times during the course of consideration of the first eight draft trusteeship agreements by the Fourth Committee, it was deferred each time until all the other provisions had been agreed upon.

The draft resolution was presented to the General Assembly on February 9, and was adopted unanimously by that body.[29] The resolution, in so far as it pertained directly to the trusteeship system, welcomed the declarations so far made by certain of the mandatory states of their intention to place their mandates under trusteeship, and invited the mandatories to undertake negotiations "in concert with the other states directly concerned," designed to draft trusteeship agreements in time for submission to the second part of the first General Assembly.

[25] *Ibid.*, p. 25.

[26] *Ibid.*, p. 29. The subcommittee was composed of the representatives of Australia, Belgium, Canada, China, Czechoslovakia, France, the Netherlands, New Zealand, the Soviet Union, Syria, the Union of South Africa, the United Kingdom, the United States, Uruguay, and Yugoslavia.

[27] United Nations Document A/C.4/21.

[28] *Official Record of the First Part of the First Session of the General Assembly, Fourth Committee, Trusteeship* (January-February, 1946), pp. 35.

[29] *Official Records of the First Part of the First Session of the General Assembly, Plenary Meetings* (January-February, 1946), pp. 376, 590-91.

The First Session of the General Assembly, Part II. During the period between the first and second parts of the first General Assembly, the mandatory powers took it upon themselves to draft trusteeship agreements, deciding in each case for themselves which states were in fact directly concerned.[30] Thus the United Kingdom sent draft agreements for Tanganyika, Togoland, and the Cameroons to France, Belgium, and the Union of South Africa "for comment" and to the other members of the Big Five "for information purposes." [31] France submitted draft agreements for Togoland and the Cameroons to the United Kingdom, as a state directly concerned, and communicated the terms "for information purposes" to the rest of the Big Five, Belgium, and the Union of South Africa.[32] Belgium likewise considered only the United Kingdom as a state directly concerned while communicating the terms of its draft for Ruanda-Urundi "for information" to the other members of the Security Council.[33] Australia and New Zealand exchanged views concerning New Guinea and Western Samoa only with each other, the United Kingdom, and France.[34] In each case this was done without prejudice to any final decision on a definition of states directly concerned, but it is interesting to note that in no case was either of the two criteria previously proposed (Yugoslavia's inclusion of the Big Five generally, or the Arabs' "essential interest" idea) made use of by the mandatory state. Be that as it may, the reconvened General Assembly saw eight draft agreements ready for submission. The General Assembly, upon receipt of these, referred them to its Fourth Committee for consideration.[35]

Before the detailed consideration of each of the eight draft trusteeship agreements took place, Committee Four engaged in extensive general discussion in the course of which two items of importance to this study emerged. The first of these concerns the interest in the fate of the trust peoples displayed by representatives of former dependent areas. At the fifteenth meeting of the committee the delegate from India, for example, during a speech on the general nature of the trusteeship agreements stated that:

the final object, which was the autonomy of those territories, should be clearly

[30]Apparently as early as January, 1946, there had been preliminary discussion among the United Kingdom, France, and Belgium on the question of placing mandates under trusteeship, but the actual drafting of texts and formal submission of these to other states did not occur until the summer. The New York *Times,* June 26, 1946.

[31] United Nations Document A/117.

[32] *Ibid.*

[33] *Ibid.*

[34] *Ibid.*

[35] *Official Record of the Second Part of the First Session of the General Assembly, Plenary Meetings* (October-December, 1946), pp. 933, 1477.

stated, and . . . the right of the natives to election and participation in the administration should be affirmed in detail. In particular it should be explicitly stated that no racial discrimination and no monopoly would be admitted in theory or fact. Freedom of speech, freedom of the press, freedom of assembly, and freedom to present petitions would have to be guaranteed. No authority should be given to establish a base without the approval of the United Nations. . . . Finally, it was desirable that, as with the Americans in the Philippines, a date limit for the transitional regime should be fixed.[36]

This quotation indicates generally the point of view of those states recently emerged from colonial status—a point of view that has remained vigorous and outspoken during the ten years the trusteeship system has been in operation, and which constitutes a continuous and concerted pressure in the direction of full and speedy attainment of the aims of trusteeship.

The second notable point about the general preliminary discussion in Committee Four is illustrated by the remarks of Mr. Bailey of Australia concerning the respective roles of the administering authority and the Trusteeship Council in a trust territory:

A clear distinction should be drawn between the governmental function of the administering authority and the advisory function of supervision assigned by the Charter to the Trusteeship Council.

The administering authority was accountable to the United Nations for its administration, but the administration itself was the function of the administering Power. The role of the Trusteeship Council was that of supervisor and not that of administrator.[37]

This view, at one time or another expressed or implied by most of the administering authorities, is important when viewed alongside the position of such states as India and the Philippines that the United Nations was the real administering authority while the individual administering state was merely the agent of the international body. It is worth while to keep this divergence of interpretation in mind, for it lies behind much of the debate in the Trusteeship Council—and likewise in the Fourth Committee—on the administration of the various trust territories.

In order to expedite the detailed consideration of the draft agreements, the Fourth Committee at its twentieth meeting appointed a subcommittee before which any member of the committee could place proposed modifications to any and all of the drafts.[38] After brief general discussion, the subcommittee decided to consider one draft agreement first rather than to deal simultaneously with all eight. That chosen was the draft for Western Samoa and the procedures developed in connection

[36] *Ibid., Fourth Committee, Trusteeship Part I* (November-December, 1946), p. 70.

[37] *Ibid.*, p. 95.

[38] *Ibid.*, pp. 116, 120.

with the consideration of this "pilot run" are important since in the main they were used for the other seven agreements.[39] Further, with regard to the questions raised concerning the draft agreement for Western Samoa, it was understood, though not formally, that a decision taken for Western Samoa would in general be followed by the Fourth Committee with respect to the other drafts. This held true in the main, although there were one or two exceptions. This discussion, therefore, will concentrate primarily on the procedures and problems concerned with the Western Samoa draft. Important differences between the decisions made with regard to this agreement and the other seven will then be noted.

Before the subcommittee continued its article by article examination of the agreements it was unanimously decided to request the Secretariat to prepare a paper on the procedure to be followed.[40] The memorandum submitted by the Secretariat,[41] and adopted unanimously at the third meeting of the subcommittee, outlined the course of procedure as follows:

(1) Article by Article consideration of the draft agreement.

(2) Preliminary examination confined to inquiries concerning the meaning, implications, or interpretation of specific articles. (One or two meetings.)

(3) All suggested changes to specific parts of an agreement to be sent, in writing, to the Secretary of the subcommittee and the administering authority within twenty-four hours after the end of the preliminary consideration.

(4) Final Article by Article examination. At this stage the administering authority indicates its willingness to accept suggested modifications.

(5) Final decision on the draft as a whole.

With the acceptance of this procedure the subcommittee went on to the specific provisions of the draft agreement. But while the preliminary article by article examination was supposed to be "confined to inquiries concerning the meaning, implication, or interpretation of specific articles," many of the delegates introduced specific modifications at that time. Thus in practice the preliminary examination served primarily as a sort of notification period, during which the administering authority was given notice that such and such a state would recommend specifically such and such a change in the draft when it came time for final article by article consideration—although some of the representatives did reserve their proposals until the latter stage. Because of this development in the procedure for considering the draft agreements much of the discussion in the later stage was a repetition of the former. This study, therefore, will not follow the actual process of the subcommittee hearings, but instead select the major points discussed in either or both of the two

[39] The agreements for Nauru, the Pacific Trust Territory of the United States, and Italian Somaliland will be dealt with separately.

[40] *Official Record of the Second Part of the First Session of the General Assembly, Fourth Committee, Trusteeship, Part II* (November-December, 1946), p. 9.

[41] United Nations Document A/C.4/Sub. 1/4.

"readings" of the drafts. Without going into each and every proposed change—there were upward of two hundred seventy-five—it is possible to single out several questions of general importance.

One of these arose in connection with Article 3 of the Western Samoa agreement which provided that the administering authority should have "full powers of administration, legislation and jurisdiction over the territory . . . as an integral part of New Zealand. . . ."[42] There was immediate reaction to the phrase "as an integral part." The reader will remember that this phrase was in one respect crucial to the formation of the mandates system, as it was the crux of the differences between the "B" and "C" mandates—and the "C" mandates were devised to insure that various territories, among them Western Samoa, were brought under the mandates system. Thus it should not have been surprising to find the phrase repeated in the proposed trusteeship agreement for Western Samoa. Notwithstanding, Mr. Menon, the delegate from India, asserted that the "peoples of the trust territories were latently independent," and that if the trust territories were made integral parts of the administering states "rebellion or secession would be necessary for the realization of their independence."[43] In his aversion to the phrase Mr. Menon was supported mildly by the United States delegate (who suggested "as if it were an integral part"), and more strongly by the Soviet delegate.[44] In reply, the representative of New Zealand, Sir Carl Berendsen, disavowed any intention, past, present, or future, of making Western Samoa an integral part of New Zealand. The latter merely wanted the right to administer it as an integral part—that is, to apply such of the laws of New Zealand as were appropriate to the local conditions.[45] Later Sir Carl told the subcommittee that to make the matter completely clear his government was prepared to accept the phrase "as if it were an integral part," as suggested by the American delegate and as found in the draft for New Guinea.[46] This, however, was unsatisfactory to the Soviet representative who requested a formal vote on his amendment to delete the phrase. The amendment was adopted by the subcommittee, and the article in question was approved as amended.[47]

[42] United Nations Document A/160, p. 4.

[43] *Official Records of the Second Part of the First Session of the General Assembly, Fourth Committee, Trusteeship, Part II* (November-December, 1946), p. 11.

[44] Both India and the Soviet Union submitted formal amendments to delete the phrase in question. United Nations Documents A/C.4/Sub. 1/9 and A/C.4/Sub. 1/15.

[45] *Official Records of the Second Part of the First Session of the General Assembly, Fourth Committee, Trusteeship, Part II* (November-December, 1946), p. 11.

[46] *Ibid.*, p. 46.

[47] *Ibid.*, p. 47. The vote on the amendment was 9 in favor, 7 against, with 1 abstention; the vote on Article 3, as amended, was 10 in favor, 2 against with 5 abstentions.

With regard to this deletion, however, it must be kept in mind that in terms of compelling the New Zealand government to accept the deletion, the decision meant nothing more than an expression of opinion, a *voeu*, of the subcommittee. The New Zealand government could reject the proposal and the original text would then have to be voted on. Suppose, then, that the original text had been voted down after such a refusal. If New Zealand still declined to modify its position the original wording would be voted on by the subcommittee as part of a vote on the entire draft. This process would be repeated in the Fourth Committee and finally in the General Assembly. In other words, there would always be tremendous pressure on those states objecting to the phrase not to vote against the entire draft since the goal was to get the territory quickly under trusteeship. Of course there would undoubtedly be corresponding pressure on New Zealand to modify its position, but the crucial point is that in the last analysis the General Assembly approves or rejects the drafts as a whole, and there consequently exists considerable incentive for the various delegations to overlook certain undesirable features of the drafts in order to attain the greater end of putting the territories under the trusteeship system. In this particular instance the New Zealand delegate informed the subcommittee that his government was prepared to accept the deletion, in the interests of harmony, and the draft was so modified.[48]

A second important question raised about the Western Samoa draft concerned a possible time limit for the period of trusteeship, by the end of which the territory was to be made self-governing or independent. During the preliminary discussion of the draft, Mr. Menon of India, pointing to the example set by the United States in the Philippines, suggested a similar timetable for independence for Western Samoa, together with provision for automatic revision of the agreement at an agreed future date.[49] It is interesting to note that this oral suggestion of the Indian representative involved an apparent attempt to change the letter if not the spirit of the Charter. The latter speaks of "self-government or independence," clearly indicating the possibility of a territory securing local autonomy *within* a particular political framework such as the British Commonwealth of Nations or the French Union. Whether this oversight on the part of Mr. Menon was intentional or not is not clear since when it came time for formal written amendments, self-government as well as independence was included in the Indian proposals. The immediate reaction of Sir Carl Berendsen to the Indian suggestion was that, although New Zealand earnestly desired the independence of Western Samoa, "the attainment of independence would depend on many

[48] *Ibid.*, p. 83.

[49] *Ibid.*, p. 15.

factors," and "the fixing of the time limit would therefore be completely impractical." With regard to the revision of the terms of the trusteeship agreement Sir Carl pointed out that all agreements would "be constantly reviewed by the Trusteeship Council," so that any specific provision was unnecessary verbiage in the agreement.[50]

Despite this apparent unwillingness on the part of New Zealand to accept modifications of this sort, when the formal amendments were submitted they included proposals for a time limit both for the attainment of political maturity and for revision of the agreement.[51] With regard to both of these proposals, it was argued that while there was nothing to be said against the principle involved, setting time limits for either or both revision of the agreement and the attainment of self-government or independence meant rigidifying a purposely flexible arrangement, and might convey the impression to the Samoans that attainment of self-government would be blocked until the fixed date. Further, the question arose of how to select the proper period during which a territory was to become prepared to "go it alone," for there exists always the possibility that an area may be given independence or self-government before it is capable of assuming the full responsibilities concomitant with such status. Finally, it was argued that the appropriate place to take up such questions was the Trusteeship Council, which would have the requisite knowledge to deal with these matters—knowledge which the subcommittee did not possess.[52]

Actually, what seems evident from the discussion was the desire on the part of the administering state to get as little committed in writing as possible—a natural point of view—while those states favoring the proposals wanted more specific assurance than was provided in the Charter that the trusteeship system would not be merely disguised annexation, as it was more than once charged the mandates system had been. When it came to a vote, both the Soviet and Indian proposals were rejected, however, and the draft agreement remained unchanged in this respect.[53]

---

[50] *Ibid.*

[51] Relevant amendments were proposed by the delegates from the Soviet Union and India. United Nations Documents A/C.4/Sub. 1/9 and A/C.4/Sub. 1/15. The Soviet proposal was confined to recommending an unspecified time limit for revision, while that of India included (a) a ten year limit before revision and (b) an unspecified limit by which time the territory was to be self-governing or independent.

[52] *Official Records of the Second Part of the First Session of the General Assembly, Fourth Committee, Trusteeship, Part II* (November-December, 1946), pp. 97-102.

[53] *Ibid.*, p. 102. The Indian proposal for a time limit for the attainment of self-government or independence was defeated by a vote of 4 in favor, 10 against, with 3 abstentions. The Indian proposal for a time limit of 10 years before revision of the agreement was defeated by a vote of 5 in favor, 9 against, with 3 abstentions. The Soviet proposal for an unspecified time limit before revision was defeated by a vote of 6 in favor, 8 against, with 3 abstentions.

Although rejected by the subcommittee, the idea of a time limit for the attainment of self-government or independence did not die, and became a very important consideration in connection with the former Italian colonies.

Another question of more than passing importance raised during the examination of the draft agreement for Western Samoa was with regard to immigration. Noting the absence of what they conceived to be satisfactory provisions on the subject, the Chinese and Indian delegates pressed for the inclusion of a paragraph similar to Article 7 of the "B" mandates which provided for equality of immigration rights as between nationals of member states and nationals of the mandatory.[54] While to Western eyes the right of immigration may not appear very fundamental, to those peoples who have historically felt the brunt of exclusion policies this was a crucial point for which they were prepared to exert considerable pressure. Sir Carl Berendsen answered these delegates by pointing to Article 76(d) of the Charter, which insures "equal treatment in social, economic, and commercial matters for all members of the United Nations and their nationals, and also equal treatment for the latter in the administration of justice. . . ." These words, however, did not specifically spell out the right of immigration, and satisfied neither the Chinese nor Indian delegates.

In addition to the above mentioned reference to Article 76(d) of the Charter, the chief argument against the proposal was that the interests of the indigenous inhabitants were paramount and if immigration conflicted with those interests immigration would have to be controlled. This argument was apparently telling, for after short debate, during which the New Zealand delegation assured the subcommittee it had no desire to discriminate except in the interests of the Western Samoans themselves, the Chinese amendment was rejected.[55]

The fourth important question brought up with regard to the draft agreement for Western Samoa occasioned perhaps more discussion than any other single item in the debates of the subcommittee. This concerned Article 10 of the agreement, and is of sufficient importance to be quoted in full:

> The administering authority shall ensure that the trust territory of Western Samoa shall play its part, in accordance with the Charter of the United Nations, in the maintenance of international peace and security. To this end the administering authority shall be entitled:
>
> (1) to establish naval, military and air bases and to erect fortifications in the trust territory;

[54] *Ibid.*, pp. 13, 14-15. United Nations Documents A/C.4/Sub. 1/10 and A/C.4/Sub. 1/15 contain the amendments in question.

[55] *Ibid.*, p. 91. The vote was 1 in favor, 7 against, with 9 abstentions.

(2) to station and employ armed forces in the territory;

(3) to make use of volunteer forces, facilities and assistance from the trust territory in carrying out the obligations toward the Security Council undertaken in that regard by the administering authority, as well as for local defence and the maintenance of law and order within the trust territory;

(4) to take all such other measures in accordance with the Purposes and Principles of the Charter of the United Nations as are in the opinion of the administering authority necessary to the maintenance of international peace and security and the defence of Western Samoa.[56]

The crucial point raised about this article concerned the functions to be performed by the Security Council. Arguing that only paragraph (3) came under the jurisdiction of the General Assembly, the Indian and especially the Soviet delegates maintained that action taken by the administering authority with respect to paragraphs (1), (2), and (4) should be supervised by the Security Council, and submitted amendments to that effect.[57]

This line of reasoning was "under no circumstances" acceptable to the New Zealand representative.[58] His position may be summed up in this way: (a) The neutralization of mandates had been disastrous as shown in World War II. (b) As a result, the Charter removed this restriction. (c) Article 82 of the Charter left it to the administering authority to decide whether a territory should be designated as strategic and New Zealand had decided Western Samoa should not be so designated.[59] (d) The concept of strategic areas had been adopted to prevent undue interference in territories where such interference could not be tolerated. Such a restriction on supervision was not required in Western Samoa.

Against this reasoning the Soviet delegate, with support from Mr. Menon, held that Article 84 of the Charter—upon which Article 10 of the agreement was based—was limited in scope to matters referring to the defense of the territory with local volunteers, and in any event did not empower an administering authority to establish military bases and station its own forces in the territory.[60] The latter came under Articles

[56] United Nations Document A/160, pp. 6-7.

[57] United Nations Documents A/C.4/Sub. 1/15 and A/C.4/ Sub. 1/9.

[58] *Official Records of the Second Part of the First Session of the General Assembly, Fourth Committee, Trusteeship, Part II* (November-December, 1946), p. 60.

[59] Article 82 of the Charter reads: "There may be designated, in any trusteeship agreement, a strategic area or areas which may include part or all of the trust territory to which the agreement applies. . . ."

[60] Article 84 of the Charter reads: "It shall be the duty of the administering authority to ensure that the trust territory shall play its part in the maintenance of international peace and security. To this end the administering authority may make use of volunteer forces, facilities, and assistance from the trust territory in carrying out the obligations towards the Security Council undertaken in this regard by the administering authority, as well as for local defence and maintenance of law and order within the trust territory."

82 and 83 of the Charter and hence must be approved by the Security Council.[61] Stated another way by the Indian delegate, the argument was simply that the only condition under which the trust territory could become the site of military bases would be on the basis of the needs of international peace and security, and that would entail jurisdiction of the Security Council.[62]

As a way out of this apparent impasse the Chinese delegate proposed that paragraphs (1), (2), and (4) of Article 10 be deleted, and suggested that arrangements for permitting the trust territory to play its part in the maintenance of world peace be made under Article 43 of the Charter between the administering authority and the Security Council.[63] This, however, proved unacceptable, and when all the talking was over the Soviet, Indian, and Chinese proposals were successively voted down. Article 10 was then adopted in its original form.[64] It is doubtless idle to speculate on which group interpreted the Charter "correctly." The main point is that the interpretation of the administering authority was adopted, creating a precedent with respect to the other trust territories, and the Security Council was prohibited from exercising control over this aspect of trusteeship. Whether this in itself, in view of the subsequent difficulties arising over the use of the veto in the Security Council, was for better or for worse with respect to the trust territories is arguable, although it is difficult to imagine what additional benefits would have accrued if the other interpretation had been accepted.[65]

Another question of fundamental importance to the trusteeship system was raised by a proposal of the Indian delegate that the administering authority should be the United Nations. This was introduced in the form of an amendment to the draft agreement for Western Samoa to the effect that New Zealand was "to act on behalf of the United Nations, who shall be the administering authority. . . ." [66] While, given the general purpose of the trusteeship provisions in the Charter, such an amendment would seem to raise a question of emphasis only, the difference in

[61] *Official Records of the Second Part of the First Session of the General Assembly, Fourth Committee, Trusteeship, Part II* (November-December, 1946), p. 60.

[62] *Ibid.*, p. 61.

[63] *Ibid.*, p. 62.

[64] *Ibid.*, pp. 79-80, 82.

[65] In this connection the remarks of John Foster Dulles, the American delegate, are interesting and perhaps revealing: "Mr. Dulles then referred to the hope of the peoples of the world that the appropriate provisions of the Charter would be implemented and that the reduction and limitation of armaments could soon become a reality. . . . There was, however, a gap between the hopes of the world and their practical realization . . . the use of the veto power in the Security Council was destroying the confidence of many nations in that organ. For these reasons, the Soviet proposal was looked upon with some scepticism." *Ibid.*, p. 67.

[66] United Nations Document A/C.4/Sub. 1/15.

emphasis is important. The real question at issue was who in the last analysis was actually going to administer a trust territory.

When viewed in this light, and remembering the remarks of Mr. Bailey of Australia on the relationship of the administering authority and the Trusteeship Council,[67] it is not surprising that Sir Carl Berendsen, far from accepting the proposed change, argued its unacceptability for two reasons: (1) New Zealand, with twenty-five years of experience in Western Samoa, knew the area best; it would thus be impractical to have divided authority; (2) as a result of the Treaty of Berlin, the Samoans had had an unhappy experience with international administration, and New Zealand was opposed to inflicting it upon them again.[68]

In this view Sir Carl was supported by all the mandatory powers on the subcommittee, many of whom added other reasons, such as the need for continuity and the desirability of giving the trust peoples a clear idea of who was the administering authority.[69] Actually, the Indian proposal was never pressed to a vote, and after a good deal of discussion the text of Article 2, which provided that New Zealand should be the administering authority, was adopted by a considerable margin.[70]

One additional aspect of the discussion on this question deserves notice, as it points up an interpretation of the subcommittee discussions held in general by the mandatories and other powers friendly to them, but not held by others, including India and the Soviet Union. In defending New Zealand's position on this issue, Mr. Cote of Canada argued that the subcommittee's function was to ascertain whether or not the proposed trust agreements were in conformity with the Charter, and *not* to negotiate. Therefore, he felt constrained to approve any article not violative of the Charter.[71] The attitude of other delegations was that suggestions could and should be made, and further that if an amendment were decided upon which was unacceptable to the administering authority, there should be no consideration given to approving the agreement as a whole.[72] The significance of this divergence of viewpoint is, of course, the absence of a consensus on the proper function of the subcommittee, and for that matter, of the General Assembly itself, in the approval of the trust agreements. What lay behind the difference was the question of the extent

[67] See above, p. 55.

[68] *Official Records of the Second Part of the First Session of the General Assembly, Fourth Committee, Trusteeship, Part II* (November-December, 1946), pp. 33-34.

[69] *Ibid.*, pp. 38-39.

[70] *Ibid.*, p. 42. The vote was 13 in favor, with 4 abstentions.

[71] *Ibid.*, p. 38.

[72] This point of view was not specifically spelled out until the discussions in the Fourth Committee after the work of the subcommittee had been completed; but it obviously underlay much of the discussion in the subcommittee.

to which nonadministering states would have a voice in the determination of the terms of agreements.

When the subcommittee to consider the eight draft agreements had been appointed, it was agreed that any member of the United Nations could appear before the subcommittee for the purpose of submitting and defending proposed modifications. The only state which took advantage of this opportunity was Byelorussia, whose representative pressed for the inclusion of a clause designed to insure that the indigenous population would be consulted on the question of their political regime, such consultation to be under the direction of the Trusteeship Council.[73] There were really two elements in this proposal: (1) assuring the key position of the Trusteeship Council in the supervision of the trust territories, and (2) insuring the right of the indigenous inhabitants to be consulted on the form of their political regime.

The proposal was rejected,[74] largely on the ground that while the principles involved were not unacceptable, they were already implicit in the Charter, and hence it was not necessary to spell them out in the trusteeship agreement.[75] Again the reluctance of the mandatory powers to accept any provision which was not absolutely essential to an agreement became manifest. Of course, following the line of reasoning of the Canadian delegate, Mr. Cote, it would be virtually impossible to modify any of the agreements—and this line of reasoning was obviously never carried to its logical extreme. The point is, however, that whenever or wherever possible the mandatory states maintained that a given amendment was an unnecessary limitation on the administering authority because in their unamended form the draft agreements were consonant with the Charter. From this position, then, it would be easy to blame the failure of any agreement to be adopted on those states dissatisfied with the agreement. Such appears to have been the basic—and successful—strategy of the mandatory states.

In addition to these important proposed modifications, there were numerous minor changes proposed for almost all the articles in all the draft agreements. Without going into each question, it is possible to generalize that in most cases, as with the specific proposals considered above, the amendment was directed toward the increased protection of the native inhabitants[76] or to a statement of steps leading to ultimate self-government or independence.

---

[73] *Official Records of the Second Part of the First Session of the General Assembly, Fourth Committee, Trusteeship, Part II* (November-December, 1946), p. 154. The amendment is document A/C.4/Sub. 1/24. This proposal concerned, of course, all the trusteeship agreements, not just that for Western Samoa.

[74] *Ibid.*, p. 160. The vote was 6 in favor, 9 against, with 2 abstentions.

[75] *Ibid.*, pp. 154-57.

[76] For example, with regard to Article 6 of the draft agreement for Western

In general most of the discussion of the other seven draft trusteeship agreements was pretty much a rehash of what had already been said concerning Western Samoa. Thus the questions of fortifications, consultation, and the time limit were all brought up again, and again defeated. There were, however, a few new and different questions discussed, as well as one previously discussed question to which the subcommittee gave a different answer.

The latter concerned administering the trust territories "as an integral part of the territory" of the administering authority. This had been deleted from the draft for Western Samoa upon recommendation of the subcommittee, but when the same question came up with regard to the African mandates, the subcommittee failed to recommend similar action. The primary contention upon which France, Belgium, and the United Kingdom rested their opposition to the elimination of the phrase was that while Western Samoa was an isolated territory,[77] the African territories were joined physically to other territories of the administering states. They all specifically repudiated the notion that the phrase in question was designed to diminish the political individuality of the trust territories, and maintained that it was solely a matter of administrative convenience and common sense.[78] The point was made, especially by the British representative, that the language did not mean "as an integral part of the metropolitan state," but only as a part of the territory of that state which adjoined the trust territory.

This explanation did not satisfy those opposed to the phrase, nor did statements by the Belgian and French representatives that they were willing to accept as a substitution "as if it were an integral part," as appeared in the Australian draft for New Guinea. Pressed to a vote, however, both the elimination of and the substitution for the phrase were defeated.[79]

One important question brought up in connection with the draft agreements for the seven other mandates was the matter of constituting the

Samoa (prohibiting the slave trade and forced labor, and placing a limitation on arms traffic and liquor), the Chinese delegate sought the inclusion of narcotic drugs on the list of prohibited items. *Ibid.*, p. 13. Lest the reader get the impression that New Zealand desired to promote the use of narcotics it should be mentioned that Sir Carl Berendsen pointed out that narcotics were controlled under a separate convention, and later agreed to the Chinese suggestion even though pointing out its redundancy.

[77] The draft agreement for New Guinea contained the phrase "as if it were an integral part." United Nations Document A/153.

[78] *Official Records of the Second Part of the First Session of the General Assembly, Fourth Committee, Trusteeship, Part II* (November-December, 1946), pp. 118-22.

[79] *Ibid.*, p. 123. The vote to delete the phrase was 7 in favor, 9 against, with 1 abstention; to substitute "as if it were an integral part": 3 in favor, 3 against, with 11 abstentions.

trust territory into an administrative union with the other territories of the administering authority. This practice had been acceded to by the Permanent Mandates Commission, and all the drafts for the African territories, as well as that for New Guinea, contained a provision on the point. The chief objection to such a provision, of course, was the possibility that it might lead to annexation. Thus the Soviet delegate spoke of the attempt to place the trust territories "in the same category as colonies,"[80] and the Indian representative expressed concern over "the inevitable tendency for administrations having reactionary policies to influence the policy in neighboring territories."[81] It is interesting to note that at least some of the delegates who favored deletion of the article in question categorically declared that they had nothing against the idea of some form of union, but were opposed only to the specific proposals, which they felt would lead to annexation. As stated by the Soviet delegate, a union of territories having the same legal system was perfectly acceptable, but the unions proposed were for territories with differing legal frameworks.[82]

In general, the mandatory states repeated their remarks made in connection with the "integral part" issue, arguing for the convenience of the arrangement and renouncing any thought of diminishing the respective territories' individuality.[83] After a good deal of discussion, the proposal to eliminate the right of the administering authority to create administrative unions was defeated, while at the same time it was agreed to include in the Rapporteur's report a statement to the effect that such unions were not regarded "as giving powers to the Administering Authority to establish any form of association between the Trust Territory and adjacent Territories which would involve annexation of the Trust Territory in any sense or would have the effect of extinguishing its status as a Trust Territory."[84]

It is not difficult to argue that with this decision the subcommittee agreed to the possibility of disguised annexation so imminent in the minds of some of the delegates, while salving its conscience with the innocuous declaration in the Rapporteur's report. On the other hand, the respective positions of the subcommittee and the prospective administering authorities must be kept in mind. Neither the Soviet Union nor India (the most vociferous dissidents) actually were going to have to administer trust territories. Further, neither the subcommittee nor the

[80] *Ibid.*, p. 124.

[81] *Ibid.*, pp. 124-25. The Indian delegate's remarks referred specifically to Tanganyika and Kenya.

[82] *Ibid.*, p. 124.

[83] *Ibid.*, pp. 126-34.

[84] *Ibid.*, 131, 132-34.

General Assembly itself was in a position to force the administering authorities to do anything. The success of the entire trusteeship system depends to a major extent on the willingness of the administering authorities to cooperate with the United Nations agencies. With this in mind, it is more difficult to criticize the subcommittee, the Fourth Committee, or the General Assembly for acquiescing in provisions of the trusteeship agreements which might not please all those who claimed to champion the rights of dependent peoples. The potential alternative, annexation—in fact, if not in form, as shown in the case of South West Africa—always remains, its eventuality depending upon how far the administering authorities consider themselves pressed.

One other new question was raised in connection with the seven other draft agreements. This concerned the right of the administering authority to create monopolistic enterprises for the benefit of the native inhabitants. Disclaiming any opposition to the principle of public monopolies or in some cases even private monopolies, for the benefit of the indigenous peoples, the United States delegate nevertheless asserted that this should be limited by necessary safeguards, such as the assurance of no discrimination on the grounds of nationality in the selection of nongovernmental agents of monopoly, and prior review by the Trusteeship Council when monopolies other than "fiscal monopolies or essential public works" were created.[85] The delegates from India and China proposed similar amendments, but withdrew theirs in favor of the American proposal.[86] After some discussion of the matter, a working party was appointed to draft a proposal reconciling the texts of the draft agreements with the U. S. proposal.[87]

The administering authorities, as it turned out, were dubious only about the prior notification of the Trusteeship Council concerning a proposed monopoly. In the words of the British delegate, for example, "such a procedure would give to the Trusteeship Council an administrative duty which it was not empowered, under the Charter, to exercise." The upshot of this was that the principle of prior notification of the Trusteeship Council was defeated,[88] although the provision assuring nondiscrimination was incorporated into the agreements.

The significance of this lies not merely in the extent to which monopolies would be limited or controlled, but also in the question of the degree of supervision the Trusteeship Council would have. Again it

[85] *Ibid.*, p. 142. United Nations Document A/C.4/Sub.1/53 contains an American amendment embracing these proposals.

[86] *Ibid.*

[87] *Ibid.*, p. 144. The working party was made up of representatives from Australia, Belgium, China, France, India, the United Kingdom, and the United States.

[88] *Ibid.*, p. 170. The vote was 3 in favor, 7 against, with 7 abstentions.

illustrates that while the administering states were willing to submit their mandated areas to the Trusteeship System, they desired to be as free as possible to deal with any problems that might arise in the territories with as little "interference" as possible by the United Nations. If the substance of the point is comparatively minor, the approach to the whole trusteeship system illustrated by the point is not.

At the end of its discussion of the text of the draft agreements, the subcommittee proceeded to vote on each of the agreements as modified by the acceptance on the part of the administering state of changes adopted by the subcommittee. Of the delegates most articulate in proposing modifications only the delegate of the Soviet Union announced his intention to vote against the agreements, while the delegates from India and Iraq announced they would abstain as an indication that their delegations had not as yet made up their minds whether or not the agreements were acceptable. The Soviet decision was ostensibly based on the failure to incorporate four major modifications into the agreements: (1) the deletion of the "integral part" phrase in certain of the agreements; (2) the denial of the administering authority's right to incorporate a trust territory into a fiscal or other union with neighboring territories; (3) the provision that fortification of a trust territory came under the supervision of the Security Council; and (4) the fixing of a time limit for revision of the agreements.[89] In general, with regard to all the proposed drafts, the Soviet Union and its two satellites on the subcommittee (Czechoslovakia and Yugoslavia) voted against, India and Iraq abstained, and the rest voted in favor of the agreements. China abstained in the case of the draft agreement for New Guinea and voted in favor of the others. Hence the vote on the New Guinea agreement was eleven in favor, three against, with three abstentions, while on the other it was twelve in favor, three against, with two abstentions.[90] In view of the obvious inclination of Czechoslovakia and Yugoslavia to vote with the Soviet Union, this voting represents a fair degree of consensus. Before the drafts could be sent on to the Fourth Committee proper, however, there remained the "states directly concerned" question which the reader will recall had been considered earlier, but had been postponed. Now the subcommittee could no longer avoid dealing with the problem, and as its last effort it turned its attention to the feasibility of defining the troublesome phrase.

The discussion was precipitated by the Indian delegate's contention that his state was directly concerned in Tanganyika, and that his government could not accept an American suggestion that all states should

[89] *Ibid.*, p. 190.

[90] *Ibid.*, pp. 186-93.

forego their claim to be considered as states directly concerned.[91] This was followed by a statement of the Soviet delegate that until the issue was settled, the agreements were not in conformity with the Charter since the states directly concerned could not be said to have in fact negotiated the agreements. His contribution to a definition of the phrase was that in any case it would include the members of the Big Five.[92] This would, of course—although the Soviet delegate was vague on this point when pressed—give the Soviet Union a veto on any and every proposed trusteeship agreement, something which the mandatory states could hardly be expected to accept. Actually, what appears to have lain behind the Soviet proposal was not so much a desire to participate in the negotiations of all trusteeship agreements, but rather to secure for itself the right of taking part in any negotiations concerning the former Italian colonies, particularly Libya.[93] That other members of the Big Five were aware of this was demonstrated by their absolute refusal to accept any such general definition of the phrase.

After a great deal of discussion the chairman asked the delegates of the United States and the Soviet Union to consult informally and try to draw up an acceptable definition.[94] Four days later Mr. Dulles, of the United States, reported failure to reach a solution and requested permission to submit his proposal which provided for the approval of the agreements by the General Assembly "without prejudice to future determination of the 'states directly concerned.'"[95] This was opposed by Mr. Novikov of the Soviet Union who argued that the issue was still on the agenda and proposed the formation of a subcommittee to attempt a definition.[96] There followed considerable debate, during the course of which most of the arguments already made were reiterated. When the matter came to a vote the American proposal was adopted.[97] It was pointed out that all this meant was that it was unnecessary for each state to press its claim as a state directly concerned, but if it wished to it could. But, of course, it should not be forgotten that if a state did so press its claim and this was evaded by the mandatory state, the General Assembly, acting on the basis of this proposal, could still approve the agreement.

---

[91] *Ibid.*, pp. 172-73.

[92] *Ibid.*, p. 174.

[93] See below, pp. 81 ff.

[94] *Official Records of the Second Part of the First Session of the General Assembly, Fourth Committee, Trusteeship, Part II* (November-December, 1946), p. 186.

[95] *Ibid.*, p. 201.

[96] *Ibid.*

[97] *Ibid.*, p. 209. The vote on the Soviet proposal was 4 in favor, 10 against, with 3 abstentions; on the American proposal: 13 in favor, 3 against, with 1 abstention.

Thus it seems perfectly logical for the Soviet delegate to argue that the decision contravened Article 79 of the Charter and that consequently the trusteeship agreements were all invalid, as indeed he did.[98] And the possibility of evasion just mentioned was nicely illustrated shortly after the adoption of the American proposal. The Indian delegate took advantage of the interpretation of the United States resolution and pressed his government's claim to be considered as a state directly concerned in Tanganyika—to which the British representative replied that while note would be taken of the claim, it could not be accepted "because . . . there was not as yet a definition of the states directly concerned." [99] Despite such criticisms of the subcommittee's evasion of the question, it must be kept in mind that there was little likelihood of agreement on any general definition, and therefore there existed a real possibility for long delay in establishing the trusteeship system pending agreement on the issue. The phrase is obviously ambiguous and subject to varying interpretations, and it seems unfair to be critical of the subcommittee, and the United Nations generally, for going ahead with the trusteeship system despite the fact that the states directly concerned in any given territory were not specifically determined. Politics, international as well as national, is, after all, the art of the possible—and the attainment of the possible may well mean the circumvention rather than the overpowering of obstacles.

With the acceptance of the American proposal the question remained of how to alter the preamble of the draft agreements so as to bring them into conformity with this decision. In most cases the preambles contained specific references to Article 79 of the Charter, and it was suggested that the deletion of this reference would in substance carry out the decision. This idea was acceptable to some of the mandatory states, but not to France and Belgium, who took the position that the agreements were either valid—hence there was no need to delete the reference to Article 79—or invalid; and they were prepared to settle this issue in the subcommittee. It was eventually agreed, however, that those two states would delete the entire preamble of their respective trusteeship agreements, and leave it to the General Assembly to formulate the text of the preambles.[100] As the agreements finally emerged from the subcommittee the preambles merely omitted any reference to Article 79 and thus, in effect, the definition of the "states directly concerned" was bypassed.[101]

[98] *Ibid.*

[99] *Ibid.*, p. 213.

[100] *Supplementary Report of Sub-Committe 1.* United Nations Document A/C.4/69 Add.1. This contained the subcommittee's recommendation for the General Assembly's resolution on the subject.

[101] In this connection the Soviet delegation went on record as declaring that in the conclusion of the agreements "the provisions of Article 79 . . . were not complied with." *Ibid.*

The Fourth Committee's review of the work of its subcommittee amounted largely to a reintroduction of various amendments which had failed of adoption in the subcommittee. Of these, three are important because the subcommittee's decision was reversed by the superior body. This was done with respect to the "integral part" question [102] and with respect to the time limit for review and revision of the agreements.[103] Thirdly, an Indian proposal assuring that all rights of sovereignty were to be surrendered to the indigenous inhabitants upon termination of the trusteeship was adopted.[104]

Called upon to state whether these amendments were acceptable to them, the mandatory powers unanimously declared in the negative on each point.[105] In general the reasons given were the same as had been stated in the subcommittee. And again it was emphasized that from the point of view of the mandatory states, the question to be asked by the Fourth Committee was simply: Is the proposed agreement violative of the Charter? If not, the mandatory powers argued that the committee should feel constrained to approve it.

This attitude was resented by some members of the committee, who felt that it constituted undue pressure on them to accept undesirable features of the agreements or risk getting no agreements. Thus the Chilean delegate stated that "In substance what the Committee had been told was that either the draft agreement must be approved in a form wholly acceptable to the mandatory powers or there would be no Trusteeship Council." Deploring this, he felt it would be better to have no Council than to impair the prestige of the United Nations in the eyes of the world by approving faulty agreements.[106] Despite sentiments such as these the committee proceeded to approve the agreements (*without* the last three generally applicable amendments which it had adopted) by a substantial majority, although many of the delegates expressed dissatisfaction with the agreements, and explained their votes in terms of wanting to establish the trusteeship system at all costs.[107]

As its last relevant act in connection with organizing the Trusteeship

[102] By a vote of 16 to 15, with 3 abstentions, the phrase was deleted from all agreements in which it appeared. *Official Records of the Second Part of the First Session of the General Assembly, Fourth Committee, Trusteeship, Part I* (November-December, 1946), p. 141.

[103] The vote was 20 in favor, 14 against, with 1 abstention. In addition a Chinese proposal providing for a 10-year time limit for review was adopted by 20 votes to 7 with 8 abstentions. *Ibid.*, p. 147.

[104] The vote was 19 in favor, 16 against, with 2 abstentions. *Ibid.*, p. 152.

[105] *Ibid.*, pp. 160-65. This excepts, of course, the positions of New Zealand and the United Kingdom with regard to the agreements for Western Samoa and Tanganyika, respectively, neither of which contained the "integral part" phrase.

[106] *Ibid.*, pp. 171-72.

[107] *Ibid.*, p. 174. The vote in each case was 35 to 8, with no abstentions.

Council, the Fourth Committee adopted a proposal recommending that the General Assembly take cognizance of the fact that conditions for the establishment of the Trusteeship Council had been fulfilled, and proceed to constitute that body.[108]

When, on December 13, 1946, the Fourth Committee's Report and suggested resolution setting up the Trusteeship Council were presented to the General Assembly,[109] the delegates of both India and the Soviet Union, who had opposed the adoption of the agreements in the Fourth Committee, reiterated their objections. The Soviet representative, however, went further than did the representative of India, in that he proposed that the General Assembly adopt a resolution declaring (A) that the proposed trusteeship agreements were unconstitutional because (1) the states directly concerned had not been consulted; (2) the provisions in some of the agreements that the territory should be administered "as an integral part" of the territory of the administering authority amounted to annexation in contravention of the avowed purpose of the trusteeship system; and (3) the provision for establishing military, naval, and air bases did not provide for Security Council supervision; and (B) for these reasons the agreements were unacceptable to the General Assembly and the mandatory states were called upon to submit new draft agreements.[110]

After brief discussion this resolution was voted upon and decisively defeated.[111] It is of interest to note that despite the opposition of India to the proposed agreements the representative of that state did not vote in favor of the Soviet resolution, but instead abstained, together with other states whose attitude toward the agreements had been something less than enthusiastic.[112] This illustrates one of the basic considerations in connection with the approval of the first eight agreements: the desire to set the trusteeship system in motion was sufficiently strong to outweigh a considerable amount of dissatisfaction with the agreements for all but the Soviet Union and its followers. And, from the discussion in the Fourth Committee and its subcommittee, it does not seem too much to say that the mandatory states were well aware of this and took full advantage of it to prevent as much as possible any limitation on their general authority in the territories.

The same desire to get the trusteeship system going was manifested in

[108] *Ibid.*, p. 180.

[109] *Official Records of the Second Part of the First Session of the General Assembly, Plenary Meetings* (October-December, 1946), pp. 1265-67.

[110] *Ibid.*, pp. 1282-83.

[111] *Ibid.*, p. 1286. The vote was 6 in favor, 34 against, with 11 abstentions.

[112] These states included Colombia, Ecuador, Egypt, Ethiopia, Guatemala, India, Iran, Iraq, Liberia, Philippine Republic, and Saudi Arabia.

the final vote on the draft agreements by the General Assembly, which followed immediately the defeat of the Soviet proposals. In each case the only states actually voting against the agreement, with the one exception of Liberia, were the Soviet Union and the other Communist-controlled countries. The agreements for New Guinea, Ruanda-Urundi, Western Samoa, Tanganyika, British Cameroons, and British Togoland were approved by a vote of forty-one in favor, six opposed, with five abstentions. Those for the French Cameroons and Togoland were approved forty-one in favor, five against, with six abstentions.[113] The next day, with the Soviet Union, Byelorussia, Yugoslavia, and the Ukranian S.S.R. not taking part because of their position that the agreements violated the Charter, the General Assembly elected Mexico and Iraq for three-year terms on the Trusteeship Council.[114] Following this it directed the Secretary-General to convoke the first session of the Trusteeship Council not later than March 15, 1947.[115]

Thus almost eighteen months to the day after the Charter was signed at San Francisco, the conditions necessary for the establishment of the Trusteeship Council were at last fulfilled. In pursuance of his instructions, the Secretary-General sent out a provisional agenda for the first session of the Trusteeship Council and called upon the member states to submit the names of their delegates. All but the Soviet Union replied, and the Trusteeship Council convened for the first time on March 26, 1947. The reasons for the Soviet boycott of the Council were not made explicit, although the presumption is that it was based on its position that the trusteeship agreements were unconstitutional and that therefore the Trusteeship Council itself was without legal basis.

Other than Italian Somaliland, which will be discussed in a separate chapter, two more territories have been brought within the trusteeship system, and we turn now to a brief mention of the conclusion of the agreements for these territories.

The Trust Territory of the Pacific. The reader will remember that the submission of a draft trusteeship agreement for the former Japanese mandate now under American jurisdiction had been delayed, primarily because of difficulties within the United States, specifically concerning the fear on the part of some members of the military and Congress that our strategic interests would be imperiled if fortification of these islands were made subject to Soviet veto. This fear was based, of course, on the assumption that any former Japanese mandate placed under trusteeship

[113] *Ibid.*, pp. 1287-88. The shift from abstention to opposed was by Poland. Other abstainers were Colombia, Czechoslovakia, Ecuador, India, and Venezuela.

[114] *Ibid.*, pp. 1322-23.

[115] *Resolutions Adopted by the General Assembly During the Second Part of its First Session*, p. 122. Resolution 64 (I).

by the United States would be classified as strategic and thus be under the aegis of the Security Council rather than the General Assembly. It was an easy enough matter to remove the basis of this fear and still keep the territory strategic by simply providing for fortification in the trusteeship agreement, which was in fact done.[116]

The draft agreement was submitted on February 17, 1947, and the Security Council soon afterward proceeded to examine it. A major portion of the debate in the Security Council ostensibly involved the "constitutional" question of whether or not the Security Council could approve an agreement settling the disposition of certain territories formerly mandated to Japan in the absence of a peace treaty formally ratifying such disposition. On this point the Pacific powers, Australia and New Zealand, were particularly interested; what lay behind this "constitutional" question was the desire of these states to make sure that all belligerents in the war against Japan had "the right to join in any decision which is part of the peace settlement with Japan. We say that the disposal of these islands is part of the peace settlement." [117] The issue was resolved when the Security Council invited all the states in the Far Eastern Commission to partake in the discussion, at which time Australia's delegate withdrew his proposal to suspend approval of the agreement until such time as a treaty with Japan had been signed.[118]

With the exception of the classification of "strategic" the draft for the former Japanese mandate followed in general the terms of the first eight agreements, which will be summarized below. The Soviet Union took the lead in proposing three important modifications to the draft: (1) to delete the phrase "as an integral part of the United States" from the article describing the authority of the administering state; (2) to add "independence" to the goal of self-government; and (3) to change article 15 from: "The terms of the present agreement shall not be altered, amended or terminated without the consent of the administering authority" to read: "The terms of the present agreement may be altered, supplemented, or terminated by decision of the Security Council." [119]

With regard to the first two of these proposals, the American representative, Mr. Warren Austin, acquiesced, but he firmly rejected the third.[120] This was, of course, to be expected in view of the fears expressed by those in this country opposed to trusteeship because of the Security Council supervision with its attendant possibilities of Soviet veto of our

[116] United Nations Document S/281.

[117] *Security Council, Official Records Second Year, no. 26, 119th Meeting* (17 March 1947), p. 519.

[118] *Ibid., no. 30, 123rd Meeting* (28 March 1947), pp. 626-28.

[119] *Ibid., no. 20, 113th Meeting* (26 February 1947), p. 414.

[120] *Ibid., no. 23, 116th Meeting* (7 March 1947), pp. 473-75.

fortification plans. When this issue came to a vote the Soviet proposal was defeated and the original wording was accepted.[121]

Other proposals were made, but on the whole they were of only minor importance, and generalizing, it is possible to say that as compared with the approval of the first eight agreements by the General Assembly, the United States agreement for the former Japanese mandate passed the Security Council with almost no difficulty. In its slightly amended form the agreement was approved unanimously on April 2, 1947, and ratified by the United States government on July 18.[122] On September 8, 1951, the Treaty of Peace with Japan was signed in San Francisco. Under Article 2, paragraph (d) of that treaty: "Japan renounces all right, title and claim in connection with the League of Nations Mandate System, and accepts the action of the United Nations Security Council of April 2, 1947, extending the trusteeship system to the Pacific Islands formerly under mandate to Japan." [123]

Nauru. Other than former Italian Somaliland, the last territory to be placed under the trusteeship system to date was the island of Nauru. This territory, a tiny island in the Southwest Pacific, had been administered jointly by the United Kingdom, New Zealand, and Australia under the mandates system, the latter state acting as day-to-day mandatory. Consequently the draft trusteeship agreement was submitted jointly by these three powers. The General Assembly turned the draft over to its Fourth Committee, which, after general discussion, appointed a subcommittee to consider the agreement, following generally the same procedure used with respect to the first eight agreements.[124] This subcommittee, however, was of a different composition than the other in that it followed the composition of the Trusteeship Council—that is, it was composed of an equal number of administering and nonadministering states. At the time of submission of the Nauru agreement, October, 1947, the General Assembly was in the process of selecting two new states as members of the Trusteeship Council; action necessitated by the adoption of the agreement for the Territory of the Pacific Islands. Since this selection had not as yet been made, the Fourth Committee elected India and Yugoslavia to sit on the subcommittee together with the regular members of the Trusteeship Council.[125]

One point only is worth mentioning with regard to the subcommittee's

[121] *Ibid., no. 31, 124th Meeting* (2 April 1947), p. 679.

[122] *Ibid.*, p. 680. *Japanese Peace Conference* (State Department Publication No. 4392, International Organization and Conference Series II, Far Eastern 3), pp. 303-9.

[123] *Japanese Peace Conference*, p. 314.

[124] *Official Records of the Second Session of the General Assembly, Fourth Committee, Trusteeship* (October-December, 1947), p. 28.

[125] *Ibid.*

consideration of the draft for Nauru, since in general the agreement followed the first eight drafts with the exception that it was shorter and less detailed in its provisions. This point concerns the position taken by the former mandatory powers in general that since the General Assembly had approved the other eight agreements there was a compelling presumption that it would approve this one—since it contained no significant additions nor omissions.[126] This view was, as might be expected, specifically rejected by the delegates of some of the nonadministering states. In particular, the Soviet delegate reiterated his objection to a provision providing fortification of the territory without Security Council supervision, and to the lack of any definition of states directly concerned.[127] A Soviet amendment providing for Security Council supervision of fortifications was rejected, but the provisions on this point were modified to the extent that any such fortification was to be in accordance with Article 84 of the Charter.[128]

Other proposed amendments were actually nothing more than a detail of general provisions and were rejected as being unnecessary in view of the obligation already undertaken by the administering authority as signatories of the Charter. The original draft was approved by the subcommittee with the sole modification mentioned above.[129] The Fourth Committee's consideration of the agreement followed the pattern set with regard to the first eight. The Soviet Union again voiced its objections, they were again rejected, and the committee approved the agreement without further change by a vote of forty-one to six.[130] The General Assembly did the same ten days later with the Soviet bloc alone voting against it.[131]

It might be well at this point to summarize briefly the important provisions of the agreements, and to note one or two important points which emerge from the discussion of the process by which the mandates were placed under the trusteeship system. In general, all the agreements contain provision for the following:

(1) Definition of the boundary of each territory placed under the system.
(2) Designation of the administering authority of the trust territory.
(3) The obligations of the administering authority under Article 76 of the Charter (which sets forth the basic objectives of the trusteeship system).

[126] See the remarks of the Belgian delegate, M. Ryckmans, at the 29th meeting of Subcommittee 1. United Nations Document A/C.4/SC.1/SR.29.

[127] United Nations Document A/C.4/SC.1/SR.30.

[128] United Nations Document A/C.4/SC.1/SR. 33 and 34.

[129] United Nations Document A/C.4/SC.1/SR.34.

[130] *Official Records of the Second Session of the General Assembly, Fourth Committee, Trusteeship* (October-December, 1947), p. 104.

[131] *Ibid.*, Plenary Meetings, p. 571.

(4) The rights of the administering authority in legislation, administration and jurisdiction; in constituting the territory into a customs, fiscal or administrative union with adjacent territories under the control of the administering authority; in establishing naval, military and air bases.
(5) Promotion of the educational, cultural, and political development of the inhabitants of the territory.
(6) Protection of the economic rights of the inhabitants, and the assurance of freedom of religion and speech.
(7) Annual reports to the General Assembly by the administering authority on the basis of a questionnaire to be formulated by the Trusteeship Council.
(8) Approval of the terms of the Agreement and of any alteration or amendment thereof by the General Assembly.[132]

The fourth item raises the question of whether or not there is any real distinction between strategic and nonstrategic areas. That is, if an administering authority of a nonstrategic trust territory may establish military, naval, and air bases, how is this territory any different from a strategic territory? The only real difference, it would seem, is that by somewhat arbitrarily classifying a territory as strategic the administering authority is (1) subject to ultimate Security Council supervision rather than to General Assembly supervision, and (2) able to close some areas to international inspection. But this is very different from what was supposedly envisaged at San Francisco. There, the basis of the distinction was that some areas were more crucially concerned in the preservation of international peace than were others, and so should be dealt with in a different manner. The Security Council, the body whose main task lay in the preservation of international peace and security, should supervise the administration of these territories. Actually, what seems to have happened was that each administering state considered its territories to be concerned in world peace, and that the assumption that lay behind the original distinction—that is, some areas were more involved in the preservation of world peace than others—was not in fact realistic. Does it follow then that the Security Council should supervise all bases in the nonstrategic areas? That is, are the bases themselves strategic areas? It is certainly possible to argue this if the distinction between strategic and nonstrategic territories is to have substance. The point is, however, that when the agreements for the nonstrategic territories were concluded this was not the interpretation given by the General Assembly.

This discussion points up what is perhaps the most important difference between the mandates and the trusteeship agreements. In the former, fortification was expressly prohibited—they were to be removed from the vicissitudes of international strife. But, with the memories of the threat provided when Japan illegally fortified its Pacific mandate, the

[132] Items (7) and (8) are not applicable to the agreement for the Pacific Islands. The list is based on a summary in *Yearbook of the United Nations, 1946-47*, p. 577.

trust agreements in each case specifically provided for fortification in the interests of international peace and security.

Other than this, there is little difference between the terms of the mandates and trusteeship agreements that is not implicit in the difference between the Charter and the Covenant.[133] This might be expected, however, since the trust territories so far considered were all formerly mandates, and with one exception, were under the same administering authority as before. When we examine the trusteeship agreement for former Italian Somaliland it will be seen that the differences become much more extensive.

At least one writer,[134] in commenting upon the differences between the mandates and trusteeship systems, has pointed to the fact that where the mandates were divided into "rigid" categories, no such categorization has occurred with regard to the trust territories and hence the advantage of flexibility of the latter over the former is claimed. This may well be true in principle, but the present writer can find little evidence of this flexibility in the agreements for the first ten territories brought within the trusteeship system. Perhaps the real importance of this distinction will be manifested in the future when territories other than former mandates are placed under trusteeship. This seems to be the case with respect to former Italian Somaliland, but it is difficult to render judgment on the basis of this one territory.

[133] The comparison is, of course, between the "B" mandates and the African trust territories, and the "C" mandates and the trust territories in the Pacific. None of the "A" mandates became trust territories.

[134] Ralph Bunche, "The Trusteeship System and Non-Self Governing Territories in the Charter of the United Nations," *Department of State Bulletin*, Vol. 13, (July-December, 1945), p. 1041.

CHAPTER FOUR

Former Italian Somaliland

The trusteeship agreement for Somaliland under Italian administration has been singled out for special consideration in part because of the number of differences between it and the other agreements, and in part because the negotiations leading up to its adoption illustrate the interrelation of the trusteeship system with the more general problems of international politics, particularly the struggle between East and West. One of the main differences between the mandates and trusteeship systems is that where the former was largely isolated from the great power rivalries of the day, the trusteeship system, from almost the very beginning of its existence, has been affected by the East-West struggle. This is true generally, but it is particularly so with respect to the disposition of the colonies detached from Italy at the end of World War II.[1]

There are at least three important ways in which the negotiations concerning the trusteeship agreement for Somaliland differ from those of the first ten agreements. First, in the case of the latter, the administering states submitted to the General Assembly or the Security Council proposed agreements to which amendments could be suggested, but which in the last analysis could not be changed unless the administering state in each case agreed. While it is true that Italy submitted a draft agreement for Somaliland, the Trusteeship Council regarded itself as being under no such limitation. That is to say, the Council took an active part in the actual negotiation of the agreement—with marked results. Secondly, the actual disposition of all three of the former Italian colonies in Africa was left by the Big Four to the General Assembly, with the understanding that any disposition made by it would be considered binding.[2] Here, then, was one of the few cases in which an agency of the United Nations

[1] The three colonies in question were Libya, Eritrea, and Italian Somaliland. An excellent discussion of this phase of trusteeship may be found in the unpublished doctoral dissertation of Joseph John Sisco, "The Soviet Attitude Toward the Trusteeship System," University of Chicago, 1951. The present writer is indebted to this work for the chronology of events prior to submission of the question to the General Assembly, as well as for other information cited.

[2] The Charter (Article 77) provides that territories to be placed under trusteeship shall include "territories which may be detached from enemy states as a result of the Second World War. . . ." This, however, in view of subsequent events, i.e., the decisions with respect to Libya and Eritrea, must be interpreted as non-mandatory. By the Treaty of Peace with Italy (Article 23), "Italy renounces all right and title to the Italian territorial possessions in Africa . . . The final disposal of these possessions shall be determined jointly by the Governments . . . of the Big

was given the power to make binding decisions, not subject to a single-nation veto. Third, when the agreement had been negotiated and the territory placed under the trusteeship system, Italy became the first, and so far the only, administering authority not a member of the United Nations. While the Charter says nothing on this point it is not unreasonable to suppose that it was assumed that all administering authorities represented on the Trusteeship Council would, by the nature of the organization be members of the United Nations. At least in part, all three of these elements of uniqueness concerning Somaliland are the result of the great power struggle, as will be seen during the course of this chapter.

Although Somaliland was the only one of the three colonies that eventually found its way into the trusteeship system, it must be kept in mind that the General Assembly decisions concerning the three territories were by no means isolated from each other; rather it is nearer to the truth to say that the final disposition was in the nature of a "package deal." It is impossible, therefore to discuss Somaliland without some mention of Libya and Eritrea, even though this study is concerned only with trust territories.

Big Four Negotiations. While the Italian colonies had been mentioned at Yalta, San Francisco, and Potsdam, the various positions of France, England, the United States, and the Soviet Union were not made explicit until the London Conference of Foreign Ministers in September, 1945. At that time the positions of these states may be summed up as follows: France, in general, favored the return of the colonies to Italy, either directly or in the form of trusteeship. Its principal consideration in following this line was that a liberation of the Arabs from the Italians in North Africa might well jeopardize its own position in that area [3]—a fear which, in view of later events in Tunisia and Morocco, seems more than a little justified. The British position was complicated by the fact that during the war the Coalition Government had more than once unequivocally stated that in no case would any of the Italian colonies be

Four within one year from the coming into force of the present Treaty, in the manner laid down in the joint declaration of February 10, 1947, issued by the said Governments, which is reproduced in Annex XI." Annex XI provides, *inter alia*, that "The final disposal of the territories concerned . . . shall be made by the Four Powers in the light of the wishes and welfare of the inhabitants and the interests of peace and security, taking into consideration the views of other interested Governments. If . . . the Four Powers are unable to agree upon their disposal within one year from the coming into force of the Treaty . . . the matter will be referred to the General Assembly of the United Nations for recommendation." *Treaties of Peace with Italy, Bulgaria, Hungary, Roumania and Finland*, Department of State, Publication 2743, European Series 21, pp. 13, 18-89. The treaty entered into force September 15, 1947.

[3] C. Grove Haines, "The Problem of the Italian Colonies," *Middle East Journal*, Vol. II (1947), p. 420. James F. Byrnes, *Speaking Frankly*, p. 95.

returned to Italian rule.[4] By the end of the war, however, Britain had its own interests in the Mediterranean and the Gulf of Aden to consider. In general it favored the division of Eritrea between the Sudan and Ethiopia (this would satisfy the latter's desire for an outlet to the sea), and supported the United States plan for collective trusteeship for the other two colonies. American policy was not completely formulated until just prior to the London Conference. Before that time there had been two general groups within the State Department on the issue. One group favored the return of the colonies to Italy, while the other favored collective trusteeship; the first reflected growing apprehension concerning Soviet influence in Africa, while the latter was motivated by a desire to implement and strengthen the United Nations.[5] By the time of the London Conference the collective trusteeship position had won out, and Mr. Byrnes, the American Secretary of State, proposed it generally for all the colonies, with the exception that there should be a minor territorial adjustment between Ethiopia and Eritrea in favor of the former. There was to be a ten-year time limit on the trusteeship for Libya and Eritrea, though not for Somaliland.[6]

At this stage of the negotiations the Russians completely rejected the principle of collective trusteeship, and argued instead for individual trusteeships for each of the three colonies with an unconcealed desire that the Soviet Union should administer one of them, preferably on the Mediterranean. This undoubtedly would have meant that Libya would be divided, at least temporarily, into its three constituent parts of the Fezzan, Cyrenaica, and Tripolitania. The latter was most frequently mentioned as the area possibly to be put under Soviet administration.[7] The other powers, particularly France and the United Kingdom, reacted rather strongly against this proposal, indicating that even at that early date they had begun to be fearful of Soviet influence in the Mediterranean area and wanted to prevent it if possible.[8]

The Italian and Arab governments had by this time also formulated policies with regard to the colonies and had made their views known to the Big Four. As might be expected, Italy favored the return of her colonies, preferably as colonies, secondarily in the form of trusteeship,

[4] *The Times* (London), September 22, 1942.

[5] Sisco, p. 211. The term "collective trusteeship" may mean either two or more states acting as the administering authority, or the United Nations itself acting as such. The American idea of collective trusteeship referred to the United Nations acting as administering authority.

[6] *A Decade of American Foreign Policy*, Senate Document No. 123, 81st Congress, 1st Session, p. 53.

[7] The New York *Times*, September 19, 1945. Byrnes, p. 96.

[8] Byrnes, p. 95. Later, British Foreign Minister Bevin called the Soviet desire for a North African trusteeship "an effort to cut across the throat of the British Empire." The New York *Times*, April 29, 1946.

while the Arabs desired to create two independent states, Tripolitania and Cyrenaica, out of Libya, or, as a second choice, have those two areas put under the trusteeship system.[9]

No definite agreement as to the disposal of the colonies was reached in London, although the "principle of trusteeship" was generally accepted—whether collective or individual was the question. One important result of the conference, however, was the crystallization of British policy to permit the Soviet Union to exercise as little influence as possible in Africa, a policy which the United Kingdom was willing to pursue even to the extent of reversing its position on the return of the colonies to Italy in any form. From the time of the London Conference the British sought, according to one student of the subject, to convince the United States of the danger of letting the Soviet Union into Africa by the device of collective trusteeship.[10]

In the period between the London Conference and the Paris Conference in April, 1946, the two most noteworthy developments were the deterioration of East-West relations, and the emergence of a strong and potentially victorious Communist Party in Italy. In view of this it is not surprising to find the Soviet Union at Paris coming a little closer to the French position of returning the colonies to Italy in the form of trust territories. The Soviet plan still called for individual trusteeships, but in each case there was to be an Italian assistant to the top administering official. Later in the conference, the Soviets indicated they would be willing to support the French plan for Italian trusteeships in return for outright cession of Trieste to Yugoslavia.[11]

Meanwhile the British had presented a new plan calling for the independence of Libya and a British trusteeship for Somaliland.[12] The American position at this time was still that of favoring collective trusteeships, though by no means so actively as at the London Conference. The United States rejected the Soviet proposal and entertained doubts about the British proposal for Somaliland; the second shift in Soviet policy, the return of Italy's colonies to that country in the form of trusteeships, was acceptable to the United States—providing a time limit of ten years was placed on the trusteeships for Libya and Eritrea—but this in turn proved unacceptable to the British, primarily because of strategic considerations in Cyrenaica.[13] Thus, while the Paris Conference saw apparent progress made toward a settlement of the question, agreement among the Big Four was not reached. It is interesting to note the shift in Soviet policy which at the time accomplished two purposes: (1) it divided the

[9] Sisco, p. 210.

[10] *Ibid.*, p. 219.

[11] The New York *Times*, May 7, 1946.

[12] *Ibid.*, April 29, 1946.

[13] Sisco, pp. 227-31.

West, the United States and France being willing to accept the principle of Italian trusteeship, the British not; and (2) it served to bolster the position of the Communist Party in Italy. In addition, Italian trusteeship would serve to substitute a lesser power for a greater power in Mediterranean Africa. These proposals, and the considerations underlying them, demonstrate how the supposedly humanitarian question of colonies can become enmeshed in the power struggle on the general international scene. Nor was the question to become disentangled from the East-West struggle when it was turned over to the General Assembly for settlement.

At Paris the Big Four had been able to arrive at one important decision concerning the Italian colonies. Pursuant to Annex XI of the Treaty of Peace with Italy, it was decided that a commission of investigation should be sent to the colonies to determine the wishes of the indigenous inhabitants as they pertained to the disposition of the areas.[14] The Commission visited the three areas in the winter and spring of 1947-48, and though the results of it investigations were not conclusive, it was able to get some idea of the local sentiment on the question of the disposition of each territory.

Specifically it reported that the most vocal and best organized groups in Libya favored that territory's independence as a united state, although what percentage of the population was represented by those groups was difficult to ascertain.[15] The inhabitants of Eritrea were split along religious lines. The Christians (about 45 per cent of the population) favored annexation by Ethiopia, while the Moslems (about 40 per cent of the population) desired eventual independence with the United Kingdom trusteeship in the interim. The other 15 per cent were divided between those who favored the return of Italian rule and those Christians opposed to joining Ethiopia. Here again, however, the Commission was doubtful as to the validity of its sampling of opinion.[16]

In Somaliland, the Commission found the "strongest force" to be the Somali Youth League, which favored a ten-year period of trusteeship under the joint administration of the Big Four. The League also expressed violent opposition to either Italian or Ethiopian rule. About 30 per cent of the population seemed to be opposed to the Somali Youth League, and favored instead trusteeship under a single government (not necessarily excluding Italy) "which would insure peace and security." [17]

[14] Members of the Commission were F. E. Stafford (United Kingdom), Chairman, John E. Utter (United States), Burin des Rogers (France), and Artemy Feodorov (Soviet Union). N. I. Klimov replaced Feodorov while the Commission was in Libya. See F. E. Stafford, "The Ex-Italian Colonies," *International Affairs*, Vol. XXV (1949), p. 47.

[15] *Ibid.*, pp. 53-54.

[16] *Ibid.*, p. 49.

[17] *Ibid.*, pp. 50-51.

The Commission's activities in Somaliland were impaired by the outbreak of a riot in Mogadishu (the capital of the territory), in which fifty-one Italians and fourteen natives were killed. As a result the Commission was not able to make as extensive a survey of opinion as it wished.[18] The results of the Commission's investigation were sufficiently inconclusive to allow a variety of interpretations of the evidence gathered. Thus each member could, as each did, interpret that evidence to support its own position.[19]

By August, 1948, other interested powers had had an opportunity to present their views and ten out of nineteen indicated they favored the return of one or more of the colonies to Italy in the form of trusteeship,[20] a position apparently not in accord with the views of the native inhabitants. As the deadline (September 15, 1948) approached when the question had to be decided or referred to the General Assembly, the Soviet Union asked for another meeting of the Big Four, and, after some hesitation on the part of the United States, such a meeting took place in Paris late in the summer of 1948.

This meeting is of importance primarily as the point at which East and West both reversed their positions, at least in part; they were influenced, no doubt, more than a little by the results of the Italian elections. The United States and Great Britain now proposed that Somaliland be placed under the trusteeship system with Italy as the administering authority, while the Soviet Union favored what was originally the American plan—collective trusteeships.[21] This "double reverse" was, of course, a reflection of the political situation: the West attempting to keep the Soviet Union out of Africa, the Soviet Union endeavoring to get at least its foot in the door through collective trusteeship. If this course of events did nothing else for the Soviet Union, it at least cleared the propaganda air, for from this point on that state could, as it did, in arguing for collective trusteeships, charge the West with imperialist designs on Africa—a position it could take only with difficulty when it was supporting Italy as an administering state. Needless to say, no agreement was reached at this conference, and it was therefore decided to send a letter to Mr. Trygve Lie, Secretary-General of the United Nations, informing him of the failure of the Big Four to reach agreement on the disposition of the Italian colonies, and that pursuant to the Treaty of Peace with Italy, the matter was being referred to the General Assembly.[22]

---

[18] *Ibid.*, p. 50.

[19] The official report of the Commission is not available. The later debates in the General Assembly, however, reveal the way each of the states on the Commission interpreted the evidence.

[20] The New York *Times*, August 10, 1948.

[21] Sisco, pp. 243-44.

[22] *Yearbook of the United Nations, 1948-49*, p. 256.

Negotiations in the Third General Assembly. When talking about the United Nations there is sometimes a tendency to view that organization as something completely apart from the various governments which make up its membership—to view it, that is to say, as an agency separate from, and perhaps superior to, the governments of the sixty member states. But when the Big Four send delegations to the United Nations, although the machinery of negotiation may be different from that of a Foreign Ministers Conference, the governments remain the same. There is no sudden metamorphosis from positions based on national interests to an objective international viewpoint when, for example, delegates from the Soviet Union and the United States meet in the General Assembly instead of in Paris or Moscow.

Thus, when the disposition of the former Italian colonies was turned over to the General Assembly it should not be surprising that the positions of the Big Four did not, at least at first, materially change. The significance in the change in machinery lay rather in the fact that now all sixty members of the United Nations would be taking part in the decision. Much of the impetus for a given decision would still come from the Big Four, but other groups could now suggest solutions and, more important, whenever two-thirds of the General Assembly lined up behind any given solution it would succeed regardless of what the minority felt. Submission of the problem to the General Assembly meant, then, not that any solution would be necessarily more "objective" than one reached by the Big Four, but that the negotiations would take place among sixty governments, any forty of which could force a decision.

When the General Assembly convened in September, 1948, it was soon obvious that the Western powers, with the exception of the United Kingdom, wanted to delay a final settlement of the issue, while the Soviet Union pressed for early consideration. The British, with the backing of the United States for a British trusteeship in Cyrenaica, wanted quick disposal which would include this feature. France, on the other hand, wanted to delay a decision until such time as it was sure its interests in North Africa would be protected. The United States, while willing to support the British plan for Cyrenaica, preferred a year's delay in the settlement of Eritrea.[23] Perhaps because of this lack of unity in the West, the Soviet Union pressed for early consideration and proposed that the question be dealt with at once in an *ad hoc* committee. This proposal was defeated, however, and the matter was not actually taken up until the second part of the third session, April and May, 1949, and then in the First Committee.[24]

At the first meeting which dealt with the former Italian colonies, the

[23] Sisco, pp. 253-54.

[24] *Ibid.*, p. 254. *Yearbook of the United Nations, 1948-49*, p. 257.

Chairman of the First Committee presented a request from the government of Italy that a representative of that state be allowed to participate in the discussions. This was acceptable to the committee, but only after it was agreed that representatives of the indigenous inhabitants of the territories in question also be allowed to present their views.[25] In the general discussion at this time the question of the legality of Italy, a nonmember state, acting as an administering authority arose. On this point, M. Chauvel of France stated:

It had never been stated, either by the four Powers or by any of the Governments consulted, that the fact that Italy was not a Member of the United Nations excluded it from participation in the Trusteeship System. But if a legal argument were brought forward, it would be simply the reply that Article 81 of the Charter mentioned "one or more States," and did not refer to a Member of the United Nations. . . . A similar case, that of a State which was an Administering Authority, but which left the United Nations, had been foreseen in a declaration made by the representatives of the United States and the United Kingdom, to the effect that if a State left the United Nations for reasons which reflected no discredit upon it, and if it stated that it would continue to observe the rules of Trusteeship, there was no reason for that trusteeship to be taken from it.[26]

This interpretation received the general assent of the members of the First Committee and was not seriously disputed thereafter.[27]

The committee, after a good deal of discussion on the point, decided to resolve the question of hearing representatives of the indigenous inhabitants by appointing a subcommittee to report to the full committee "on the extent to which those parties or organizations of indigenous inhabitants represent substantial sections of opinions in the territory in question" and, taking into account the report of the Commission of Enquiry which had been sent to the territories by the Big Four, make recommendations on whether and if so how such representatives should be heard by the committee.[28]

When, nine days later, the subcommittee made its first report only three parties had so far appeared before it with requests to present their views to the First Committee: (1) the Moslem League of Eritrea; (2) the Nuova Eritrea Pro Italia Party; and (3) the Somali Youth League. The subcommittee found it difficult to make any assessment as to the size and importance of the various groups, primarily because it had no way

[25] *Official Records of the Third Session of the General Assembly, Part II, First Committee* (April-May, 1949), p. 2.

[26] *Ibid.*, p. 9.

[27] For a minor exception to this see below, p. 115.

[28] *Official Records of the Third Session of the General Assembly, Part II, First Committee* (April-May, 1949), p. 46. The committee was composed of the representatives of Brazil, Egypt, France, Haiti, India, New Zealand, Norway, Poland, the Soviet Union, the United Kingdom, and the United States.

to verify the evidence presented by each of the groups as to its size and representativeness.[29] Until this verification could be completed, however, the subcommittee concluded that in any case each of the three groups represented "substantial sections of opinion" and recommended they each be heard in turn.[30] The procedure for hearing these groups recommended by the subcommittee and adopted by the committee was as follows:

(1) The representatives should be invited to the table of the Committee to make a general statement of their views.
(2) They should then remain at the disposal of the Committee for the purpose of giving any additional information which Committee members desire.
(3) The representatives could then make brief concluding statements if they wish.[31]

Three points emerge from this first report of the subcommittee. First, the United Nations in considering the disposition of the former Italian territories was definitely attempting to ascertain the wishes of the native inhabitants, and the First Committee had developed a procedure for so doing. In the entire history of the formation of both mandates and trusteeship systems this was, in effect, the first time this had been attempted by an international body. Second, the First Committee through its subcommittee attempted to assess the groups requesting hearings so that a qualitative as well as quantitative measurement of native opinion could be made. Third, it was already becoming obvious that, in the absence of impartial on-the-spot investigations, this assessment of the various groups was hazardous and imprecise at best. Despite this difficulty, however, the action taken by the First Committee augured well for those who hoped that the trusteeship system would in fact as well as principle take into account the wishes of the trust peoples. The crucial question remained, though, to what extent these wishes would actually affect the final disposition of the territories in question.

The First Committee, following the procedure recommended by its subcommittee, listened to representatives of the various indigenous groups cleared by the subcommittee. Ultimately, representatives of some thirty-odd groups appeared before the subcommittee, although only about one half requested to be heard, since many of the organizations overlapped.[32] With reference to Somaliland the subcommittee noted a dozen organizations whose views, together with the subcommittee's assessment of their

[29] *First interim report of Sub-Committee 14 to the First Committee.* April 19, 1949. United Nations Document A/C.1/439, p. 1.

[30] *Ibid.*, p. 2.

[31] *Ibid.*

[32] *Third Interim Report of Sub-Committee 14 to the First Committee.* (26 April, 1949). United Nations Document A/C.1/442.

respective positions in the territories may be summarized in chart form as follows:

Organization	*Membership*	*Policy*
Somali Youth League	100,000 300,000 followers (relatives and dependents of active members)	(1) United Nations Trusteeship for not more than ten years (2) Strong opposition to restoration of Italian administration in any form
Somalia Conference	180,000 360,000 supporters	Italian trusteeship for thirty years; ultimate independence
Hamar Youth Club	1,587	Same as Somali Youth League
Patriotic Beneficence Union	80,788	Member of the Somalia Conference
Hisbia Dighil Mirifle	60,871 300,000 supporters	Member of the Somalia Conference. President recently changed to the view of the Somali Youth League, but evidence shows this was due to external pressure.
The Union of Africans in Somalia	5,000	Member of the Somalia Conference
Somali Young Abgal Association	30,000	Adheres to program of Somalia Conference
Hidait Al Islam Bhidle and Mobilem	10,618 (60,000 including families of members)	Member of the Somalia Conference
Bimal Union	300	Claimed by the Somalia Conference
Italian Representative Committee	Claims to represent all Italians living in Somaliland. Total membership not listed	Return of the Italian administration under United Nations supervision
Arab Community	25,000	"Such a Government as would guarantee security, free trading, protection of property, etc."
Local Born Young Arabs	1,800	Same as Arab Community

Granting the best of intentions on the part of the First Committee to determine objectively the wishes of the indigenous populations, almost insurmountable obstacles prevented any agreement on the substance of the evidence offered. And even if there had been agreement on this point, the question still remained of how much weight to attach to such evidence. In the case of Somaliland, for example, by combining groups of similar views and leaving out groups claiming comparatively small membership it is fair to say that about one half favored eventual independence with Italian trusteeship in the interim, the other half independence within ten years with a United Nations (i.e., collective) trusteeship meanwhile.[33] Further, the second group in any case violently opposed Italian trusteeship.[34]

On what are these facts based? The claims of the groups involved to the Four Power Commission and the subcommittee. In the absence of any kind of a census, records of political activity (e.g., voting), or sample polling, this evidence is questionable at best. But assuming for the moment its correctness, the Somali Youth League not only opposed Italian administration in any form, but at one point threatened forceful resistance to it, even though it came as a result of a United Nations decision. The Somalia Conference, on the other hand, was much milder in its position and was willing to acquiesce in any decision reached by the General Assembly. Should the latter's slightly greater numerical strength outweigh the more adamant stand of the former? Further, even if this question be decided, the Charter itself does not specifically provide that the wishes of the indigenous inhabitants be taken into account in the approval of the trusteeship agreements; but even if this is implied in the case of the Italian colonies, few were prepared to argue that it was to be the sole factor in the decision. If not the sole factor, then how much weight should be given to those views? The point of all this is to illustrate that it is one thing to accept the principle that it is a good thing to take the wishes of the indigenous inhabitants into account when disposing of territories, but that it is quite another to implement this principle in practice, even under the most auspicious of conditions. Add to these questions the general East-West struggle, and the complexity of the decision is such that one may be pleasantly surprised if any of the inhabitants concerned are pleased with the decision.

After the various representatives of the native populations had been heard, the First Committee, upon the suggestion of the United States delegate, appointed another subcommittee—this one to consider various

[33] This grouping was reflected in the hearing before the First Committee, where only representatives of the Somali Youth League, and its subordinates, and the Somalia Conference, and its subordinates, actually spoke. *Official Records of the Third Session of the General Assembly, First Committee, Part II* (April-May, 1949), pp. 96-98.

[34] *Ibid.*, p. 344. Mr. Issa of the Somali Youth League told the First Committee that his organization would fight the return of Italian administration "to the death."

draft resolutions which had been submitted to the First Committee on the disposition of the colonies and to formulate its recommendations for the First Committee.[35] In general the proposed solutions at this time may be summarized under five general headings: (1) the United States-British position: British trusteeship over Cyrenaica, postponement of the disposition of Tripolitania, division of Eritrea between Ethiopia and the Sudan, and Italian trusteeship over Somaliland; (2) the Soviet bloc position: United Nations trusteeship for each of the colonies (with the exception of giving Ethiopia an outlet to the sea in Eritrea), in which, in each case, a United Nations administrator would be assisted by an advisory committee whose membership was to include representatives of the Big Four; (3) the Latin American bloc: British trusteeship over Cyrenaica, Ethiopian outlet to the sea in Eritrea, the return to Italy of the remainder of the territories involved; (4) the Arab states' position: Libya united and independent, or at most a brief trusteeship leading to independence, opposition to return of the colonies to Italy; (5) the Asiatic delegations' position: collective trusteeship, but differing from the Soviet proposal in not providing for Big Four participation in administration.[36]

It was obvious that in order to obtain the necessary voting strength in the General Assembly some kind of compromise would have to be reached. After attempts made in this direction, particularly between the Latin American and Arab-Asiatic blocs, failed,[37] there seemed little chance of reaching agreement on the question during the third session of the General Assembly. During the meetings of the subcommittee to consider the various proposals, however, it was announced that Foreign Minister Bevin of the United Kingdom and Count Sforza of Italy had reached an agreement which followed the Anglo-American plan with these changes: (1) Tripolitania would be placed under Italian trusteeship in 1951, meanwhile remaining under British administration; (2) the Fezzan would be placed under trusteeship with France as the administering authority; (3) all of Libya would be granted independence in ten years.[38]

This compromise received the support of France and the Latin

[35] *Ibid.*, pp. 270-71. Members were Argentina, Australia, Brazil, Chile, Denmark, Egypt, Ethiopia, France, India, Iraq, Mexico, Union of South Africa, the Soviet Union, the United Kingdom, and the United States.

[36] Benjamin Rivlin, "The Italian Colonies and the General Assembly," *International Organization*, Vol. 3 (1949), p. 466. The specific proposals for each group may be found in Documents A/C.1/446, A/C.1/433, A/C.1/449, A/C.1/453, and A/C.1/448 respectively. In addition the Australian delegate submitted a proposal (A/C.1/447) to postpone settlement, meanwhile appointing a special committee to study further and report on the problem.

[37] Rivlin, pp. 466-67.

[38] The New York *Times*, May 10, 1949.

American states, which was sufficient to secure its adoption in the form of a proposed resolution by the subcommittee,[39] but it was bitterly attacked by the Soviet bloc and the Arab states when the subcommittee reported back to the First Committee. The latter group, speaking through the representative of Iraq, charged that the subcommittee had exceeded its terms of reference in that the Bevin-Sforza proposal had not been submitted to the First Committee. This was followed by a demand on the part of the Polish delegate that since the draft resolution contained a completely new solution, the representatives of the indigenous groups should be re-invited by the committee to comment on the proposal, as well as on other proposals, specifically those of the Soviet Union and Iraq.[40] Concerning Somaliland, the position of the representatives of the Somali Youth League and the Somali Conference remained unchanged—that is, the latter was willing to accept the proposal, the former bitterly opposed it.

After this final hearing of the indigenous groups, the committee proceeded to vote on the subcommittee's proposal (embodying the Bevin-Sforza agreement), after first rejecting substitute proposals by Iraq, the Soviet Union, and India.[41] The voting on the proposal was done paragraph by paragraph with amendments offered to almost every part of the resolution. In general there was little change made in the resolution with the important exception that in the paragraph dealing with the disposition of Eritrea, the proposal to incorporate the Western Province into the Sudan was rejected.[42] There was one significant vote, however, that augured trouble for the proposal in the General Assembly. The paragraph providing for Italian trusteeship over Tripolitania was the pro-Italian concession of the Bevin-Sforza agreement designed to attract the Latin American states. This paragraph was adopted by a vote of thirty-two to seventeen with eight abstentions,[43] less than the required two-thirds needed in the General Assembly. If this proved to be an accurate forecast of the voting in the latter body, it could be assumed that the Latin American bloc would vote against the resolution as a whole. In its amended form the entire resolution was adopted by a vote of

[39] *Report of Sub-Committee 15 to the First Committee.* May 11, 1949. United Nations Document A/C.1/466, pp. 4-7. The vote in the subcommittee was 10 to 4 with 1 abstention.

[40] *Official Records of the Third Session of the General Assembly, Part II, First Committee* (April-May, 1949), pp. 325-26.

[41] Iraq (Document A/C.1/455): Libya to be granted immediate independence. Soviet Union (Document A/C.1/433/Rev.1): collective trusteeships. India (Document A/C.1/488): collective trusteeships for Libya and Somaliland; further investigation of the wishes of the natives in Eritrea. *Ibid.*, pp. 377-80.

[42] *Ibid.*, p. 394. The vote was 16 in favor, 19 against, with 21 abstentions.

[43] *Ibid.*, p. 393.

thirty-four to sixteen, with seven abstentions, and sent on to the General Assembly for final approval.[44]

When the latter body voted on the resolution both the paragraphs providing for Italian trusteeship (over Tripolitania and Somaliland) failed to get the necessary two-thirds majority by one vote.[45] Then the resolution as a whole, or what was left of it, suffered a thumping defeat, fourteen in favor, thirty-seven against, with seven abstentions, the Latin American bloc now opposing the measure as a result of the paragraph by paragraph voting.[46] There was nothing else to be done now except to try again at the fourth session of the General Assembly.

What is the significance of this failure to solve the problem during the third session? One competent observer has maintained that it added to the prestige of the United Nations if only because in rejecting the Bevin-Sforza agreement, the General Assembly refused to accept a solution opposed by the indigenous population in the territories.[47] In other words, the West, operating in the realm of power politics, was not able to force through a solution based on expediency ulterior to the needs and desires of the dependent peoples concerned.

The present writer has some difficulty in accepting this point of view. In the first place, taking the information given by the subcommittee, those groups in Somaliland opposed to Italian administration were outnumbered by those who were willing to accept it. But more important, since there is no exact method of assessing the importance of the two general groups in question, is Mr. Rivlin's assertion that the United Nations rejected "a solution based on pure expediency" and showed that "principle is a moderating force on power politics."[48] What, in fact, was that "expediency?" It was the desire on the part of the West to insure the prevention of a Soviet foothold in the continent of Africa. Thus if the welfare of the dependent peoples is the principle involved, and if there is a suspicion that Soviet influence in dependent areas does not lead to the increased welfare, all things considered, why is not the prevention of Soviet influence in Africa a matter of "principle"? The point is that no power, other than Italy, was apparently prepared to assume the trusteeship for Somaliland; that a United Nations trusteeship meant some Soviet influence in the administration of that territory; and that no group or state was prepared to argue that Somaliland was as yet ready for independence.

[44] *Ibid.*, p. 394.

[45] *Official Records of the Third Session of the General Assembly, Part II, Plenary Meetings* (April-May, 1949), pp. 587, 593.

[46] *Ibid.*, pp. 595-96.

[47] Rivlin, p. 469.

[48] The quoted phrases are from *ibid.*, p. 470.

One other alternative suggests itself: why not follow the Asiatic proposal of having joint trusteeship without including the Soviet Union in the administering group? This would have the advantage of satisfying the request of the Somali Youth League as well as keeping the Soviet Union out of Africa. The answer here is undoubtedly at least twofold: (1) the Latin American states, whose acquiescence was virtually necessary for any decision, pressed for Italian administration in at least one of the territories, and (2) Western aid in the direction of helping Italy "re-establish" her prestige in Africa doubtless aided the pro-West DeGasperi government as against the Communists in Italy. The dichotomy between "expediency" and "principle" fails to take into account the basic fact that territorial questions can no more be dissociated from the general vicissitudes of international politics than can, say, atomic energy. To expect otherwise is to condemn the United Nations for failure to achieve what no national government has been able to achieve with respect to domestic issues. The rejection of the Bevin-Sforza solution did not, then, demonstrate the triumph of principle over expediency, but only that the competing interests within the United Nations had as yet failed to compromise their views sufficiently to achieve the required two-thirds majority.

Negotiations in the Fourth General Assembly. If the fourth session of the General Assembly was to have any more success than the third in dealing with the problem of the disposal of the former Italian colonies it was clear that there would have to be a modification in the positions taken by at least some of the interested states. Of the states taking the most active interest in the question, the proceedings in the third session of the General Assembly, and during the early part of the fourth session, revealed four major groups. Group one consisted of the major powers in the West who by this time were agreed on the basic policy of keeping the Soviet Union from exercising influence in Africa. This view manifested itself in the refusal on the part of these powers to consider collective trusteeship which would include the Soviet Union for any of the colonies. To this group Italy may be added, after the victory of the DeGasperi government at the polls. There was a minor divergence of opinion within the group as to precisely what positive disposal should be made, but all were agreed in their opposition to the Soviet plan of collective trusteeship.

The second group was the so-called Latin American bloc, whose primary concern was to see that Italy was accorded, in one form or another, some control over her former colonies. Since this group of states collectively amounted to almost one-third of the General Assembly's membership, it had, with very little outside support, an effective veto over any final decision. The third group consisted of the Arab states, chiefly concerned with the fate of Libya and desiring, specifically, unification and independence for that area. It was the Arab states in the third session of the General Assembly who were instrumental in voting down Italian trusteeship for Tripolitania, and thus effectively defeating the solution based on the Bevin-Sforza plan. The fourth group was, of course, the Soviet Union and its satellites, bent on exercising as great a degree of influence in Africa as possible, supporting first a Soviet trusteeship in Tripolitania, then Italian trusteeship, then collective trusteeship, as circumstances dictated.

In addition to these general groups, Ethiopia pressed very strongly for what it conceived to be its legitimate interests which included incorporation of at least the southern and eastern parts of Eritrea into Ethiopia and prohibition of Italian jurisdiction in any form in Somaliland. From this grouping, and remembering the events of the third session of the General Assembly, it becomes obvious that the best chance for a solution, from the point of view of the West, was to modify their proposals in the direction of Libyan independence enough to bring Arab acquiescence, but not enough to alienate the Latin Americans. This, as will be seen, was precisely what happened.

When the First Committee considered the question at the fourth session of the General Assembly, it turned its attention first to hearing the revised proposals of various interested states. As might be expected from the above discussion, the Western powers had modified their stand to the extent of proposing independence for Libya in the near, if not immediate, future.[49] There was still some disagreement within Western ranks as to the actual implementation of this principle, however. The United Kingdom and France preferred recognizing their own, and Italy's special interests in the Fezzan, Tripolitania, and Cyrenaica by providing for independence for each of the three component parts of Libya separately, with aid being administered to the various areas by the major power most vitally concerned there—Italy in Tripolitania, France in the Fezzan, and the United Kingdom in Cyrenaica.[50] The United States and China, on the other hand, spoke of a united, independent Libya, "at a definite date in the near future."[51] The Soviet Union, meanwhile, had modified its position in such a way as to appeal to the Arab states by calling for the immediate independence of Libya plus the withdrawal of all foreign troops and the removal of all foreign military bases.[52] The

[49] *Official Records of the Fourth Session of the General Assembly, First Committee* (September-December, 1949), pp. 20-22.

[50] *Ibid.*, p. 26.

[51] *Ibid.*, pp. 22, 33.

[52] *Ibid.*, p. 22. The Soviet proposals were circulated in United Nations Document A/C.1/487.

position of most of the other states, with respect to Libya, and of all states with regard to Eritrea and Somaliland remained for the most part unchanged.

After a good deal of invective discussion, the chairman of the First Committee, Mr. L. B. Pearson of Canada, suggested the formation of a subcommittee to consider requests by various representatives of the native populations. This proposal was adopted unanimously and an eleven-member subcommittee was thereupon appointed.[53] Of the representatives of the various groups in Somaliland the subcommittee recommended hearing those of the Somali Youth League and the Somalia Conference.

Before this occurred, however, the representative of the United Kingdom was closely questioned in the First Committee about an allegation that the British administration in Somaliland had taken steps to suppress, without justification, the Somali Youth League. The British explanation of this was to point out that on October 5, 1949, demonstrations of a violent order were being planned to protest proposals made in the First Committee concerning Somaliland. The British administrative officials, facing a tense situation, proceeded to close temporarily *all* political clubs, regardless of party.[54] When Mr. Issa of the Somali Youth League testified before the committee, however, he repeated the charge that the British had discriminated against the League because the latter refused to accept the Western plan for Italian trusteeship for the area.[55]

The present writer has been able to find no clear evidence supporting the British or the League concerning these charges, but regardless of where the truth lay, the episode did little to change any delegate's mind as to the final disposition of the territory. It did serve, however, to intensify the growing bitterness between East and West on the committee. Other than this, the representatives of both the Somali Youth League and the Somalia Conference had nothing to add to their previous statements made during the third session of the General Assembly. They merely called each other "terrorists" and "traitors."

Actually there was little discussion of Somaliland or Eritrea as compared with Libya during this phase of the proceedings. This was true undoubtedly because the latter provided the crucial issue. The Arab states, while not particularly fond of seeing Italy in East Africa, were primarily interested in the fate of Libya. The real question was, then, could a solution be found for Libya to which both the Arabs and the Latin Americans agreed? And the reason why so much turned on this

[53] *Ibid.*, p. 28. The subcommittee was composed of representatives of Brazil, Egypt, France, Haiti, India, New Zealand, Norway, Poland, the Soviet Union, the United Kingdom, and the United States.

[54] *Ibid.*, p. 56.

[55] *Ibid.*, pp. 78-79.

question was that the three areas were not considered separately, but any solution had to be in the nature of a "package deal." This was insisted upon by the Latin Americans, among others, to insure that if the Arabs had their way with respect to Libya, Italian interests would be protected in East Africa.[56]

After the various representatives had been heard, an Argentine resolution calling for the creation of a subcommittee to consider and report on the various proposed solutions was adopted.[57] This subcommittee held twenty-nine meetings between October 11, and November 4. The subcommittee at the outset had before it six draft resolutions,[58] of which four contained recommendations regarding Somaliland. Later, new draft resolutions were submitted, as well as an amendment to one of the latter resolutions.[59] Rather than consider the detailed provisions of each of the drafts, the subcommittee proceeded to vote on the various principles involved and considered detailed recommendations only after these principles had first been agreed upon. A drafting group of five members was charged with the task of preparing draft resolutions embodying the decisions of the subcommittee.[60] As Somaliland was the only one of the three colonies eventually to find its way into the trusteeship system, we shall follow through the subcommittee's work on that area only. But it is necessary to summarize the decisions made with respect to the other territories, especially Libya, since the interrelation of the decisions for each of the three areas remained an important consideration throughout the entire process of arriving at a solution.

With regard to Libya[61] the subcommittee proposed that the territory be constituted an independent state, effective not later than January 1, 1952. The form of government, unitary or federal, together with a constitution for the state should be decided upon by representatives of the inhabitants of the three constituent parts of the state. To assist the Libyans in the formation of a constitution it was recommended that a United Nations Commissioner be appointed, to be aided by a Council composed of the representatives of Egypt, France, Italy, Pakistan, the United Kingdom, and the United States, one representative of each of

[56] Rivlin, p. 466. See also the remarks of Mr. Issa of the Somali Youth League, *ibid.*, p. 79. The "package deal" nature of these negotiations has also been confirmed for the writer by Mr. Jack Harris, Senior Officer, Department of Trusteeship, United Nations, in a conversation on April 22, 1952.

[57] *Official Records of the Fourth Session of the General Assembly, First Committee* (September-December, 1949), p. 82.

[58] *Report of Sub-Committee 17 to the First Committee,* November 1, 1949. Document A/C.1/522, p. 1.

[59] *Ibid.*, p. 2.

[60] *Ibid.*, pp. 1-2.

[61] For the specific proposals see *ibid.*, pp. 16-17.

the three regions of Libya, and one representative of the minorities in the area. It is interesting to note that the subcommittee rejected the Soviet bloc proposals providing for (1) immediate independence, (2) inclusion of a representative of the Soviet Union on the proposed Council, and (3) the withdrawal of "all foreign troops and military personnel," and the liquidation of "all military bases" within three months, the latter two by majorities of at least two to one in each case.[62]

Concerning Eritrea the subcommittee faced a vexatious problem. Most of the delegates accepted the claim of Ethiopia for at least an outlet to the sea, but dividing Eritrea between Ethiopia and the Anglo-Egyptian Sudan smacked too much of an old-time division of the spoils. Since the Four Power Commission report had stated that the wishes of the natives in that land had not been as definitely ascertained as in the cases of the other two colonies, however, the final disposition of Eritrea could be side-stepped by the subcommittee by a recommendation that a United Nations Commission be established for further consideration of the Eritrean question, including a more complete ascertainment of the wishes of the indigenous population. A resolution to that effect was adopted by a substantial majority,[63] while a Soviet-sponsored proposal that Eritrea should be made independent in five years, being placed under United Nations trusteeship in the interim, was voted down.[64]

With regard to Somaliland,[65] the subcommittee first adopted the principle that the territory should become independent by a unanimous vote. The next question concerned the time interval during which independence was to be achieved. By close margins the subcommittee rejected proposals for five and ten year time limits, and by a large majority adopted the proposal that the territory should become independent in ten years, unless at that time the General Assembly should decide otherwise. There followed the crucial vote on the Soviet plan to place the territory under the trusteeship system with the organization itself as the administering authority. Here there was a definite alignment of forces, the Soviet and Arab blocs, together with Liberia, voting in favor of the proposal, the Western powers and the Latin American bloc voting against it. It was thus defeated twelve votes to nine.

The importance of the "package" nature of the decision with regard to the three colonies is here illustrated. A combination of Soviet and Arab states had been sufficient to muster enough strength to defeat the Bevin-Sforza plan in the third session of the General Assembly, and it

[62] *Ibid.*, pp. 2, 4, 7.

[63] *Ibid.*, p. 14. The vote was 15 to 3, with 2 abstentions.

[64] *Ibid.* The vote was 9 to 5, with 7 abstentions.

[65] The decisions regarding Somaliland noted in this, and the following, paragraph, are found in *ibid.*, pp. 10-12.

could be assumed that a similar group would do the same to the proposal for Italian trusteeship in Somaliland. If this occurred, however, it was obvious that the Latin American states might very well vote against the immediate independence of Libya as provided in the present plan. Since one solution was closely tied in with the other, the Arabs would be forced to choose between their desire for an independent Libya and the prevention of Italian influence in Somaliland—with every indication that they would choose the former.

After the defeat of the Soviet proposal, a recommendation for a collective trusteeship administered by three states (not including the Soviet Union) was also defeated, the Arab states voting in favor, the Soviet bloc and India abstaining. Finally, the proposal for Italian trusteeship was adopted, the Soviet and Arab blocs voting against, India abstaining. The subcommittee then decided by large majorities that a declaration of constitutional principles "guaranteeing the rights of the inhabitants of Somaliland and establishing institutions designed to insure the inauguration, development and subsequent establishment of self-government," should be annexed to the trusteeship agreement, and that a draft declaration submitted by India [66] should be "taken into account" by the Trusteeship Council and the administering authority when the agreement was drafted. The final substantive recommendation adopted by the subcommittee was an Argentine proposal that the Trusteeship Council should negotiate with the administering authority the draft of a trusteeship agreement for submission not later than the fifth session of the General Assembly.[67]

The subcommittee reported back to the First Committee on November 4, 1949, and the latter body completed its consideration of the proposals on the twelfth. After the arguments were restated the First Committee adopted the subcommittee's proposals for Libya with a few minor changes. This was after they rejected a Soviet-sponsored amendment to grant immediate independence to Libya and to replace France, the United Kingdom, and the United States on the Advisory Council with Czechoslovakia, Haiti, and the Ukranian S.S.R. After turning down a Polish amendment to the section on Eritrea which encompassed the Soviet plan for United Nations trusteeship, the committee adopted a Burmese amendment to the subcommittee's recommendations which provided for the composition of the Commission on Eritrea. Burma, Guatemala, Norway, Pakistan, and the Union of South Africa were selected to serve.[68]

Turning to the territory of Somaliland, the procedure used for dis-

[66] This proposal may be found in United Nations Document A/C.1/SC.17/L.6.

[67] *Ibid.*, p. 12.

[68] *Official Records of the Fourth Session of the General Assembly, First Committee* (September-December, 1949), pp. 221-26, 242-49.

cussion of the subcommittee's proposals was to take up each paragraph separately, considering amendments to each as the particular paragraph was dealt with. After the paragraph by paragraph vote, the entire proposal was voted on; finally, the proposals for all three territories were voted on as a unit—that is, as one single resolution recommended by the First Committee to the General Assembly. Discussion on Section B of the subcommittee's proposals, dealing with Somaliland, was involved and acrimonious. From these discussions, however, important decisions both negative and positive concerning proposed amendments to the subcommittee's recommendations emerged. They illustrate the types of questions faced and how they were dealt with by the First Committee.

Turning first to those amendments which proved to be unacceptable to the committee, the most important were those of the Soviet bloc, sponsored in the main by the Polish representative. These consisted of proposals (1) to limit the duration of the trusteeship period to three, rather than ten years, and (2) to provide for United Nations rather than single-nation trusteeship.[69] The second of these was, of course, crucial, for the vote in the First Committee could be considered an adequate forecast of the General Assembly vote. The issue remained in doubt, however, because the Arabs abstained on the second question, though voting in favor of the first amendment. Both were defeated by large majorities.[70]

The only other significant unsuccessful amendment was that of Liberia, whose delegate introduced a proposal providing for a Commission similar to that recommended for Eritrea and having the same objectives.[71] If adopted this would have fundamentally changed the entire subcommittee proposal, and would have undoubtedly alienated the Latin Americans with respect to the recommendations as a whole. In defense of the motion it was argued that the wishes of the inhabitants of Somaliland had by no means been fully ascertained, an argument which in view of the conflicting claims of the Somalia Conference and the Somali Youth League, had a distinct air of creditability about it. Nevertheless, the First Committee rejected this motion and proceeded to use the subcommittee's recommendation as the basis for further discussion.[72]

Of those changes made by the First Committee by far the most important was the addition to the subcommittee's resolution of a paragraph

[69] United Nations Document A/C.1/529.

[70] *Official Records of the Fourth Session of the General Assembly, First Committee,* pp. 230, 233. The votes were, respectively: 35 to 18, with 6 abstentions, and 35 to 8, with 16 abstentions.

[71] United Nations Document A/C.1/527.

[72] *Official Records of the Fourth Session of the General Assembly, First Committee* (September-December, 1949), pp. 227-29. The vote was 40 to 11, with 8 abstentions.

calling for the establishment of an advisory council to "aid and advise" the administering authority. The feeling behind this amendment was the obvious reluctance on the part of many delegates to entrust the administration of Somaliland to Italy alone.[73] Two amendments along this line were submitted: the first, by the Lebanese delegate,[74] called for a council consisting of five (unnamed) states; the second, by the Argentine delegate,[75] provided for two representatives on the council, specifically a Latin American and an Arab. These two were compromised during the discussion, and a joint Lebanese-Argentine amendment providing for an advisory council of three (representatives of Colombia, Egypt, and the Philippines) was offered.[76] Before this could be voted on, however, the committee first had to consider a Polish amendment providing that three representatives of the local population be added to the advisory council, a Chinese proposal that the members of the advisory council be invited to participate without vote in the debates of the Trusteeship Council "on any question relating to this territory," and another Polish proposal that the word "advisory" be deleted from the Argentine-Lebanese amendment.[77]

All these were defeated by substantial majorities, and the joint Argentine-Lebanese amendment was adopted overwhelmingly, Ethiopia alone voting against it.[78] Another amendment adopted by the First Committee reversed a decision made in the subcommittee. This was with reference to the clause in the subcommittee's resolution that Somaliland be accorded independence in ten years "unless at the end of that period the General Assembly decides otherwise." The Philippine representative, arguing that "to give and take back at the same time was an ambiguous and unwise

[73] *Ibid.*, p. 227. Mr. Arce, of Argentina, stated that this proposal was "aimed at allaying the anxieties of Pakistan and of certain other delegations which did not think that Italy should administer Somaliland alone."

[74] United Nations Document A/C.1/530.

[75] United Nations Document A/C.1/532.

[76] *Official Records of the Fourth Session of the General Assembly, First Committee* (September-December, 1949), p. 237.

[77] The Chinese amendment and the first Polish amendment are found in United Nations Documents A/C.1/540 and A/C.1/538, respectively. The second Polish amendment was apparently offered from the floor.

[78] *Official Records of the Fourth Session of the General Assembly, First Committee* (September-December, 1949), pp. 237-38. The voting was as follows:

	Against	*For*
First Polish amendment:	33	9
	17 abstentions	
Chinese amendment:	25	6
	27 abstentions	
Second Polish amendment:	37	14
	8 abstentions	
Argentine-Lebanese amendment:	1	48
	10 abstentions	

policy," proposed the deletion of the phrase giving the General Assembly this discretionary power. The deletion was adopted, receiving its support from the Arab, Asiatic, and Soviet representatives, while the Latin Americans split on the question.[79] The only other significant modification of the subcommittee's recommendations was the decision to substitute the words "be guided by" for "take into account" in the clause referring to consideration by Italy and the Trusteeship Council of the annex of constitutional principles proposed by the Indian delegation.[80] Finally, based on combined proposals of Argentina, Chile, and Mexico,[81] two new paragraphs were added to the subcommittee's resolution, providing for the undertaking by Italy of the provisional administration of the territory at a time agreed upon by that state and the United Kingdom, after giving assurances that such temporary administration would be in accordance with the relevant provisions of the Charter. The advisory council was to commence its duties when the Italian government began its provisional administration.[82]

The decisions reached in the First Committee provide an interesting commentary on the role of the General Assembly in the settlement of the Italian colonies question. With reference to Somaliland, the Western proposal for Italian trusteeship was accepted in substance; but the smaller states, less motivated by ulterior considerations of the East-West struggle, were able to modify the original plan to the extent of having an advisory council of three small states created to "oversee" directly the Italian administration with a view to making sure that Italy's protestations of renouncing Fascist philosophy and adhering to democratic principles were implemented in practice in the territory. The significance of this lies in the fact that while so-called power considerations were very much a part of the negotiations surrounding the disposition of the Italian colonies, including Somaliland, nevertheless considerations of a more "idealistic" nature such as the protection and well-being of the native inhabitants involved, were woven into the settlement in the form of such provisions as that concerning the advisory council and the Indian annex of constitutional principles. The point is that while it is idle to talk about United Nations settlement of the problem based solely on enlightened interest in the welfare of the Africans, it is also incorrect to view the decision as one of merely disguised division of spoils among the mighty, with no consideration given to the native peoples. A correct analysis obviously lies somewhere in between, and to the extent that it does, it shows that

[79] *Ibid.*, pp. 229-30. The vote was 33 to 22, with 4 abstentions.

[80] *Ibid.*, p. 239. The vote was 50 in favor, with 7 abstentions. The amendment, sponsored by the Indian delegate, may be found in United Nations Document A/C.1/537.

[81] United Nations Documents A/C.1/541, A/C.1/545, and A/C.1/548.

[82] *Official Records of the Fourth Session of the General Assembly, First Committee* (September-December, 1949), pp. 254-59.

the General Assembly is, in a meaningful sense, an assembly composed of small as well as great powers.

After finishing paragraph-by-paragraph consideration of each of the three parts of the subcommittee resolution, the First Committee proceeded to vote on the Preamble and each of the three sections, all of which were adopted by large majorities, as was the resolution, in its amended form, as a whole.[83]

The General Assembly considered the resolution of its First Committee at its two hundred forty-ninth and two hundred fiftieth plenary meetings on November 19 and 21, 1949. During the discussion members of the Soviet bloc reiterated their opposition to the proposed solution, while most of the other states voiced their approval, though many had reservations about specific parts of the proposals. Following the same procedure used in the First Committee, the General Assembly voted on each of the three sections of the resolution separately, then on the resolution as a whole. On the final vote only Ethiopia remained adamant in its opposition, while the Soviet bloc, Sweden, and France abstained.[84] The General Assembly had thus reached a decision on the complicated problem given to it over a year previously. It remained now for the Trusteeship Council and Italy to negotiate the agreement under which Somaliland would be actually placed under the trusteeship system.

Drafting the Trusteeship Agreement. Pursuant to the resolution passed by the General Assembly, the Trusteeship Council met in special session on December 8, 1949, to begin work on the drafting of a trusteeship agreement for Somaliland. Before the Council could discuss the problem, however, the question arose of whether or not other states should be invited to participate, without vote, in the discussions of the Council pertaining to Somaliland. Specifically, the states involved were Italy, Egypt, and Colombia (as members of the Advisory Council; the Philippines were at that time a member of the Trusteeship Council), India, as the author of the annex of constitutional principles, and Ethiopia, as a state directly concerned. After some discussion, and over the objection of the Soviet representative, the Chairman of the Council invited Italy to take a seat at the Council table, which ruling was sustained.[85] After more lengthy discussion, representatives of the other states were similarly

[83] *Ibid.*, pp. 260-61. The voting was as follows:
Section A (Libya): 50 to 0, with 8 abstentions
Section B (Somaliland): 47 to 7, with 4 abstentions
Section C (Eritrea): 47 to 5, with 6 abstentions
The resolution as a whole: 49 to 1, with 8 abstentions.

[84] *Ibid., Plenary Meetings* (September-December, 1949), p. 302. Libya received its independence January 1, 1952. Eritrea became an "autonomous unit federated with Ethiopia under the sovereignty of the Ethiopian crown. . . ." *United Nations Yearbook*, 1951, pp. 277-85.

[85] *Trusteeship Council, Official Records, Second Special Session* (December 8-20, 1949), pp. 7-9.

invited, with the reservation that the invitation to the Ethiopian representative was without prejudice to the question of what constitutes a "state directly concerned." [86]

The Council then turned its attention to a draft resolution submitted by the New Zealand [87] delegate calling for a special committee of six to be appointed to make a preliminary study of the question. Membership on the committee was to consist of three administering and three non-administering states. To this the French representative added an amendment to the effect that the special committee was to "carry out this work, with the advice, in so far as it may be necessary, of . . . Colombia, Egypt, Ethiopia and India." [88] During the course of the debate on these proposals, one item of importance arose. This concerned an implicit divergence of opinion on the position of Italy in the draft of the trusteeship agreement. On the one hand, the administering states, especially the United Kingdom, assumed that the Italian draft would serve as the basis of discussion in the committee.

The Philippine delegate, however, argued that the Trusteeship Council must take the initiative. Accordingly, he submitted three amendments to the draft resolution, the aims of which were to (1) transfer initiative from Italy to the Trusteeship Council in the drafting of the agreement; (2) provide for the expression of views of the indigenous population of Somaliland before the special committee; and (3) provide that the observations of any delegation who may have participated in the work of the committee could be recorded so that the full Council could hear the views of the representatives of the local population.[89] Objections were made to all three of these amendments on the following grounds: (1) Italy would have to implement the provisions of the agreement, so it should submit its draft proposals; (2) the General Assembly had not deemed it necessary to provide for further hearing of the native inhabitants, and there was therefore no justification for introducing the procedure now, and (3) keeping records of the special committee's actions would prevent full and frank discussion.[90]

After further arguments on both sides the Council proceeded to reject the first and third of the Philippine amendments, adopting the proposal providing for the hearing of the native inhabitants. Then rejecting a counterproposal by the Soviet representative, the Council adopted the amended New Zealand draft resolution and designated the membership

[86] *Ibid.*, pp. 11-16.

[87] United Nations Document T/L.1.

[88] *Trusteeship Council, Official Records, Second Special Session* (December 8 to 20, 1949), p. 18.

[89] *Ibid.*, p. 28.

[90] *Ibid.*, p. 30. The arguments summarized are those of Mr. Fletcher Cooke of the United Kingdom.

of the committee as follows: administering authorities: France, the United Kingdom, and the United States; nonadministering authorities: the Philippines, Iraq, and the Dominican Republic.[91]

The Special Committee on Somaliland met in Geneva from January 9 to January 19, 1950. Although the Philippine proposal that initiative in the drafting of the agreement should lie with the Council had been voted down, this did not mean that the general procedure for considering the proposals submitted by Italy was the same as that used in the Fourth Committee for the first eight agreements. In those cases, as was noted, the question was one of the appropriate United Nations organs approving an agreement submitted to the General Assembly. Here, even though Italy's draft was used as the basis for discussion, there was nothing to prevent other states from submitting either amendments or complete sets of proposals of their own. Nor was the "sword of Damocles," which hung over the head of the Fourth Committee in the form of the administering authority's "ultimate veto," present at the Special Committee's sessions. Or perhaps it is more correct to say that the sword was much smaller and of doubtful temper—that is, Italy could of course absolutely refuse to accept some part of the agreement if pressed too far; but the pressure to accept was now on the administering authority, where before it had been on the Fourth Committee and the General Assembly.

Italy's draft, then, served as the basis of negotiation, but the agreement which emerged from the Committee was in fact based on *negotiation*, and was not merely a revised set of Italian proposals. In addition to the Italian draft, the Philippines submitted a draft agreement, the Dominican Republic offered a series of statements to serve as bases of discussion, and Iraq proposed an annex covering educational policy in the territory.[92] The Italian draft was very similar to the agreements reached during the course of discussion in the Fourth Committee. Most of the modifications made to that draft were based on the Philippine proposals, the Dominican Republic proposals being referred to very little because the Philippine proposals covered the same ground and were more specific.

Without following through the step-by-step negotiations of the Special Committee, it is sufficient to note three or four of the most important changes made in the Italian draft—all of which were in the direction of further insuring the protections of the rights of the native population and limiting those of the administering authority.

---

[91] *Ibid.*, pp. 33-35.

[92] These proposals may be found in the following United Nations Documents:
Philippines: Document T/440
Dominican Republic: Document T/AC.18/L.3
Iraq: Document T/AC.18/L.6
Italy: Document T/429

The first of these changes concerned, simultaneously, the Advisory Council provided for in the resolution passed by the General Assembly, and the goals of administration in the territory. The Italian draft, in enumerating the duties of the Advisory Council, did so in very general terms, and went no further than the Charter in providing for the administrative objectives in the territory. The Philippine proposals, on the other hand, were much more specific in providing that the administering authority and the Advisory Council should work out programs for the benefit of the trust population. A comparative table of proposals illustrates this difference: [93]

Italy	*Philippines*
The advisory Council, which shall have its headquarters at Mogadishu, shall assist the Administering Authority: (a) in problems of primary importance respecting the political, economic, social and educational advancement of the inhabitants of the Territory; (b) in programmes of a general nature reflecting the economic prosperity of the Territory; (c) in problems relating to the participation of the Territory in the maintenance of international peace and security; (d) in questions regarding the annual reports of the Administering Authority to the organs of the United Nations; (c) in any dispute, as referred to in Article 17 of the present Agreement, which may arise; (dispute between the administering authority and a member of the United Nations) (f) in all other matters concerning which the Administering Authority may request advice.	The advisory Council shall be fully informed by the Administering Authority on all matters relating to the political, economic, social and educational advancement of the inhabitants of the Trust Territory, including legislation appertaining thereto, and may make to the Administering Authority such observations and recommendations as it considers likely to be conducive to the attainment of the objectives of this Agreement. The Administering Authority shall seek the advice of the Advisory Council on all measures envisaged for the inauguration, development and subsequent establishment of full self-government for the Territory, particularly in respect of: (a) the establishment and development of organs of self-government; (b) the plan for the economic and financial development of the Territory; (c) the programme for educational advancement; (d) the policies of labour and social advancement; (e) the annual budget of the Territory; (f) the plan for the transfer of the functions of Government to a duly constituted independent government of the Territory;

[93] Cf. United Nations Documents T/429 and T/440.

The object in quoting the specific provisions is to show the difference in emphasis involved. Technically, the provisions in the Italian draft included those of the Philippine proposal since the former, in general, provided for carrying out the objectives of the Charter, and the latter could go no further than the Charter. Nevertheless it is one thing to be committed, as an administering authority, to availing oneself of the assistance of the Advisory Council "in problems of primary importance respecting the political . . . advancement of the inhabitants of the Territory," and quite another to undertake to establish and develop "organs of self-government." Further, where the Italian draft provided that the administering authority "shall avail itself of the cooperation of an Advisory Council" the Philippine draft stated that the administering authority "shall be aided and advised" by an Advisory Council. Again, perhaps merely a difference of emphasis—but significant in that the latter wording, especially when offered as a substitute for the former, provides for a stronger position of the Advisory Council in the territory.

The Philippine proposals, with one exception, were adopted by the committee and substituted for the Italian text.[94] The one exception was the clause providing that the administering authority should consult the Advisory Council on the annual budget. The Philippine and Iraq delegates felt that this should be included, but the other four members of the Committee argued that it would be too great a handicap on the administering authority. And it seems reasonable to argue that if the Advisory Council members were not going to contribute funds for the administration of the territory, as they were not, then the administering authority should not have to consult them about finances.

In addition to accepting, in general, the Philippine proposals as to the functions of the Advisory Council the committee also approved three additional articles, based on the Philippine proposals, which provided (1) assurance of free access for members of the Advisory Council to such sources of information as were necessary for the Council to carry out its duties, (2) diplomatic privileges and immunities for members of the Advisory Council in the territory, and (3) that states members of the Advisory Council, if not members of the Trusteeship Council, could participate without vote in the debates of the Council on questions specifically relating to Somaliland, and could make such reports (oral or written, separately or jointly) as they felt necessary.[95]

A second important question which arose during the negotiation of the agreement for Somaliland in the Special Committee concerned the

[94] *Committee for Italian Somaliland, Summary Record of the Ninth Meeting* (January 13, 1950), United Nations Document T/AC.8/SR.9, p. 3.

[95] *Committee for Italian Somaliland, Summary Record of the Fifteenth Meeting* (January 17, 1950), United Nations Document T/AC.18/SR.15, p. 3.

degree to which the territory could be militarized. The Italian draft followed the provisions of the agreements already in existence in providing that the administering authority had the power to establish "whatever military, naval, and air installations are necessary for the defence of the territory," and to maintain its own armed forces, as well as raise volunteer contingents, in the territory, for the maintenance of internal order as well as to help maintain international peace and security. The Philippine proposals, however, would have limited this to the raising of volunteer forces, with the number of those recruited from outside the territory subject to approval by the Trusteeship Council, and would have prohibited altogether the establishment of bases or the erection of fortifications in the territory.

There was a good deal of discussion concerning this question. The Italians, supported by the British, felt that the territory must be prepared to defend itself when it became independent and that a prohibition of fortification was unjustified. The Ethiopian delegate expressed the view that the building up of security for Somaliland was by definition a threat to the security of his state. The Iraq delegate argued that the Philippine proposals were satisfactory because Somaliland had no strategic value at all, and therefore did not need fortification.[96]

As might be expected, a compromise was reached. The Italian delegate went on record as declaring that any Italian forces in the territory would never be larger than the British forces then present, and further agreed that any measures taken for the defense of the territory would be only after prior consultation with the Advisory Council. With these reservations, Italy was accorded the same military powers as were the other administering authorities in nonstrategic territories.[97] The second reservation, however, provided for considerably more direct international supervision of the military program within the territory than had been provided in the first eight agreements.

A third important limitation placed on the administering authority, following negotiations in the Special Committee, concerned the possible transfer of land rights to non-indigenous persons. In the Italian draft, this was not to be done without "the previous consent of the competent authorities." The Philippine proposals, however, prohibited the transfer of land rights to non-indigenous persons except "on lease for a period to be determined by law." The principal objection to the Philippine proposal was voiced by the Italian representative who maintained that there was a danger in the absolute prohibition of land transfer; the United

[96] *Ibid., Summary Record of the Sixth Meeting* (January 12, 1950), United Nations Document T/AC.18/SR.6, pp. 3-8.

[97] *Ibid.*, p. 5. The second reservation was made at the suggestion of the American representative.

Kingdom representative, accepting this argument, suggested that land transfer could be made subject to approval of the Trusteeship Council. This, however, was unacceptable to representatives of both Iraq and the Philippines, who argued that prohibition of land rights transfer was an essential protection for the native inhabitants.[98]

After further discussion, it was agreed that the administering authority could not permit the acquisition by non-indigenous inhabitants of land rights in the territory except "on lease for a period to be determined by law," unless a majority of the indigenous members of the Territorial Council agreed.[99] This last codicil was later changed to read two-thirds of the total membership of the Territorial Council.[100] Further, in cases involving agricultural land in excess of one thousand acres, the administering authority was compelled to request the advice of the Advisory Council which in turn was to make a detailed report on such alienation to the Trusteeship Council.[101]

The importance of these decisions concerning land rights is greater than it might seem at first glance. The alienation of native-owned land to non-indigenous persons has long been a source of both social and economic difficulties in parts of Africa—and with the controls written into the trusteeship agreement the discretion of the administering authority was severely limited. The difference between the provisions in this respect as between the Italian draft and the draft agreement as it emerged from the Special Committee is the difference between the latter and the first eight agreements. If the land rights in Somaliland specifically are not worth as much as the paper on which the negotiations concerning them were recorded, the principle of limiting the discretionary powers of the administering authority is as important a difference as may be found between the agreement for Somaliland and those for the other African trust territories.

Another important change made in the Italian draft was based on a draft of an Educational Annex submitted by the delegate from Iraq which provided for detailed assurances that due regard be given to the teaching of Islamic religion and the Arabic language in all stages of education; that elementary education be for no less than five years, be free, and be promulgated as widely and rapidly as possible; that students be given the opportunity to study in foreign universities; that teacher training institutions should be established; that the working of the United

[98] *Ibid., Summary Report of the Seventh Meeting* (January 12, 1950), United Nations Document T/AC.18/SR.7, p. 5.

[99] The Territorial Council is explained below, pp. 110-11.

[100] *Committee for Italian Somaliland, Summary Report of the Seventh Meeting* (January 12, 1950), United Nations Document T/AC.18/SR.7, pp. 6-7.

[101] *Ibid.*, p. 7.

Nations be taught; and that "education, on all levels, shall be free and democratic and shall work to eradicate any discrimination based on class, race, sex, religion, or political consideration." [102]

This proposal was little discussed in the Special Committee proper, being largely settled through the process of "informal" negotiation.[103] The upshot of the negotiation was that, in a new article, the administering authority recognized the importance of education, but was specifically committed only to seeing that qualified university students could study outside the territory, and that in all educational institutions the activities of the United Nations were taught.

Finally, two new articles added to the Italian draft provided specifically that the territory would become an "independent sovereign state" within ten years, and that the administering authority should submit to the Trusteeship Council at least eighteen months before the expiration of the trusteeship a plan "for the orderly transfer of all functions of the Government to a duly constituted independent government of the Territory." [104] The provisions stemmed directly from the Philippine draft and were obviously designed to implement the agreement reached by the General Assembly that Somaliland would achieve its independence in ten years.

Resolution 294 (IV) of the General Assembly providing for the placing of Somaliland under trusteeship also called upon the Trusteeship Council to include in the trusteeship agreement an annex of constitutional principles based on the draft annex submitted by India. This draft is significant as an indication of what principles were thought important by a state recently emerged from colonial status, and is therefore worth summarizing:

1. Sovereignty is vested in the people of the territory.
2. An administrator, appointed by the administering authority should be the executive authority in the territory.
3. To assist the administrator, the latter should appoint a Territorial Council of five representatives of the principal political parties or organizations in the territory.
4. The administrator should consult and be guided by the advice of the Territorial Council in all matters except those relating to defense and foreign affairs.
5. The administrator, with the consent of the Territorial Council (enlarged by such other representatives as he should choose to summon for the purpose),

[102] United Nations Document T/AC.18/L.6, p. 3.

[103] *Committee for Italian Somaliland, Summary Report of the Thirteenth Meeting* (January 16, 1950), United Nations Document T/AC.18/SR.13, p. 7. *Ibid., Summary Report of the Fourteenth Meeting* (January 17, 1950), United Nations Document T/AC.18/SR.14, p. 11.

[104] *Ibid., Summary Report of the Eighth Meeting* (January 13, 1950), United Nations Document T/AC.18/SR.8, pp. 8-9.

should normally act as the legislative authority, with the proviso that in exceptional circumstances, subject to United Nations control, the administrator could promulgate necessary ordinances.

6. The judiciary should be appointed by the administrator, and not be removable except with the consent of the United Nations.

7. All authorities in the territory should "respect human rights and fundamental freedoms for all without distinction as to race, sex, language, or religion."

8. The United Nations may amend the above rules.[105]

In addition to this Indian draft, the representatives of Italy and the Philippines submitted draft declarations[106] and the Special Committee proceeded to work out a final draft based on all three sets of proposals. The chief additions made to the Indian draft by the committee were (1) a provision making the indigenous population citizens of the territory; (2) a provision insuring that Islamic and local customary law would be applied where appropriate in the judicial system; and (3) a detailed spelling out of individual rights together with an acceptance by Italy of the Universal Declaration of Human Rights as a standard of achievement in the territory.

The first two of these occasioned little discussion,[107] but the last was a compromise, after long discussion, between the Philippine position that the Bill of Rights in the Italian Constitution should apply in the trust territory, and the list of rights—less inclusive—submitted by the Italian representative. The compromise entailed keeping the Italian list relatively unchanged, but adding the provision concerning the Universal Declaration of Human Rights.[108]

What were perhaps the thorniest issues concerned the provisions for the establishment and duties of the administrator and the Territorial Council. Specifically, there were three questions which the committee had to resolve. The first concerned the membership of the Territorial Council. The Indian draft in effect called for a representation of indigenous population only, and to this point of view the Iraq and Philippine delegates subscribed. Other members of the committee, however, agreed with the Italian representative that it would be necessary to have some non-indigenous members on the Territorial Council if only because the native population lacked, as yet, adequate experience in government.

[105] United Nations Document T/420, paraphrased.

[106] United Nations Document T/429, pp. 11-12, and T/440, pp. 12-14.

[107] *Committee for Italian Somaliland, Summary Report of the Tenth Meeting* (January 14, 1950), United Nations Document T/AC.18/SR.10, p. 6. *Ibid., Summary Report of the Twelfth Meeting* (January 16, 1950), United Nations Document T/AC.18/SR.12, p. 8.

[108] *Ibid., Summary Report of the Eleventh Meeting* (January 14, 1950), United Nations Document T/AC.18/SR.11, pp. 8-9. *Summary Report of the Thirteenth Meeting* (January 16, 1950), United Nations Document T/AC.18/SR.13, pp. 3-8.

The proposal of the latter group was that at least one half the members of the Territorial Council be indigenous.[109]

The discussion on this issue raised the second, and broader, question of the general nature of the Territorial Council. The nonadministering states on the committee argued that the Territorial Council should be broadly representative of the indigenous population because it would in time develop into the legislative body of the territory. The other states viewed the Territorial Council more as a small advisory body to the administrator.[110] The compromise finally reached on both these questions was one of ambiguity. The Territorial Council was to be "broadly representative of the people of the Territory," and the legislative authority of the territory was to be "normally exercised by the Administrator after consultation with the Territorial Council until such time as there shall have been established an elective legislature." [111]

The third question concerned the responsibility of the administrator for decisions relating to defense and foreign affairs. While the Indian draft had called for responsibility to the United Nations for such decisions, the United States and the United Kingdom, supporting Italy, argued that the administrator should be responsible only to the administering authority; otherwise the chain of responsibility would be broken, with resulting confusion of responsibilities of the administering authority. The compromise effected here was offered by the French representative and resulted in the main in a victory for the nonadministering states on the committee in that it provided for responsibility of the administrator to the Trusteeship Council.[112] To this extent, then, the idea of direct international supervision was brought into the agreement.

Other than comparatively minor changes, the only further modifications of the Indian draft made by the committee was the addition of a preamble and the deletion of the article providing for the amendment of the declaration—the latter, apparently, in view of the fact that the main body of the agreement provided for its amendment, and the Declaration of Principles formed an integral part of the agreement.

The modifications in both the main body and the annex of the agreement discussed above are by no means all that were made. They do, however, represent the most important ones in terms of the question of how much actual negotiation, as opposed to mere approval or disapproval of the Italian draft, occurred in the committee. Actually, in terms of

[109] *Ibid., Summary Report of the Tenth Meeting* (January 14, 1950), United Nations Document T/AC.18/SR. 10, pp. 8-9.

[110] *Ibid.*, p. 9.

[111] *Ibid., Summary Report of the Eleventh Meeting* (January 14, 1950), United Nations Document T/AC.18/SR.11, pp. 3-5.

[112] *Ibid.*, pp. 6-7.

time and effort spent, much of the discussion in the committee involved questions which, while important to the particular states concerned, are not relevant to this study. For example, several meetings were devoted, at least in large part, to the issue of how the boundary between Ethiopia and Somaliland should be determined, and several other meetings were used to work out an acceptable formula to provide for the transfer of administering functions from the United Kingdom to Italy, and arrangement for provisional government in the interim.

With regard to the points discussed, it is difficult to assess the actual process of negotiation in the committee for the reason that some of the important decisions were reached during "informal" discussions, of which no record is available, while many of the decisions reached in the committee proper occasioned little if any actual dispute. It may be fairly said, however, that the records of the committee indicate a real spirit of negotiation on the part of all member states. At no time did any of the representatives manifest an attitude of absolute refusal to have their points of view modified. To be sure several times the committee seemed to split along administering versus nonadministering authority lines, but this was certainly to be expected in view of the obvious importance which both groups attached to various articles in the agreement, particularly those concerning limitations on the rights of the administering authority. Certainly this much can be said: the nonadministering states on the committee exercised a real influence on the terms of the agreement, and any reference to Somaliland being placed under Italian trusteeship as being little more than disguised annexation [113] flies in the face of the facts as revealed by the records of the Special Committee.

The Special Committee completed its work on January 19, 1950,[114] and submitted its report [115] to the Trusteeship Council for consideration during its sixth session. The latter body considered the report from January 20 to 27, 1950, during which time the Soviet Union was not represented on the Council. The most significant general aspect of the discussion in the Trusteeship Council was the recognition on the part of the administering authorities that the draft agreement as submitted by the Special Committee did in fact represent a considerable advance

[113] Soviet bloc reaction to the General Assembly decision on Somaliland implied this charge more than once. Typical were the remarks of Mr. Kiselev (Byelorussian S.S.R.): "the United States, the United Kingdom and France, faithful to their traditional colonial policy had paid no heed to the wishes of the indigenous population and had sought only to satisfy their own imperialistic interests." *Official Records of the Fourth Session of the General Assembly, Plenary Meetings* (September-December, 1949), p. 288.

[114] Actually the committee met one more time, on January 26, at the request of the Trusteeship Council, to reconsider the drafting of one clause.

[115] United Nations Document T/449.

over the other agreements in terms of more specifically spelling out the rights of trust peoples and increasing the machinery of international supervision, with the consequent anxiety as to the precedent-making possibilities of the agreement. The Australian delegate, for example, while applauding the work of the committee, took pains to assert that in his view the agreement did not "constitute a new departure or create a new precedent for the definition of the functions of the administering authority and its obligations under the Charter."[116] It did constitute, however, corroborative evidence that the nonadministering states on the Council took their position seriously and did not particularly mind putting the administering authorities on the defensive.

Specifically, the Council, in dealing with the Special Committee's draft, made three substantive modifications, none of which has great intrinsic importance, but which are worth noting as an indication of the fact that the trusteeship system evolves through little battles, and that it, like Rome, will not be built in a day. The first of these concerned the article providing for "special investigations and inquiries as the General Assembly or the Trusteeship Council may deem necessary." The Belgian delegate doubted that the General Assembly was concerned with "investigations and inquiries," and pointed out that such a provision was not found in the Charter. Upon assurance that Article 87 was sufficient justification[117] for such a provision in the agreement, the representative of Belgium then moved to replace the phrase in question with "as provided for in Article 87 of the Charter. . . ." This was adopted by a close vote and, as amended, the article was approved.[118]

The second modification concerned the right of the members of the Advisory Council, collectively or individually, to make statements or written reports to the Trusteeship Council. The Special Committee's draft provided that this might be done "as may be necessary for the Trusteeship Council's proper consideration of . . . questions relating to the Territory."[119] The question arises: who is to decide when this is necessary? Obviously if it were any agency other than the Advisory Council — the administering authority, for example — its supervisory powers would be considerably more curtailed than if left to its own

[116] *Trusteeship Council, Official Records, Fourth Year, Sixth Session* (January-April, 1950), p. 8.

[117] Article 87 of the Charter reads, in part, "The General Assembly and, under its authority, the Trusteeship Council, in carrying out their functions, may: . . . c. provide for periodic visits to the respective trust territories at time agreed upon with the administering authority; and d. take these and other actions in conformity with the terms of the trusteeship agreements."

[118] *Trusteeship Council, Official Records, Fourth Year, Sixth Session* (January-April, 1950), pp. 11-13. The vote on the amendment was 5 to 4, with 2 abstentions.

[119] *Ibid.*, p. 22.

discretion. Here the nonadministering powers won the victory, for the article in question was changed to spell out the latter interpretation.

The third modification made by the Trusteeship Council was similar to the second. Where the Special Committee's draft provided that in cases involving the alienation of agricultural land in excess of one thousand acres the administering authority should request the advice of the Territorial Council, the Trusteeship Council added the words "in advance," with the obvious purpose of insuring the Territorial Council its proper role in the making of such decisions.[120]

Going behind the formal positions of the Council members on each of these relatively minor points, the discussion indicates on the one hand the constant desire on the part of the administering authorities to keep international supervisory machinery to a minimum—that is, in American terms, to construe Charter provisions strictly wherever possible. The nonadministering states on the Council, on the other hand, continually try to exert pressure toward a greater amount of international supervision in order to insure further the protection of native rights.

In its slightly amended form the entire agreement was approved unanimously by the Trusteeship Council on January 27, 1950,[121] and thereafter submitted to the Fifth Session of the General Assembly for final approval. That body immediately turned the draft agreement over to its Fourth Committee which considered it from November 10 to December 2, 1950.

In addition to the draft agreement the Fourth Committee also had before it a progress report of the Advisory Council,[122] which had been functioning in the territory since April 1, the date on which the administration of the territory had been transferred from British to Italian jurisdiction. This report indicated that the Italians had not been hesitant about proceeding to implement the provisions of the agreement, and in fact had already consulted the Advisory Council on two issues: the composition of the Territorial Council and the languages other than Italian to be taught in the schools. It was further evident to the Advisory Council that the Somali Youth League, which had at one time vowed armed resistance to Italian administration in any form, had—though apparently with some misgivings—cooperated with the administering authority and had called upon its adherents to do likewise. In general the report indicated approval of Italy's administration, though declaring it too early to make more than a tentative appraisal, and noted the complex political, social, and particularly economic problems which would have to be solved before the territory achieved its independence.

[120] *Ibid.*, p. 27.

[121] *Ibid.*, p. 47.

[122] This report was circulated as United Nations Document A/C.4/178.

Considering that the report was submitted by three states, at least two of which (Egypt and the Philippines) could certainly not be accused of partiality in favor of Italy, it might be expected that the Fourth Committee would approve the draft agreement in comparatively short order. Such in fact was the case. Other than the Soviet bloc, almost all the delegates expressed their general satisfaction with the agreement, although many had reservations on specific points.[123] The representative of the Somali Youth League, once more invited to speak on the subject, complained as to the immigration and land alienation provisions of the agreement, but in general made no further attempt to have the committee turn down the agreement.[124]

The Ethiopian representative, however, raised two objections to the entire agreement and urged the committee not to approve it. Specifically, he argued (1) that Italy, not being a member of the United Nations, could not assume the responsibilities of an administering authority, and (2) that Ethiopia, as a "state directly concerned," had not approved the agreement, hence it was not consonant with Charter provisions. The first argument was not pressed, but the Ethiopian representative submitted a resolution [125] to the effect that the United Nations was unable to proceed further in the consideration of an agreement for Somaliland because of the second point. This, after much discussion, was rejected by a large vote, as was a later Ethiopian proposal that the entire issue be submitted to the International Court of Justice for an opinion.[126]

Following this, the committee proceeded to vote on a resolution jointly sponsored by Argentina, Colombia, Denmark, India, Iraq, Norway, Pakistan, the Philippines, and the United States, calling upon the General Assembly to approve the draft agreement in view of the declarations made by the administering authority before the Fourth Committee of his country's desire to implement the Charter and the agreement, and to prepare Somaliland for "independence in a spirit of justice, peace, liberty, and progress." [127] This was adopted by a vote of forty-four to five, with one abstention,[128] and the agreement was sent on to the General

[123] The Egyptian delegate, for example, wanted assurance that Italy "would seek the advice on all matters referred to in article 3 of the draft agreement." *Official Records of the Fifth Session of the General Assembly, Fourth Committee* (September-December, 1950), p. 216.

[124] *Ibid.*, p. 233. A representative of the Somalia Conference voiced approval of the draft agreement. *Ibid.*, p. 235.

[125] United Nations Document A/C.4/L.102.

[126] *Official Records of the Fifth Session of the General Assembly, Fourth Committee* (September-December, 1950), p. 237.

[127] United Nations Document A/C.4/L.104/Rev.1.

[128] *Official Records of the Fifth Session of the General Assembly, Fourth Committee* (September-December, 1950), p. 237.

Assembly unchanged. It will be noted that the procedure in the Fourth Committee in this instance differed from that used in connection with the first eight agreements, in that there was no article by article discussion of provisions. This was undoubtedly due primarily to the fact that the agreement itself had been negotiated by a United Nations body and the basic issues of how much protection was to be given to the indigenous inhabitants and how much control to the administering authority had already been fought out. The General Assembly, with no general debate, approved the agreement at its three hundred sixteenth plenary meeting on December 2, 1950,[129] thereby officially beginning the ten-year period of Italian trusteeship.

Generally speaking, it seems that the United Nations fulfilled its task remarkably well with regard to Somaliland. Certainly the agreement represents considerable advancement in terms of protection for the indigenous population and international supervision. That many of the agreement's provisions were the result of compromise and were completely satisfactory to neither administering nor nonadministering states is obvious. That considerations of "power politics" entered into the general question of the disposition of Somaliland is also evident. But the very fact that most of the member states, and all of the major powers, did take an active interest in the question, and that an agreement was reached, provides a basis for calling that achievement a success.

It is probably a safe postulate about the United Nations to say that to the extent that a decision has been reached "objectively," with little discussion and less disagreement, to that extent the decision is meaningless. When, however, a question seems of vital concern to the major powers, and of interest to most others, and a decision is hammered out, surely this reflects a successful completion of the type of task the United Nations was designed to perform. Interest clashes, perhaps even bitterness, then compromise—that is the stuff of which peaceful international decisions are made. There would seem to be a few other issues raised in the United Nations which, on this basis, can be put more completely on the credit side of that organization's ledger.

[129] *Ibid., Plenary Meetings* (September-December, 1950), p. 550. The vote was 44 to 6.

Part II

Functioning

CHAPTER FIVE

The Mechanics of the Trusteeship Council

The heart of the trusteeship system is the international supervision of the administration of trust territories. Before the details of this supervision can be explained, however, it is necessary to summarize the mechanics of the working Trusteeship Council in order to understand better Council activities. This chapter is designed to furnish this basic information as a background to the specific description of the major aspects of the trusteeship system.

Membership. The Charter, it will be remembered, provides that the Council shall be composed of an equal number of administering and non-administering states, always including the Big Five, and that each member "shall designate one specially qualified person to represent it." In addition, the Rules of Procedure of the Council provide that each representative may have such alternates and advisors as he desires. In practice, most of the states on the Council have made use of this provision, and alternates have often temporarily acted for the representative.

The Charter states that the nonadministering states on the Council shall be elected for three year terms by the General Assembly. While nothing in Chapter XIII mentions using geographic distribution as a criterion in the selection of nonadministering states, in practice there have always been at least two Latin American states, one Middle Eastern state, and one Far Eastern state on the Council, accounting, all told, for the entire elected membership from the second session on, as the table on the next page indicates.

From this table it can be seen that at all times Council membership has included at least one state which has been under colonial administration within the lifetime of its representative. Thus at least one of the members can be looked for to defend the views of the inhabitants of the trust territories if only in this indirect manner. In practice almost all of the elected representatives, in particular the delegates from Iraq and the Philippines, have taken the lead in presenting proposals on behalf of the trust peoples.

One of the questions arising in connection with making states rather than private individuals members of the Trusteeship Council was whether the official representatives would have the necessary competence in the field of colonial administration to perform their functions adequately.

COUNCIL MEMBERSHIP

Session	*Administering Authorities*	*Big Five Non-administering States*	*Elected*
First	Belgium France Australia New Zealand United Kingdom	United States China U.S.S.R.	Mexico Iraq
Second, Third, Fourth, and Fifth	Belgium France Australia New Zealand United Kingdom United States	China U.S.S.R.	Mexico Iraq Costa Rica Philippines
Sixth and Seventh	Same	Same	Argentina Dominican Republic Iraq Philippines
Eighth and Ninth	Same	Same	Thailand Dominican Republic Argentina Iraq
Tenth and Eleventh	Same	Same	Same, except El Salvador replaced Argentina which resigned
Twelfth	Same	Same	Same, except Syria replaced Iraq
Thirteenth, Fourteenth, Fifteenth, and Sixteenth [1]	Same	Same	El Salvador Syria Haiti

[1] With the admission of Italy to the United Nations in the fall of 1955, that country became a regular member of the Trusteeship Council by virtue of its position as an administering authority. At present, therefore, the total membership of the Council has been increased to fourteen.

In practice any fears along this line have not materialized, for the individual delegates have, in general, been experts in the field—or, as in the case of the representatives of some of the nonadministering states, as near experts as may be found. Further, those representatives not as informed as others have the opportunity of rapidly gaining firsthand information through the supervisory functions of the Council. Thus the possible disadvantages of not following the Permanent Mandates Commission's principle of private, rather than governmental, representatives is largely offset by the more intimate relationship of Council members with the territories provided in the trusteeship system.[2]

The Charter left it to the Council to provide for the selection of its President. Accordingly, the Council, in its Rules of Procedure, provided for the election of a President and Vice-President, "by secret and separate ballots, . . . at the beginning of its regular session in June." [3] The selection of both President and Vice-President follows the principle of rotation between administering and nonadministering members. Further, the two positions themselves rotate between administering and nonadministering members.

The Rules of Procedure provide that the President may appoint an alternate to "participate in the proceedings and to vote in the Trusteeship Council." [4] Mr. Sayre did so during his term,[5] but the practice has not been regularly followed.

Soviet Attendance at Council Sessions. Although the Soviet Union, under the terms of the Charter, has permanent membership on the Trusteeship Council, it should be noted that its delegation has not been present at all Council sessions. Specifically, the Soviet Union was not represented at the first, second, sixth, and seventh sessions. The ostensible reason behind the absence at the first two sessions was the "unconstitutionality" of the Trusteeship Council, since the trusteeship agreements providing the basis for organizing the Council were not negotiated in pursuance of the Charter.[6] At the time of the sixth and seventh sessions the Soviet Union was boycotting United Nations bodies generally over the issue of the admission of Communist China.

Absence of the Soviet delegate insures, of course, a majority of administering authorities on the Council, in addition to removing a severe

[2] The device most suitable for providing Council members with firsthand knowledge and experience concerning the trust territories is the visiting mission. This has been recognized by the Council in its appointments of various mission members. See below, p. 185.

[3] United Nations Document T/1/Rev.2, Rule 19.

[4] United Nations Document T/L/Rev.2. Rule 22.

[5] Mr. Benjamin Gerig, at that time the American alternate delegate, substituted for Mr. Sayre.

[6] See above, pp. 70, 72.

critic of administering authorities' policies. In effect, however, this does not seem to have been very important in the functioning of the Council since, as will be explained, the administering authorities do not need a majority to protect their interests, and other nonadministering states on the Council have been as vociferously critical of the administering authorities as the Soviet delegate. Indeed, it might be argued that by attending Council sessions the Soviet Union does more harm than good for its avowed role as "friend to the native peoples." There is a certain reluctance on the part of many of the nonadministering states on the Council to be on the same side of an issue as the Soviet Union. Hence a violent attack on some aspect of an administering authority's policies in a territory followed by a resolution condemning the policy by the Soviet representative might well not receive as much support as the same attack and resolution if sponsored by another nonadministering state.[7]

Italy and the Advisory Council for Somaliland. While there is nothing in the Charter which prevented Italy, a nonmember of the United Nations, from assuming the administration of a trust territory, this situation did create the need for defining Italy's position on the Trusteeship Council. The underlying problem in this connection was that only United Nations members were eligible for Council membership.[8] The question was, then, how to reconcile the fact that Italy was an administering authority, but not a member of the Council? Article 5 of the Trusteeship Agreement for Somaliland provides that Italy may designate an accredited representative to be present at the meetings of the Trusteeship Council at which reports on, or petitions concerning, Somaliland are considered. But this left unanswered such questions as: could Italy be represented at discussions of problems relating to the trusteeship system generally, or could the Italian representative request that items be placed on the provisional agenda for any given session? It was necessary, in other words, for the Council to define specifically Italy's place on that body. Similar questions had to be answered with respect to the Advisory Council.

Accordingly, at its eighth session, the Council created a committee of six to draft, using a Secretariat working paper as a basis for discussion, such additional rules of procedure as were necessary to spell out the relationship of both Italy and the states on the Advisory Commission for Somaliland to the Trusteeship Council.[9] This committee held three meetings (February 5, 6, and 8, 1951) and reported back to the Council on February 20.[10] In general, the committee followed the recommenda-

[7] This point was confirmed for the writer by Mr. Benjamin Gerig who, as alternate American delegate to the Trusteeship Council, has often taken an active part in Council debates.

[8] Article 86.

[9] *Trusteeship Council, Official Records, Eighth Session* (January-March 1951), p. 9.

[10] *Ibid.*, p. 94. United Nations Document T/L.123.

tions of the Secretariat's working paper, with the notable exception that where the former would have confined Italy's participation in Council discussions to those subjects relating to Somaliland, as provided in the Trusteeship Agreement, the latter provided that the Italian representative could also participate "upon invitation of the President . . . in the deliberation on general questions relating to the operation of the trusteeship system."

Specifically, the committee recommended eight additional rules of procedure to regulate Italy's status, of which the six substantive ones may be summarized as follows:

(1) Italy shall be invited to designate a special representative to be present at all sessions of the Council and participate without vote in discussions relating specifically to Somaliland, and, at the President's invitation, to participate in discussion of general questions relating to the trusteeship system.
(2) Italy shall be notified, as a rule, at least thirty days in advance, of the beginning of each session of the Council and of the provisional agenda in each case.
(3) Italy may request inclusion of items in the provisional agenda if they relate to Somaliland or the general operation of the trusteeship system.
(4) Italy may request a special session of the Council.
(5) The Italian representative may propose resolutions, motions, or amendments on questions dealing with Somaliland or the general operation of the trusteeship system.
(6) The Italian representative may request that a statement of his views be appended to any report or resolution of the Council relating to Somaliland or the general operation of the trusteeship system.

In effect, these rules meant that Italy had the same status as other administering authorities with two exceptions: its representative could not vote on any issue, nor can he discuss questions specifically relating to any territory other than Somaliland. In view of the natural reluctance of the representatives of administering authorities to criticize one another's administrations in the territories, it is the first exception which was really the crucial distinction in status.[11]

In the main, the committee's recommended supplementary rules concerning the Advisory Council for Somaliland provided for keeping that body *au courant* with Council activities. In addition, however, they stipulated that:

The Secretary-General shall communicate to the members of the Trusteeship Council, without delay, any request of any of the Governments of States Members of the Advisory Council for Somaliland who are not members of the Trusteeship Council to be represented during the deliberations on general questions relating to the operation of the International Trusteeship System

[11] Italy became a regular member of the Council beginning with the seventeenth session (February-April, 1956) as a result of its admission to the United Nations in the fall of 1955.

included in the provisional agenda, or which may have been added to the agenda by the Trusteeship Council. . . .[12]

Thus it was envisaged that the Advisory Council members not on that Council might, subject to Council approval apparently, have the same expanded rights of participation as the Italian representative.

When the Council discussed the committee's recommendation the only real issue was that concerning this expanded right of participation of both Italy and the Advisory Council members. The debate arose over an Argentine amendment to delete the sentence in the first additional rule providing for participation of the Italian representative in the deliberations on general questions, since it was unnecessary. After some discussion this amendment was withdrawn, but the administering authorities insisted on voting to delete the words "upon the invitation of the President." This proposal was carried in a close vote.[13] Thus Italy's participation in discussions on general questions is not subject to even the President's invitation.

This action presaged further debate on the similar provision with regard to the Advisory Council members. The administering authorities, France in particular, wanted to limit the members of the Advisory Council to participation in discussion concerning Somaliland only, and moved to delete the above-quoted paragraph. The representative of Iraq, however, argued that this was not justified in view of the decision with regard to Italian participation. When the paragraph in question came to the vote the result was deadlocked (five in favor, five against, with two abstentions).

As a compromise, the Argentine delegate suggested that the Advisory Council members be permitted to participate in deliberations concerning general questions "connected directly or indirectly with Italian Somaliland." This, however, was not acceptable to the Belgian representative who still pressed for deletion of the original provision. The Belgian argument was that since Article 11 of the Trusteeship Agreement for Somaliland provided for participation of Advisory Council members in discussions concerning Somaliland only, supplementary rules increasing the scope of participation would violate the agreement. As the Thailand delegate pointed out, this argument could be applied to Italy as well, however. Actually these considerations of legality were not the real question.

What mattered was the fact that the administering authorities and Argentina wanted Italy to have as much right of participation as possible, while the other members of the Council wanted to limit this to some

[12] United Nations Document T/L.123.

[13] *Trusteeship Council, Official Records, Eighth Session* (January-March, 1951), p. 98. The vote was 6 to 5, with 1 abstention.

extent. Conversely, the nonadministering states desired equal rights of participation for Advisory Council members with the Italian representative, while the administering authorities were opposed to it, since it would open the door to increased criticism by nonadministering states of the administering authorities generally with regard to the full and speedy attainment of the goals of trusteeship.

When the vote was taken for the second time, the deletion was adopted.[14] Members of the Advisory Council for Somaliland not represented on the Council are thus limited in their participation in Council discussions to those questions specifically related to Somaliland.

Voting. The Charter provides that each member of the Council shall have one vote and that decisions "shall be made by a majority of the members present and voting." This has been expanded by the Council's Rules of Procedure to provide that in case of a tie vote "a second vote shall be taken at the next meeting, or by decision of the Trusteeship Council, following a brief recess." If the vote then remains tied, the proposal is defeated.

When taken together with the provisions governing membership, what these voting provisions do, in effect, is to emphasize the importance of the necessity for cooperation among the members of the Council. That is, on any point at issue, if the administering authorities are unanimously opposed to a proposal it cannot pass. The same is true, of course, whenever the nonadministering states are unanimously agreed, but in practice this favors the administering authorities since any limitation of their prerogatives, any criticism of their administrations, any increase in the rights of the trust peoples must come in the form of positive Council action. Inaction leaves the situation as is. Thus action taken by the Council to implement Charter provisions on trusteeship must come about through some measure of cooperation between administering and nonadministering states on the Council.

This division of the Council into administering and nonadministering states may seem unfortunate to those who would hope for an "objective" administration of Council functions. Several times in the debates of the Council, representatives have deplored the fact that voting so often follows this division. Nevertheless, the division does exist and it is not unreasonable to assume that it must exist as long as the Council contains representatives from nonadministering states who desire to see the trust territories and their inhabitants, reach that state of self-government or independence provided by the Charter in as short a time as possible. It is only natural that the administering authorities feel that many proposals are unrealistic in that they attempt to "build Rome in a day," and it is

[14] *Ibid.*, p. 105.

only natural that the nonadministering states on the Council often feel that the administering authorities want to move too slowly, if at all, in carrying out the aims of trusteeship.

With this in mind, the advantage of having equality of representation as between administering and nonadministering states on the Council becomes apparent. It would avail nothing if all sorts of laudable resolutions were passed by the Council only to be disregarded by the administering authorities. Yet there are obvious merits in having those states pressed for action by representatives of nonadministering states. With equality of representation between the two groups, cooperation is necessary, and the voluntary basis of the trusteeship system is recognized. In such circumstances, when the Council does take action it is meaningful action.

That action is taken is largely the result of the fact that the administering authorities do not like to be put in the position of uniformly opposing all suggestions. On the other hand, they will not, of course, be pressed too far—the voting and membership provisions merely recognize this. What often happens is that a proposal made by the representative of a nonadministering state is not acceptable to the administering authorities, but a compromise proposal involving something more than inaction on the matter will be. Thus the accepted version will be the result of compromise and concomitantly of cooperation. These considerations have already been illustrated in connection with the negotiation for the trusteeship agreement for Somaliland, and they hold true for the normal functioning of the Council, as will be seen.

Sessions. The Charter leaves it to the Council to provide for its sessions in its Rules of Procedure, with the proviso that the rules "shall include provision for the convening of meetings on the request of a majority of its members." The Executive Committee of the Preparatory Commission, apparently following the practice of the Permanent Mandates Commission, suggested that the Trusteeship Council meet in regular session once each year.[15] When the Preparatory Commission met, however, it amended this to two sessions per year.[16] This was accepted by the Council with the modification that one session begin in November, the other in June of each year.[17] In addition, special sessions may be held at the request of (1) a majority of Council members (2) the General Assembly, (3) the Security Council, or (4) Economic and Social Coun-

[15] *Report by the Executive Committee to the Preparatory Commission of the United Nations*, p. 58.

[16] *Preparatory Commission, Committee 4, Trusteeship, Summary Record of Meetings* (November-December, 1942), p. 11.

[17] *Trusteeship Council, Official Records, First Year, First Session* (March-April, 1947), pp. 107-8.

cil. To date the Trusteeship Council has held five special sessions, all of which were concerned with procedural matters only.[18]

The Council found that it was difficult to meet in November, and after one session (the second) had met during that month the date was moved up to January.[19] Thus the Council now meets regularly in January and June of each year.

Procedure. One final point about the mechanics of Council functioning should be kept in mind as the details of the supervisory functions of the Council are discussed. This concerns the emphasis placed by Council members on the procedural aspects of any given question. This appears to be a hallmark of any international organization for, as Sir Carl Berendsen said during the first session of the Council, "There appears to be no subject which attracts more strongly the attention of an international body, which arouses in it a greater zest and enthusiasm, than the totally ancillary subject of procedure." [20]

In reading the records of the Council sessions one cannot help being impressed with the truth of those remarks. The tempting reaction is, of course, to become impatient with the Council and feel that it could accomplish much more if it spent less time on procedure and more on substantive matters. Yet, it must be remembered that procedures themselves often have an effect on any substantive decision.

In implementing the Charter provisions on trusteeship, therefore, the Council must move cautiously, and what may appear as an over-lengthy discussion of a small matter of procedure many times will turn out in fact to be the debate on a substantive issue. This point will become more evident as the supervisory functions of the Council are described, but it should be kept in mind at all times in order to appreciate fully the nature of Council activities.

---

[18] The dates of these sessions were as follows: first, 27 September, 1949; second, 8 to 20 December, 1949; third, 22 November, 1950; fourth, 18 December, 1951. The first, third, and fourth special sessions determined the opening date of the next regular session. The second special session created the Committee on former Italian Somaliland. See above, pp. 102-4. The fifth special session considered the report of the special mission to the Togolands. See below, p. 235.

[19] *Trusteeship Council, Official Records, Fifth Session* (June-July, 1949), pp. 5-7.

[20] *Trusteeship Council, Official Records, First Year, First Session* (March-April, 1947), p. 35.

CHAPTER SIX

Annual Reports

The Charter contains two provisions affecting the submission of annual reports by the various administering authorities on the conditions in each of their respective trust territories. Article 67 provides: "The General Assembly and, under its authority, the Trusteeship Council, in carrying out their functions may:

a. consider reports submitted by the administering authority. . . ." and Article 88 states: "The Trusteeship Council shall formulate a questionnaire on the political, economic, social and educational advancement of the inhabitants of each trust territory, and the administering authority for each trust territory within the competence of the General Assembly shall make an annual report to the General Assembly on the basis of such questionnaire."

Since this was the principal method of supervision used by the Permanent Mandates Commission it was to be expected that it would be carried over in trusteeship. Neither the Constitution of the Permanent Mandates Commission nor its rules of procedure provided for a questionnaire to serve as the basis for the annual reports, but in practice the Commission, following the usual practice of League committees, adopted questionnaires for each of the three types of mandates.[1] Thus both annual reports and questionnaires to serve as the basis for those reports in the trusteeship system found their predecessors in the mandates system.

Rules of Procedure. The Preparatory Commission drafted provisional rules of procedure for the Trusteeship Council, and in so far as these pertain to annual reports they were little changed by the Council when the latter formulated its rules of procedure on the basis of the Preparatory Commission's proposals.[2] What few changes were made were for the benefit of the administering authorities. The most significant of these was the substitution of the phrase "four months from the termination of the year to which it refers" for "one month before the session" at which the report was to be considered in the rule providing for the time of submission of the annual reports. Other changes included the deletion

[1] Hall, p. 190.

[2] *Trusteeship Council, Official Records, First Year, First Session* (March-April, 1947), pp. 342-424. In addition to the Preparatory Commission's suggestions, the Secretariat submitted a list of draft rules of procedure. United Nations Document T/4.

of the provisions that the questionnaire should be "comprehensive and detailed," and that the administering authorities should report on the steps taken to implement the goals of trusteeship. Both of these, however, have been at least partially reinstated in practice. The entire revised rules of procedure were adopted on April 23, 1947.[3] As they refer to questionnaires and annual reports they may be summarized as follows:

1. (68) Provision for the transmission of the questionnaire to the administering authorities.
2. (69) Provision for the modification of the questionnaire.
3. (70) Provision for cooperation with the Economic and Social Council and the specialized agencies in the preparation of the questionnaire.
4. (71) Provision that the questionnaire shall be sent to the administering authorities at least six months before the expiration of the year covered by the first annual report. The questionniare will remain in force from year to year without specific renewal.
5. (72) Provision that the administering authorities shall submit their annual reports, based on the questionnaire, within four months from the end of the year to which it refers.
6. (73) Provision that each administering authority will furnish 400 copies of each annual report.
7. (74) Provision for a special representative of the administering authority to be present at the examination of each annual report.
8. (75) Provision that each special representative may participate in the discussions of the Council concerning the report on the territory within his competence, except those discussions relating to the specific conclusions and recommendations of the Council.[4]

The only subsequent change in these rules occurred at the fourth session of the Council (January 24 to March 25, 1949), when rule 72 was changed to read "six" instead of "four" months, to give the administering authorities more time in which to prepare their reports.[5]

As the result of a timetable which the Council worked out for considering annual reports those for the six African trust territories were considered sometimes as much as a year after the end of the year covered by reports.[6] This eventually led to a proposal [7] by the Syrian delegate to the Council that the administering authorities be requested to submit, approximately one month in advance of each relevant session, a summary of the more important events and developments occurring in each territory during the period between the end of the report and the convening of the Council.

[3] *Ibid.*, p. 597.

[4] See United Nations Document T.1/Rev. 1. The numbers in parentheses refer to the actual rule number.

[5] *Trusteeship Council, Official Records, Fourth Session* (January-March, 1949), pp. 20-22.

[6] See below, pp. 139-40.

[7] United Nations Document T/L.446.

Despite some hesitancy on the part of some of the administering authorities,[8] the proposal was adopted,[9] but in the form of an invitation to the administering authorities to give favorable consideration to the matter, rather than as a change in the rules of procedure.

One interesting proposal which has so far failed of adoption was brought up at the first session, when the rules of procedure were being considered, and reintroduced at the fourth session of the Council. This concerned the possibility of having representatives of the indigenous population of the territories present during the examination of the annual reports, with the same rights as the special representatives of the administering authorities. The debate on this proposal at the fourth session was sharp and the voting split along administering versus nonadministering states lines. Eventually, the Council voted down both a Soviet proposal that: "The population of the Trust Territories has the right, in the name of its social, cultural and educational organizations as well as its representative bodies of self-government if such exist in the Trust Territories, to send their representatives to participate without vote in the consideration by the Trusteeship Council of the annual reports of the Administering Authorities as well as all other questions relating to these Territories." [10] and a Philippine substitute proposal that: "the inhabitants of the Trust Territory may designate a special representative of their own with the same privileges and functions as the special representative of the Administering Authority. . . ." [11]

It also voted down a proposal that representatives of nongovernmental agencies could participate without vote in Council discussion of the annual reports.[12]

This issue is a good illustration of a phenomenon about Council voting in general. It is obvious from the composition of the Trusteeship Council that if that body is to be effective its activity must be based on cooperation between administering and nonadministering states. Many of the nonadministering states on the Council (China, Mexico, and Iraq especially), realizing this, are often prone to abstain from voting on an issue on which the administering authorities are lined up solidly—thus preventing the appearance of a deadlock. Hence, as in the case of the

[8] The Belgian representative, for example, argued, that the supplementary report was "unnecessary and undesirable . . . and the local administration could not assume the additional burden imposed by the draft resolution." *Trusteeship Council, Official Records, Fourteenth Session* (June-July, 1954), p. 12.

[9] The vote was 8 to 3 with 1 abstention. *Ibid.* In its final form the proposal appears as Trusteeship Council Resolution 997 (XIV).

[10] United Nations Document T/235.

[11] United Nations Document T/238.

[12] *Trusteeship Council, Official Records, Fourth Session* (January-March, 1949), pp. 89, 106.

Soviet and Philippine proposals, the voting in the Council may be six to five or six to four.

The Questionnaire. While no annual reports were due during the first session of the Council, there was the problem of formulating the questionnaire on which future reports would be based. As might be expected, some of the former mandatory powers, Belgium in particular, suggested using the Permanent Mandates Commission questionnaire on the grounds that it had been perfected over a period of a quarter century, and no hastily devised new set of questions could possibly be as adequate. If necessary, the Commission's questionnaire could be revised in due course.[13] The nonmandatory states on the Council, however, while admitting that the Permanent Mandates Commission questionnaire should be taken into consideration felt that the Council should formulate its own set of questions. The representative of Mexico, for example, was: "absolutely against the proposals of the representative of Belgium, that this Council, in disregard of Article 88 of the Charter, should say to the administering authorities: 'Go and make the reports the way you have always made them for the Permanent Mandates Commission,' because this was the Trusteeship Council and not the Permanent Mandates Commission." [14]

After a general discussion of the question there was agreement that a committee should be appointed to draft a questionnaire based on the Commission's questionnaire and others which had been, or might be, submitted.[15] Following a further agreement that the committee be composed of two administering states (one with a territory in Africa, the other with a territory in the Pacific), and two nonadministering states (one a permanent member of the Council, the other not), the President appointed representatives of the United Kingdom, Australia, the United States, and Mexico.[16]

This committee, under the chairmanship of Mr. Chinnery of Australia, met eleven times in the period April 15 to April 23, 1947, and reported back to the Council on April 25.[17] In addition to the proposals before the committee, a compilation of questions on economic advancement

[13] *Trusteeship Council, Official Records, First Year, First Session* (March-April, 1947), pp. 362-63.

[14] *Ibid.*, p. 363.

[15] The United States (United Nations Document T/24), the United Kingdom (United Nations Document T/6), France (United Nations Document T/11) and the Secretariat (United Nations Document T/9) had each submitted draft questionnaires.

[16] *Trusteeship Council, Official Records, First Year, First Session* (March-April, 1947), p. 393.

[17] *Ibid.*, p. 614. The report of the committee is contained in United Nations Document T/AC.2/1.

was submitted by the Secretariat [18] and a draft set of questions on labor was put forward by a representative of the International Labour Organization.[19] Representatives of the latter organization and UNESCO collaborated with the committee on sections relevant to their interests.[20]

With the exception of the proposals of the Secretariat and the ILO, the committee used the United States draft as the basis for discussion.[21] This draft, with necessary modifications, was based on the Permanent Mandates Commission questionnaire, but was more detailed, and covered a wider range of topics. The draft questionnaire produced by the committee was both detailed and inclusive. In addition to over two hundred fifty questions, the questionnaire included a statistical appendix necessitating the compilation of tables on a variety of subjects. A list of the sections of the questionnaire and appendix gives an idea as to the amount of information asked:

A. Brief Introductory Descriptive Section
B. Status of the Territory and Its Inhabitants
C. International and Regional Relations
D. International Peace and Security, Law and Order
E. Political Advancement
    1. General Administration
    2. Judicial Organization
F. Economic Advancement
    1. General
    2. Public Finance, Money and Banking
    3. Taxation
    4. Commerce and Trade
    5. Monopolies
    6. Land and Natural Resources
    7. Agriculture, Fisheries, and Animal Husbandry
    8. Industry
    9. Investments
    10. Transport and Communications
    11. Public Works
G. Social Advancement
    1. General
    2. Social Conditions
    3. Standards of Living
    4. Status of Women
    5. Human Rights and Fundamental Freedoms
    6. Labour Conditions and Regulations
    7. Public Health
    8. Sanitation
    9. Drugs

[18] United Nations Document T/AC.2/SR.4.

[19] United Nations Document T/AC.2/SR.6.

[20] United Nations Document T/AC.2/1.

[21] *Ibid.*

10. Alcohol and Spirits
11. Population
12. Social Security and Welfare
13. Housing and Town Planning
14. Penal Administration

H. Educational Advancement
1. General
2. Schools and Curriculum
3. Adult, Mass and Community Education

I. Publications

J. Research

K. Suggestions and Recommendations. This concerns the implementation of General Assembly and Trusteeship Council resolutions.

L. Summary and Conclusion

APPENDIX

Tables on:

1. Population
2. Administrative Structure of Government
3. Justice and Penal Administration
4. Public Finance
5. Taxation
6. Trade
7. Enterprises and Business Organizations
8. Housing
9. Production
10. Labour
11. Cost of Living
12. Public Health
13. Education

The committee submitted its draft with the recommendation that it be considered provisional and that it should be revised in the light of Trusteeship Council experience. On this basis, the Council decided to send out the questionnaire with an accompanying letter inviting comments and suggestions for eventual improvement.[22] Following this, the Council proceeded to discuss the questionnaire with a view to making some changes before it was sent out for the first time. Actually, little was done along these lines. A few provisions were deleted, either because the Council agreed they were redundant or were too vague to permit a precise answer.[23] Two or three new questions were added to spell out the information desired in greater detail, and a few amendments were

[22] *Trusteeship Council, Official Records, First Year, First Session* (March-April, 1947), p. 627.

[23] The most important of these was a question concerning the amount of armed forces in each territory, the defense bases maintained for security, and annual expenditure on them. This was deleted on the suggestion of the British representative, who pointed out that the Charter called for information on the political, economic, social, and educational conditions in the territory, *not* military conditions. There seemed to be no opposition to the deletion. *Ibid.*, p. 635.

made to certain questions to obtain greater clarity. In the main, however, the draft questionnaire was adopted intact,[24] and was sent to the administering authorities to provide the basis for the first annual reports.

In doing this the Council emphasized two points. One was that the administering authorities were asked to include in the first annual reports an outline of "the main features of the administration of the territories during the period for which no reports have been submitted to the League of Nations," including laws, regulations, and ordinances passed during that period. The second was to emphasize the provisional nature of the questionnaire and to hope that "the administering authorities themselves will be able to advise upon the most satisfactory means of presenting the desired information, and to suggest alternative questions which may prove to be a greater value in relation to local conditions." [25]

Both these *voeux* were expressed by the committee and adopted by the Council to be sent, in the form of an explanatory preface, with the questionnaire to the various administering authorities. In addition, the Council, at the twenty-sixth meeting of its first session, decided to transmit the provisional questionnaire to the Economic and Social Council and the specialized agencies for comments and suggestions on those parts of the questionnaire which dealt with matters lying within their respective competences.[26]

While the questionnaire adopted at the first session was merely provisional, the Council, during its second through sixth sessions,[27] deferred consideration of revising it, in each case to give the administering authorities, ECOSOC, and the specialized agencies additional time to propose changes. Meanwhile, of course, the administering authorities were sending in their annual reports based on the provisional questionnaire. Thus what started out to be a temporary set of questions was becoming more and more permanent. Indicative of this were the remarks of the Belgian representative at the seventh session of the Council, June, 1950, when the question of revising the questionnaire was again considered. It was this delegate who had been the most critical of the original questionnaire and who had wanted to emphasize its provisional nature. Now, however, this same delegate, M. Ryckmans, argued that "the Belgian Government and the local authorities of Ruanda-Urundi had become accustomed to replying to the Questionnaire, although they realized that it was far from perfect. The Belgian Government feared that any alterations in that

[24] *Ibid.*, p. 686. The questionnaire was issued as United Nations Document T/44.

[25] United Nations Document T/44, p. 3.

[26] *Trusteeship Council, Official Records, First Year, First Session* (March-April, 1947), p. 693. For the resolution providing for the transmission of the questionnaire see *Resolutions Adopted by the Trusteeship Council During its First Session,* p. 8. Resolution 8.

[27] The sixth session ended April 4, 1950.

document would further complicate the work of the local authorities." [28]

This illustrates a characteristic of the Trusteeship Council which is difficult to describe specifically, but which the observer can discern: a kind of Newton's law of inertia acting in international organization, by which a procedure, once accepted, even if only "provisionally," is very difficult to modify to any considerable extent. It is a good example of why the Council apparently "wastes" so much time in the discussion of procedures—a phenomenon otherwise often inexplicable to the observer.

At its seventh session (June 1 to July 21, 1950) the Council appointed a committee of two—representatives of the Dominican Republic and Belgium—to undertake preliminary consideration of revising the questionnaire, and report back to the Council before the end of the session on how the work of revision should be pursued.[29] The committee reported at the twenty-seventh meeting, suggesting the formation of a committee of four to "undertake revision of the Provisional Questionnaire with a view to eliminating all duplications and ambiguities, taking into account all comments and suggestions made by the Economic and Social Council and its commissions, specialized agencies, members of the Council, and suggestions . . . made by the individual members during the second session of the General Assembly." [30]

When the Council discussed this report the question of the form of the annual reports arose. Some of the administering authorities desired to present their reports in narrative fashion rather than simply answer each of the questions. The nonadministering states on the Council, however, were dubious about this. What lay behind the divergence of viewpoint on this apparently insignificant question was the desire on the part of the administering authorities to make certain that their reports could include all facts casting a favorable light on the administration of their territories, while the nonadministering states were fearful that a report cast in narrative fashion might omit unfavorable material. Because of this difference, the committee of four appointed by the Council on the above recommendation was also instructed to consider the form of the annual reports.[31] Representatives of Belgium, the Dominican Republic, Iraq, and the United Kingdom, were appointed to the committee which was to report back to the Council at its eighth session. The Secretariat was asked to prepare a working paper including all suggestions and comments so far made, including its own suggestions as to the proposed revision of the questionnaire.

[28] *Trusteeship Council, Official Records, Seventh Session* (June-July, 1950), p. 60.

[29] *Ibid.*, p. 62.

[30] United Nations Document T/L.95.

[31] *Trusteeship Council, Official Records, Seventh Session* (June-July, 1950), pp. 239-40.

When the committee met, on February 19, 1951, it decided that the Secretariat's working paper [32] should be submitted to the administering authorities for their further comments, and in its report to the Council [33] it proposed a resolution to that effect.[34] This resolution was adopted by the Council, which also requested the Secretariat to prepare further documentation for the committee, based on such observations as were forthcoming. The committee was instructed to report back during the ninth session.[35]

At least two of the administering authorities, France and Belgium, had not prepared comments on the Secretariat's working paper by the time the committee was to report to the ninth session of the Trusteeship Council, so the committee recommended,[36] and the Council adopted, a resolution [37] calling for a final report of the committee at the Council's tenth session, and requesting those administering authorities who had not as yet submitted their comments to do so prior to October 31, 1951.

The committee held three meetings during the tenth session of the Council and reported to the Council on March 26, 1952,[38] having adopted both its report and an attached revised questionnaire unanimously. Although the new questionnaire had been unanimously adopted, the British and Belgian representatives on the committee had attached reservations: (1) the administering authorities could submit reports in narrative form if they desired, provided that the reports contained an index to the pages and paragraphs in which answers to each question in the questionnaire could be found; (2) five years should elapse before the Council undertook further revision of the questionnaire; (3) information on matters which did not vary from year to year need not be repeated in each report; (4) information already given to specialized agencies could be appended to, rather than included in, the annual reports.[39] When the committee's report was discussed by the Council some of the non-administering states objected to those reservations, and pressed for adoption of the questionnaire without them. This issue was not joined during the tenth session, however, for at the suggestion of the American repre-

[32] United Nations Document T/AC.32/L.1.

[33] United Nations Document T/L.128.

[34] *Trusteeship Council, Official Records, Eighth Session* (January-March, 1951), p. 120.

[35] *Official Records of the Eighth Session of the Trusteeship Council, Resolutions,* p. 2. Resolution 304 (VIII).

[36] United Nations Document T/911.

[37] *Official Records of the Ninth Session of the Trusteeship Council, Resolutions,* p. 1. Resolution 342 (IX).

[38] *Trusteeship Council, Official Records, Tenth Session* (February-April, 1952), p. 169. The report of the committee is contained in United Nations Document T/L.246.

[39] United Nations Document T/L.246.

sentative, final action on the committee's report was deferred until the eleventh session at which time members of the Council were to have submitted such further comments on the revision of the questionnaire as they desired.[40]

No further comments were forthcoming and the eleventh session of the Council saw the adoption of a revised questionnaire some five years after the first efforts at revision had been made. Before this, however, the Council adopted an amendment sponsored by the Dominican Republic delegation designed to insure protection of the dignity of women in the territories, in accordance with a resolution of the Economic and Social Council [41] to that effect. The question of the British and Belgian reservations to the questionnaire was again discussed with the Council dividing along administering versus nonadministering state lines on the issue. This was eventually settled by taking three separate notes on the report of the committee on the questionnaire. The proposals before the Council were:

1. The Council decides to adopt the questionnaire . . .
2. without prejudice to the form of the reports,
3. reservations of the individual members of the Council having been entered in the Council's official records.

The first and third proposals were adopted, the second rejected. The amended proposal was then adopted unanimously with two abstentions.[42] The upshot of the voting was that while the Council had adopted the revised questionnaire, the administering authorities considered themselves free to submit their reports in such form as they thought best, while the Council reserved the right to disapprove the form in which they were submitted if it so desired.

The discussions surrounding the adoption of the revised questionnaire point up two characteristics of the Trusteeship Council which are true generally. The first is that, as was mentioned in Chapter Four, Council decisions are more often than not concerned with comparatively small issues of interpretation rather than dramatic questions. All the Council members accepted the need for revising the questionnaire; all accepted the revision proposed; the issues involved were those of interpretation. It is in the settlement of these kinds of questions that the trusteeship system is evolving, with constant pressure from the nonadministering states for increased international supervision, and constant reluctance on the part of the administering authorities to acquiesce in this. The

[40] *Trusteeship Council, Official Records, Tenth Session* (February-April, 1952), p. 172.

[41] United Nations Document E/2237.

[42] *Trusteeship Council, Official Records, Tenth Session, 414th Meeting* (June 5, 1952), pp. 1-3. United Nations Document T/PV.414.

second characteristic is related to the first. It is, simply, that the Council, because of the nature of its composition, cannot reach any decision opposed by the administering authorities *en masse*. Greater international supervision, increased rights and protections for the indigenous inhabitants of the trust territories, anything desired by the nonadministering states must in the last analysis be acceptable to at least one of the administering authorities — and the latter show such cohesiveness as a voting bloc that a defection of one administering authority is rare indeed. The Council has really only two courses open to it. Either the lines could be drawn between the administering and nonadministering states with the latter *demanding* and the former tending to *refuse* Council actions, or, as is the case, cooperation between the administering and nonadministering states can produce, albeit gradually, reasonable success in the implementation and development of Charter provisions on trusteeship.

When the General Assembly's Fourth Committee considered the revised questionnaire, many of the delegates urged that further revision be undertaken with a view to developing a separate questionnaire for each territory. To this end a jointly sponsored proposal calling upon the Council to "undertake the preparation of separate questionnaires for each territory" was introduced at both the seventh and eighth sessions of the General Assembly.[43] At the latter session, the Belgian representative offered an amendment designed to relieve the Council of the additional work load entailed in the proposal. This called for the creation of a subcommittee consisting of representatives of El Salvador, Haiti, India, and Syria "to study such changes as may be necessary to adapt it [the questionnaire] to the special conditions of each territory and to submit its conclusions to the fourteenth session of the Trusteeship Council.[44] The latter was then invited to carry out the terms of the original proposal on the basis of the work of the subcommittee.

After considerable discussion, the Fourth Committee adopted both the amendment and the revised proposals by considerable majorities.[45] The General Assembly, without further debate, adopted the proposal at its eighth session.[46]

As of the sixteenth session of the Council, the subcommittee had not

[43] United Nations Documents A/C.4/L.253 and A/C.4/L.319.

[44] United Nations Documents A/C.4/L.325 and Rev.1.

[45] *Official Records of the General Assembly, Eighth Session, Fourth Committee* (September 16-December 7, 1954), pp. 496-522. The vote on the amendment was 32 in favor, 3 against, with 17 abstentions; on the proposal as amended: 43 in favor, 4 against, with 5 abstentions.

[46] *Official Records of the General Assembly, Eighth Session, Plenary Meetings* (September-December, 1953), p. 455. The vote was 41 in favor, 4 against, with 5 abstentions.

completed work on a questionnaire for any of the territories, but was at that time revising that for New Guinea.[47]

Council Consideration of Annual Reports. The consideration of the annual reports of the mandatory powers had been the heart of the League of Nations mandates system, and when the Council, during its second and third sessions considered the procedure to be used in its examination of annual reports it had League precedent to guide it. Based on that, a Secretariat memorandum on the subject,[48] and proposals by the President of the Council, a working procedure for the examination of reports was devised. In general this procedure followed that of the Permanent Mandates Commission in providing (1) that a general discussion of the report should precede the more detailed examination; (2) that the special representative should be on hand to answer questions; (3) that small working groups should be appointed to specialize in certain aspects of all the reports (economic advancement, for example), and that members of these groups should have the first opportunity to submit observations and ask questions concerning that section of a report about which they had special competence; (4) that all members of the Council could make such observations and ask such questions as they liked about any phase of a report; (5) that the Council, after the above four steps, would appoint a drafting committee to formulate comments and recommendations on the report; (6) that the final report of the Council would include observations and recommendations approved by the Council, but any member had a right to ask for a recommendation or observation not having Council approval to be included as an individual or minority opinion.[49]

If any generalization can be made about this procedure it is that while the Council has more or less followed the six steps outlined, it has attempted several variations of each step, and at no time has it considered itself bound by any set procedure. For example, the Rules of Procedure provide, as noted above, that six weeks must elapse between the receipt of a report by the Secretary-General and the opening day of a Council session, if the report is to be considered during that session. Nevertheless, the Council, at its third session, waived this rule with regard to the reports concerning Ruanda-Urundi and Tanganyika, which had been received one day and one week late, respectively.[50]

To date, the greatest problem in connection with scheduling considera-

[47] Second Progress Report of the Sub-Committee on the Questionnaire. United Nations Document T/1163, dated 8 March, 1955.

[48] United Nations Document T/94.

[49] *Trusteeship Council, Official Records, Second Session, Second Part, 31st Meeting* (March 5, 1948), United Nations Document T/SR.57, p. 10.

[50] *Trusteeship Council, Official Records, Third Session* (June-August, 1948), pp. 8-16.

tion of the annual reports has been the failure of the administering authorities to submit their reports on time. This has led to requests for supplementary information as well as appeals for greater promptness. At its fourteenth session, for example, the Council adopted a report of a committee on control and limitation of documentation, which urged, *inter alia*, the strict application by the administering authorities of Rule 72 (concerning submission of reports).[51] At its third special session (November 22, 1950), the Council proceeded in effect to waive the time limit again, by providing that at its ninth session it would consider the reports on the African trust territories for both 1948 and 1949 in order to catch up on its work. This was necessary because the Council spent much of its time at its earlier session on special problems such as drafting a statute for the City of Jerusalem and negotiating the draft trusteeship agreement for Somaliland. At its eleventh session the Council, in order to equalize the work load between the winter and summer sessions decided to examine annual reports in accordance with the following schedule: Winter Session: All African territories except Somaliland; Summer Session: Somaliland and all territories in the Pacific.[52]

The administering authorities on the Council were somewhat dubious about assigning special responsibility for particular phases of each report to working groups. While this procedure had precedent in the practice of the Permanent Mandates Commission, the administering authorities argued that members of the Trusteeship Council were governmental representatives and *not* experts, as had been the case under the League.[53] While defeated in their opposition to the idea at the time, in practice the informal groups have given way to general questioning by all members on each section of the reports. This may have been due to the Soviet representative's reluctance to take part in any informal group, reserving his right to ask questions on any and all sections of all reports. At any rate from the third session on the groups have not been appointed, and no preference is shown to any particular members of the Council with regard to questioning the special representative on particular aspects of the report.

Perhaps the most important modification of the general procedure for considering annual reports came at the fourth session of the Council when, at the President's suggestion, the Council decided that written as well as oral questions could be submitted to the special representa-

[51] *Trusteeship Council, Official Records, Fourteenth Session* (June-July, 1954), p. 159. The report was circulated as United Nations Document T/L.477.

[52] *Trusteeship Council, Eleventh Session, 453rd Meeting,* United Nations Document T/PV.453, pp. 7-10.

[53] *Trusteeship Council, Official Records, Second Session, Second Part, 30th Meeting* (March 4, 1948), United Nations Document T/SR.56, p. 10.

tives.[54] This proposal was adopted primarily to speed up the process of considering the annual reports. Many of the questions asked with regard to the first reports had been of a detailed and technical nature, and the Council felt that these could well have been answered in written form, while oral questions could concentrate on eliciting fuller explanations of ambiguous parts of the reports. After some difficulty at its sixth session with regard to a deadline for the submission of written questions,[55] the Council has since laid down a time limit with respect to each annual report.

Undoubtedly the utilization of written as well as oral questions has done much to alleviate the burden of business on the Council. The dangers in such an innovation lie at either extreme: it might develop into a limitation of the right of oral questioning,[56] or might merely duplicate much of the oral questioning and thus further aggravate the condition the Council is attempting to ameliorate. So far there certainly seems to be no limitation on oral questioning even though the written questions occasionally run to voluminous proportions. The Council at its fourteenth session, however, in an attempt to streamline its procedure for considering annual reports, provided that comments by members could be made during the question period, rather than rigidly separating the question period from the general discussion of each report.[57]

The annual reports, following the general outlines of the questionnaire, are uniformly divided into component parts—i.e., general, political, economic, social, and educational conditions in the territory. The practice of the Council is to discuss each section separately, with each Council member being free to ask such questions and make such observations as he wishes. At first the Council attempted to discuss the substance of the annual reports, the reports of the visiting missions, and petitions separately. Both as a means of gaining a better idea of conditions in a terri-

[54] *Trusteeship Council, Official Records, Fourth Session* (January-March, 1949), pp. 2-12.

[55] *Trusteeship Council, Official Records, Fourth Year, Sixth Session* (January-April, 1950), pp. 67-68. The specific problems arose in connection with the Annual Report on Tanganyika for 1948. When the Council began consideration of the report, no written questions had been submitted. The Philippine representative pressed for delay in consideration of the report until such time as written questions had been submitted, while the Belgian delegate argued that it was too late for written questions. The matter was resolved by the British representative's offer to answer such questions as were submitted "as best we can," with the understanding that in the future time limits would be fixed for the submission of written questions.

[56] This point of view was taken by the Soviet representative who opposed the submission of written questions. *Trusteeship Council, Official Records, Fourth Session* (January-March, 1949), p. 5.

[57] *Trusteeship Council, Official Records, Fourteenth Session* (June-July, 1954), p. 159. The proposal adopted was part of the Report of the Committee on Control and Limitation of Documentation. United Nations Document T/L.477.

tory as a whole and of using its time more efficiently, however, the Council has developed the practice of referring to petitions of a general nature from the territory concerned, as well as the most recent report of a visiting mission to the territory, at the time the annual report on the territory is considered.

The Council took considerable time in evolving some sort of steady practice concerning the drafting of recommendations and observations on the annual reports. At first committees of four were assigned to draft recommendations for each territory. Then, because several members wanted to participate in the drafting of recommendations for all reports, a committee of the whole was used. This device proved cumbersome, however,[58] and at its seventh session the Council went back to committees of four.[59] At its sixth session, the Council adopted a resolution [60] providing for the form of its recommendations and observations.[61] They were to consist of three parts: Part I, an outline of the general conditions in the territory as stated in the annual report; Part II, conclusions and recommendations of the Trusteeship Council; Part III, observations of individual members of the Council representing their opinions only. Part III may, of course, include observations of the administering authorities concerned.

What has been said, while applying specifically to nonstrategic areas, applies generally to the reports on the Pacific Trust Territory administered by the United States. The only difference is, of course, that the conclusions and recommendations of the Council are submitted to the Security Council. With regard to Somaliland, however, there is an important modification. In this case the members of the Advisory Council are invited to comment on the annual report for that territory as well as to take part in the questioning of the special representative. While the terms of the trusteeship agreement for Somaliland do not provide for the submission of an annual report by the Advisory Council, in practice working papers of that body have been circulated in the form of a report and are used as a source of supplementary information on the territory.

The participation by the Advisory Council in the discussion concern-

[58] *Trusteeship Council, Official Records, Fifth Session* (June-July, 1949), pp. 120-22. At this session the committee of the whole was divided into three subcommittees. *Ibid.*, pp. 229-33.

[59] At its fourteenth session, the Council recommended, as an aid to the drafting committees, that Council members should submit proposals to the Trusteeship Council in the form of draft conclusions or recommendations. *Trusteeship Council, Official Records, Fourteenth Session* (June-July, 1954), p. 159.

[60] *Resolution Adopted by the Trusteeship Council During its Sixth Session*, p. 6. Resolution 123 (VI).

[61] *Trusteeship Council, Official Records, Fourth Year, Sixth Session* (January-April, 1950), p. 241.

ing the reports from Italy on Somaliland, puts the Italians on a different footing than the other administering authorities. The presentation of reports to the Council is an administering authority's best chance to cast a favorable light on its administration. Petitions, of course, uniformly complain of certain action—or lack of action—on the part of the administering authority. Visiting missions, while not concerned merely with what is wrong in the territories, must necessarily concentrate on the more important problems facing each territory rather than praising the already accomplished measures of the administering authority, if they are to fulfill adequately their function. The annual reports taken in conjunction with the testimony of the special representatives, on the other hand, give the administering authorities their best, not to say only, chance to point to achievements in their respective territories. This opportunity is considerably reduced in the case of Italy, however, in view of the fact that representatives of the Advisory Council in Somaliland take part in the Council discussion along with the special representative.

On the other hand, it is sometimes the case that members of the Advisory Council come to the aid of the Italian representative. This occurred during the ninth session of the Council, for example, when the Soviet delegate, in questioning the special representative of Italy in connection with the annual reports on Somaliland for 1950, referred to a petition alleging the looting of a prisoner's property by the local administration. In reply the special representative referred to an Advisory Council document [62] which contained a statement to the effect that the whole matter had been satisfactorily settled.[63] Later at the same session the Philippine representative on the Advisory Council concluded that "the Italian government and the special representative (the chief administrator in the territory) deserved high praise. . . ." [64] Whether criticism or praise, the testimony of the Advisory Council members obviously has the appearance of being on a sounder basis than that of other Trusteeship Council members and discussions of the reports on Somaliland are consequently in the nature of objective analyses rather than a series of charges and refutations, as is the case with regard to reports on other territories.

The annual reports submitted to the Trusteeship Council are not dissimilar to those submitted under the mandates system, except of course that they are longer and more detailed, following the questionnaire. They provide a wealth of information on all phases of life in the territories, though naturally they tend to accentuate the achievements of the ad-

[62] United Nations Document A/AC.33/W.34.

[63] *Trusteeship Council, Official Records, Ninth Session* (June-July, 1951), p. 32.

[64] *Ibid.*, p. 42.

ministering authorities and gloss over some of the problems which have yet to be solved. Members of the Council can and do, however, ferret out omissions or evasions, and in this they are considerably aided by the petitions from the territory as well as by the reports of the visiting missions.

Through the first six sessions of the Council it was customary for that body to include a separate section on annual reports in its reports to the General Assembly. From the seventh session on, the material on each territory gleaned from annual reports is combined with that of petitions and the visiting missions' reports in one separate section on conditions in each territory generally. At its fourteenth session the Council, pursuant to a request of the General Assembly to all United Nations organs that they scrutinize their documentation with a view to reducing it,[65] and in line with a Secretariat suggestion in this regard, decided to give a comprehensive report on each territory only once every three years, coinciding with the Council's examining of the visiting mission's report on the territory.[66] The Council's practice has been to summarize its observations and recommendations on each part of the report and to recommend action to the administering authority concerned. The Council's recommendations are of necessity both general and on the whole mild. Often this is not so of the remarks made by individual members in Part III of the report. A good illustration of this may be found in connection with the report on the Cameroons under French administration for 1948. With regard to racial discrimination in the territory the Council noted many petitions on the subject, noted that the administering authority had taken measures to eliminate it, and urged the French government to continue its efforts in this regard. Individual members, however, stated that "the Council should not be satisfied until conditions of complete equality were achieved between the European and the African" [67] and that "the continued existence of racial discrimination in the Territory was disappointing in view of the assurances given to the Council last year that all vestiges of discrimination had been removed . . . So long as any distinction or difference in treatment of any kind was applied between the European and the African, it could not be reasonably claimed that all vestiges of discrimination had been removed." [68] These statements by nonadministering states on the Council were followed by those of the representatives of the United Kingdom and France, the former pointing

[65] *Resolutions Adopted by the General Assembly at its Eighth Session*, p. 47. Resolution 789 (VIII).

[66] *Trusteeship Council, Official Records, Fourteenth Session* (June-July, 1954), p. 159.

[67] *Report of the Trusteeship Council Covering Its First Special Session, Its Second Special Session, and Its Sixth and Seventh Sessions*, 23 July, 1949-21 July, 1950, p. 57. The remarks were those of the Philippine delegate.

[68] *Ibid.* The remarks were those of the Chinese delegate.

to progress that had been made on the problem,[69] the latter re-affirming that any discrimination was by private individuals and that it was therefore unfair to hold the administering authority accountable.[70]

As was true of the Permanent Mandates Commission, the heart of the consideration of annual reports is the questioning of the special representative. As was noted in Chapter One, the idea of the special representatives emerged when the Council of the League decided that the Commission should be composed of private experts rather than governmental representatives. And even though the Trusteeship Council was made up of the latter, the procedure proved so useful to the Mandates Commission that it was carried over in the trusteeship system. The chief advantage to the Council of such a procedure is that the special representative is always an official, often the highest official, of the administration in the territory concerned, while the representative of the administering state on the Council, although often having had considerable experience in colonial administration, is no longer in close personal touch with the territory.

The chief advantage to the administering authority is the presence of someone capable of answering on the spot any questions raised concerning the annual report, defending the administration of the territory in the process. In the case of the Permanent Mandates Commission talking with the special representatives was as close as many of the Commission members ever got to the territories. While this is not true of the Trusteeship Council members in all cases—since all may serve on visiting missions at one time or another—it is true with respect to some of the territories for most of the nonadministering states.[71] Written reports are, after all, comparatively dead things as against the personal testimony of a competent person who thoroughly knows a territory. Verbal presentation by the latter can help to enable the Council members to get more of a "feel" for the conditions in the territories and further help to create a better understanding of the problems faced by the administering authorities.

The Council's Rules of Procedure provide that each special representative "should be well informed on the territory involved." In practice this has come to mean that he is a top official in the administration. This is true undoubtedly because it behooves an administering authority to have the best available person on hand. While the presence of such an emi-

[69] *Ibid.* The British delegate referred specifically to the equalization of pay for European and African teachers.

[70] *Ibid.*, p. 58.

[71] Since the term of office for nonadministering states on the Council is three years and since each territory is regularly visited only once every three years, a nonadministering state could visit each territory only if all nonadministering states were represented on each mission, which as will be seen below, is not the case.

nently qualified official helps to further the cooperative spirit between administering and nonadministering states on the Council, so necessary to the adequate performance of that body's functions, it should not be assumed that all is sweetness and light during the question period. In the first place, there are always members of the Council who represent states which have arrived at an independent status comparatively recently. These members are always on a sharp lookout for any derogation of what they conceive to be the rights of the trust people. Secondly, for better or worse it is obvious that the Soviet representative on the Council has a constant "official distrust" of the administration of all trust territories. His questions are usually from the point of view of one who "knows" that something is wrong in the territory under consideration and is determined, by cross-examination, to discover every possible weakness in the position of the administering state.

It is difficult for the observer not to believe that many of the questions of the Soviet representative are designed to reinforce an overall propaganda position of being a friend to oppressed peoples all over the world rather than to elicit specific information about the territory under discussion. There is no reason to expect the Soviet representatives at the United Nations to take an anti-West position in the General Assembly, for example, and manifest a spirit of good will toward the West in the Trusteeship Council.

Soviet actions in this respect have produced two notable effects in the Council. First, whether asked "in good faith" or not, questions of the Soviet representative serve to keep the administering authorities on their toes. Perhaps it is not particularly pleasant to be constantly badgered about small details when the broad picture of administration shows real progress, but such badgering does tend to make one think of those details before the next annual question period—and hence to do something about them. From another point of view, however, the Soviet representative aids the administering authorities no end. During some sessions he has not been there, thus assuring administering authority victory on any issue forced to a showdown. Even when he is present, however, the vicissitudes of the East-West struggle are such that many nonadministering states on the Council, China being the best example, hesitate to support him and so line up on the side of the East even in the "nonpolitical" Trusteeship Council. The Trusteeship Council is political, and the cold war exists in the Council whether one would wish it that way or not. The result is that while unfavorable comments about the administration of the territory may be made, when it comes to voting the administering authorities usually have the last word on what goes into Council recommendations—hence, in part, the mildness of those recommendations as noted above.

One of the sections of the provisional questionnaire concerned the implementation by the administering authority of recommendations made by the Trusteeship Council and the General Assembly or Security Council. While the annual reports included this information from the very beginning the reports adopted by the Trusteeship Council for submission to the General Assembly contained no such special section. Quite obviously one of the most important functions that annual reports can perform is to indicate to the Council what steps have been taken to better conditions in a territory in the year between two annual reports; and the Council would, of course, be most interested in those steps taken as a result of recommendations by it. This point became of great interest to nonadministering states both on the Council and in the Fourth Committee of the General Assembly, and after the submission of the first three reports by the Trusteeship Council to the Assembly, the latter body urged the Council to include special sections on the matter in its future reports.[72]

The Council considered this recommendation at its sixth session and decided that in the future its drafting committees on the annual reports should indicate for each of the sections of the report (i.e., political, economic, social, etc.) what steps had been taken to implement the recommendations previously made by the Council.[73] The only reservation to this voiced by the administering authorities was that the dates on which particular recommendations had been made should be included in the Council reports to the Assembly. In this way the administering authorities could protect themselves against charges of failure to implement fully the Council's recommendations if, for example, a recommendation had been of a sweeping nature and had been made just a year previous to the submission of a given report.

This development in Council procedure for the consideration of annual reports marks a significant departure from the underlying philosophy of the Permanent Mandates Commission. In the latter body the spirit was one of supervision *and* cooperation. In its own words: "Supervision and co-operation are functions which though neither incompatible nor in conflict with one another, may yet be accompanied with genuine difficulties when they have to be carried out simultaneously. If the task of the Mandates Commission were merely to supervise the administration of the mandated territories, it would be natural that, in all difficult cases, it should propose to visit these territories itself, or should recommend the holding of enquiries on the spot." [74]

---

[72] *General Assembly, Official Records, Fourth Session, Resolutions,* Resolution 320 (IV), 322-24 (IV).

[73] *Trusteeship Council, Official Records, Fourth Year, Sixth Session* (January-April, 1950), p. 597.

[74] *Minutes of the Permanent Mandates Commission, Eighth Session* (1926), p. 200.

Now members of the Trusteeship Council would never for a moment admit that their task is not one of cooperation as well as supervision. The question is one of emphasis. As may be readily seen from the passage just quoted, the shift in emphasis was implicit in the terms of the Charter, but the Council, and particularly the administering authorities have been reluctant to explicitly recognize this shift. The question is often touched on, but in the official records of the Council it is more often than not passed over.

The decision to make specific reference to implementation of Council recommendations, however, is a manifestation of the emphasis on supervision. While the discussion concerning the question was not couched in these terms, the purpose of the proposal could admit no other interpretation. In one sense the shift from equality of collaboration and supervision to increased emphasis on supervision goes ever farther. While the Permanent Mandates Commission rarely made recommendations which had a bearing on the future,[75] some of the nonadministering states on the Council continually press for the implementation of steps leading to self-government or independence.

Since the administering authorities themselves must acquiesce in any Council recommendation, by no means all of the proposals of these non-administering states are accepted by the Council. Nevertheless it must be said that one group within the Council manifests very little desire for cooperation with the administering authorities except where the latter are willing to consider steps leading toward the end of the period of trusteeship for a territory. The number of states in this group obviously varies with the changing of Council membership, as well as the changing climate of world politics. The Soviet Union has, of course, been at the forefront in criticizing administering authority policies, and the Philippine delegate has been the most active of the nonpermanent members of the Council in this respect. The position of China has changed somewhat since the Communization of that state, the Nationalist delegate naturally not wanting to side with the Soviet Union.

This whole question is, like everything else concerning Council activities, complicated by the role played by the Soviet representative. When criticisms and demands for increased supervision by the Council, however stringent, are made in good faith, that is one thing. When, however, both administering and nonadministering states on the Council become convinced that criticisms and proposed recommendations are made with a view to overall propaganda affects, and to improving conditions in the trust territories only incidentally, they serve only to weaken the criticisms of other nonadministering states and to strengthen the solidarity of the administering authorities against further implementation of the trusteeship provisions of the Charter.

[75] Hall, p. 49.

Where the consideration of annual reports had been the main activity of the Permanent Mandates Commission, it has been considered less important by the Trusteeship Council for the simple reason that the devices of petitions and, especially, visiting missions provide members of the Council with a closer and more intimate view of conditions in the territories. The reports do, none the less, play a vital role in the activities of the Council. In the first place not all the nonadministering states can visit all the territories, and petitions taken alone would present a one-sided and obviously unfair picture of the total conditions in a territory.

Secondly, the reports have become the central core of information on the basis of which conditions in the territories have been reviewed. That is, the reports of the visiting missions and petitions raising questions of a general nature about a territory are considered along with the annual reports, so that from all three sources, plus information given by the special representative, the drafting committee can formulate observations and recommendations on the territory.

Third, with the continuous pressure placed by the nonadministering states on the administering authorities to improve conditions in their territories, it is necessary to allow the latter to present their side of the story in the interests of complete understanding of the conditions in the territories. This function the annual reports, in conjunction with the special representative's remarks, can perform.

Finally, the reports plus the oral and written answers of the special representative give the most complete information on the territories. Supervision, no matter how well-meaning, cannot be fruitful if conditions in the territories are not fully known, let alone understood. As will be seen below, visiting missions of necessity cannot do the research and investigation necessary to produce anywhere near the amount of information contained in a single report. Certainly, then, the annual reports play a vital role in the functioning of the trusteeship system. As a device by which the administering authorities can adequately present their views, they are important; as a means of assembling information on the territories, they are crucial.

CHAPTER SEVEN

Petitions

From the point of view of the inhabitants of the trust territories the consideration of petitions is undoubtedly one of the most important functions performed by the Trusteeship Council. While the visiting missions can ascertain the abridgment of rights of the trust peoples by the administering authorities, petitions provide the most direct means for representation of the native viewpoint on the Council. Petitioning occurred under the mandates system, but it was strictly regulated and, on the whole, little used as compared with the practice so far evident under the trusteeship system; and the increased importance of that device in the trusteeship system is a good indication of the difference between mandates and trusteeship with regard to the relationship of the international supervisory body and the dependent peoples involved. Where annual reports tend to make a case in favor of the administering authority concerned, petitions may be viewed as the case for the opposition, with the implication that the Trusteeship Council sits as judge. This analogy is not completely correct, of course, but it does illustrate the important fact that under the trusteeship system much more formal attention is paid to the position of the inhabitants of the trust territories than was the practice under the mandates system.

Rules of Procedure. That the administering authorities were aware of this is shown by the records of Council debates concerning the rules of procedure governing petitions. Nowhere are the respective positions of administering and nonadministering states on the Council with regard to the rights of the inhabitants of the trust territories and the supervisory powers of the Council more strikingly contrasted than in the discussion concerning petitions. As in other instances the issue was seldom clearly joined, but there is a noticeable difference of emphasis all through those discussions. The administering authorities were perfectly willing to admit that "it is indeed the very essence of democracy to provide for the expression and consideration of the views of all individuals," [1] but "far more important is this: we must, at all times, be careful not to impugn or impair the authority of the Administering Power." [2] The nonad-

[1] *Trusteeship Council, Official Records, First Year, First Session* (March-April, 1947), p. 78. The quotation is from the remarks of Mr. Makin of Australia.

[2] *Ibid.*, p. 83. The quotation is from the remarks of Sir Carl Berendsen of New Zealand.

ministering states, on the other hand, agreed that "There is no reason to prejudice the interests of the Administering Power" but they also emphasized the aim of "according the utmost latitude and freedom to present petitions. . . ." [3]

The Council spent much more time drafting, and drew up considerably more Rules of Procedure for petitions than for either annual reports or visiting missions—great importance was attached to the subject by all members. Since many of the fundamental principles concerning the handling of petitions evolved at this stage, it is necessary to consider in some detail the problems met by the Council in formulating its rules governing petitions. Later the development of petitioning through the ten years of Council functioning will be explained.

When the Council, at its first session, turned to the question of implementing the Charter's provisions for petitions,[4] it had before it the Provisional Rules of Procedure drawn up by the Preparatory Commission as well as suggested revisions to these Rules in the form of a Secretariat memorandum.[5] As they pertained to petitions, the former was brief and generalized, differing from the rules developed by the Permanent Mandates Commission in providing for (1) submission of petitions directly to the Secretary-General and (2) oral petitions, and in omitting (1) criteria for rejecting petitions and (2) provision for administering authority comment on petitions.[6] The latter proposals were based on the experience of other major organs of the United Nations as well as on the discussions in the Fourth Committee surrounding the adoption of the first eight trusteeship agreements.

With regard to the other parts of the Rules of Procedure the Council used the Preparatory Commission's draft as a basis of discussion and adopted or amended those proposals. In view of the importance of petitions, however, it was agreed that the Council would first agree on basic principles. On this basis, the President of the Council, Mr. Francis Sayre of the United States, submitted an Outline of Discussion [7] containing several major questions to be answered by the Council. The Council accepted the President's proposal to use this as a guide and proceeded to discuss the various questions raised in the Outline.

---

[3] *Ibid.*, p. 89. The quotation is from the remarks of Mr. Khalidy of Iraq.

[4] Article 87 of the Charter provides, in part that "The General Assembly and, under its authority, the Trusteeship Council . . . may . . . accept petitions and examine them in consultation with the administering authority.

[5] *Trusteeship Council, Official Records, First Year, First Session, Supplement*, pp. 2-11, 29-60.

[6] The Mexican, Philippine, and Egyptian delegates took the lead in sponsoring these changes from League practice. *Preparatory Commission, Committee IV: Trusteeship*, p. 4.

[7] United Nations Document T/21.

The first of these concerned the origin of petitions. On this point there was general agreement that petitions might originate either from within or outside a trust territory.[8] This had been the practice under the Permanent Mandates Commission, and there could be little opposition to the principle that the Trusteeship Council should have access to information about the territories under its jurisdiction whether the source of information lay within or without those territories.

The second general question concerned the form of petition—specifically, whether or not oral petitions would be accepted. On this point the British representative argued that, while oral petitions should not be completely excluded, oral hearings "should be limited to petitions which had previously been communicated in writing." [9] Agreeing with this, the Belgian delegate urged that as a matter of principle petitions should be formulated in writing as a general rule; oral presentation would be the exception.[10] The main consideration in the minds of the administering authorities was to insure that they would have full knowledge of the subject matter of any oral petition *before* it was taken up by the Council, so that they might be prepared to present their side of the question. This was acceptable to other members of the Council, and it was decided that oral petitions, while not unacceptable per se, would be considered only "in exceptional cases." Oral presentation in support of a previously submitted written petition, not subject to the same limitation, was also provided for if the Council consented.[11]

The next question—the mode of transmission of petitions— provides an illustration of the difference in emphasis as between administering and nonadministering states alluded to above. All the Council members agreed that petitions could be transmitted to the Council through the Secretary-General directly, through the administering authority concerned, or through the visiting missions. But debate waxed long over what was to be "the normal mode of transmission." The nonadministering states argued that the visiting missions should develop into the most useful channel for petitioning since it would probably prove true that many questions could be settled by a mission on the spot, without referring the matter to the Council.[12] The administering authorities, however, wanted petitions to go through the local administration. Even accepting the usefulness of the visiting missions, they argued, the missions should turn over all petitions to the local authorities. Then, if the matter could not be set-

[8] *Trusteeship Council, Official Records, First Year, First Session* (March-April, 1947), pp. 80-81.

[9] *Ibid.*, p. 82.

[10] *Ibid.*, pp. 82-83.

[11] *Ibid.*, pp. 158-59, 179.

[12] *Ibid.*, pp. 87-88.

tled, the local authorities could send it on to the Trusteeship Council.[13] The primary concern of the administering authorities was, of course, to make sure that they had ample notice of petitions so as not to be caught unprepared in the Council. Further, they feared that any short-circuiting of their position in the line between trust peoples and Trusteeship Council would impair their authority in their territories.

The position of the nonadministering states on this point was nicely summed up by Mr. Khalidy of Iraq: "If you want to accuse Mr. X, you do not submit the accusation to Mr. X. That is to say, petitions are mostly, if not always, some sort of accusation, and if the inhabitants are to present accusations against the Administering Authorities to the Administering Authorities, then why have the Trusteeship Council at all? [14] In the end the Council decided that all three methods of transmission were acceptable, and that any limitations on any of these methods would be decided in connection with the fourth general question: functions and duties of the transmitting agencies.

The chief issue which arose in connection with this fourth question was whether the Secretary-General had the duty to circulate a petition immediately upon receipt, or whether he could wait until the administering authority concerned had attached its comments to the petition. Relevant to this was the additional question of how long an administering authority should have to attach its comments. With regard to the second point there was general agreement that the administering state should have at least two months to consider and comment on petitions concerning its territories. The question then was: should the petitions be circulated in the interim? It was argued that doing so would be manifestly unfair to the administering authorities since the issues might be prejudiced.[15] On the other hand, it was urged that publicity in any case was unavoidable and there were obvious advantages in having other Council members in possession of petitions before they were discussed by the Council.[16] This issue was forced to a vote, and by a margin of one (five to four) it was decided that petitions should be circulated immediately to all Council members.[17]

This represented a clear victory for the nonadministering states on the Council, and the fact that the administering authorities readily acquiesced in the decision was a measure of their genuine willingness to cooperate—although it should be noted that the administering authorities had impaired neither their right to make comments on petitions nor the oppor-

[13] *Ibid.*, p. 87.

[14] *Ibid.*, p. 90.

[15] *Ibid.*, p. 94. The remarks of Mr. Makin of Australia.

[16] *Ibid.*, pp. 95-96. The remarks of Mr. Nervo of Mexico.

[17] *Ibid.*, p. 135.

tunity to be fully prepared when the Council discussed those petitions. The Council also decided, with little debate, that the visiting missions could comment on petitions received by them, but that the Secretary-General could not.[18]

The Council next turned its attention to the problem of screening petitions. Under the mandates system certain types of petitions, including those submitted anonymously, were screened out,[19] and while the Preparatory Commission had not provided for such screening in the Provisional Rules of Procedure, the French representative submitted a proposal [20] that the Council create, at the beginning of each session, an *ad hoc* committee to classify and screen petitions. Included in this proposal were criteria by which the committee could be guided in determining which petitions were unacceptable.[21] The Council accepted the idea of this committee, but there was a good deal of discussion concerning whether its activities should be confined to classifying petitions or whether it could screen them as well. The question of anonymous petitions, especially, caused much debate and is important not only per se, but as an indication of the differences of opinion among members of the Council on the respective positions of the Council and the administering authorities in the trusteeship system. Thus the Iraq representative felt that "petitions, once outside the hands of the petitioners, become the property and the right of this Council." He, therefore, "envisaged the responsibilities of the *ad hoc* committees as purely preliminary; that is to say, I thought of it as something like a credentials committee. It would screen, it would recommend, study and report, but it would not have the power to reject or throw out any petitions, not even anonymous ones." [22] The Belgian delegate, however, while admitting that "Through anonymous denunciations I have on occasion learned of certain situations which were not as they should be," nevertheless asserted that "There is a serious difference . . . between the Administering Authority's consideration of all information brought to its knowledge inasmuch as it is responsible for the proper administration of the Territory, and the Trusteeship Council's consent to consider anonymous denunciations as petitions." [23]

In the end it was decided to permit the Secretary-General to screen

[18] *Ibid.*, p. 121.

[19] See above, p. 20.

[20] United Nations Document T/15.

[21] *Trusteeship Council, Official Records, First Year, First Session* (March-April, 1947), pp. 141-42. The criteria followed that used by the Permanent Mandates Commission.

[22] *Ibid.*, pp. 136, 142.

[23] *Ibid.*, p. 137.

out petitions "which are manifestly inconsequential," [24] while the *ad hoc* committee would undertake preliminary examination of petitions, but "No appraisal of the substance of the petitions shall be made by it. . . ." [25] There was no limitation placed on anonymous petitions in the Rules, but the administering authorities could raise the point of their acceptability in individual cases, and this they have done. In addition to the question of anonymous petitions, the inadmissibility of petitions directed against the judgment of the courts in the territories was raised. The Permanent Mandates Commission had refused to accept these, and the Council was agreed that a similar rule should exist for the Trusteeship Council, with the reservation that petitions against laws giving rise to particular judicial decisions were not, by that fact, unacceptable.[26]

Following this discussion, the Council turned its attention to its procedure for handling petitions. This had already been considered to some extent with the approval of the *ad hoc* committee for preliminary examination of petitions. In addition, the Council now decided that the Secretary-General should make a preliminary classification of petitions, that, following the practice of the Permanent Mandates Commission, the administering authorities would have the right to appoint special representatives to be present when petitions concerning their territories were examined, and that the Council could "grant, control, limit, or deny oral hearings," in support of written petitions.[27]

Concerning the disposition of petitions, there was some argument concerning the channels through which the Secretary-General should acknowledge the receipt of a petition. The administering authorities naturally desired that all petitions be acknowledged through the territorial administration, and they considered a Mexican suggestion that all petitions, regardless of their source, be acknowledged directly to the petitioner as "absolutely inadmissible." [28] When the Mexican proposal was voted on the result was a tie.[29] The Rules of Procedure omit reference to acknowledgement by the Secretary-General of the receipt of a petition. He must, however, inform both the administering authority concerned and the petitioner of such action as the Council takes on each petition.[30]

[24] A list of inconsequential petitions, with a summary of their contents, is communicated by the Secretary-General to all Council members. United Nations Document T/1/Rev.2. Rule 85.

[25] *Trusteeship Council, Official Records, First Year, First Session* (March-April, 1947), p. 385. United Nations Document T/1/Rev.2. Rule 90.

[26] *Ibid.*, p. 150.

[27] *Ibid.*, pp. 156-57, 159.

[28] *Ibid.*, pp. 161-62.

[29] *Ibid.*, p. 169. The vote was 4 to 4.

[30] United Nations Document T/1/Rev.1. Rule 93.

Finally, the Council agreed that provision should be made for emergency and summary procedure for petitions, should the need arise, and that the functions of the Trusteeship Council and the Secretary-General with regard to petitions from strategic territories should be "governed by Article 83 of the Charter and the terms of the relevant Trusteeship agreement." [31]

In sum, the Rules of Procedure on petitions as formulated at the first session of the Council provide that: (1) the Council may consider petitions if they concern the affairs of one or more trust territories or the operation of the trusteeship system; (2) petitions may originate either within or outside a trust territory and may be presented in writing or, in exceptional circumstances, orally; further, the Council may hear oral presentations in behalf of previously submitted written petitions; (3) petitions may be submitted to the Secretary-General either directly, through the administering authority concerned, or through the visiting mission, and will be circulated by the Secretary-General to the members of the Council promptly upon receipt by him; (4) the administering authority concerned may submit observations on any petition affecting a territory under its administration and may appoint a special representative to be present at Council discussions of the petition; (5) an *ad hoc* committee on petitions will be established at each session of the Council to undertake preliminary, but nonsubstantive, consideration of petitions; (6) petitions are inadmissible if directed against the judgments of courts of the administering authority, or if they concern disputes with which the courts have competence to deal; (7) the Secretary-General shall inform both the petitioner and the administering authority concerned of the results of Council consideration of each petition; (8) petitions relating to strategic areas are governed by Article 83 of the Charter and the terms of the relevant trusteeship agreement.

There are three main differences between the rules governing petitions as between the mandates and trusteeship system. First, under the latter petitions can be submitted in three ways; the former permitted submission only through the administering authorities. Secondly, the trusteeship system envisages oral petitions and, more normally, oral elaboration of written petitions, neither of which was provided for in the Permanent Mandates Commission. Third, more generally, petitions are provided for as normal procedure under the trusteeship system, where under mandate they were viewed as an exceptional practice, and, in fact, were submitted only by the inhabitants of the "A" mandates. What was really only a latent possibility under mandates has thus become a reality under trusteeship.

Submission of Petitions. The Council has so far received literally thou-

[31] *Ibid.*, Rule 93.

sands of petitions, not including addenda,[32] by far the greatest number of these concerning the territories in Africa.[33]

The petitions themselves show a wide variety both as to source and substance. Petitioners have ranged all the way from well-organized political groups[34] to a schoolboy hoping the cost of education could be reduced so that he could continue his schooling.[35] The substance of the petitions has been as varied as the petitioners. In addition to requests for the amelioration of specific grievances and more general demands for the early fulfillment of the goals of trusteeship, the Council has had to consider such communications[36] as an indignant denial by the wives of a native ruler in the Cameroons that they grudged "sharing husbands,"[37] and a plan for "universal colonial and mandate trusteeship under the United Nations."[38]

While the Council's Rules of Procedure permit consideration of petitions originating outside of as well as within the territories, there have been comparatively few of the former.[39] Usually these are either from humanitarian organizations interested in dependent peoples, or from individuals pleading the cause of a friend or relative within a territory. Thus the St. Joan's Social and Political Alliance was a steady petitioner during the early sessions of the Council.[40] The organization was particularly interested in the status of women in the territories. On the other hand, the Council received a number of petitions from a Mrs. K. Maier, who lived in Germany, in behalf of a relative about to be repatriated to that country from Tanganyika.[41]

[32] Addenda are supplementary information supplied by the petitioners either voluntarily or at the request of the Council.

[33] At its seventeenth session (February-April, 1956), the Council was faced with the unique problem of how to dispose of 20,000 separate communications coming from one territory, the French Cameroons. "Council to Survey Progress in Five African Trust Territories," *United Nations Review,* Vol. 2, No. 9, March, 1956, pp. 7, 35.

[34] United Nations Document T/Pet.4/16, submitted by the Cameroons National Federation, which included more than 20 local organizations.

[35] United Nations Document T/Pet.6/134.

[36] The word "communication" in Council usage has two meanings. On the one hand it means any and all written statements received by the Secretary-General, including petitions. On the other hand, it is used to denote written statements not really classifiable as petitions (addresses of welcome to visiting missions, for example), and thus distinguishable from petitions proper. The meaning, in this chapter as in Council records, is revealed by the context in each case.

[37] United Nations Document T/Pet.4/48.

[38] United Nations Document T/Pet./General 14.

[39] This statement is made on the basis of considering petitions emanating from territories immediately adjacent to trust territories as originating within a trust territory. Many petitions concerning the Togolands, for example, are sent from the Gold Coast. These have been considered as emanating from the trust territories.

[40] For an example see United Nations Document T/Pet.4/2.

[41] United Nations Documents T/Pet.2/28, 32, 33, and 37.

If the administering authorities hoped that the normal method of submitting petitions would be through the local administration they must so far be very disappointed, as this has not proved to be the case. With the exception of those concerning Somaliland, most of the petitions have been submitted to the visiting missions, and the remainder have for the most part been sent directly to the Secretary-General.[42] With regard to Somaliland most of the petitions have been submitted through the Advisory Council.

One noteworthy development with regard to the submission of petitions is the tendency for petitioners to become impatient with the Council, and attempt to submit their grievances to some other United Nations body. Thus some petitions [43] have been addressed not to the Council, but to the Fourth Committee of the General Assembly, while at least one other [44] requested that the Council turn over consideration of a matter to the General Assembly. Further, from its seventh session on, the General Assembly's Fourth Committee has regularly granted oral hearings to the indigenous inhabitants of the trust territories.[45] For the most part the General Assembly, after hearing the petitioner, refers the matter to the Trusteeship Council for consideration. The latter body then takes up the question in connection with its general consideration of the particular trust territory. This development is one manifestation of the Charter's ambiguity concerning the respective jurisdictions of the General Assembly and the Trusteeship Council—an ambiguity that has not, as yet, been cleared up.[46]

The number of petitions has been on the increase each session of the Council. This is due in part to the fact that petitioners tend to petition several times on the same subject, and in part, undoubtedly, to the growing awareness on the part of the indigenous population of their right of petition.[47] The vast number of petitions is not really indicative of the number of grievances or requests involved since very often—in addition to petitioners repeating themselves—petitions from different sources concern the same problem. The outstanding example of this is the so-called

[42] One petition was sent to the Secretary-General via the government of the Soviet Union.

[43] United Nations Document T/Pet.6/309, for example.

[44] United Nations Document T/Pet.6/238.

[45] To date the oral hearings have been given primarily to the inhabitants of Somaliland and the French Cameroons.

[46] See below, pp. 205-10.

[47] Another noticeable trend related to this is that more and more native, as distinguished from European, residents submit petitions. For example, during the first two sessions of the Council most of the petitions emanating from within the territories were from European settlers. By the seventh session, out of 182 petitions received by the Secretary-General, less than a dozen were from European residents of the territories.

Ewe question, which has been before the Council since its inception. This concerns the request of the Ewe people that they be unified under a single administering authority, instead of being under British and French administration in the Togolands.[48] Some one hundred and seventy-odd petitions concerning the Ewe people have been submitted—and this does not include petitions requesting unification of the Togolands, which affect the Ewe question.[49]

The administering authorities have not hesitated to make use of their right to comment on the petitions submitted. In general, these observations take the form of statements of the general background of the situation giving rise to the petition, followed by a recommendation as to Council action on the matter.

Often the administering authority categorically denies the allegations of a petitioner, but in many instances the validity of the complaint is recognized. In the latter case, the administering authority usually brings the Council's attention to such steps as have been taken to ameliorate the conditions complained of. Where a petition involves two or more trust territories the administering authorities concerned submit a joint memorandum.

In addition to the original observations, the Council sometimes calls for supplementary information as the result of its discussion of a petition. This takes the form of an addendum to the observations.

Procedure for Consideration of Petitions. No other problem has given the Council more trouble than the development of an effective procedure for the handling of petitions. Broadly, the problem is one of reconciling the necessity of keeping up with its work with the goal of not impairing this important right of the inhabitants of the trust territories. During the first sixteen sessions of the Council the general trend has been consistently in the direction of speedier processing of petitions at the expense of giving full consideration to each and every communication directed to the Council. While this trend might seem to vitiate an important aspect of trusteeship, it has been necessitated by the tremendous number of petitions received by the Council, and has been accepted by most of the nonadministering states, albeit with some regret. The Council's handling of petitions to date may be divided into three general stages: the first through the fifth sessions, the sixth through the ninth sessions, and the tenth session to the present.

[48] For a summary of the main aspects of this question see Benjamin Gerig and Vernon McKay, "The Ewe Problem: A Case Study in the Operation of the Trusteeship Council," *Department of State Bulletin,* Vol. XXIV (January-June, 1951, pp. 128-37. See, also, below, pp. 231-32.

[49] An organization known as the Togoland Progress Party has submitted numerous petitions expressing the desire for unification. In the process it has deprecated the Ewe movement, since the latter involves only part of the total population of the Togolands.

At the first session of the Council, that body adopted its President's suggestion that the procedure used in dealing with petitions follow that of the Permanent Mandates Commission, which may be outlined as follows: first, a general hearing of the petitions, including questioning the special representatives of the administering authorities concerned; second, the appointment of a drafting committee to formulate proposed resolutions based on Council discussion; and third, consideration by the Council of the committee's recommendations.[50] In general, this procedure was used by the Council during its first five sessions, except that the *ad hoc* committee was dispensed with at the third and fifth sessions (the Council used the Secretariat's classification of petitions),[51] and the drafting committee was not appointed at the fourth session, the Council preferring to reach its conclusions on the petitions in plenary meeting.[52]

Two other developments worthy of note occurred during this period. At the third session of the Council the decision was made to postpone the consideration of general questions raised in petitions until such time as the annual report and the latest visiting mission's report on the areas concerned were discussed.[53] Thus a distinction was made between specific or personal petitions, and those concerning general conditions in the territories—the latter being discussed when the annual reports and visiting mission's reports are considered. This distinction has played an increasingly important part in Council consideration of petitions.

During the Council's fourth session the Secretariat requested the Council to instruct it as to what action it should take with regard to (1) confidential petitions, (2) lengthy petitions (some of the petitions were running over three hundred pages), and (3) the problem of the time limit for the submission of administering authority observations on the petitions (the observations were forthcoming long after the petitions were received). At the sixth meeting of this session the Council agreed that the Secretary-General should inform the senders of confidential petitions that under the Council's Rules their petitions must necessarily be made known to the administering authorities, and ask the petitioners if they still wanted to submit their petitions. It was further agreed that the Secretariat should summarize lengthy petitions, with the proviso that any member of the Council could request copies of the full petitions if he desired. Finally, to speed up the process of obtaining administering authority observations on petitions, it was agreed that the Secretary-

[50] *Trusteeship Council, Official Records, First Year, First Session* (March-April, 1947), p. 519.

[51] *Ibid., Third Session* (June-August, 1948), pp. 18-19; *Fifth Session* (June-July, 1949), p. 47.

[52] *Ibid., Fourth Session* (January-March, 1949), pp. 18-19.

[53] *Ibid., Third Session* (June-August, 1948), pp. 78-79.

General should send a copy of each petition to the local authority in the territory concerned so that the necessary information concerning the petition would reach the home government sooner.[54]

In connection with the first decision, the Council agreed that anonymous petitions would be handled in the same way as confidential petitions, and that they would not be immediately circulated as unrestricted documents.[55] The question of anonymous petitions has given the Council a great deal of difficulty. The administering authorities have been uniformly opposed to receiving them on the grounds that they promoted irresponsible attacks on the administration of a territory—attacks which are difficult to repudiate specifically since the petitioner is unknown. The nonadministering states on the Council, however, have argued that, granting the justice of the administering authorities' position, a petition should not be considered unacceptable merely because it is anonymous; rather the Council should judge each on its merits. This question is not of considerable intrinsic importance in view of the few anonymous petitions so far submitted, but it does indicate the difference in approach of the administering and nonadministering states toward the right of petitions, especially as regards the limitation of that right.

The sixth session of the Council saw fundamental changes made in the handling of petitions. Noting the increasing number of petitions during the first five sessions of the Council, the General Assembly, at its fourth session (October-December, 1949), recommended to the Council that it review its procedures for examining and disposing of petitions with a view to developing more expeditious methods, while at the same time not impairing the rights of the petitioners.[56] When the Council considered this resolution it referred it, together with a French proposal to permit the *ad hoc* committee to make recommendations on petitions,[57] to a committee composed of the representatives of Argentina, Australia, Belgium, Iraq, the Philippines, and the United States.[58] This committee accepted the substance of the French proposal and in its report to the Council[59] recommended that the Rules of Procedure be changed to the extent that:

The *ad hoc* Committee on Petitions shall be empowered:
(a) to undertake preliminary examination of written petitions and of any

[54] *Ibid., Fourth Session* (January-March, 1949), pp. 65-69.

[55] *Ibid.*, pp. 66-71.

[56] *Official Records of the Fourth Session of the General Assembly, Resolutions,* p. 38. Resolution 321 (IV).

[57] United Nations Document T/384.

[58] *Trusteeship Council, Official Records, Fourth Year, Sixth Session* (January-April, 1950), p. 4.

[59] United Nations Document T/L.8.

observations which the Administering Authority concerned may have circulated . . .

(b) to invite the representative of the Administering Authority concerned or the petitioner to furnish additional information which the Committee may deem necessary.

The *ad hoc* Committee shall make a report to the Trusteeship Council on each petition considered by it together with its recommendations as to the action to be taken by the Council in each case.

This recommendation was adopted by the Council unanimously.[60] The committee continued to meet during the course of the sixth session, and later submitted a final report[61] to the Council. Included in this report were a number of further recommendations with regard to changes in the Rules of Procedure governing petitions, the crucial one of which concerned the possibility of speeding up the process of considering petitions by limiting the number of communications eligible to be classified as petitions. With regard to this last point the position of the administering authorities represented on the committee had been that only those signed communications requesting the redress of specific grievances should qualify as petitions. All other communications should be classified as such and circulated under Rule 24 of the Council's Rules of Procedure, which provided merely that the Secretariat should circulate information relevant to trusteeship to all Council members. Opposed to this point of view, some of the nonadministering states argued that this would impair the right of petition.[62] The result, "a hard-won compromise," in the words of the Philippine representative, was that no specific definition of petitions, as distinct from communications, was made by the committee. Rather, all petitions would be placed in one of three categories, their treatment depending upon their classification:

(a) Petitions calling for intervention of the Council for the redress of a grievance or the modification of a policy.
(b) All other petitions except
(c) Petitions which are
 i. Manifestly inconsequential
 ii. Not within the competence of the Trusteeship Council
 iii. Merely expressions of appreciation for Council activities.

Petitions in category (a) would continue to be treated in the regular manner. Those in category (b) would be circulated to Council members with a reference, if appropriate, to any petitions dealing with the same subject matter. Those in category (c) would be listed, together with a

[60] *Trusteeship Council, Official Records, Fourth Year, Sixth Session* (January-April, 1950), p. 92.

[61] United Nations Document T/L.13.

[62] Summary records of the meetings of the committee are not available, but the respective positions of its members are revealed in Council discussions of the committee's report.

brief summary of each, and the list circulated to Council members. Any petition in categories (b) or (c) could, at the request of a Council member, be placed in category (a). While the committee's report did not state this, what the committee had in mind with reference to category (b) were petitions repetitious of matters already raised, and general questions which the Council concerned itself with during the course of its consideration of the annual reports and the reports of the visiting missions.

When this proposal was discussed by the Council, the administering authorities were uniformly opposed to its adoption. They argued that the crucial question—the limitation of the number of communications specifically defined as petitions and dealt with accordingly—had not been met. The nonadministering states, on the other hand, pointed to the fact that the administering states on the committee had approved its report; why were they objecting now? [63] After further argument it was agreed to drop the entire proposal and continue to handle petitions as before. Both the proposal and the discussion surrounding it are important as manifestations of the administering and nonadministering states' positions on the question of petitions generally. Both, of course, accepted the principle of petitioning. The question was how far would that principle have to be limited in order that the Council might give adequate consideration to petitions? The nonadministering states were prepared to go no further than the proposal of the committee; the administering authorities saw no improvement in the proposal. There the matter rested—though not permanently.

One other decision of the Council made during its sixth session is important. In a report of the *ad hoc* committee on petitions, the committee asked the Council for instructions as to the disposition of an anonymous petition.[64] The arguments concerning anonymous petitions in general were again discussed, and in the end the Council adopted an American-sponsored resolution providing that "the communication circulated as T/Pet.3/16 *being an anonymous petition*, calls for no action by the Council as a petition." [65] An Iraq amendment to strike out the italicized words of the resolution was subsequently rejected.[66] The vote on the proposal, taken together with the rejection of the amendment, finally settled the issue of anonymous petitions. With the phrase in question included, the Council decision was one of principle, and not merely on the specific communication.

[63] *Trusteeship Council, Official Records, Fourth Year, Sixth Session* (January-April, 1950), pp. 186-87.

[64] *Ibid.*, p. 263.

[65] *Ibid.*, pp. 266-71.

[66] *Ibid.*, p. 271.

When the Council granted its *ad hoc* committee on petitions the power to make substantive recommendations it created, in effect, a "little Trusteeship Council," for the recommendations of the committee are uniformly accepted by the Council with little, if any change. The committee followed the same procedure used by the Council in the consideration of petitions, with the exception that the chairman was asked to draft recommendations based on committee discussion of each petition, thus acting as the counterpart of the Council's drafting committee. At its third meeting, the chairman of the committee, Mr. Peachey of Australia, suggested, and the committee adopted, a proposal that the Secretariat be requested to prepare draft reports of the committee which would include, successively, the following points with regard to each petition: (1) a summary of the petition, (2) observations of the visiting mission, where appropriate, (3) observations of the administering authority concerned, (4) previous action taken by the Council on the subject matter of the petition, (5) a summary of the discussion in the committee, including any comments of the special representative of the administering authority concerned, and (6) the recommendation of the committee.[67] The committee also followed the practice of the Council in recommending that general questions raised in petitions be considered by the Council when the annual reports and the reports of the visiting missions on the territory concerned were examined.

In addition to following the Council's procedure with regard to petitions, the committee, during the sixth and seventh sessions of the Council, considered several petitions under general headings rather than individually. Thus all petitions relating to educational advancement within a territory could be considered together, and a single resolution applicable to all recommended. In this way the committee was able to avoid discussing the same questions repetitiously.[68]

During the eighth and ninth sessions of the Council, a representative of the Soviet Union was appointed to the committee, and at both sessions he voiced protest against the committee's practice of recommending specific action only on "personal petitions" (the phrase is his), and delaying consideration of those raising general questions until such time as the next annual report on the territory was considered.[69] He argued that in many respects the general questions, such as over-all social or economic policy within a territory, were more crucial than petitions calling for specific redress of grievances, and that delay in consideration

[67] *Ad Hoc Committee on Petitions, Summary Record of the Third Meeting,* February 1, 1950, p. 11. United Nations Document T/AC.20/SR.3.

[68] See, for example, Trusteeship Council, Seventh Session, *Fourth Report of the Ad Hoc Committee on Petitions.* United Nations Document T/L.101.

[69] *Ad Hoc Committee on Petitions, Summary Record of the First Meeting,* February 13, 1951, p. 2. United Nations Document T/AC.34/SR.1.

of the former was a violation of the right of petitioning under the Charter. The committee, nevertheless, continued to make this *de facto* distinction in petitions, and it thus has developed into an important aspect of the Council's procedure.

The *ad hoc* committee operated during the sixth through the ninth session of the Council. At the latter session the Council was in receipt of another General Assembly resolution on the subject of petitions.[70] This called upon the Council to consider the advisability of taking three major steps to improve further its procedure for handling petitions:

a. Transforming the *ad hoc* committee into a Standing Committee of Petitions.
b. Calling upon the administering authorities to submit their observations within the two month time limit after the receipt of a petition.
c. Requesting the administering authorities to submit each year special information on action taken on the recommendations of the Council with respect to petitions concerning their respective territories.

The matter was referred by the Council to its *ad hoc* committee on petitions. When the committee considered the resolution at its nineteenth and twenty-second meetings[71] two important questions arose. First, it became evident that the administering authorities were opposed to the creation of a standing committee since the purpose of it would be to permit the committee to sit between Council sessions in order to enable its consideration of petitions to keep pace with their submission. This would mean either that special representatives of the administering authorities would not be on hand during the committee's consideration of some petitions, or that they would have to spend what in the administering authorities' view was far too much time at Council headquarters. Second, the Secretariat was concerned over the problem of classifying communications— that matter, it will be recalled, had been left in abeyance at the sixth session of the Council. The Secretariat's representative felt that the committee might, during the period between Council sessions, undertake the preliminary classification of communications. As matters stood, many documents considered by the committee as petitions were really only expressions of appreciation, or raised matters upon which the Council had previously taken action. If these could be circulated as communications, for information purposes only, the committee could spend more time discussing petitions proper.

Neither of these questions, the one very much related to the other, was settled at this time. The committee's report[72] merely recommended

[70] *Resolutions adopted by the General Assembly during the period* 19 September to 15 December, 1950, p. 51. Resolution 435 (V).

[71] Untied Nations Documents T/AC.41/SR.19. (7 August, 1951) and T/AC.41/SR.22 (14 August, 1951).

[72] United Nations Document T/L.224.

that the Council urge the administering authorities to submit their observations within the prescribed time limit, and that Council members give further thought to the question of creating a standing committee on petitions. The Council adopted the committee's report, while rejecting a Soviet proposal which would insure that all petitions on the agenda for a given session would be considered at that session, and not postponed until the annual reports were considered.[73]

Informed of this action by the Council, the General Assembly, at its sixth session passed another resolution [74] recommending that the Council

a. Create a Standing Committee on Petitions to meet in between as well as during Council sessions.
b. Devise a procedure for the preliminary examination i.e., classification of petitions.
c. Call upon the administering authorities to submit information on actions taken on Council recommendations on petitions.

When the Council considered this resolution at its tenth session it referred it to a committee of four.[75] The committee held three meetings in February and March, 1952,[76] and made suggestions [77] on both of the questions left unresolved at the ninth session of the Council, as well as suggesting action with regard to the third point raised in the General Assembly resolution. In essence, the committee agreed that a Standing Committee on Petitions should be created, to meet both during and between Council sessions. To allay the fears expressed by the administering authorities concerning the absence of special representatives at committee meetings when the Council was not in session, the committee proposed that the Standing Committee conduct "preliminary examination of petitions on which observations by the Administering Authority are available; . . . formulate any questions to be submitted to the Administering Authority, or to the special representative . . ." and "complete, whenever possible, its examination of those petitions which the Administering Authority agrees to have examined in the absence of the special representative." With respect to the question of classifying petitions, "the Committee was of the opinion that all communications containing requests, complaints and grievances seeking action by the Trusteeship Council should continue to be handled in accordance with the established

[73] *Trusteeship Council, Official Records, Ninth Session* (June-July, 1951), pp. 321-23.

[74] *Resolutions adopted by the General Assembly during its Sixth Session* (November, 1951-February, 1952), p. 55. Resolution 552 (VI).

[75] *Trusteeship Council, Official Records, Tenth Session* (February-April, 1952), p. 6. The committee was composed of the representatives of Belgium, the Dominican Republic, Thailand, and the United States.

[76] United Nations Documents T/AC.43/SR.1-3.

[77] United Nations Documents T/L.243.

procedure for examination of petitions. However, communications concerning general problems to which the attention of the Council has already been called and on which it has taken decisions or made recommendations, as well as anonymous communications . . . should be screened by the standing committee . . . which should decide whether any of them ought to be treated as a petition." [78]

This recommendation meant, of course, the acceptance of the original administering authority position: only petitions for redress of specific grievances should be processed as petitions; others should be circulated for information purposes only. The acceptance of this by the nonadministering states on the committee was due primarily to the overriding fact that it was becoming increasingly difficult for the Secretariat and the *ad hoc* committee to process the virtual flood of petitions addressed to the Council. As a concession to those who feared an impairment of the right of petition two safeguards were recommended by the committee. The first, mentioned above, was that the Standing Committee could treat any communication as a petition if it so desired. The second was that any member of the Council could request that a communication be considered as a petition, though this request is subject to Council approval.

When the Council considered these recommendations,[79] the only voice raised in opposition to them was that of the Soviet delegate who argued against the proposals on two grounds. First, he felt that the Council could not delegate its authority to consider petitions to another body, and second, he again objected to the division of petitions into categories of general and personal, especially in view of the fact that in the future, rather than waiting to consider the former in conjunction with annual reports, the Council would take no specific action on them at all. Despite these objections the proposals of the committee were overwhelmingly approved.[80]

It was agreed, however, that these decisions would be considered temporary, and the Standing Committee on Petitions was asked to report on their validity to the Council at its twelfth session.

The report [81] was not made until the Council's fourteenth session, because of the desire of the committee to gain more experience with the new procedure. In general the committee expressed approval of the procedure with the following suggested modifications:

1. Because the administering authorities had been uniformly late in submitting observations to petitions, it was suggested that the time limit

[78] *Ibid.*, pp. 2-4.

[79] *Trusteeship Council, Official Records, Tenth Session* (February-April, 1952), pp. 87-88.

[80] *Ibid.*, p. 88. The vote was 11 to 1.

[81] United Nations Document T/L.465.

for this should be increased from two to three months after the receipt of a petition "on the understanding that the administering authorities would undertake to submit observations on all petitions within this time limit." [82]

2. The committee found it difficult to keep up with its work on the basis of its schedule and suggested that it be permitted to meet as often as necessary.

The Council, after very little discussion, adopted these proposals and modified its Rules of Procedure accordingly.[83]

The Standing Committee on Petitions has operated from the tenth session on.[84] Its procedures follow those of the *ad hoc* committee with the exception, of course, that petitions raising general questions are handled in a different manner. The precise procedure to be used was discussed by the committee in connection with one hundred and thirty-one petitions which it had decided "wholly concerned general problems to which the attention of the Council had already been called and on which it had taken decisions or made recommendations." [85] The committee, over Soviet objections, decided that the normal procedure for dealing with petitions would not be applied to these. Instead it prepared a topical index which indicated for each territory concerned the general problems raised, and recommended that the Secretary-General be requested to reply to each of the petitioners "that the problems mentioned had been brought to the attention of the Council . . . in connection with the examination of conditions in the Trust Territories concerned," and to inform the petitioners of what action, if any, the Council had taken on the questions.[86]

Oral Presentations. The Council's Rules of Procedure envisaged a distinction between oral presentation in behalf of a previously submitted written petition and oral petitions. In practice, however, the Council has been concerned primarily with the former. If there is any discernible trend in this connection it is that the Council is becoming somewhat more liberal in permitting oral petitions and presentations—probably due to the practice in the General Assembly's Fourth Committee of hearing petitions from trust territories.

[82] *Ibid.*

[83] *Trusteeship Council, Official Records, Fourteenth Session* (June-July, 1954), p. 13. The vote was 9 in favor, with 3 abstentions.

[84] Members of the Standing Committee are chosen each session, though the principle of rotation is not strictly adhered to. The committee is always composed, however, of 3 administering and 3 nonadministering states.

[85] Standing Committee on Petitions, *Summary Records of the Fourteenth, Sixteenth, Nineteenth,* and *Twentieth Meetings* (May 19, 20, 22, June 2, 1952), United Nations Document T/C.2/SR.14, 16, 19, 20.

[86] Standing Committee on Petitions, *Eighth Report* (June 3, 1952), United Nations Document T/L.268, pp. 1-2.

The Council has, in general, divided along administering versus non-administering state lines in interpreting its Rules of Procedure with respect to oral petitioning. The former have argued that appearing before the Council was a privilege to be granted by the Council only in special circumstances. Thus while the administering authorities concerned (France and the United Kingdom) were perfectly willing to grant an oral hearing to a representative of the Ewe people [87] concerning the possible unification of those people under a single administering authority, the British delegate distinguished this case sharply from the request of a Mr. Fortis, a resident of the United States, to be heard in connection with his petition concerning Tanganyika.[88] The latter request, the British representative argued, "should not be recognized because it was a petition presented by a person who had no direct relations with the Trust Territories. The Council should confine the right to oral presentation to persons residing in the Trust Territories or in close relation to the Territories." [89]

Representatives of the nonadministering states, on the other hand, argued that making oral presentations was not a privilege, but a right. Thus the Mexican delegate asserted that the reasoning of the British delegate in the case of Mr. Fortis's request was "not in accordance with the principles of the Charter," since the criterion of residence was nowhere stated as a prerequisite to oral presentations.[90] He argued that the substance of the petitions alone should be the determining factor in the Council's decision. The Soviet delegate went even further. His position was that if the Council agreed to examine a petition "it could not refuse the petitioner the right to be heard." [91]

The Council rejected Mr. Fortis's request [92] and, in general, while all members of the Council have been willing to accept the criterion of "substance" in principle, the granting of an oral hearing has been restricted to those petitioners whose requests raise important general questions in the territories—recognized as such by the administering authorities concerned—and who will be greatly affected by the settlement of those questions.

After the creation of the *ad hoc* committee the Council adopted the

[87] *Trusteeship Council, Official Records, Second Session: First Part* (November-December, 1947), p. 48. The petition involved is United Nations Document T/Pet.6/5, T/Pet.7/6. The twofold document number indicates the petition concerns two territories, in this case both the Togolands.

[88] United Nations Document T/Pet.2/40 and Add.1. The petition alleged that several of the administering authority's policies and practices in Tanganyika were "inimical to the interests of the indigenous inhabitants."

[89] *Trusteeship Council, Official Records, Third Session* (June-August, 1948), p. 21.

[90] *Ibid.*, p. 22.

[91] *Ibid.*, p. 23.

[92] *Ibid.*, p. 29. The vote was 4 against, 3 in favor, with 3 abstentions.

practice of submitting to the committee requests for oral hearings not agreed to by the administering authorities concerned. The idea behind this was that the committee, in considering the substance of the written petition involved, could recommend appropriate action to the Council.[93] This practice has been followed with respect to the Standing Committee as well.

When a petitioner is heard by the Council, the practice has been to allow him to give an opening statement after which various members of the Council may submit questions. In one instance, the Council heard five petitioners, representing various shades of opinion on the same question.[94] This might prove to be an important precedent with respect to the possibility of increasing the degree of native participation in Council activities, but at present it is impossible to forecast with certainty on this point.

Council Action on Petitions. As was the case with regard to the *ad hoc* committee on petitions, the Council invariably accepts the recommendations of its Standing Committee. If any generalization can be made about these recommendations it is that the action they call for is extremely mild. In the case of petitions raising general questions which are regularly considered by the Council in connection with its examination of annual reports and reports of its visiting missions, the Council uniformly calls the attention of the petitioner to this procedure, and informs him of such decisions as the Council has made in connection with the reports.

With respect to petitions raising specific questions, the most the Council does is to recommend that the administering authority concerned review its policy or actions with regard to the petitioner(s) in a spirit of leniency. Very often the Council merely refers to the observations of the administering authority and decides that no action is called for. Occasionally it will direct a visiting mission to investigate a matter raised in a petition. This policy of mild recommendations has not, of course, been acceptable to all members of the Council. The Soviet delegate particularly has continually pressed for more strongly worded resolutions. For example the *Fourth Report* [95] of the Standing Committee on Petitions, containing recommendations on six petitions from Somaliland, proposed that the Council decided that no action was called for in the case of three, called for additional information from the administering authority on two, and concluded that the matter raised in one was within the competence of the local courts. The Soviet delegate on the committee, however, voted against all these recommendations on the grounds that they

[93] *Trusteeship Council, Official Records, Seventh Session* (June-July, 1950), pp. 19-21.

[94] *Ibid.*, pp. 147-59, 161-72, 173-80.

[95] United Nations Document T/L.257 (March 28, 1952).

did "not take into consideration the interests of the indigenous inhabitants and do not recommend the Administering Authority to take urgent measures to satisfy the requests of the petitioners and to put an end to the violation of the rights and interests of the indigenous population." [96]

In spite of these objections, there are good reasons why Council resolutions on petitions at most "invite" [97] the administering authorities to review their policy rather than "demand" that certain steps be taken. In the first place, if there is a direct conflict in the reporting of the factual situation the Council, in the absence of other evidence, has no other choice but to accept the word of the administering authority. If it did not it would, in effect, be questioning the honesty of one of its members. This explains why so many times a Council resolution will read to the effect that having noted the observations of the administering authority concerned on the petition, the Council decides that no action is called for.[98]

Secondly, viewing the matter in broader perspective, the Council can never afford to forget the cooperative basis on which it is organized. As with annual reports and visiting missions, it would be of little avail for the Council to chastise an administering authority only to produce a recalcitrant attitude on the part of the latter. In the last analysis the trusteeship provisions of the Charter can be implemented only to the extent that the administering authorities concur. This does not mean that the nonadministering states on the Council should not, or do not, press the administering states to take action on matters raised in petitions. It does mean, however, that the latter can be pressed only so far, and Council resolutions going beyond that point would not only be valueless—they would also tend to break down the cooperative spirit so necessary to effective Council operation. Whether some of the nonadministering states like it or not, there can be no trusteeship system without administering authorities.

One development in the direction of making the right of petition more effective came as the result of a General Assembly request that the Council consider the possibility of asking the administering authorities to

[96] *Ibid.*, p. 1.

[97] It should be noted that "invite" in diplomatic language has more of the connotation of "request" than it has in ordinary usage. Thus a Council "invitation" is somewhat stronger than a personal "invitation."

[98] For example, a petitioner claimed (United Nations Document T/Pet.11/48) that two applications for compensation from the administering authority (Italy), for the loss of a leg suffered while on duty as a *gendarme,* had been ignored. The administering authority observed (United Nations Document T/959) that there was no evidence that the petitioner had in fact ever filed an application. On this basis the Council decided that no action was called for. *Ibid.*, p. 8.

furnish special information on action taken by them on Council recommendations concerning petitions.[99] As a result, beginning with its tenth session, the Council, on the recommendation of its Standing Committee on Petitions, has made such requests where it felt the question raised in a petition warranted it, although so far these have been confined to requests for additional information on questions for which the Council feels there is not sufficient information to enable it to reach a conclusion.

The Role of the Visiting Missions. As noted above, the visiting missions have been the recipients of an increasing number of petitions. Some of these are investigated while the missions are in the territories,[100] but in so far as the missions consider petitions on the spot they are faced with the same problems as the Council. As a result the committee on the examination of petitions [101] recommended, and the Council adopted, the policy of empowering the visiting missions to classify communications in the same manner as the Council. One problem which remained unsolved, however, was the fact that visiting missions were continually flooded with communications—to the point where their itinerary did not permit adequate, on the spot investigations of many petitions. As a result the 1952 mission to West Africa suggested that in the future "fixed periods should be set aside at regular intervals . . . for the primary purpose of enabling each mission to review the communications and other information it has received . . . and to carry out necessary investigations into the more important petitions." [102] The Council, without objection, adopted these proposals thereafter requesting visiting missions "to consider the suggestions" when arranging their itineraries.[103]

In some respects the visiting mission plays the leading role in the disposition of many petitions. This results from the fact that the missions can investigate firsthand not only the questions raised in petitions submitted directly to them, but also those questions raised in other petitions about which the Council has some doubt. In other words, the visiting missions are capable of furnishing the "other evidence," in the absence of which the Council has no choice but to accept the administering authority's word on a matter. Thus the terms of reference for missions often direct them to investigate questions raised in petitions, as well as

[99] See above, p. 165.

[100] See below, pp. 186-88.

[101] This was the committee appointed at the tenth session of the Council whose report (United Nations Document T/L.234) was discussed above.

[102] Report of the United Nations Visiting Mission to Trust Territories in West Africa, 1952, on procedures of visiting missions. United Nations Document T/1044 and Corr. 1.

[103] *Trusteeship Council, Official Records, Twelfth Session* (June-July, 1953), p. 338.

to investigate those petitions received by it which the missions feel warrant such investigation.[104]

The missions' comments on petitions serve, of course, as the best objective analysis of the actual situation, and as such are important to the Council. For example, during the tenth session of the Council, the Standing Committee on Petitions considered a petition from Chinese residents of New Guinea [105] asking that the Council investigate their status as aliens in the territory with a view to requesting the administering authority (Australia) to grant them the right of permanent residence. At the time, the petitioners were residing in New Guinea under immigration exemption due to expire shortly.

The administering authority commented [106] that the whole matter of immigration was under examination, but decisions had not as yet been made. The visiting mission to the territories in the Pacific, however, had observed [107] that there existed possibilities for real hardship on many Chinese residents of New Guinea, particularly the petitioners, and suggested that the administering authority "review the matter of immigration as a whole in a sympathetic spirit."

Had there been no mission comments on the petitions, the Council might well have satisfied itself with noting that the administering authority was studying the matter, and deciding that no further action was called for. As it was, however, the Committee recommended, and the Council adopted, a resolution providing, *inter alia*, that the Council

> *Recommends* that the Administering Authority grant further immigration exemptions to the petitioners . . . before or at the expiration of their present exemptions and pending a decision on their application for permanent residence;
>
> *Requests* the Administering Authority to inform the Trusteeship Council, in its next annual report, of the results of its examination of the questions raised in the petition and of action taken or being taken thereon. . . .[108]

Whether or not the provision in the Charter for petitioning under the trusteeship system has been fully implemented is difficult to say. Certainly

[104] For example, the terms of reference for the second visiting mission to West Africa directed the mission to "give attention . . . to issues raised . . . in petitions received by the Trusteeship Council relating to those Trust Territories in West Africa," and "to investigate on the spot, after consultation with the local representative of the Administering Authorities concerned, such petitions received, as in its opinion, warrant special investigation." *Official Records of the Eleventh Session of the Trusteeship Council, Resolutions*, pp. 2-3. Resolution 465 (XI).

[105] United Nations Document T/Pet.8/4 and Add. 1 and 2.

[106] United Nations Document T/859.

[107] United Nations Document T/791.

[108] *Trusteeship Council, Official Records, Tenth Session* (February-April, 1952), p. 176. *Official Records of the Tenth Session of the Trusteeship Council, Resolutions*, pp. 4-5. Resolution 438 (X).

the Council has not proved to be a sort of international court of appeals with special jurisdiction over the trust territories, as at least one member of the Council apparently would like to have it. Is the right, then, meaningful for the inhabitants of the trust territories? Certainly the requests by petitioners for the transfer of problems from the Council to the General Assembly indicates that in the eyes of some petitioners the answer to this question is "no." On the other hand, it seems unreasonable to expect the Council—in view of the basis on which it was organized—to attempt to redress any and all alleged grievances brought to its attention. It is perhaps not the petitioners' fault that they do not fully understand the voluntary nature of trusteeship—but it is not the Council's fault either.

The real value of petitioning would seem not to be along the lines of specific redress of grievances. Rather its value is that of providing a channel through which native viewpoints can reach the Council. Thus, when a number of petitions from a territory emphasize the inadequacy of some particular aspect of administration—say, education—it is reasonable to suppose that the Council should give special attention to this in its examination of the conditions in the territory, as, in fact, it does.

It is in this more general representation of the views of the indigenous inhabitants that petitions serve their most useful purpose. Seen in this light, petitions provide the natural counterpart of the administering authorities' annual reports.

CHAPTER EIGHT

Visiting Missions

The Council is "dealing now with a question of real and fundamental importance. We are turning new ground, and we will all do well to ponder, and ponder if necessary at length, to ensure that we turn that ground carefully and properly, and that the furrow is straight. It is new ground and it is delicate ground." [1] So spoke Sir Carl Berendsen of New Zealand when the Council first began to consider rules of procedure to govern visiting missions. His words were certainly true in respect to visiting missions as compared with annual reports and petitions for, while the League of Nations Council sent out one or two investigatory commissions to mandated territories, the Permanent Mandates Commission did not. While there was nothing in the Covenant or the Constitution of the Commission which prevented it from using this device, the weight of opinion on both the Council and Commission was against it.[2] The chief argument against the idea in the Commission was that such visits would create unnecessary difficulties for the administration in the territory. As Lord Lugard said: "it was impossible for the Commission to adopt the policy of challenging the whole administration of any mandatory Power by visiting the territory in order to listen to all who criticised it. Such a course would be a signal for trouble." [3]

At San Francisco the American draft of suggestions for trusteeship included the idea of empowering the Trusteeship Council "to institute investigations." While none of the proposals submitted by mandatory powers to the conference contained a similar provision, those states acquiesced in the idea, subject only to a change of wording to: "make periodic visits at times agreed upon with the administering state." [4] Thus Article 87 of the Charter reads, in part: "The General Assembly, and under its authority, the Trusteeship Council, in carrying out their functions, may . . . provide for periodic visits to the respective trust territories at times agreed upon with the administering authority. . . ." With regard to strategic areas, of course, the Security Council, with the as-

[1] *Trusteeship Council, Official Records, First Year, First Session* (March-April, 1947), p. 41.

[2] Hall, p. 204.

[3] *Minutes of the Permanent Mandates Commission, Seventh Session* (1925), p. 128.

[4] See above, p. 36.

sistance of the Trusteeship Council, provides for these visits subject to the limitation that "the extent of its applicability to any areas closed for security reasons" may be determined by the administering authority.[5] All trusteeship agreements provide for visiting missions either by repeating the substance of Article 87 of the Charter, or by referring to it.

The draft rules of procedure for the Council, prepared by the Preparatory Commission, contained four rules relating to visiting missions. In substance these provided that (1) the Council could make provision for periodic visits "for information or enquiries or for any other purposes within the Charter;" (2) the Council must give one month's prior notice to an administering authority of its intention to send a mission; in case of disagreement the exact time of the visit would be decided by the President of the Council and the administering authority concerned; (3) the Council could designate the members of the missions who should "preferably be from among non-nationals of the administering authority;" it could also avail itself of the services of experts; (4) the Council could conduct special investigations to the extent provided in any trusteeship agreement; and (5) the Council should publish the findings of each mission unless "in the general interest" it should decide to postpone publication temporarily. When the Council, in formulating its own rules of procedure, discussed these provisions it made several important modifications in, as well as additions to, the Preparatory Commission's proposals.

The first of these concerned the provision that visiting missions could be made for any purpose under the Charter. Some of the representatives of administering authorities argued that such a rule was much too broad and dangerously vague in scope. Thus the New Zealand delegate stated that the phrase in question "really goes too far. It must surely be confined to any other purpose within the Charter relating to the Trusteeship Council. I suggest that this Council has no authority at all to go beyond the purposes of the Trusteeship Council."[6] There was general acceptance of this view, and the rule was modified to read that visits to the territories would be made "with a view to achieving the basic objectives of the International Trusteeship System."

The second modification concerned the sending of special missions to the territories. At the outset of the discussion on this provision, the Australian representative suggested deleting it altogether since the Council, should the occasion arise, would be competent to insert such a rule in its procedure; and in any case none of the trusteeship agreements provided for special missions.[7] The Council, however, by an informal show of

[5] The quotation is taken from the agreement for the Trust Territory of the Pacific, under U.S. administration, United Nations Document S/318.

[6] *Trusteeship Council, Official Records, First Year, First Session* (March-April, 1947), p. 443.

[7] *Ibid.*, pp. 454-55.

hands, decided to formulate some rule on the subject. Rather than accept the Preparatory Commission's proposal, though, the Council adopted a substitute rule submitted by the American representative, modified by the Chinese delegate, omitting any reference to the trusteeship agreements and providing simply that the Trusteeship Council might "in agreement with the administering authority, conduct special investigations and enquiries. . . .[8] This assured the acceptance of the idea of special missions, while at the same time assuring the administering authorities that no special mission would be sent in contravention of their wishes.

The third change involved the publication of the visiting missions' reports. Concerning this proposed rule, the New Zealand delegate inquired "whether in publishing these reports we should not arrange to publish at the same time any comment on them which the Administering Authority may wish to make. I suggest that that might be an advantage, and that we might be able to meet that situation by inserting the words 'in consultation with the Administering Authority' before the word 'publish'." [9] By accepting this the Council would have permitted the administering authority concerned to participate actively in the formulation of visiting mission reports on each territory. The representatives of both Iraq and Mexico were very dubious about this suggestion. In the words of the Iraq delegate, the reports were those of the Council alone. "They have nothing to do with the Administering Authority, except of course that the territory is theirs in trust and we have visited it. I cannot see, therefore, how it could be justified that when we have visited a Trust Territory and have come to a conclusion, we have to consult the Administering Authority before we publish our report. It is our report, and I think such a procedure as suggested by the New Zealand representative would be going far beyond our mandate as a Council." [10] As a compromise between the New Zealand suggestion and the opposition voiced by the representatives of Iraq and Mexico, the British delegate suggested that the reports be published "together with any observations by the Administering Authority and by the Council." [11] This recognized that the reports were those of the Council, solely, at the same time providing the administering authorities an opportunity to submit written comments on those reports. This was acceptable to the Council generally and the rule was changed accordingly.

The fourth modification of the rules of procedure concerning visiting missions dealt with the question of membership of the missions. The specific issue was: would the mission members be individuals appointed by

[8] *Ibid.*, 456-61.
[9] *Ibid.*, p. 469.
[10] *Ibid.*, p. 471.
[11] *Ibid.*

and responsible to the Trusteeship Council, or would the Council designate governments who in turn would each appoint a qualified individual? Speaking against the first principle, the representative of Iraq argued (1) that the Council could not so restrict members of the Council, forcing them to send particular individuals; (2) that a given person might be needed by his government in a different capacity and "this would present us with a difficulty." [12] He therefore urged that as a matter of principle members of the visiting missions should be Council members—who in turn would appoint individual representatives—and not particular individuals. In opposition to this, the representatives of China stated:

> I think I start from a premise that is somewhat different from that which motivated my colleague from Iraq. As I see it, a visiting mission is really representative of the Council. The visiting mission is sent to a Trust Territory by the Council to investigate and inquire into certain things which the Council wants to know. Therefore, I think the mission does not represent any Government; it represents the Council. For that reason, I think it is wise to make the personnel of that mission a choice of the Council rather than individual Governments. That mission will be responsible not to any individual Government but to the Council. It will have to report back to the Council. Therefore, I am inclined to think that the members should be chosen on their personal merit and competence.[13]

In this connection, the same delegate urged further that a clause be inserted providing that all expenses for the visiting missions be borne by the United Nations and not the individual states whose nationals were members of the mission.[14] In the ensuing discussion there was manifest agreement on the principles espoused by the Chinese representative, as well as the further principle that individuals appointed should preferably be one or more representatives on the Council. This, as well as the proposals of the Chinese representative, were incorporated into the rules.

The draft rules of procedure drawn up by the Preparatory Commission omitted any specific reference to the terms of reference of the visiting missions. The Secretariat, however, proposed the following rule in its draft: "The Trusteeship Council shall define the terms of reference of each visiting mission and shall give to the members of the mission such special instructions as it may consider appropriate." [15] The Belgian delegate suggested that this should be modified to the extent of providing that the terms of reference should be defined by the Council "in agreement with the Administering Power." His principal argument for this modification was based on the fact that in some cases (Ruanda-Urundi, for in-

[12] *Ibid.*, pp. 438-39.

[13] *Ibid.*, p. 440.

[14] An American proposal on the subject had provided for the latter. *Ibid.*, p. 438.

[15] United Nations Document T/4, Rule 92.

stance) the trusteeship agreements provided for joint (that is, Council—administering authority) discussion on terms of reference.[16]

Opposed to this suggestion, the Mexican delegate declared that the Charter provided for consultation with the administering authorities only on the time of the visit. Hence the Belgian proposal would be unduly restrictive on the Council.[17] While it was true that this would seem to contradict the terms of the agreement for Ruanda-Urundi, it was conceivable that future agreements might not contain such a restriction. The obvious compromise, suggested by the American representative, was to provide that the terms of reference should be drawn up by the Council "in accordance with the respective trusteeship agreements." [18] This was acceptable to all the members of the Council, and the rule was adopted in that form.

The discussion on the rules of procedure concerning visiting missions again shows the tendency for the administering authorities to protect themselves against what they might consider undue interference by the Council, while the nonadministering states attempted to insure as much Council supervisory powers as possible. The discussion also illustrates that by compromise it is possible to work out decisions satisfactory—or at least acceptable—to almost all members of the Council. It cannot be too often emphasized that it is in this spirit—and it might be said, this spirit alone—that real progress can be made in the implementation of the Charter provisions for trusteeship.

Before the Council considered the problems connected with sending out its first regular mission it sent one special mission to investigate a specific question, as provided in the Rules of Procedure. At its first session the Council received a petition from certain local leaders of Western Samoa requesting that that territory be granted self-government, with the advice of and under the protection of New Zealand. It further requested that the division of Samoa into its present component parts [19] be temporarily "left in abeyance." The petition thus raised the fundamental question of terminating the trusteeship for the territory. Sir Carl Berendsen, the New Zealand representative on the Council, pointed to this and therefore asked the Council to investigate the matter on the spot before

[16] *Trusteeship Council, Official Records, First Year, First Session* (March-April, 1947), pp. 435-36.

[17] *Ibid.*, p. 435.

[18] *Ibid.*, p. 436.

[19] By a treaty of December 2, 1899, Samoa was divided into East and West components under the respective jurisdiction of the United States and Germany. During the first world war, New Zealand forces occupied German Samoa, and following the war the territory was mandated to New Zealand. The United States has remained in control of Eastern Samoa. Samuel Flagg Bemis, *A Diplomatic History of the United States,* (Revised Edition), p. 474.

any final decision was reached. The Council agreed and proceeded to consider the establishment of a mission for that purpose.[20]

While at least one member of the Council (the representative of Belgium) felt that the mission to be created should be the first of the regular visiting missions, there was general agreement that it should be a special body, instructed to report on the specific question raised by the petition. After some discussion a committee was appointed to "formulate recommendations for the consideration of the Trusteeship Council" with regard to the proposed terms of reference of the mission.[21] The committee recommended [22] that the mission be composed of three members: two from the Council, the other an expert on colonial administration from a nonadministering state not represented on the Council. The committee further recommended that another committee be set up to select the actual members of the mission. There was a good deal of debate on this last recommendation, some members of the Council feeling that the actual selection of the members of the mission was a job for the Council itself. The issue was compromised by the establishment of a committee of nine—that is, all the Council members present.[23]

The terms of reference directed the mission to "(1) investigate the petition . . . and (2) to visit Western Samoa for this purpose and remain in the Territory for a sufficient period to ascertain all the relevant facts and to report back to the Council. . . ." [24]

The mission visited Western Samoa during July and August, 1947, and reported back to the Council during the first part of its second session (November 20-December 16, 1947). It recommended [25] a number of changes in the administration of Western Samoa by which the indigenous inhabitants of that area would achieve a greater measure of self-government, but did not advocate the termination of the trust at that time. The Council, acting on the mission's report, resolved that "the people of

[20] *Trusteeship Council, Official Records, First Year, First Session* (March-April, 1947), pp. 547-58.

[21] *Ibid.*, p. 564. *Resolution Adopted by the Trusteeship Council During its First Session*, p. 3. Resolution 3. The committee consisted of representatives from France, Mexico, the United Kingdom, and the United States.

[22] *Ibid.*, p. 575-76.

[23] *Ibid.*, p. 612.

[24] *Resolutions Adopted by the Trusteeship Council During its First Session*, p. 3. Resolution 4. The committee of 9 recommended the appointment of Mr. Francis Sayre (United States), Mr. Pierre Ryckmans (Belgium), and Mr. Awni Khalidy (Iraq) to the mission. While this did not follow the prior decision to include the national of a nonmember state, the committee also recommended that mission members could be accompanied by experts. Subsequently Dr. Cruz-Coke of Chile (not a Council member) substituted for Mr. Khalidy who found it impossible to take part in the mission. *United Nations Weekly Bulletin*, Vol. 2 (1947), pp. 661-62.

[25] United Nations Document T/46.

Western Samoa should be accorded such measure of self-government as indicated in the report of the . . . mission," and that they be accorded increasing responsibilities in self-government pending the attainment of full self-government "as soon as they are capable of assuming the responsibilities involved." [26]

The Council, in creating this special mission, discussed two points which are significant in view of the debates surrounding the establishment of the various periodic missions. The first concerned the question of whether or not members of the mission were to be states or private individuals. Even though this had apparently been settled during consideration of the Rules of Procedure the question was again raised by the Belgian representative, and was answered by the President, Francis B. Sayre of the United States, to the effect that individuals, not states, would be mission members. This ruling was accepted by the Council with no apparent disagreement at the time. It was to arise later, however, and the decision here is important as a precedent for the regular visiting missions. The second matter was the question of experts. While many of the members of the Council were in favor of choosing experts in colonial administration the representative of Iraq pointed to long and unfortunate experience with commissions of experts in the Middle East. The matter was resolved by providing that while at least two of the members of the mission would be Council members, they could be assisted by recognized experts.[27]

Other than this the Council's action with regard to Western Samoa had no particular significance for the later visiting missions, since it was generally agreed that it would not in any way create precedents—although it did in the two instances noted above—with respect to the regular missions. The action by the Council does demonstrate, though, the value of providing for special missions. It would have been obviously very difficult, if not impossible, for the Council to reach a fair decision of the question raised by the petition in the absence of on-the-spot investigation. Regular visiting missions must deal with conditions in the territories generally, rather than with a specific issue, and since time has proved to be of the essence with these missions, it seems a good idea for the Council to have established the precedent of sending a special mission in a case like this. The question raised certainly warranted it. To date no other special missions have been sent out; [28] specific questions have been investigated by the regular missions where the Council felt special reference to them was necessary. It seems likely that the special missions will be reserved for

[26] *Trusteeship Council, Official Records, Second Session: First Part* (November-December, 1947), p. 274, *Resolutions Adopted by the Trusteeship Council During its Second Session*, pp. 2-3. Resolution 13 (II).

[27] See above, p. 176.

[28] See, however, below, pp. 234-35.

fundamental questions such as a request for the termination or transfer of a trusteeship—and, for questions such as these, the device seems admirably suited.

While the Rules of Procedure adopted by the Council laid the basis for the sending of periodic missions and settled many questions concerning them, much was left either vague or unsaid, and remained to be implemented when the Council actually began sending the missions. In general the procedure involved consists of four major steps: (1) deciding when and where the mission is to go; (2) deciding the composition of the mission; (3) drafting the terms of reference for the mission; and (4) considering the report of the mission.

Where and When to Go. The Charter and the Rules of Procedure provide for periodic visits to the trust territories. How often is "periodic"? Considerations such as the availability of members, the willingness of the administering authorities to receive missions, availability of funds, and the location of the trust territory all combined to produce a Council decision that the territories would, for the purpose of sending visiting missions, be divided into three groups: East Africa (Tanganyika, Ruanda-Urundi, and Somaliland) and West Africa (the Cameroons and the Togolands) and the Pacific. One mission is sent each year to one of the areas. Thus each territory is visited regularly every three years.[29] That decided, it remained for the Council to determine which general area to start with. This was done by the simple expedient of the delegate from the United Kingdom suggesting, with the concurrence of the Belgian representative, that the first mission be sent to East Africa.[30] The second mission was sent to West Africa, the third to the Pacific, and since that time the Council has followed this system of rotation. Other than the desire not to have a mission conflict with Council sessions in timing, the major consideration as to what period an individual mission will spend in a territory, is, in the case of the African territories, weather. In connection with the first mission to East Africa, for example, while some members of the Council desired the mission to leave immediately (winter, 1947-48) and thus be able to report to the Council at its next session, the administering authorities concerned pointed out that if this were done the mission would be visiting the territories during the rainy season which would severely handicap its functioning. July through October being the dry season of the year in the area, the British and Belgian representatives suggested that time for the mission's visit, and in the end this was adopted by the Council.[31]

[29] *Trusteeship Council, Official Records, First Year, First Session* (March-April, 1947), pp. 703-29.

[30] *Trusteeship Council, Official Records, Seventh Session* (June-July, 1950), p. 259.

[31] *Ibid.*, p. 566.

Experience of the first three regular missions showed that one of the chief problems was proving to be that the members of the missions often felt they did not cover enough ground in the areas. At the seventh session of the Council the suggestion was made that two visiting missions be sent to East Africa.[32] This, however, was not adopted, the chief arguments against it being the expense involved, the unavailability of Council members, and the fact that there was nothing to prevent one mission from temporarily dividing, each part then concentrating on a separate area. The latter practice has been employed subsequently, and to date no more than one mission at a time has been sent to any of the three general areas.

The Composition of the Missions. The discussion in the Council over the Rules of Procedure with respect to the visiting mission had apparently settled the principle that the missions were to be composed of individuals rather than states, such persons to be responsible to the Council and not their respective governments. The Soviet representative had not been present at that time, however, and when the Council, at its third session, discussed the sending of its first mission, that delegate took exception to this decision. He argued that the Council itself was composed of states and that logically its visiting missions should be constituted in the same way.[33] This interpretation was again rejected by the Council,[34] but in practice the issue seems to have been compromised. The position of the Council when it actually came to appointing members was delicate. It was generally accepted that in so far as possible a mission's composition should include members of the Council, thereby providing them with firsthand contact with the territories. Suppose, then, that the Council refused to accept a representative on the Council as a member of a mission? This would obviously cause at least embarrassment, at most a breakdown in the cooperative spirit so necessary to that body's efficient functioning. Or suppose the actual member himself could not join the mission. It might well be embarrassing if the Council were then to choose a national of some other state. If the replacement were to come from the same state, how would the Council know the best man to pick? The Council, with these considerations in mind, has developed the practice of letting individual states nominate their representatives for visiting missions, while reserving to itself the final approval. Since disapproval of any nomination would naturally produce embarrassment, this approval is, in effect, largely formal. Thus while members of the mission are private persons, they are nominated by the governments concerned, and the Council selection of the composition of the mission is actually one of states rather than indi-

[32] *Trusteeship Council, Official Records, Seventh Session* (June-July, 1950), p. 259.
[33] *Trusteeship Council, Official Records, Third Session* (June-August, 1948), p. 215.
[34] *Ibid.*, pp. 215-20.

viduals. This is further borne out by the fact that on every mission there has been an equal division of members from administering and nonadministering states.[35]

In connection with this last point the Council was called upon to consider a recommendation by members of the General Assembly that for its second and succeeding missions, the composition should include: "one representative of an Administering Authority, one representative of a non-administering member of the Council, and one representative of a Member of the United Nations not represented on the Council." [36] This would, of course, have meant that the compositon of the mission would reflect a two to one ratio as between nonadminstering and administering states. As might be expected the administering authorities reacted rather strongly against this suggestion,[37] and the Council has not adopted it. Nor has it yet accepted the suggestion of the Mexican representative that representatives of the specialized agencies be appointed to the missions.[38] The predominant feeling has been that since the size of the missions must be limited, all members of missions should be members of the Council so as to make sure that as many members as possible see the conditions in as many trust territories as possible.[39]

The size of the missions has been largely determined by two factors: expense and the difficulties in connection with the missions' functioning in the territories. That is, not only have the missions been limited in size by the availability of funds, but the physical conditions in the territories in many instances do not permit a large party to function adequately. To take an extreme example, the representative of Australia on the Council pointed out that while the administering authority in Nauru would welcome a mission, if more than a few persons arrived they would have to sleep outdoors since there were few enclosures on the islands. Moreover, he would not be responsible for more than a small mission in the case of New Guinea, both in terms of comfort and physical danger.[40] While

[35] At the third session the representative of Iraq urged that the mission to East Africa include a majority of members from nonadministering states. This proposal was rejected. *Ibid.*, p. 220.

[36] *Trusteeship Council, Official Records, Fourth Session* (January-March, 1949), p. 57. The proposal, a suggestion of the Indian delegate, may be found in United Nations Document T/230.

[37] *Trusteeship Council, Official Records, Fourth Session* (January-March, 1949), pp. 57-59.

[38] *Ibid.*, p. 59.

[39] The feeling of the Council on this point was summed up by the American representative: "it was . . . essential that each member of the Council should have an opportunity of visiting and getting to know for himself at least one of the territories in which the Trusteeship System functioned." *Ibid.*, p. 51.

[40] *Trusteeship Council, Official Records, Second Session: First Part* (November-December, 1947), p. 119.

conditions in the other territories are doubtless better in this connection, none apparently are able to handle a large group with any degree of efficiency. Consequently the missions have consistently been composed of four members of the Council, with sufficient aids from the Secretariat and local clerical help bringing the number to around a dozen.

While never explicitly recognizing it as a principle, the Council has adopted the policies of rotation and seniority for membership on the missions. Thus, France, China, Australia, and Costa Rica were represented on the first mission, the second mission was composed of nationals of the United States, Belgium, Iraq, and Mexico, and the third, of nationals of France, China, the Philippines and the United Kingdom. If the Council member himself cannot serve, the practice has been to have him, after consultation with his government, suggest a substitute for Council approval.[41] In the case of a substitution being proposed while the Council is not in session, the President has been authorized to approve the new appointee.[42]

With regard to the equality of representation as between administering and nonadministering states on the missions, the representatives of France, during the second session of the Council, took the position that the administering authorities concerned should be represented on each mission. The argument in favor of this suggestion was that the mission would be better able to perform its duties with a member who had a sound knowledge of the conditions in each territory. In opposition it was stated that the local authorities could supply all the needed information thus making unnecessary the member from the administering authority, and further that it would appear bad in the eyes of public opinion if the administering authority should seem to be a judge in its own cause.[43] The latter view was accepted by the Council and, although the national of an administering authority whose territory was to be visited was appointed to one mission, it was with the understanding that he would not accompany the mission to the territory concerned.[44]

A national of the Soviet Union has so far not been a member of any of the visiting missions. When that state's representative on the Council was asked to be a member of the third mission (to the Pacific), he replied that he could not accept,[45] and no substitute nomination was forthcoming.

[41] Mr. Woodbridge of Costa Rica substituted for that state's representative on the Council, Mr. Canas, on the first visiting mission. *Trusteeship Council, Official Records, Third Session* (June-August, 1948), pp. 218, 245.

[42] *Trusteeship Council, Official Records, Fifth Session* (June-July, 1949), pp. 16-17.

[43] *Trusteeship Council, Official Records, Second Session, Second Part, 34th Meeting* (March 17, 1948), United Nations Document T/SR 60, pp. 15-16.

[44] *Trusteeship Council, Official Records, Fifth Session* (June-July, 1949), pp. 257-58.

[45] *Ibid.*, p. 257.

Subsequently the Soviet delegate has taken the position that no administering authority should be represented on any mission [46] and has, apparently, consistently refused to serve as long as the principle of equal representation has been adopted by the Council.

In sum, the visiting missions are uniformly composed of the nationals of four Council members—two administering, two nonadministering states. The Council decides, on the basis of seniority and rotation, what states' nationals should make up the mission's membership, and, after nominations are made by those states, approves the members as individuals responsible collectively to the Council. It has rejected suggestions to weight the mission's membership in favor of nonadministering states' nationals or to ask members of specialized agencies to serve. It has also consistently refused to appoint a national of a state whose territory is to be visited by the mission, with the one exception noted. In essence, then, the composition of the visiting missions reflects the basic principle of the functioning trusteeship system: equality of representation—which necessitates cooperation between administering and nonadministering states if the Council, and hence the system, is to function adequately.

Terms of Reference. Drafting the terms of reference for each mission has occasioned perhaps more difficulty than any other single aspect of the visiting missions. Broadly, the problem can be stated as the question of how detailed the instructions should be. The administering authorities have consistently urged general terms, leaving a large measure of discretion to the mission itself. The nonadministering states on the Council, on the other hand, have argued for detailed instructions, taking the position that the Council should require the missions to investigate specific problems.

The issue arose during consideration of the terms of reference for the first regular mission, at the third session of the Council. At that time the American representative introduced a draft resolution, the substantive parts of which included two directives to the mission: (1) the mission was to "observe the developing political, economic, social and educational conditions in the Trust Territories . . . their progress toward self-government or independence, and the efforts of the respective Administering Authorities to achieve the other basic objectives of the International Trusteeship System;" (2) the mission was "to give attention, as may be appropriate in the light of discussion in the Trusteeship Council and resolutions adopted by the Council, to issues raised in and in connection with the annual reports . . . and in petitions . . . relating to those Trust Territories." [47] Mr. Sayre, the American delegate, pointed out that these terms were left purposely vague to give the mission wide discretion.

[46] *Trusteeship Council, Official Records, Eighth Session* (January-March, 1951), p. 14.

[47] *Trusteeship Council, Official Records, Third Session* (June-August, 1948), p. 284.

Objections to this vagueness were voiced by representatives of the non-administering states, particularly those of the Soviet Union and the Philippines. The latter proposed two amendments, one to each of the two directives. The first, that the words "this and" should be substituted for the word "the" following "achieve" in the first directive, was accepted by the Council. The second, to add the phrase "and with special reference to," followed by a list of important topics, to the second directive was opposed by all the administering states on the grounds that it placed too great a limitation on the mission's discretion. The argument used by the latter was that in listing some topics, by implication those not listed would not fall within the purview of the mission. When the issue came to a vote there was an even division of administering and nonadministering states so that the Philippine amendment failed of adoption.[48] The American draft, with the one Philippine amendment and minor drafting changes, was thereupon approved.[49]

Representatives of the Soviet Union and the Philippines again raised the question of including specific items for investigation in the missions' terms of reference when the Council, at its fifth session, was considering the terms of reference for its second visiting mission (to West Africa). The former pressed for inclusion of instructions to investigate (1) the extent to which indigenous political parties were active in the political life of the territories, (2) how Charter provisions concerning the development in economic and social fields were being implemented, and (3) questions raised by petitions, including both those received by the mission and those previously submitted to the Council.[50] The Philippine delegate desired only that the mission be directed to investigate on-the-spot petitions received by the mission which it felt were sufficiently important to warrant such special consideration.[51] These proposals were in the form of amendments to the draft resolution on the terms of reference for the mission (drawn up by the Secretariat), the draft being similar with one exception to the one adopted for the first mission. While the Philippine amendment was adopted, the Soviet proposals were rejected.[52] Again the argument of the desirability of vagueness in the terms of reference was used, this time backed up by the assertion that the general terms used for the first mission had proved adequate.[53] The chief difference in the terms of reference as between the first and second visiting missions, in addition

[48] *Ibid.*, p. 289. The vote was 6 to 6.

[49] *Ibid.*, pp. 289-90. The vote was 11 in favor, with 1 abstention.

[50] *Trusteeship Council, Official Records, Fifth Session* (June-July, 1949), pp. 21-23, 25.

[51] *Ibid.*, p. 24.

[52] *Ibid.*, pp. 25, 28-29.

[53] *Ibid.*, p. 26-27.

to the Philippine amendment, was the inclusion of a reference to specific questions raised in petitions received by the Council.[54] This stemmed from a Council decision with regard to action on petitions, and occasioned no debate at this time.

At its fourth session, the General Assembly adopted a resolution[55] which, *inter alia*, recommended to the Trusteeship Council that it should: "Direct visiting missions to report fully on the steps taken towards the realization of the objectives set forth in Article 76b of the Charter, under the headings of political, economic, social and educational advancement, and in particular, on the steps taken towards self-government or independence." When the Secretariat submitted draft terms of reference for the first mission to the Pacific Islands to the Council at its sixth session, it included a paragraph incorporating the substance of this resolution.[56] The administering authorities did not at all like the special emphasis placed on "steps taken towards self-government or independence," and suggested deleting everything after the reference to Article 76b of the Charter. Some of the nonadministering states, however, took the position that if the complete phraseology were not included in the terms of reference the Trusteeship Council would be showing a lack of respect for the General Assembly. The representative of China, for example, argued that the Council was not at liberty to give the visiting mission instructions "as far removed from the General Assembly resolution as those suggested by the representative of the United Kingdom" (i.e., accepting the deletion mentioned above). The discussion pointed to an eventual deadlock on the issue until the Belgian delegate introduced a compromise. This was to the effect that the visiting mission should "take into account the desire expressed by the General Assembly in its Resolution." The Argentine delegate agreed to this if "the desire expressed by" were deleted. To the combined Argentine-Belgian proposal most of the Council members agreed. Further discussion was postponed, however, pending informal consultation. The informal consultation produced no further agreement, and when the Council again resumed discussion of the question a Dominican Republic proposal encompassing the substance of the Belgian-Argentine proposal was passed over the objections of both the Philippine and Argentine representatives.[57] Thus the final terms of the paragraph involved were: "*Directs* the Visiting Mission to investigate and to report as fully as possible on the steps taken in the four above-mentioned Trust Territories

[54] See above, p. 170.

[55] *Official Records of the Fourth Session of the General Assembly, Resolutions*, p. 38. Resolution 321 (IV).

[56] United Nations Document T/451.

[57] *Trusteeship Council, Official Records, Fourth Year, Sixth Session* (January-April, 1950), pp. 56-58.

towards the realization of the objectives set forth in Article 76b of the Charter, taking into account the terms of the General Assembly resolution 321 (IV) of 15 November 1949. . . ." [58]

The issue was not completely settled, however, for following its regular procedure the Council still had to consider the resolution in question when it considered Assembly resolutions generally. When this occurred, later in the sixth session, the delegates from the United States and Iraq submitted a joint draft resolution which "took note of" the Assembly resolution and further noted "that steps have already been taken or are being taken by the Council to carry out [the recommendation]." [59] This, of course, referred to the action taken by the Council in connection with the terms of reference for the mission to the Pacific. The representatives of the Philippines and Argentina now, however, took this opportunity to raise again the question of placing special emphasis on steps taken toward the achievement of self-government or independence by offering a substitute draft resolution by which the Council agreed "to recommend to all Visiting Missions to report fully . . . in particular the steps taken toward self-government or independence." [60] This proposal, after further discussion, was defeated by a tie vote, and the American-Iraq draft adopted.[61]

Even though the proposal to spell out the terms of Article 76b of the Charter and lay special emphasis on self-government or independence was defeated, the inclusion of the directive to report "as fully as possible" on the realization of the objectives of Article 76b marked a significant addition to the terms of reference. Again we see the manifestation of the emphasis on supervision which is characteristic of the position taken by the representatives of nonadministering states on the Council; again we see the reluctance of the administering authorities to "go too far" in the implementation of Charter provisions; we further see the terms of reference growing progressively more specific for each visiting mission.

During its ninth and eleventh sessions the Council considered terms of reference for its second missions to East and West Africa, respectively. In connection with the former, the Soviet representative again introduced the three amendments to the draft terms of reference that he had made when the Council had created its second mission—the first sent to West Africa. Those were again rejected.[62] The draft terms, submitted by the

[58] *Ibid., Resolutions,* p. 1. Resolution 115 (VI).

[59] United Nations Document T/L.7.

[60] United Nations Document T/L.41.

[61] *Trusteeship Council, Official Records, Fourth Year, Sixth Session* (January-April, 1950), p. 589.

[62] *Trusteeship Council, Official Records, Ninth Session* (June-July, 1951), pp. 180-81.

representative of Iraq,[63] were similar to those of previous missions with the exception of an added paragraph calling on the visiting mission to "report on the results achieved up to the present in the provision of information about the United Nations to the peoples of the Trust Territories under resolution 36 (III) . . . and to undertake the duties enumerated in resolution 3111 (VIII) on the same question." This new paragraph was amended by the Council to the extent of substituting the words "examine, in consultation with the Administering Authorities" for "report," and substituting the words "measures taken and to be taken" for "results achieved." In this form the paragraph was included in the terms of reference and passed the Council by unanimous vote, with the Soviet Union abstaining.[64] Essentially the same process occurred at the eleventh session of the Council in connection with the terms of reference for the second visiting mission to West Africa.[65]

So far, then, the principle of general terms of reference, leaving much discretion to the mission, had been adhered to; this has been modified, however, largely as the result of General Assembly resolutions recommending that certain questions be specifically investigated and by Council decisions to the same effect. Even in the case of inclusion of specific items in the terms of reference, though, the instructions are of a general nature, as can be seen by comparing the terms of the draft paragraph submitted by Iraq for the terms of reference for the second visiting mission to East Africa and the terms as finally approved by the Council. What lies behind this issue of general versus specific terms of reference is the more fundamental question of emphasis on supervision as against cooperation. If the purpose of the visiting missions is to "educate" members of the Council—particularly representatives of nonadministering states—in the problems faced by the various administering authorities in their trust territories and thus create more understanding on the Council, then the broad terms of reference are certainly adequate. Specific terms, on the other hand, indicate an emphasis on supervision: the mission is "requested to report on action taken, or the results achieved in connection with" such and such a problem. The divergence of viewpoint is seldom explicitly recognized by members of the Council, but it is there nonetheless. And the discussions surrounding each mission's terms of reference manifest it, as well as show again the development of the trusteeship system is a gradual process of the reconciliation of such divergencies.

Consideration of the Missions' Report. The reports of the missions reveal that their activities in each territory may be described as being in

[63] United Nations Document T/L. 190.

[64] *Trusteeship Council, Official Records, Ninth Session* (June-July, 1951), p. 181.

[65] *Trusteeship Council, Official Records, 453rd Meeting* (22 July, 1952), United Nations Document T/PV.453, pp. 2-3.

the nature of half judge, half jury. On broad questions of policy such as the desirability of administrative unions, the missions report on the existing conditions resulting from a union and leave it to the Council to determine whether the union is justified. On the other hand, the missions have not been reluctant to point out and evaluate the particular effects of a given policy. For example, in the report of the first mission to West Africa, concerning the effects of the administrative union of the Cameroons under British administration with Nigeria, the mission stated: "The fact that the economy of the Trust Territory and its finances are integrated with those of Nigeria should have no disadvantageous effect on the Territory." [66] Similarly, in the report on New Guinea made by the second mission to the Trust Territories in the Pacific, the mission, reporting on the immigration policies of the administering authority, concluded that "A number of Chinese businesses in New Guinea . . . inevitably face extinction at the death of their owners. The granting of permission for entry of permanent substitutes under such circumstances appears to the Mission to be logical and necessary. The Mission hopes that the Administering Authority will review the matter of immigration as a whole in a sympathetic spirit." [67]

Since each mission operating in a territory is, in effect, a guest of the administering authority, there might be some reason to suppose that too often the investigation would be something in the nature of a guided tour on which the mission members would see only those things favorable to the administration. This possibility is offset, however, by the fact that (1) the missions may receive petitions from the native inhabitants, (2) any attempt by the administering authority to steer a mission clear of "sore spots" would undoubtedly result in a petition to that effect being submitted to the Council, and (3) by dividing itself into two parts, the mission can get off the main track, as it were, and into the local areas for firsthand investigation. To date there has been no complaint by members of the mission against the administering authorities in this regard. On the contrary, it is not uncommon for the mission to compliment the latter on their cooperation with the mission in its work in the territory.

Another possible hindrance to the usefulness of the missions as on-the-spot representatives of Council supervision is the fact that the individual territories are visited regularly only once in three years. This could lead to an attitude on the part of the local authorities of "preening for inspection time" and not worrying very much in the interim. This is apparently

[66] *Trusteeship Council, Official Records, Seventh Session* (June-July, 1950), *Supplement No. 2. Reports of the United Nations Visiting Mission to Trust Territories in West Africa,* p. 17.

[67] *Trusteeship Council, Official Records, Eighth Session* (January-March, 1951), *Supplement No. 4, Reports of the United Nations Visiting Mission to Trust Territories in the Pacific, Report on New Guinea,* p. 18.

not the case, however, for the reason that it is manifestly impossible to "preen" an entire territory unless it is continually kept that way. That is, the various agents of the administering authority working in a territory cannot very well change conditions in their areas overnight in preparation for a mission visit. This is particularly true, again, because the native inhabitants can and do communicate directly with the members of the mission.[68]

The Council has so far faced and answered two questions arising in connection with its consideration of the reports of its visiting missions. Each of these in its own way has again reflected the more fundamental issue of cooperation as against supervision. The first arose during the fourth session when the report of the first visiting mission was submitted to the Council. The Belgian representative strongly urged that consideration of the report be temporarily deferred since neither his government nor that of the United Kingdom had as yet made comments on the report as both were entitled to do under the Rules of Procedure. Representatives of both these states preferred to discuss the report of the mission with the annual reports on the territories, which gave further reasons for delay. The President of the Council, Mr. Liu Chieh (China), however, pointed out that delay would be unfortunate for two reasons. First, this would mean a delay in the consideration of petitions received by the visiting mission. Second, the report itself would lose much of its value if the consideration of it were deferred until the next session. In answer, the Belgian and British representatives agreed to discuss the report provisionally for the purpose of considering matters raised in the petitions.[69] When the Council proceeded to do this, however, a motion by the French representative to defer consideration until the fifth session was adopted.[70] In part to overcome this difficulty the Council has subsequently considered all visiting missions' reports in conjunction with the annual reports on the territories involved.

The second question concerned what action the Council should take after considering a report. When the Council had completed its examination of the first mission's report during its fifth session, the Mexican representative suggested that since the report of the visiting mission was technical in nature the Council should not vote on it. Rather, material in the report, plus recommendations made by the mission, and observations made on the report, should be included in reference documents prepared by the Secretariat for use of the drafting committee in connection with the ex-

[68] This general point was confirmed for the writer in a conversation in November, 1952, with Mr. Henry A. Fosbrooke, Senior Government Sociologist, Tanganyika Territory. Mr. Fosbrooke was formerly a District Commissioner in the Territory.

[69] *Trusteeship Council, Official Records, Fourth Session* (January-March, 1949), pp. 118-23.

[70] *Ibid.*, p. 447.

amination of annual reports.[71] After discussion of this suggestion, during which the Philippine representatives expressed reservation, the Mexican delegate agreed that the Council should also invite the administering authorities concerned "to give most careful examination to the conclusions of the Visiting Mission." This was acceptable to the Philippine representative provided that the phrase "as well as the comments made thereon by the members of the Trusteeship Council" was added. Both the Mexican and Philippine proposals were accepted by the Council which passed a resolution embodying the revised Mexican suggestion.[72] In subsequent resolutions on the missions' reports the Council has added a paragraph drawing attention to the fact that in formulating its conclusions and recommendations with respect to annual reports and petitions "the observations and conclusions of its Visiting Mission and the observation of the Adminstering Authorities concerned were taken into account. . . ." [73]

The form of the visiting mission's reports follows that of the annual reports in that they are organized under the major headings of Political, Economic, Social and Educational Development; the precise questions considered under each heading, however, vary with the circumstances in each territory. Council consideration of the report is much like that with regard to the annual reports, with the chairman of the mission taking the place of the special representative in elucidating any part of a report not clear to some member. As explained above, the only action taken by the Council on the reports is to resolve that material in them, together with comments by the administering authorities concerned as well as other members of the Council, will be taken into consideration in the formulation of the Council's conclusions and recommendations on conditions in the territories concerned.

Revision of the Organization and Functioning of the Visiting Missions. The General Assembly, at its fifth session, passed a resolution which, after noting the valuable contributions made to the functioning of the trusteeship system by the first three visiting missions, called upon the Council to undertake a review of the "organization and membership as well as the methods and functioning of the Visiting Missions," taking into account the advisability of:

(a) Arranging for the visiting mission to remain long enough in each territory to be able to fulfill its tasks adequately.
(b) Reducing the number of trust territories to be visited by each mission.
(c) Ensuring the greatest possible flexibility in the itinerary of each mission.

[71] *Trusteeship Council, Official Records, Fifth Session* (June-July, 1949), p. 260.

[72] *Ibid.*, pp. 261-64.

[73] The specific quotation is from the resolution on the Reports of the Visiting Mission to West Africa. *Official Records to the Seventh Session of the Trusteeship Council, Resolutions,* p. 60. Resolution 298 (VII).

(d) Extending the duration of visits without diminishing their number.

(e) Continuing to include in the terms of reference of each visiting mission the examination of specific problems.

(f) Continuing to include in their terms of reference provision to examine certain petitions on the spot.

(g) Selecting membership primarily from the members of the Trusteeship Council.

(h) Directing missions to take every opportunity to inform indigenous inhabitants of the functioning of the trusteeship system.[74]

At its eighth session, the Council, on the suggestion of the representative of the Dominican Republic, created a committee composed of the chairmen of the first three visiting missions, and the representative of Argentina,[75] to consider the resolution and recommend appropriate Council action. The committee met twice and reported to the Council on February 23, 1950,[76] making suggestions on each of the eight points covered in the Assembly resolution. It agreed in principle with points (a), (c), (d), (f), and (g). With regard to (b), the committee felt that one mission each was sufficient to cover the territories in both east and west Africa, but thought that two missions should be sent to the Pacific every three years. While accepting point (e), the committee felt that "caution should be exercised so as not to overload the missions with the examination of too many problems." Agreeing with point (h), the committee submitted a draft Statement for use by the visiting missions, containing the necessary information.

When the Council discussed the report of its committee, there was general agreement on the recommendations, with the major exception of the Statement designed to inform the peoples of the trust territories of the functioning of the trusteeship system. Some of the members of the Council, the representative of Iraq in particular, felt that the Statement was much too vague and desired a more specific description of the organization of the Council and the system generally. At the suggestion of this delegate, the committee, enlarged to six (representatives of Australia and the Dominican Republic were added), was directed to revise its proposals in the light of Council discussion.[77] The enlarged committee redrafted the Statement and the Council, at its ninth session, unanimously adopted its report, although the Australian representative had some doubts about sending two missions to the Pacific every three years.[78]

[74] *Resolutions adopted by the General Assembly during the period 19 September to 15 December 1950*, p. 50. Resolution 434 (V).

[75] *Trusteeship Council, Official Records, Eighth Session* (January-March, 1951), pp. 15-17.

[76] United Nations Document T/L.120/ *Trusteeship Council, Official Records Eighth Session* (January-March, 1951), p. 114.

[77] *Trusteeship Council, Official Records, Eighth Session* (January-March, 1951), pp. 118-19.

[78] *Trusteeship Council, Official Records, Ninth Session* (June-July, 1951), pp. 7-8.

Also at its ninth session the Council, consistent with the recommendations of its committee on visiting missions, in sending out the second mission to East Africa, decided to have the mission visit all three territories, spending about as much time in each territory as had the first mission to the area.[79] Noting this, the General Assembly at its sixth session, passed a resolution again recommending that the Council review the organization and functioning of visiting missions with respect to (a) increasing the duration of each visit by each mission; and (c) achieving these ends without diminishing the frequency of visits to each territory.[80]

The Council considered this resolution at its tenth session. At the same time it had before it a resolution of the Economic and Social Council [81] concerning the advisability of appointing women as members of visiting missions, and a Special Report of the Second Visiting Mission to East Africa,[82] containing proposals for the modification of the organization and functions of the visiting missions. A Committee on Visiting Missions composed of the representatives of Australia, the Dominican Republic, Thailand, and the United Kingdom was appointed to consider all three documents and make recommendations on that basis to the Council.[83] The committee held four meetings (March 4, 6, 17, and 25, 1952), and reported back to the Council on March 27.[84] In addition to the three documents mentioned, the committee also heard the views of a number of former members and chairmen of the missions as well as Secretariat officers who had accompanied missions.

The Special Report of the Second Visiting Mission to East Africa contained a number of observations based on the actual experiences of the mission. Its principal recommendations embraced six major points. (1) Advance preparations for a mission should be as thorough as possible, including the preparation by the Secretariat of briefs on the conditions in each territory to be visited. This would save the mission considerable time in organizing its activities upon arrival in the territories. (2) The missions should spend more time talking with officers of the local administration and leaders of local political and social groups, even at the expense of curtailing widespread geographic coverage of a territory. (3) With respect to East Africa, the difficulties attendant in visiting the territory in the rainy season were not insurmountable, and there are manifest advantages

[79] *Ibid., Resolutions*, p. 2. Resolution 344 (IX).

[80] *Resolutions adopted by the General Assembly during its Sixth Session* (November, 1951-February, 1952), p. 55. Resolution 553 (VI).

[81] *Economic and Social Council, Official Records, Sixth Year, Thirteenth Session Supplement I, Resolutions*, p. 36. Resolution 385 E (XIII).

[82] United Nations Document T/951.

[83] *Trusteeship Council, Official Records, Tenth Session* (February-April, 1952), pp. 15-17.

[84] United Nations Document T/L.249.

in having successive missions visit an area at different times of the year. (4) The number of communications, including petitions, received by the second mission was upward of three hundred and fifty as compared to twenty-one received by the first mission, and there was a presumption that the number would increase in the future. Therefore, it would be advisable to have the mission classify these communications, since many were for the benefit of the mission only, and it was not necessary to forward these to the Council. (5) The mission should be given wide latitude in how the statement of the functions of the trusteeship system should be presented to the indigenous inhabitants, since the levels of education in different territories varied considerably. (6) Secretariat members in charge of drafting proposals of the mission for each territory should be left in the territory after the mission had departed in order to be able to check further any doubtful points in the information gathered by the mission.

Based on these proposals and other evidence presented to it, the committee formulated its own recommendations, which included, in substance, the above suggestions plus the recommendations that the Council considered appointing women to the visiting missions (in accordance with Economic and Social Council resolution), and that terms of reference for future missions direct the missions to concentrate on the main problems in the territories rather than repeat unnecessarily an earlier mission's work. With specific reference to the General Assembly's resolution concerning the duration of each visit, the committee concluded that duration had nothing, or at most, little to do with the value of a visit. Rather, the important thing was the most efficient possible organization of the work of the mission in each territory. The committee then recommended the adoption of a draft resolution providing that "in making arrangements for future visits to the Trust Territories," the Council would take into account the principles set forth in the General Assembly and Economic and Social Council resolutions as well as the Special Report of the Visiting Mission to East Africa, together with the various observations made thereon by the committee. After short discussion the resolution was adopted unanimously by the Council, the representatives of the Soviet Union abstaining.[85]

From the point of view of achieving the most practicable division of emphasis between cooperation and supervision, the visiting missions seem to be the most important device used by the Council. Annual reports present the administering authorities' side of the story, petitions are uniformly critical of some aspect of the administration in the territories.

[85] *Trusteeship Council, Official Records, Tenth Session* (February-April, 1952), pp. 178-79. For changes in the visiting mission's role with respect to petitions, see above, pp. 172-73.

The missions, on the other hand, can form a firsthand picture of what conditions in the territories actually are. Their reports have so far demonstrated their value in this respect. That is, they not only enable representatives of nonadministering states to see clearly that talking about self-government in New York and applying it in Africa or the Pacific are two entirely different things, but they also make clear that not every criticism of the administering authorities can be dismissed as unrealistic. The visiting missions, then, perform the dual role of being the Council's most useful supervisory device while at the same time providing the best opportunity for administering and nonadministering states on the Council to achieve the degree of cooperative spirit without which all the supervision imaginable would come to naught.

CHAPTER NINE

Relations of the Trusteeship Council with Other Organs of the United Nations

The Trusteeship Council, in carrying out its functions under the Charter, is brought into contact, at least potentially, with all other organs of the United Nations as well as with many of the specialized agencies. In describing the functioning of the trusteeship system, then, it is necessary to survey the main points of contact between the Council and these other bodies.

Of the major organs of the United Nations, only the International Court of Justice has so far had no direct contact with the Council, but each of the trusteeship agreements provides that should any dispute concerning the interpretation of the agreement arise, the matter may be submitted to the Court. The other major organs, as well as some of the specialized agencies, all play important roles in the trusteeship system.

The Secretariat. The Secretariat, as the name implies, is the "pen of the Trusteeship Council." [1] It has a department devoted solely to trusteeship and information from nonself-governing territories, one division of which is concerned with the trusteeship system. The table on the next page, based on material in a United Nations publication *Organization of the Secretariat*,[2] illustrates the nature and extent of the Secretariat's tasks with respect to trusteeship.

From this table it can be seen that the Secretariat renders many more services to the Council than just the preparation of the necessary documentation. From one point of view it is the nerve center of the trusteeship system, for all contacts between the Council, the administering authorities, the indigenous inhabitants of the trust territories, and the other organs of the United Nations are maintained through the Secretariat.

In addition to its duties with respect to documentation, members of the Trusteeship Division of the Secretariat serve as secretaries for the Council, its committees, and its visiting missions. Further, they are sometimes asked not only to summarize the course of the debates, discussion, or investigations, but also to formulate draft proposals embodying the sense

[1] The phrase is borrowed from Professor Rappard, the first Director of the Mandates Section of the League Secretariat. In reply to thanks given the Secretariat by the Permanent Mandates Commission, Professor Rappard asked, "Does a man owe gratitude to his pen?" Quoted in Hall, p. 165.

[2] United Nations Document ST/APS/2, p. 25.

Section	Duties
1. Trusteeship Agreements	a. Assists Council in drafting, revising and analyzing the application of trusteeship agreements. b. Provides technical assistance to the Council with regard to drafting and revising its Rules of Procedure. c. Maintains liaison with the Advisory Council for Somaliland, and with specialized agencies and interested nongovernmental organizations on trusteeship matters.
2. Questionnaire and Technical Reports	a. Assists Council in preparation and revision of the questionnaire, and in the adaptation of it to the particular needs of each trust territory. b. Receives the annual reports and prepares analyses of and background documentation on the annual reports, and related working papers of the Council.
3. Petitions	a. Processes written and oral petitions, including: i. Acknowledgment of petitions to the petitioners; ii. Transmission of petitions to the administering authorities; iii. Transmission of comments of the administering authorities to the other Council members. b. Transmits resolutions of the Council to the petitioners and the administering authorities. c. Prepares working papers and background documentation of petitions. d. Provides secretarial services for the Committee on Petitions.
4. Visits	a. Makes plans and arrangements for visiting missions. b. Prepares background documentation on the territories to be visited.
5. Territorial Research and Analysis	a. Performs research and analysis in all matters concerning the trusteeship system. b. Provides expert assistance in the analysis of reports and petitions pertaining to trust territories.

of the Council, committee or mission on the subject at hand. For example, the Secretariat was asked by the Committee on the Examination of Petitions [3] to prepare a working paper based on its discussions,[4] and it was this working paper [5] which served as the basis for the committee's report. Also, members of the Secretariat accompanying the visiting missions formulate the missions' reports, in the first instance, on the various territories visited.

The Council's Rules of Procedure permit the Secretary-General or his representative to "make oral as well as written statements to the Council" and its committees.[6] In addition members of the Secretariat may, at the

[3] See above, p. 166.

[4] Committee on Examination of Petitions, *Summary Record of the First Meeting*, 29 February, 1952. United Nations Document T/AC.43/SR.1, p. 9.

[5] United Nations Document T/AC.34/L.1.

[6] United Nations Document T/1/Rev.3, Rule 26.

discretion of the President, be given precedence in the order of speaking.[7] To date, members of the Secretariat have not availed themselves of this right to any considerable degree. Those present at Council sessions have ordinarily confined their remarks to answering such questions as the members of the Council put to them. One writer, in discussing the political nature of the Secretary-General's role in the United Nations, has asserted that the "influence of the Secretary-General [i.e. the Secretariat] upon the operation of . . . [the Trusteeship Council] in some ways surpasses that which he asserts on the activities of the General Assembly and the Security Council. The political elements of that influence are naturally not so prominent in a nonpolitical sphere. But its total extent is perhaps greater." [8] Without going into a discussion of the over-all role played by the Secretary-General in the United Nations as compared with the League, the evidence supporting this assertion with respect to the Trusteeship Council is meager indeed. As indicated above, the Secretariat does play an important role in the functioning of the trusteeship system—a role which is not confined to mere secretarial work, but includes the substantive aspect of the formulation of draft resolutions and reports as well. But if the Secretariat's reports and drafts are largely accepted by the Council, this hardly proves the existence of "political elements of influence." Rather it means that the Council is satisfied with the impartiality of the Secretariat's work. As was the case with regard to the mandates,[9] the Secretariat's importance in the trusteeship system is a measure, not of its attempts to influence Council activities, but to provide impartial services to that body.

The Economic and Social Council and the Specialized Agencies. The importance of associating the work of the Economic and Social Council and the specialized agencies with that of the Trusteeship Council is recognized in the Charter, which calls upon the Council to "avail itself of the assistance of the Economic and Social Council and of the specialized agencies in regard to matters with which they are respectively concerned." [10]

At the beginning of the Trusteeship Council's first session the President of the Economic and Social Council, Sir Ramaswami Mudaliar of India, called on the President of the Trusteeship Council, Francis Sayre of the United States, and proposed that the two Councils appoint a joint committee to discuss the possibilities of "developing sound lines of co-operation, avoiding duplication of effort, and coordinating the work of the two Councils." [11] At its fourth session the Economic and Social Coun-

[7] *Ibid.*, Rule 53.

[8] Stephen M. Schwebel, *The Secretary-General of the United Nations,* p. 119.

[9] Hall, p. 169.

[10] Article 91.

[11] *Trusteeship Council, Official Records, First Year, First Session* (March-April, 1947), p. 106.

cil appointed its President and two other members for this purpose,[12] and late in its first session the Trusteeship Council did likewise.[13]

This joint committee met twice, in August, 1947, and submitted its report [14] with a number of recommendations, the most important of which were that:

(1) The Economic and Social Council, while empowered to make general recommendations "should not single out Trust Territories for special recommendations except with the concurrence of the Trusteeship Council."

(2) "All petitions to Organs of the United Nations emanating from or relating to Trust Territories should be dealt with in the first instance by the appropriate commissions of the Economic and Social Council regarding those parts of such petitions which concerned them."

The report, with the above recommendations, was approved by both Councils,[15] and has since served as the basis for cooperation between the two bodies.

With respect to the specialized agencies, the Council appointed a committee composed of the representatives of Mexico and Australia to participate in the drafting of the agreements bringing several of those agencies into relationship with the Trusteeship Council.[16] The report of this committee [17] explained that in the case of all the specialized agencies with which agreements had been reached before the Trusteeship Council was organized, as well as those agreements negotiated following the appointment of the Council's committee, provision was made for reciprocal representation, exchange of relevant information, and the promise of mutual cooperation between the Council and the agency concerned.[18] The Council accepted the committee's report at its second session.[19]

---

[12] *Economic and Social Council, Official Records, Second Year: Fourth Session* (February-March, 1947), pp. 221-22.

[13] *Trusteeship Council, Official Records, First Year, First Session* (March-April, 1947), p. 593.

[14] United Nations Document E&T/C.1./Rev.1.

[15] *Trusteeship Council, Official Records, Second Session, First Part* (November-December, 1947), p. 89. *Economic and Social Council, Official Records, Fifth Session,* p. 259.

[16] *Trusteeship Council, Official Records, First Year, First Session* (March-April, 1947), pp. 593, 731.

[17] United Nations Document T/50.

[18] All told the specialized agencies involved were the International Labor Organization, the Food and Agriculture Organization, the United Nations Educational, Scientific and Cultural Organization, the International Civil Aviation Organization, the World Health Organization, the International Telecommunications Union, the Universal Postal Union, the International Bank, and the International Monetary Fund. There were minor differences among the various agreements as they affected the Trusteeship Council, but in general all provided for the three items listed.

[19] *Trusteeship Council, Official Records, Second Session, First Part* (November-December, 1947), p. 91.

The Trusteeship Council, on the one hand, and the Economic and Social Council and the specialized agencies on the other, render a variety of useful services to one another. For example, the Council has called upon the International Labour Office to furnish information on immigrant labor and the breaking of labor contracts by inhabitants in the trust territories [20] in connection with its study of social advancement in the territories; it has called upon the Food and Agriculture Organization to assist its Committee on Rural Economic Development with respect to problems of land tenure and alienation in the territories; [21] and the United Nations Educational, Scientific and Cultural Organization (called UNESCO hereafter) has furnished the Council with information concerning the possibilities for study abroad by the indigenous inhabitants.[22]

As was noted previously, both the Economic and Social Council and the specialized agencies were given the opportunity to comment on the Provisional Questionnaire, and, in response to an invitation of the Council [23] UNESCO has submitted its comments on the annual reports beginning with the Council's sixth session. In addition, representatives of various specialized agencies, particularly UNESCO, the International Labour Organization, and the World Health Organization have attended Council sessions.

The Council, in turn, has received a number of requests from the Economic and Social Council. For example at its eleventh session the latter body adopted a resolution [24] expressing the hope that the purposes, principles, structure and organization of the United Nations and the specialized agencies would be taught in the trust territories. At its eighth session the Council decided to refer the resolution to the administering authorities, requesting them to "include information on the measures taken for its implementation in their annual reports on the Trust Territories." [25]

As with the example just cited, in most instances the services rendered by the two Councils are largely connected with supplying information

[20] *Official Records, Sixth Session, Trusteeship Council, Resolutions.* Resolution 127 (VI).

[21] *Official Records, Tenth Session, Trusteeship Council, Resolutions.* Resolution 421 (X).

[22] United Nations Documents T/832 and T/832 Add.1.

[23] At its fourth session the Council, on the proposal of the Philippine delegate (United Nations Document T/259), adopted a resolution recommending that the specialized agencies "should study the Annual Reports . . . with a view to making such observations and suggestions as they may consider proper in order to facilitate the examination of the Annual Reports by the Trusteeship Council. *Official Records, Trusteeship Council, Fourth Session, Resolutions,* p. 385, Resolution 47 (IV).

[24] *Economic and Social Council, Official Records, Eleventh Session* (July-September, 1950), p. 199. See also this session's *Resolutions,* p. 47. Resolution 314 (XI).

[25] *Trusteeship Council, Official Records, Eighth Session* (January-March, 1951), p. 34.

and/or bringing the action of one Council to the attention of the other. In this way information is pooled, and the goal of avoiding duplication of effort is achieved. There has been no question of delimiting the respective jurisdictions of each Council similar to the difficulties in the case of the Trusteeship Council and the General Assembly, to be discussed below. Most all the requests on both sides are for information, and where one Council has asked the other to consider taking some action, the latter has readily agreed.[26]

The Security Council. While the Charter provides that all functions of trusteeship relating to strategic areas shall be performed by the Security Council, with assistance of the Trusteeship Council,[27] it has remained for these two bodies to work out the exact nature of their relationship.

This became necessary with the approval of the trusteeship agreement for the Territory of the Pacific under American administration. At the second session of the Council, its President, Mr. Sayre, informed the other members that the Security Council's Committee of Experts had been assigned the task of considering the matter, and asked for the views of the Trusteeship Council members.[28]

Sir Carl Berendsen of New Zealand felt that no action was called for, since under the Charter the Security Council was solely responsible for strategic territories. He argued, therefore, that it was up to the Security Council to ask the Trusteeship Council for its assistance, and not the place of the latter to make overtures in this direction.[29] Most of the other members disagreed with this interpretation, however, on the ground that the Charter read "the Security Council shall avail itself" of the Trusteeship Council's assistance, thus making such action mandatory. On this basis the Council decided to appoint a committee of three to confer with representatives of the Security Council on the responsibilities of the former with respect to strategic areas.[30]

Later the Security Council appointed a similar committee and suggested a joint meeting of the two committees to be held on June 27, 1949. Before that, the Committee of Experts had recommended the adoption by the

[26] For example, by resolution 285 E(XIII) of August 27, 1951, the Economic and Social Council invited the Trusteeship Council to appoint women to serve as members of its visiting missions. Subsequently the Trusteeship Council agreed that in making arrangements for future visits to the trust territories, it would "take into account the principles set forth" in the resolution. *Trusteeship Council, Official Records, Tenth Session* (February-April, 1952), p. 179. *Official Records, Tenth Session, Trusteeship Resolutions,* p. 4. Resolution 417(X).

[27] Article 83.

[28] *Trusteeship Council, Official Records, Second Session, First Part* (November-December, 1947), p. 581.

[29] *Ibid.,* p. 583.

[30] *Ibid.,* p. 593. *Resolutions Adopted by the Trusteeship Council During its Second Session,* p. 1. Resolution 10 (II).

Security Council of a resolution by which the Trusteeship Council would be requested to: (1) subject to Security Council decisions made from time to time with respect to security conditions, perform the same functions toward strategic areas as it did for nonstrategic areas; (2) submit to the Security Council, "one month before forwarding to the Administering Authority," a copy of the Questionnaire, and any amendments thereto; and (3) submit to the Security Council "its reports and recommendations on political, economic and educational matters affecting strategic areas under trusteeship." [31]

When the joint committee met, the President of the Security Council requested the opinion of the members of the Trusteeship Council on the above proposal. The latter body considered this at its third session, where two positions on the matter were manifested. The Soviet delegate maintained that the proposed resolution "was contrary to the Charter," on the grounds that the Security Council *alone* could exercise functions with respect to strategic areas. "The time for the Trusteeship Council to act," he argued, "was when the Security Council requested its assistance." [32]

The other members of the Council accepted the proposed resolution, however, and these views were accordingly transmitted to the Security Council. The Soviet Union could, nevertheless, prevent the passage of the resolution when it came up for adoption in the Security Council by exercising its right of veto. But, in the interests of facilitating "the solution of this long drawn out question," the Soviet delegate abstained on the matter, and the resolution was passed.[33] A complementary resolution, by which the Trusteeship Council undertook to comply with the Security Council's requests, was adopted by that body at its fourth session.[34]

From the point of view of its respective relationships with the Security Council and the General Assembly, the Trusteeship Council has had in practice more leeway in its supervision of the strategic areas than with other territories. The Security Council has not attempted to make recommendations similar to those of the General Assembly; rather it merely "notes" the reports of the Trusteeship Council on conditions in the territory. Thus, while the framers of the Charter envisaged much closer Security Council regulation of strategic areas than General Assembly control of nonstrategic areas, the development of the trusteeship system so far has shown the reverse to be true.

---

[31] United Nations Document S/642.

[32] *Trusteeship Council, Official Records, Third Session* (June-August, 1948), pp. 120-23.

[33] *Security Council, Official Records, no. 18, 415th Meeting* (March 7, 1949), pp. 8-9. The vote was 8 in favor, with 3 abstentions.

[34] *Trusteeship Council, Official Records, Fourth Session* (January-March, 1949), p. 598. *Official Records of the Fourth Session of the Trusteeship Council, Resolutions* pp. 1-2. Resolution 46 (IV).

The General Assembly. With the exception of the Council itself, by far the most important part played in the trusteeship system is that of the General Assembly. Broadly, the position of the latter in the trusteeship system corresponds to that of the Council with respect to mandates in that it approves the trusteeship agreements, elects the nonpermanent members of the Trusteeship Council, and receives annual reports made by the latter on the activities of the Council as well as on the conditions in each of the trust territories.[35] Thus, while the administration in each territory is directly overseen by the Council, the general conditions in the territories, as well as the progress made toward the attainment of self-government or independence, are matters over which the General Assembly has competence.

The General Assembly has accordingly created a permanent committee, the Fourth Committee, one of the primary tasks of which is to consider conditions in the trust territories and recommend Assembly action on that basis.[36] It is this body which initially considers the reports of the Council and it is here that those reports receive their detailed consideration. Indeed, to speak of the Council's relations with the General Assembly, is really to speak of its contact with the Fourth Committee.

Where the respective positions of the Council and the Permanent Mandates Commission were clearly defined—the Commission was a subsidiary organ of the Council—the exact relationship of the Trusteeship Council and the General Assembly (actually the Fourth Committee) is ambiguous. This results from the fact that the Charter in some places appears to follow the Covenant in making the Council a subsidiary body of the General Assembly. Thus Article 83 states:

1. The functions of the United Nations with regard to trusteeship agreements for all areas not designated as strategic, including the approval of the terms of the trusteeship agreement and of their alteration or amendment, shall be exercised by the General Assembly.
2. The Trusteeship Council, operating under the authority of the General Assembly, shall assist the General Assembly in carrying out these functions.

And Article 87 carries out this idea by providing that the main supervisory duties of the Council are carried out under the authority of the General Assembly.

On the other hand, Article 7 of the Charter speaks of the Trusteeship Council as one of "the principal organs of the United Nations." Further, the composition of the Council, reflecting as it does equality of membership as between administering and nonadministering states, implies that

[35] Articles 85, 86 (c), and 88 of the Charter.

[36] Its other primary duty is to consider the information submitted under Chapter XI of the Charter, the Declaration Regarding Non-Self-Governing Territories. This concerns dependent areas not brought under the trusteeship system.

the Council is responsible for the international supervision of the administration of trust territories. It is difficult to see how the administering authorities could have accepted any other interpretation.

This ambiguity has given rise to some dispute concerning the respective jurisdictions of the Council and the Fourth Committee. When the latter body considered the first report of the Council the Soviet delegate suggested that the committee "note the Report," and transmit the observations of the committee members to the Council.[37] This procedure was adopted by the committee, and has been consistently followed.

The committee, however, has not been willing to content itself with this. Rather it has shown an increasing tendency to adopt further resolutions requesting Council action on a number of subjects brought out in its consideration of Council reports. Examples of this practice, especially with regard to petitions and visiting missions, have already been cited in preceding chapters. In addition the committee has called upon the Council to make special investigations of such things as social advancement in the trust territories,[38] rural economic development in the territories,[39] and the possibility of associating the inhabitants of the trust territories in the Council's work.[40] It has also called upon the Council to make detailed reports on progress toward self-government or independence and the Council has, since its 1953-54 report, included a separate section on this subject. The question which arises from these Assembly requests is: how far is the Council bound to comply? This in turn involves the more fundamental question of whether the Council is co-equal with, or subsidiary to, the General Assembly.

On this question the Council has again divided along administering versus nonadministering state lines. The position of the former is that while the General Assembly can make requests of the administering authorities, it cannot direct the Council to do anything. The Council, in the words of the American delegate, is "not merely an executive organ [of the General Assembly], but, as set forth in Article 7, paragraph 1, of the Charter, one of the six principal organs of the United Nations." [41] The nonadministering states, on the other hand, have argued that for the Council to fail to implement a General Assembly resolution in the precise

---

[37] *Official Records of the Second Session of the General Assembly, Fourth Committee* (October-December, 1947), p. 22.

[38] *Resolutions Adopted by the General Assembly During its Fourth Session*, p. 39, Resolution 323 (IV).

[39] *Resolutions Adopted by the General Assembly During its Fourth Session*, p. 38, Resolution 322 (IV).

[40] *Resolutions Adopted by the General Assembly During its Sixth Session*, pp. 55-56, Resolution 554 (VI).

[41] *Trusteeship Council, Official Records, Fourth Year, Sixth Session* (January-April, 1950), p. 100.

manner stipulated "would be lacking in respect to the Assembly. . . ." [42] Thus, for example, when the Council was considering a General Assembly resolution with respect to the organization and functioning of visiting missions,[43] the administering authorities favored the adoption of a resolution "taking note" of the Assembly recommendations. Opposed to this, the Philippine representative "pointed out that by merely taking note of the recommendations of the General Assembly without taking steps to implement them, the Council might expose itself to the charge of discourtesy towards, or lack of respect for, the General Assembly." [44] There followed statements by the representatives of Belgium and France which, when taken together, nicely summarized the administering authorities' position on the entire matter: They are worth quoting at some length because in substance they represent what has proved to be the Council's position:

> The representative of the Philippines has just asked whether the Trusteeship Council would not be failing in courtesy toward the General Assembly if it confined itself to noting the resolutions of the General Assembly. But I wonder whether the General Assembly is not lacking in courtesy vis-a-vis the Trusteeship Council in enjoining us to do this or that thing . . . when the General Assembly asks the Trusteeship Council to make a recommendation to the administering authorities . . . I am wondering whether the General Assembly is not exceeding its powers and showing a lack of courtesy towards the Trusteeship Council.[45]
>
> . . . .
>
> According to the Charter the Trusteeship Council is under the authority of the General Assembly, but, at the same time it is one of the three most important functional organs of the United Nations. . . . When the General Assembly addresses resolutions and invitations to the Trusteeship Council . . . it should be understood that such a decision of the General Assembly in no case reduces the rights of the Trusteeship Council and the functions which are properly and fully defined.[46]

What lies behind this constitutional question is a problem of fundamental importance to the entire trusteeship system. In the Fourth Committee the nonadministering states far outnumber the administering authorities, and it is therefore possible for one or more of the former to obtain the passage of a resolution which would never receive Council

[42] *Ibid.*, p. 61.

[43] *Resolutions Adopted by the General Assembly During its Fourth Session*, p. 38. Resolution 321 (IV).

[44] *Trusteeship Council, Official Records, Fourth Year, Sixth Session* (January-April, 1950), p. 581.

[45] *Trusteeship Council, Sixth Session, Verbatim Record of the Seventy-Third Meeting* (March 28, 1950), United Nations Document T/PV.275, p. 24. The quotation is from the remarks of Mr. Ryckmans of Belgium.

[46] *Ibid.*, p. 28. The quotation is from the remarks of Mr. Garreau of France.

approval. For example, as noted above, resolutions introduced in the Council calling for participation of the indigenous inhabitants of the trust territories in the work of the Council were defeated. The Fourth Committee, however, subsequently approved a proposal that invited the Council to "examine the possibility of associating the inhabitants of the Trust Territories more closely in its work and to report the results of its examination of this problem to the General Assembly at its seventh regular session." [47] The vote on this in the Fourth Committee is interesting. Of the administering authorities, those with territories in the Pacific will undoubtedly be little affected by the possible implementation of this recommendation, for the reason that in the cases of Nauru and New Guinea the population is too backward, and the Western Samoans have demonstrated their appreciation of New Zealand as an administering authority.[48] The administering authorities with territories in Africa, on the other hand, can envisage the possibility of local inhabitants taking regular part in Council activity—local inhabitants whose feeling toward the administering authority concerned are not always the kindest. Thus when the resolution came to a vote, the three administering authorities with African territories voted against, New Zealand and Australia abstained, and the United States voted in favor.[49]

When the Council considered this resolution at its tenth and eleventh sessions three suggestions for Council action were forthcoming. The first, a draft resolution submitted by the Soviet Union,[50] called upon the Council to decide that the indigenous people of the trust territories "have the right, in the name of their social, cultural and educational organizations and of their representative organs of self-government . . . to send their representatives to participate without vote in the consideration by the Trusteeship Council of the annual reports of the Administering Authorities and of all other questions relating to these Territories." A second, sponsored by the Salvadorean representative,[51] would have the Council select one person from each territory "to participate, with the right to speak but without the right to vote, in the examination and discussion of the annual report of the administering authority, though not in discussion

[47] *Resolutions Adopted by the General Assembly During its Sixth Session*, pp. 55-56. Resolution 554 (VI).

[48] The Pacific Trust Territory under the United States would not, of course, be affected by a General Assembly resolution.

[49] *Official Records, General Assembly, Sixth Session, Fourth Committee* (November, 1951-January, 1952), p. 242. After the vote, the American delegate informed the committee that his vote "should not be interpreted as signifying . . . support of any particular form or method of associating the indigenous inhabitants in the work of the Council."

[50] United Nations Document T/L.239.

[51] United Nations Document T/L.317, pp. 2-3.

directed to specific conclusions" on that territory. The third, a compromise suggested by the delegate to Thailand,[52] recognized the "unrestricted right" of each Council member to determine the composition of its delegation, but suggested that "the objective sought by the General Assembly resolution . . . could best be realized by the inclusion, where practicable and appropriate, of indigenous inhabitants of the Trust Territories in the respective delegations nominated to the Trusteeship Council by the Administering Authorities;" and "expressed the hope" that the latter would find it appropriate to do this. Inclusion of an indigenous inhabitant as an advisor to the administering authority's delegate to the Council would, thus, fully implement the suggested Council resolution.

The Council appointed a committee to consider these proposals and recommend action.[53] The committee hardly considered the Soviet proposal, rejected the Salvadorean recommendation, and adopted the Thailand resolution.[54] The Council, after first formally rejecting the Soviet draft, adopted the committee's proposed resolution.[55] Thus, while the Council did not ignore the Assembly resolution, it merely agreed to "hope" that administering authorities would see fit to implement it; and that hope would be fully realized if the administering authorities merely appointed a native inhabitant to their Trusteeship Council delegation.[56]

Another development has been the practice of trust peoples petitioning the General Assembly directly. When this happens it is customary for the General Assembly to refer the matter to the Council with a recommendation to that body to take into consideration the points raised in the Fourth Committee in connection with the petition(s). Again the precise relationship of the General Assembly and the Trusteeship Council remains ambiguous.

The administering authorities have voiced two complaints concerning action taken by, and comments made in, the Fourth Committee. First, they have argued that many of the representatives of nonadministering states, while meaning well, are not sufficiently competent in the fields of colonial administration, with the result that many of their proposals are unrealistic.[57] Second, the charge has been made that many proposals were

[52] *Ibid.*, pp. 6-7.

[53] *Trusteeship Council, Official Records, Tenth Session* (February-April, 1952), p. 173. The committee was composed of the representatives of El Salvador, France, Iraq, Thailand, the United Kingdom, and the United States.

[54] *Draft Report of the Committee on Participation of the Indigenous Inhabitants of the Trust Territories in the work of the Trusteeship Council.* United Nations Document T/L.317, pp. 2, 4-5, 6.

[55] *Trusteeship Council, Official Records, 454th Meeting* (July 23, 1952), United Nations Document T/L.454, p. 12.

[56] This has been done on occasion, by both the British and the French.

[57] *Trusteeship Council, Official Records, Fourth Year, Sixth Session* (January-April, 1950), p. 583.

unfounded, not merely because of the lack of knowledge, but for the purpose of political propaganda. As the British representative put it "The time had come when delegations must choose whether they intend to allow the Trusteeship Council to be undermined by political propaganda and fail in its task or whether they would make a determined effort to work in a spirit of harmony to achieve its objectives."[58]

This jurisdictional question has taken on the aspect of a running battle between the Fourth Committee and the Council, with the former not hesitating to repeat its recommendation whenever it feels the latter has not sufficiently implemented its original request. While a certain amount of impatience by the nonadministering states is understandable, it is difficult to see the value of General Assembly resolutions which serve primarily only to antagonize the administering authorities. Granted that the latter must, in the nature of things, be continually pressed to improve conditions within their territories, the Charter envisages this in providing for the Council's composition to include nonadministering states. Remembering again the voluntary nature of the trusteeship system it is doubtful if Fourth Committee sniping at the policies and practices of the administering authorities will either improve the lot of the trust peoples or significantly hasten their achievement of self-government.

[58] *Official Records of the Third Session of the General Assembly, Part One, Fourth Committee* (September-November, 1948), p. 109.

CHAPTER TEN

Toward Self-Government or Independence

The primary focus of this study is on the trusteeship system as an institution of international organization, rather than on its effects on the specific dependent territories involved. In the last analysis, however, the system must be measured not by how smoothly the machinery at United Nations headquarters functions, but by what is or is not done in the various trust territories. Regardless of how many petitions are heard, how many visiting missions are sent out, or how hard the administering authorities are pressed to defend their policies in the Council, the basic question remains: Are the aims of the system, as spelled out in the Charter, being fulfilled?

These aims—political, social and economic—cover the gamut of human relationships. To analyze every possible ramification of each in every one of the trust territories goes far beyond either the pretended competence of the writer or the essential aim of this study. It is possible, however, to single out the underlying goal for all trust territories and, on the basis of materials furnished to the Council, draw some conclusions as to the effectiveness of trusteeship. This underlying goal is, of course, the attainment of self-government or independence. Not only have Council members consistently referred to this as the main purpose of trusteeship, but the General Assembly has emphasized, and re-emphasized, its importance—calling for special reports on the trust territories with specific reference to the achievement of political maturity. Thus, while social and economic issues are of sometimes crucial importance, they are consistently treated by administering and nonadministering states alike in the context of their relationship to the political goal of self-government or independence. This study, then, will be confined to the progress so far made toward this most important of objectives.

The word progress is used advisedly; for while what constitutes "progress" in many situations is subject to considerable dispute, there exists an agreement among all states connected with the trusteeship system that political progress for the trust territories means the evolution of those territories toward self-government or independence. Here, it should be added, agreement stops. What constitutes self-government, not to mention independence, has been subject to considerable difference of opinion, implicitly at least, and this in itself remains a problem for the

Trusteeship Council; but there is no disagreement with the view that all trust territories are, or should be, moving toward self-government in some form.

Discussion of the operation of the system in this regard will be confined to the African territories. Of the four Pacific territories only one, Western Samoa, has made any appreciable progress toward self-government, and the policies of the administering state for that territory follow fairly closely those of the British. In the case of the other three, one (Nauru) is gradually losing the only means of existence for its population and plans are being made eventually to remove the islanders to another territory,[1] a second (U.S. trust) is a series of islands spread over a vast expanse of ocean for which political autonomy would not be physically practical in the foreseeable future, while the third (New Guinea) is sufficiently backward by Western standards that political development there remains in nascent form. Further, it is in Africa that the greatest contemporary manifestation of the revolt against colonialism is present, and it is therefore here that the real tests of trusteeship are to be found.

In Africa two of the territories are sufficiently unique, politically, to warrant separate discussion. Somaliland, by the terms of the trusteeship agreement, must become independent by 1960; thus there is a clear and definite end of trusteeship in sight. British Togoland voted to integrate with the Gold Coast which recently became independent, so that the period of trusteeship is over for that territory. The other African territories, while varying considerably in their political development, may be discussed together.

International Standards and Colonial Policies. While the League of Nations Covenant was explicit about the goal of independence for "A" mandates, the wording of Article 22 was at best ambiguous concerning the political goals for the other two types of territories. Reading the article as a whole, one might get the impression that the three categories of mandates were on a chronological continuum, and that since the independence of the "A" mandates was "provisionally recognized," it would be merely a matter of time until the "B" and "C" territories would achieve that goal. On the other hand, nowhere in the article was any specific reference made to independence for the latter two types, and Article 23, which included obligations of colonial powers generally, contains no allusion to it.

The mandates agreements themselves omit reference to independence,

[1] Nauru is almost totally dependent on the extraction and exportation of phosphate. The reserves of this will be exhausted within 60 years and the Australian government is already searching for possible re-location areas for the island's population. See "Nauru and the 60-Year Deadline," *United Nations Review,* Vol. 2, No. 2 (August, 1955), pp. 46-51.

and in view of specific mention of social and economic progress, the omission is significant. If independence was a goal for these mandates, then, it was at most inferable from the Covenant, and remained a remote rather than immediate end.

Statements by members of the Permanent Mandates Commission reveal no agreement on this point. Thus Lord Lugard has been quoted as saying: "The time when the bulk of the population of Tropical Africa will be 'able to stand alone in the strenuous conditions of the modern world' may not yet be visible on the horizon, but the mandates impose upon the powers which have accepted them the obligation to conduct the people toward that goal." Arguing against this point of view, however, Freire d'Andrade of France asserted, "The ideal is the slow, unforced assimilation of weak or inferior communities by strong or more highly developed communities." [2]

The conclusion remains, then, that independence or even self-government was by no means spelled out as a goal for the "B" and "C" mandates, although on occasion, as in Lord Lugard's remarks, it was alluded to. That no clear expression should have been made on this point is not surprising when it is remembered that the "C" mandates as a category were developed primarily to prevent outright and admitted annexation of the Pacific Islands and Southwest Africa, and that no one seriously argued at any time that any one of the other African territories was anywhere near ready for self-government or independence. The problem did not have to be faced simply because it was not a problem—at least in the immediate sense.

This, of course, does not mean that the Mandates Commission paid no attention to political development. It does mean, however, that emphasis was placed on the problems of reconciling the preservation of native customs and institutions with the superimposed administration of the mandatory power, and of developing native participation in government. With respect to the latter, though, this was generally confined to the institution of advisory councils.[3] The overriding impression left by the operation of the mandates system is that while self-government or independence may have been viewed as a goal for the "B" and "C" territories, certainly this end was sufficiently far in the future as to obviate definite commitments to it.

The fact that this problem was not dealt with to any degree left open a very serious question with which the United Nations Trusteeship system has increasingly had to deal. Neither mandates nor trusteeships can, quite obviously, be considered as isolated from the general picture of colonialism at any given time. And, as Duncan Hall has pointed out, any commit-

[2] Quoted in Wright, pp. 232-33. Cf. Hall, pp. 80-81.

[3] Wright, pp. 247-49.

ment to independence for territories within either system runs in the face of policies of integration pursued generally by almost all colonial states.[4] While perhaps an oversimplification, it is probably true to say that ever since the American Revolution, colonial policies of all Western European countries, as well as the Dominions, have envisaged some political development leading to self-government within an empire, or assimilation as an integral part of the metropolitan state. Independence may or may not be consonant with the former; it is obviously in contradiction of the latter. The question which the mandates system left as a heritage to the trusteeship system, then, was how to reconcile the notion of independence as a standard with colonial policies based on the assumption of the interdependence, not the independence, of mother country and dependent area. It was not the only problem left unresolved, but it was generic in the sense that before other questions of political advancement could be faced, let alone answered, this question had to be dealt with.

The development of Charter provision concerning the political goals of trusteeship, it will be recalled, went through three stages. The original State Department proposals called for eventual independence for the trust territories, but this was later omitted in favor of "self-government, as may be appropriate to the particular circumstances of each territory." This change was largely the result of discussions with the British and French, both of whom were most dubious about the goal of independence as opposed to self-government. Later, at the San Francisco Conference, the smaller powers succeeded in re-introducing the notion of independence and, further, the stipulation that whatever the termination of trusteeship it would be in accord with the "freely expressed wishes" of the people of the territory.

The final phrasing of the Charter on this point then, meant (1) that either self-government or independence could be considered the political goal of trusteeship; (2) that the nature of self-government or independence would depend on the particular circumstances of the trust territory (a concession to the colonial powers); and (3) that political development would be in accord with the wishes of the inhabitants of the trust territories (a concession to the anticolonial states).[5] Thus it was clear from the outset that self-government or independence were explicit goals of political advancement, but that—as long as the people of the trust territory consented—this advancement could take the form of self-government within a larger political entity, such as the British Commonwealth or the French Union. This much the San Francisco Conference settled; much, however, remained to be answered by the evolution of the system. In

[4] Hall, pp. 83-84.

[5] The trusteeship agreements add nothing to the Charter in this respect, merely repeating the goals spelled out in the Charter.

discussing the political development of the trust territories the attempt will be made to show to what extent these unresolved questions have been met, and to what extent they remain in doubt.

The Charter provisions left open at least three general questions. First, would a choice between self-government within some large system as opposed to complete independence be offered the trust peoples? The affirmative answer to this question might seem implicit in the Charter provisions, but in the one territory so far given an opportunity to express political preferences, the issue has not been raised in this form.

A second fundamental question with which the Trusteeship Council must deal is whether or not self-government, not to say independence, is desirable for all trust territories. That is to say, even assuming the technical possibility for self-government for each of the territories, does it make sense for each of them to be moving along separate autonomies? To take an example from Africa, neither ethnically nor economically can British Togoland or the French Cameroons be called natural units. But even if they were, would it from any point of view—and especially from that of the indigenous people in those territories—be desirable to see them develop as autonomous political entities? In other words, in an era in which increasingly the advantages of political integration, however loose, seem to outweigh the disadvantages, is it desirable to Balkanize Africa? Do the assumptions of nineteenth-century liberal nationalism make sense in the mid-twentieth century? The Charter could be easily interpreted as giving a fairly clear "Yes" to these questions; yet it is just as clear that the policies of the administering authorities reveal severe reservations to, if not direct conflict with, this interpretation.

Even if integration rather than independence is emphasized as the context in which the territories should achieve self-government, a further question remains: Does integration with another territory about to achieve independence constitute fulfillment of the goals of trusteeship? Would assimilation by the administering authority, even provided that the people living in the former trust territory be represented in the central organs of government, be a violation of the Charter? Finally, to what extent should the ethnic patterns of the various trust peoples be taken into account in determining the final status of a trust territory? When the map of Africa was drawn by European powers, little attention was paid to the location of various African tribes; the result was that a given tribe might have its members located in two or even three colonies. Should any weight be given to the desires of these people to be united under one political entity?

The answers to these questions are not to be found in the Charter, yet they are all problems with which the Council has had to deal. From this point of view, the evolution of the trusteeship system to date is the story of the way in which the Council, and the General Assembly, have met or are meeting them.

It bears repetition and re-emphasis that the trusteeship system itself, and the Council's operations within that system, do not exist in a contextual vacuum. When the various administering states placed territories under the system they did not thereby commit themselves to policies in those territories entirely different from those followed in their respective colonies. This is not to say that the trusteeship system has no influence on the practice of administering authorities. It is to say that while the trusteeship system is not a mere reflection of general contemporary colonial practice, it is not, likewise, the cause of any radical transformation of colonial policies within the various trust territories, as opposed to other dependent areas. The commitments of trusteeship involve modifications of, rather than departures from, the various administering states' policies. While an exhaustive survey of these policies is beyond the scope of this study, a general view of them is necessary to appreciate the context in which the Council must deal with political advancement.

In brief, the overriding aim of French colonial policy has been the creation of a centralized and uniformly governed empire.[6] Part and parcel of this is the policy of assimilation, by which the indigenous inhabitants of the colonies were to absorb gradually French culture and, in time, become Frenchmen. As this has been applied to Africa below the Sahara, however, the notion of association rather than assimilation was developed. This modification meant, in effect, a recognition on the part of the mother country that complete assimilation of the masses of Africans was impossible in the foreseeable future; rather emphasis was put on developing a gallicized elite among the Africans, with assimilation of the masses to come at a much later date, if ever.

As assimilation gave way to association the prior assumption that all French overseas territories were to become integral parts of France gave way to the notion of an association of territories within a Union. The latter was given constitutional expression in 1946 with the provision for such territories and their representation in the organs of the Union.

In terms of self-government or independence, however, the idea of a centrally administered empire, or Union, remained unchanged. Thus whatever emphasis was placed on self-government in French territories was in the form of representation of these territories in the Assembly of the French Union or in the French Parliament itself, rather than on the development of territorial legislatures or executives with gradually increasing autonomy. As will be seen below, this associative idea has itself undergone modifications since World War II, but at least at the inaugura-

[6] This summary of colonial policies is based largely on Eric A. Walker, *Colonies*, pp. 100-126.

tion of the trusteeship system it was the basis of colonial policy for trust as well as other territories administered by France.

Perhaps the most striking manifestation of this policy is in the field of education; here a primary goal is the development of an African elite fully acculturated to French civilization, primarily through advanced education culminating in university training in the mother country. Upon return to the territory these Africans can take over positions in the administration, thus providing for the Africanization of the government in the territory while at the same time protecting the central theme of political development toward association with—rather than independence from—France.

With respect to the trust territories specifically, French spokesmen have reiterated that upon the termination of trusteeship, the people of the territory will have the opportunity to avail themselves of one of three alternatives: (1) legal union with France, (2) association within the French Union, or (3) complete independence. Despite the apparent equality of choice among these three, it seems obvious that French policy has been and continues to be, designed to induce, cajole and to a certain extent force the inhabitants of the trust territories into choosing between the first two alternatives only.

Belgian policy in Africa must be viewed in the light of the universal notoriety connected with King Leopold's control over the Belgian Congo. With this heritage of unfortunate administration, the Belgian government has concentrated on the improvement of social and economic conditions rather than on political development. While the Belgian policy includes the notion of exerting a civilizing influence on primitive peoples, there is no attempt to Europeanize the indigenous inhabitants similar to that of the French.

In a word the hallmark of Belgian policy is paternalism: the social and economic emancipation of the African within the context of the rights of Belgians to develop the territory economically. In the case of Ruanda-Urundi, which is vastly more densely populated than the Congo, and had at the time the Belgians assumed responsibility for the territory a more advanced indigenous political development, the Belgian policy is to preserve native organization, but in no sense to introduce Western reforms in terms of the extension of suffrage, nor to allow the indigenous political organizations any governmental authority which might interfere with Belgian control of the territory.

This policy is also well illustrated by the attitude of the mother country toward education. As compared to the French, much more reliance is placed on mission schools teaching the fundamentals of morality and the requirements of earning a living at some trade. Not only is there no attempt to develop a Belgianized political elite through advanced education, but the administration frowns on Africans receiving advanced education abroad. It is pointed out that much of the difficulty in British and French territories stems from educating Africans abroad, raising undue hopes for early political emancipation, before the social and economic levels of the people have been sufficiently raised. One recent visitor to Belgian Africa summarized the administering authority's position as thinking it "madness for the British to let Africans vote when they are still economically submerged, and worse madness for the French to work out an elaborate abstract political system and then try to fit Africans into it." [7]

British colonial policy is somewhat more difficult to summarize in a few paragraphs than that of either the French or the Belgians. There is no one word such as "association" or "paternalism" by which it can be characterized. Phrases such as "the dual mandate," the "pragmatic approach," or "muddling through," have all been aptly used to describe British policy. In general, probably the best way to describe it is on the basis of several tenets, some combination of which is found in each of the territories under British control.

First, the British, especially in Africa, have followed the idea of dual mandate, under which British administration at the top is superimposed on local native political institutions. No attempt is made to displace the organs of local government, but rather gradually to improve them. Further, at the top levels, the Africanization of the administration proceeds gradually, with the ultimate aim of turning over to the inhabitants of the territory complete control of their own political destiny, with the natural hope that it will remain harmonious with British interests. With reference to the goal of self-government or independence, then, British policy recognizes this as an important, if not the main, goal of their administration.

Secondly, no attempt is made to Anglicize the indigenous people, other than to teach the fundamentals of good administration to the Africans as the latter take over the reins of government. The idea seems to be to preserve African institutions as much as possible, limited only by the requirements of Western standards of good government. Thus the British may suggest to local chiefs that more democratic methods may be used to arrive at local decisions and their advisory councils at all levels of government may be modeled along the lines of English political institutions; but essentially the method is that of reconciling British and African institutions to the extent necessary to enable the territory to go it alone.

Thirdly, the British are, above all, pragmatic. Fundamental to their policies is the notion that in each case the "particular circumstances in the territory" should determine the specific policy to be followed. Thus the policy in Tanganyika, which has a racial problem caused by large

[7] John Gunther, *Inside Africa*, p. 663.

numbers of permanently settled Europeans and Asians in addition to the African population, differs materially from that followed in the British territories of West Africa in which the population is almost exclusively African.

Fourth, the British, to a much greater extent than either the Belgians or French, permit the color bar, not only socially, but to a certain extent politically as well. While the extent of this will vary considerably, depending on the number of permanent non-indigenous inhabitants there are in a given territory, there is in general no commitment to the social equality of all people in the territory. And, politically, while Africans are not kept out of governmental organs, the underlying assumption in heterogeneous territories is the political development of Europeans, Asians, and Africans side by side, rather than the removal of all legal distinctions based on national origin.

Finally, the atmosphere of British administration is predominantly one of training the territorial inhabitants to stand on their own feet, make their own mistakes, but in any case aim at the assumption of genuine autonomy. The British are not sympathetic to specific timetables for political development, but that self-government or independence is the goal for all their territories is explicitly clear, if the precise form that such political maturity will take is not.

In examining the political advancement of the trust territories both the General Assembly and the Trusteeship Council have been concerned with three general questions: (1) What is the general political situation? (2) What has been done to develop organs of territorial government, and to what extent is that government being Africanized? (3) To what extent do the inhabitants of the territories have a voice in the determination of territorial policy?[8]

General Situation. It is, of course, a truism to say that Africa generally, and the various trust territories specifically, are tremendously variegated. Nonetheless, with regard to the latter, a few generalizations applicable to all trust territories are possible.

Fundamentally, the ultimate governing authority in all the territories remains in the hands of the administering authority; there exists in none of the territories any organs of genuine self-government as separate political entities. Further, each of these territories is joined in administrative unions with other territories of the administering powers, though—despite Soviet insistence that this violates the Charter—the Council has so far

[8] The data on which the discussion of the political advancement of the African territories is based comes, unless otherwise noted, from two documents: *Official Records, General Assembly: Ninth Session, Report of the Trusteeship Council Covering the Period from 22 July 1953 to 16 July 1954;* and United Nations Document T/L.579, Annex.

seen no dangers to the political objectives of trusteeship in this situation. Finally, there are in all the territories some organs of government, with varying amounts of authority, in which the indigenous inhabitants participate. Beyond these few statements, however, the differences are more striking than the similarities.

Essentially these differences may be accounted for in part by the differences in policies pursued within the territories by the administering state, and in part by the variety in the demographic make-up of the territories. In the West African trusts, for example, the population has remained almost completely African, while in Tanganyika, there are significant segments of both European and Asian populations. This means, in the case of the latter, the additional complicating factor of race relations in the quest for self-government, not found in the other territories. But even within the overwhelmingly African populated territories there are important differences. When the Belgians assumed the administration of Ruanda-Urundi they found two distinct, comparatively well-organized governmental systems in operation, each under its own *Mwami*, or chief. The population, by and large, was and remains a fairly distinct group. In the West African territories, however, some African boundary lines were drawn with little reference to ethnic groupings.

In the Cameroons, for example, there are important differences between the peoples in the north, where Mohammedanism prevails, and the southern sections, where Islam did not reach. Further, Western-educated Africans in increasing numbers have made their appearance primarily in the south and the articulate movement for independence comes primarily from this area.[9]

Another notable example of ethnic difficulties is to be found in the position of the Ewe people, who find themselves occupying areas in the Gold Coast, and both British and French Togoland. In this situation the complicating factor is whether any attempt should be made in the final political disposition of the territories concerned to unite arbitrarily divided ethnic groups, for this in turn might jeopardize the political development of colonies and trust territories whose tradition as separate entities goes considerably far back in history. That is to say, if the Ewes were made politically autonomous, this would in large measure be turning back the clock on twenty-five to fifty years of political development in each of the Togolands as well as the Gold Coast.

The differences in the political structure and advancement in the territories result not only from demographic distinctions. For on top of this must be placed the general colonial policies of the three administering states involved. These differences are perhaps best illustrated by the implementation of the authority granted to the administering states to

[9] Thomas R. Adam, *Modern Colonialism*, pp. 44-45.

govern the territories as "integral parts" of their own territories, and by the type of territorial government found in each of the trusts. Following the mandates system in this respect, all the territories under discussion save Tanganyika (which, it was felt, was large enough to warrant separate administration) are administered as part of neighboring colonies. Here, however, similarity stops.

In the British Cameroons this has meant the development of a federal arrangement with neighboring Nigeria under which the northern half of the territory is considered to be a part of the northern state of Nigeria, while the southern half was administered as a part of Eastern Nigeria, and now has regional status in the federation. This arrangement in itself implicitly answered the question of the long range political status of the British Cameroons, since their entire development has been made in the context of their relationship to Nigeria. That is, while independence as the ultimate goal has never been officially ruled out, the actual direction of development has been along the lines of federation with a potentially independent Nigeria. Thus the legislative and executive councils in the British Cameroons have grown up either as concomitants of developments in one of the Nigerian states—as in the case of the northern section—or as autonomous organs within a Nigerian federation, as has happened in the south. In either case, however, self-government would appear to be irrevocably connected with the future of Nigeria.

French policy, with its tradition of centralized administration in Africa, nonetheless necessarily assumes neither integration nor federation of the trust territories with other French possessions. The implicit goal of the French Cameroons and Togoland would appear to be, rather, development of individual autonomy within the French Union. How much actual autonomy this would amount to is at present an unanswerable question; but such voice as the trust peoples have had in the determination of their own affairs has been, until quite recently, effected through their representation in the central organs of the French Union rather than through organs of territorial government. In both the Cameroons and Togoland, indigenous inhabitants take part in territorial assemblies, but, as compared with their British counterparts, these bodies have admittedly few powers. Steps have recently been taken to increase the scope and powers of the territorial organs, but there is little sign of change in the basic policy of association within the French Union for the trust territories under France's tutelage.

Belgian policy, with its emphasis on social and economic advancement, has not concerned itself, even implicitly as yet, with the ultimate political status of Ruanda-Urundi. Thus the Belgians have retained direct exercise of the legislative function, although an Advisory Council was created in 1947 (to which Africans have been appointed since 1953) which advises the Vice-Governor General on ordinary executive functions. In general, the situation may be described as one in which the administering authority permits the indigenous political structure to function much on its own as long as it does not interfere with the centrally administered social and economic policies of the administering authority.

Development of Territorial Government. The development of representative organs of government within the trust territories again manifests the basic difference of questions faced and policies pursued in each of the areas. In every case, however, it would appear irrefutable that some changes have been effected during the period of trusteeship—changes in the direction of genuine political advancement. The degree of change and the implications of it are, however, something else again. Generally speaking the British have moved toward political equality of ethnic groups in Tanganyika, and the institution of federalism with Nigeria in the Cameroons; the French have promoted participation of the trust people in the organs of the Union and granted some extension of authority to organs of government within their trust territories; and the Belgians have effected a kind of constitutionalism in the structure of indigenous government.

In Tanganyika the main territorial organs of government have been an Executive Council and a Legislative Council. Membership in the former has changed from eight official (administration) and five unofficial (three Europeans, one Asian, and, beginning in 1951, one African) members to eight official and six unofficial members (two representing each of the ethnic groups). Originally, and as yet primarily, this Council acted as an advisory body to the Governor. Since 1955, however, the unofficial members have been invited to interest themselves in some of the departments of government and to assist in answering in the Legislative Council for governmental policy.

Similar changes have been made in the Legislative Council where unofficial membership has increased from fourteen (four Africans, three Asians, and seven Europeans) to thirty (ten from each of the three groups), official membership having changed from fifteen to thirty-one. The Legislative Council possesses legislative and budgetary competence for the territory, subject to the assent of the Governor.[10]

What this means, of course, is that the administering authority, through its majorities in both organs, retains effective policy-making control in the territory. But it means also that permanent residents in the territory are being given increased representation in terms of absolute numbers,

[10] At the supra-territorial level Tanganyika is loosely tied with Kenya and Uganda in the East African High Commission. Whether this will eventually develop into a federation similar to that of Central Africa depends, apparently, primarily on the evolution of race relations in the three territories. See Edwin S. Munger, "Geography of sub-Saharan Race Relations," in C. Grove Haines (ed.), *Africa Today,* p. 188.

increased responsibility in the executive function, and that Africans are now given equality of representation with the European and Asiatic populations. It should be remembered, however, that this is group rather than individual equality since the Africans far outnumber the European and Asiatic elements in the population.

At the level of local government the great majority of the population falls under control of the native authorities, based on what the British call "traditional institutions." In areas where significant numbers of non-Africans dwell mixed Councils are being introduced.

British policy with respect to self-government of dependent areas takes the form of development through three main stages: (1) gradual training of the indigenous population, but under control of the administration through its official majorities; (2) change to majority control by the inhabitants of the territory, still subject to the Governor's assent; (3) genuine autonomy. The first thing to be said about political advancement in Tanganyika is that the territory is at present in the last phase of stage one. The second point is the question of whether the British policy of the multi-racial basis of political development can succeed—this is certainly one of the great unanswered questions of southern and eastern Africa.

If ethnic grouping underlies the political development of Tanganyika, the same problem in a different aspect accounts for changes in the British Cameroons. Here, however, the question is one of differences among Africans themselves—whether federalism can bridge the cultural differences among the peoples of Nigeria, and how the development of the British Cameroons fits into the evolution of Nigerian federalism.

Essentially the answer to the latter question has taken the form of integration of the northern part of the Cameroons into the Northern Region of Nigeria, and the development of the southern Cameroons as an autonomous region within the Nigeria federal system. At the beginning of the period of trusteeship, the Cameroons had no representation in the central organs of Nigerian government, although Cameroonians were members of two of the regional councils. Under the Constitution of 1954, however, the Cameroons have representatives in the central legislature (four from the north, six from the south), and the southern section is guaranteed at least one member of the Council of Ministers—the principal instrument of policy for the Federation. Regionally, the southern section has been endowed with its own legislature in which Africans make up the overwhelming majority, as well as an executive council consisting of the Commissioner of the Cameroons as President, three ex-officio members, and four unofficial members appointed from among members of the legislature.

The northern Cameroons are at present an integral part of the Northern Region of Nigeria. Representatives of the northern section are on a consultative committee, however, which will be called upon to express its views on any proposed federal or regional legislation, and to represent the interest of the northern section in both the Northern Regional Government and to the federal authorities.

Finally, the Federal Executive Council has created a portfolio for trust territory affairs, held by a Cameroonian minister.

Under the Constitution of 1954 the central organs of the federal government have been given general legislative and executive powers, subject only to the veto of the Governor, a power which has not been used. Regionally, the southern Cameroonian bodies are in control of their local affairs, subject to the assent of the Commissioner of the Cameroons, to assure that nothing is done that would violate the trusteeship agreement.

What all this amounts to is that the British Cameroons have definitely reached stage two in their political development, but in the context of Nigerian development toward self-government, rather than as a separate political entity. When Nigeria finally becomes fully self-governing, undoubtedly the Cameroonians will—as in the case of Togoland—be given the opportunity to stay within the federation or remain under trusteeship. In view of the fact that their development has proceeded entirely along the lines of participation in the Nigerian federation, it would indeed be surprising if any future plebiscite would do more than ratify the *de facto* situation.

In the French territories considerable emphasis is placed on the capacity of the local inhabitants to participate in the policy-making organs of the French Union. Thus both the Cameroons and Togoland have been allotted deputies in the National Assembly, representatives in the Council of the Republic, and delegates to the Assembly of the French Union and the Economic Council.

At the territorial level each has an assembly (in the Cameroons consisting of two sections, one elected by citizens, the other by certain classes of noncitizens; in Togoland based on a single electoral system), but in neither case has it had anything like real legislative authority. Thus, while the assemblies can make decisions on such matters as tourist traffic, administration of movable and immovable property within the territory, local taxes, town planning and contributions, it may not pass resolutions on "political matters." Real policy-making power remains in the hands of the chief administrative officer as the representative of the French government.

Recently (1955-56) the French have instituted far-reaching changes in their African colonies which affect both trust territories. Both territorial assemblies will now be elected from a common role, and their powers will be increased, particularly in the areas of appropriations and the modification of French policy to fit the individual circumstances of the territory. Further, Councils of Government, consisting of a majority selected by the territorial assemblies and a minority appointed by the government will take over some executive functions, assuming responsibility for executive departments and, together with the assemblies, will control the local civil service.[11]

This significantly increased measure of territorial autonomy manifests the shift in the French policy from assimilation to association—a shift from a relationship that was essentially unitary to one that more closely approximates federalism. But while French delegates to both the Fourth Committee and the Trusteeship Council have repeatedly stated that when the time comes to end trusteeship the inhabitants of French trust territories will be given the opportunity to leave the French Union, the political development to date has been directed toward interdependence with, not independence from, metropolitan France.

The development of territorial organs of govern in Ruanda-Urundi, as might be expected, has not been as far-reaching as in the other territories. Belgian effort along these lines has been to constitutionalize the essentially autocratic indigenous political structure. This has been done through the institution of indigenous councils at all levels of government, each higher council being selected by the members of the lower councils. This occurs through sub-chiefdom, chiefdom, and district levels, culminating in the Councils of the two *Bami*, who are now required to obtain their respective Councils' approval of proposed measures.

Belgium's defense of this lack of political innovation is that many pressing social and economic problems must be solved before autonomy may be considered—and that as long as a working indigenous structure is in existence the administering authority would be foolish to institute reforms other than very gradually, proceeding no faster than the interest evinced by the indigenous population. This argument—especially in view of the economic problems caused by the overpopulation of the territory—is difficult to answer; but it might be observed at the same time that the Belgians do little calculated to awaken in the inhabitants of Ruanda-Urundi any interest in political affairs.

Consultations and Suffrage. The degree to which the inhabitants of the trust territories have a voice in the direction of their own affairs, either through suffrage or some form of consultation with the administering authority, is in general what might be expected in each case in view of the political status of the territory and the colonial policy of the administering state.

Thus in Tanganyika there was little if any direct consultation with the

[11] "New Deal in the French Union," *The Economist* (London), March 31, 1956, p. 683.

inhabitants until 1949. In December of that year, however, a Committee on Constitutional Development visited extensively throughout the territory, and the changes in the structure of the territorial government emanated in large measure from the desires of the inhabitants, expressed through these consultations. At the local level the government is required to satisfy itself that people in an area desire the establishment of country, town, and local councils before they are instituted. Suffrage, except in one or two predominantly European or Asiatic communities, is virtually unknown. The policy of the British in this regard is to interfere as little as possible with the traditional native authorities on the local level, while election of the Legislative Council has been postponed until that body is functioning satisfactorily as a legislature.[12] Generally speaking, the British prefer to develop the organs of territorial government until the point has been reached when they are performing both executive and legislative functions smoothly before introducing suffrage on any significant scale, while extending suffrage at the local level only as the inhabitants of various communities express a desire for it.

In the British Cameroons, the Constitutions of both 1951 and 1954 were promulgated only after extensive consultations with representatives of the Cameroons and Nigeria. It was largely as the result of such consultations that the southern Cameroons were accorded what amounts to regional status in the federation. Beginning in 1951 all taxpaying adults were eligible to vote for members of the regional legislatures, through an electoral college system. Since women are not required to pay the tax, and in practice do not, this has amounted to adult male suffrage. Under the new Constitution of 1954 members of the federal legislature are no longer selected by the regional legislatures, but are chosen by direct suffrage. Locally, the elective principle is gradually being introduced in the native authorities as the local inhabitants express a desire for it.

In the French territories consultation with the inhabitants is largely carried out, at least in theory, through the representation of the latter in the organs of the French Union.[13] While proposed local government modifications have been submitted to the Territorial Assembly of the French Cameroons, in practice there has been no direct consultation with respect to the general framework in either territory. The French Constitution lays down the principle of universal adult suffrage and this has been applied to both the Cameroons and Togoland. In the case of the former, however, there were until quite recently (spring, 1956) two categories of

[12] The Governor of the territory has been quoted as stating that in his opinion Tanganyika will be ready for elections by 1958. The New York *Times*, November 22, 1955, p. 2.

[13] These territories were also represented in the French Constitutional Assemblies of 1945 and 1946.

voters: citizens and noncitizens, a further manifestation of the policy of association. Since 1952 Togoland has had only one electoral list. The increase of the number of qualified and registered voters from 1947 to 1953 is striking:

	1947	*1953*
French Togoland	7,963	113,279
French Cameroons	15,896	580,000

This extension of suffrage is not, of course, in the least inconsistent with the gradual evolution of the territories toward the status of associated states of the French Union, since voting is for representatives in the organs of the Union, as well as for territorial organs of government.

Belgium, consistent with its general emphasis on social and economic rather than political development in Ruanda-Urundi, has confined its consultations to obtaining the views of the highest council in each of the territories, and has introduced the elective principle only occasionally in local areas as a means of political education. Intrusions into the traditional autocratic native institutions have been limited to the development of advisory councils at each level of government.

Summarizing briefly with respect to the general political development of the territories under consideration it may be said that the British Cameroons have most nearly reached the end of their period of trusteeship with the outlook being very favorable for their eventual incorporation into the independent federal state of Nigeria. Tanganyika is at a stage of increasing devolution of executive and legislative responsibility from the administering authority to the territory, with genuine control over its internal affairs still in the future. French Togoland and the Cameroons have been accorded more control over territorial affairs, but continue to be administered in the aura of eventual partnership in, rather than independence from, the French Union. Ruanda-Urundi shows the least political advancement; this because the Belgians admittedly have placed a much higher priority on the attainment of the social and economic goals of the Charter's trusteeship provisions. Within the broad limitations of economic collapse and political tyranny the desirability of this emphasis will be determined by one's own value preferences.

Somaliland. This territory is in a distinctly anomolous position. It is more difficult to envisage an autonomous status for this territory than for any other of the African trusts, while at the same time it is the only trust territory for which there has been established a definite time limit by which it must attain independence. Nor is there the likelihood that it may become a self-governing part of an Italian equivalent of the British Commonwealth or the French Union, or be integrated with a neighboring self-governing state. It is, by the terms of the trusteeship agreement, to become a completely independent state by 1960. This fact, in view of the conditions in the territory, has two important implications.

First, because of the very short period of trusteeship, there tends to exist an element of coercion in the tutelage of the administering power. The Somalis, that is to say, are going to develop—or have developed for them—Western, democratic institutions whether they like it or not. And since a great portion of the population had, at the inception of trusteeship in 1950, virtually no experience with such institutions, there is not sufficient time for the gradual reconciliation of tribal political structures with Western notions of adequate political organization.

Secondly, if the experiment with a time limit succeeds in Somaliland, this will inevitably place tremendous pressure on other administering authorities to speed the political development of their territories, despite their protestations of the dangers in moving too rapidly. There are sufficient obstacles to the successful transition of Somaliland from dependent territory to independent state that it may be fairly said: If it works for Somaliland, it can work for any other African trust territory.

These obstacles, as they affect the political development of the area, include the fact that only about 10 per cent of the land is arable, water being in very short supply.[14] Further, the land has no important mineral resources, apparently, although there exists the possibility of oil deposits.[15] If the latter should prove true, it could prove to be the economic salvation of the territory, but as yet this remains no more than a possibility. As a consequence about four-fifths of the total population are nomadic cattle raisers living under the poorest of circumstances—and adding to their difficulties is the prestige concomitant with ownership of cattle so that the meager resources of the land are continually strained by the grazing of too many animals.[16] What this means in terms of the over-all economy is that Italy has, since the beginning of its administration, contributed as a direct grant, about two-thirds of the annual budget for the territory.[17] Further financial aid has been given in the form of provision for the exportation of bananas to Italy at a price considerably higher than the world market.[18] By 1960, theoretically, some way will have to be found by which Somaliland can be made self-supporting. The Italian government has introduced a number of measures in this direction including increasing the available water supply through irrigation and well digging,

[14] "Half Way to Independence," *United Nations Review*, Vol. 1, No. 1 (July, 1954), p. 51.

[15] The New York *Times*, January 9, 1955, p. 19.

[16] "Half Way to Independence," *United Nations Review*, Vol. 1, No. 1 (July, 1954), p. 49.

[17] *Ibid.*

[18] The New York *Times*, January 9, 1955, p. 19.

promoting more efficient methods of stock breeding in the hope of developing an exportable surplus, and has attempted to settle nomadic peoples in stable agricultural communities.[19] Despite these efforts, all of which have been commended by the Advisory Council as well as the Trusteeship Council, a self-sustaining Somali economy by 1960 would seem to be an improbability, to put the matter as optimistically as possible.

The political consequences of this have been that until very recently only about one-fifth of the population was capable of political participation, and even now the vast majority of the population participates only through an indirect electoral system. Further the clan structure of the nomadic tribes is such as to make the introduction of governmental changes at the local level very difficult. To add to the original difficulties of the Italian administration, the most numerically powerful of the politically articulate groups is the Somali Youth League which, it will be remembered, was bitterly opposed to Italian administration of the territory in any form.

Political development within the territory has proceeded along essentially two lines: the Somalization of the Italian administration, and the creation and development of separate territorial organs of government. Italian administration is tri-level, culminating at the top in the Administrator who, with the advice of an Administrative Committee (composed of the Administrator, the Secretary-General of the Administration, and the heads of the government departments), holds executive and legislative powers. Beneath him are six Regional Commissioners and thirty District Commissioners. As of 1956, according to the Italian representative on the Trusteeship Council, all District Commissioners are Somalis, one of the Regional Commissioners is a Somali, and six Somalis have been appointed assistants to the Directors of various government departments and participate in the work of the Administrative Committee.[20] In general the vast majority of positions in the civil administration are manned by Somalis, and the Italians have inaugurated the Escuola Politica Administrata where the indigenous inhabitants of ability are trained to assume top level positions in the administration.[21]

The most important developments in connection with territorial organs of government[22] have been with respect to the Territorial Council (provided for in the trusteeship agreement), and the municipal councils in

[19] "Meeting the Deadline for Independence," *United Nations Review*, Vol. 1, No. 3 (September, 1954), p. 22.

[20] *General Assembly, Official Records: Tenth Session, Report of the Trusteeship Council covering the period from 17 July 1954 to 22 July 1955*, pp. 115-16.

[21] The New York *Times*, January 10, 1955, p. 4.

[22] This description of the present stage of development of territorial organs is based on *General Assembly, Official Records: Tenth Session, Report of the Trusteeship Council covering the period from 17 July 1954 to 22 July 1955*, pp. 111-16.

areas of permanent settlement. Originally appointed by the administering authority, the members of the Territorial Council have since been made elective officials. Election in the municipalities has been by direct male suffrage, while representatives of the nomadic population are indirectly elected through tribal councils. Present plans call for the introduction of direct elections throughout the territory in 1958. Ethnic considerations similar to those in Tanganyika have led to the allotment of seats in the Council on the basis of sixty for the Somalis, four each for Italians and Arabs, and one each for Indians and Pakistanis.[23]

With reference to the degree of legislative authority so far given to the Territorial Council about all that may be said at present is that it is in a transitional stage. The latest available documentation on this matter indicates that the Council exercises no real legislative power, but that the delegation of such was to be the next step (contemplated for 1956) taken in the devolution of political authority. Likewise, executive responsibility in the form of a number of governmental secretaryships with responsibilities of a ministerial nature were envisaged for the current year. This will gradually be increased as the chairmen of the standing committees in the Territorial Council, to be known as the Legislative Assembly, are appointed as parliamentary assistants to each Secretary.[24]

In the permanently settled areas, the administering authority has developed some forty-two municipal Councils, which now have fairly broad powers of decision, including the levying of taxes and control over expenditures within limits. The Somali members of these Councils, totaling two hundred eighty-one, are elected by direct male suffrage, while the remaining thirty-seven seats are appointive, distributed among the Arab, Italian, Indian, and Pakistani residents. At present these municipal councils constitute the nearest thing to effective self-government in Somaliland, and they appear to have functioned successfully. But an analysis of population and voting statistics reveals that they represent political involvement of, as yet, a small part of the population.[25]

Perhaps the most encouraging aspect of political development in Somali-

[23] The total indigenous population of Somaliland (est. 1953) is 1,263,509. In addition, there are approximately 5,000 Italians, 30,000 Arabs, and 1,000 Indians and Pakistanis. *Ibid.*, p. 107.

[24] Somali control of legislative functions and positions in the government were increased in May, 1956. As of that time the Legislative Assembly was given powers over internal affairs, except for Italian state employees and Italian contributions to Somaliland, and Somalis were nominated as Prime Minister and Ministers of the Interior, Social Affairs, Economic Affairs, Finance and General Affairs. "The Trust Territory of Somaliland Prepares for 1960," *United Nations Review,* Vol. 3, No. 2 (August, 1956), pp. 60-61.

[25] In the municipal elections of 1954 there were only 50,740 registered voters. Of these 38,119, or only about 3 per cent of the total indigenous population, participated in the elections.

land has been the continued growth and cooperative attitude of various Somali political parties, most notably the Somali Youth League. The latter, although bitterly protesting Italian administration has, along with other major parties, shown both moderation and realism. The parties to date, and there seems to be every likelihood that this will continue to be the case, have been the main agencies of political education and development of the heretofore politically untouched segments of the population. And upon their shoulders will rest those classic functions of educating and activating the electorate, if self-government is to succeed in Somaliland.

In sum, *if* the economic problems can be solved, and *if* the politically articulate part of the population can succeed in integrating the nomadic peoples into a reasonably unified democratic society, there is no reason why the experiment in Somaliland cannot succeed. The latter at present seems more nearly attainable than the former, and it may well be that an independent Somaliland will perforce remain very much dependent on Italy—or some other country—for financial aid in the future. In such an event, whether political independence can remain a fact and not become a façade, will be a crucial question for the trusteeship principle everywhere as well as for Somaliland.

British Togoland. The turning point in the history of this trust territory came in July, 1954, when the British government submitted a memorandum to the Trusteeship Council to the effect that in view of the fact that the Gold Coast was approaching a fully self-governing status, and since Togoland had been administered as an integral part of that British colony, the time had come to review the status of the trust territory. The British position in this connection was that Togoland should become a part of the self-governing Gold Coast and that the trusteeship for the area should therefore be terminated.

In order to appreciate the significance of the events occurring since that time it is necessary to keep in mind three important characteristics of the territory. First, British Togoland forms but one of two parts of the former German colony of Togoland, but the boundaries of the latter were themselves arbitrarily drawn in terms of the location of various African ethnic groups. In other words, an arbitrary division was made after World War I of an arbitrarily boundaried colony. Secondly, ethnic groups tend to follow horizontal lines which cross not only the Togolands boundaries, but extend into the neighboring territories of the Gold Coast on the west and Dahomey (French colony) on the east as well. The outstanding example of this is the Ewes, a distinct ethnic group whose people reside in the southern sections of the Gold Coast and both Togolands. Thirdly, despite the unnatural division of an unnatural former colony, a tradition of an east-west split of the Togolands has now some thirty-five years of history, and, more important, this history is one of separate administrations of the two Togolands by the British and the French.

French policy has looked toward the eventual association of French Togoland with the French Union, either as a separate "state" or as part of Dahomey. British administration has operated from the premise of a unitary relationship between the Gold Coast and British Togoland, with the obvious implication that the future of the latter—in British eyes at least—would depend on the fate of the former. Neither the British nor the French have made any significant attempts to coordinate their respective policies with a view to the eventual emergence of a united independent Togoland.

Yet from almost the very inception of the trusteeship system the Council has been besieged with petitions and oral statements, especially from representatives of the Ewe people, for action leading to the eventual unification of Togoland. If opinion on this issue was fairly uniform throughout the territories, undoubtedly much more pressure would have been exerted by the Council on the administering authorities to accede to the wishes of these petitioners. But, partly due to the tradition of separateness of the two administrations, and partly due also to the apathy, not to say opposition, of the northern peoples to the desires of the southern population (which includes the Ewes), there has never been substantial evidence that a majority of the population favored integration of the Togolands, at least in the absence of the guarantee that a unified Togoland would be a completely independent Togoland.

Attempts have been made, at the urging of the General Assembly and the Trusteeship Council, to alleviate some of the hardships and inconveniences caused by the division between British and French administrations, culminating in the creation of a short-lived Joint Togoland Council. But regardless of cooperation between British and French in this connection, it has been implicit in the administrations of both powers that the ends of colonial policy of each took precedence over the idea of a united Togoland as the final goal of trusteeship.

British administration in Togoland has consistently viewed that territory as forming an integral part of the Gold Coast. Thus from the outset the territory had no separate legislative or executive organs, but was represented in the territorial organs of the Gold Coast. Further, the territory was not administered as a unit within the general framework of Gold Coast government, but was divided between north and south. The following excerpt from a Trusteeship Council Report on conditions in the territories indicates the nature of the administration. After describing the executive and legislative bodies in the Gold Coast the Report continues:

> Togoland was not represented in these organs as a separate entity, but the Southern Section was entitled to return two rural members and one traditional

member to the Legislative Assembly, while the Northern Section was represented in the Northern Territories electoral college. By these means six Togolanders obtained seats in the Assembly.

. . . .

The Administering Authority considers that geographical, economic and other factors, and not least the common tribal origin of large parts of the population on both sides of the frontier, demand that in the interests of the people . . . the Trust Territory should be administered as an integral part of the Gold Coast. It considers further that the same factors, which include substantial differences between the peoples of the Northern and Southern Sections of the Territory—the same differences as those existing between the northern and southern parts of the Gold Coast—also make it impracticable to administer Togoland as an integral unit within the Gold Coast framework, but require that the Northern Section of Togoland should be closely associated with the Northern Territories of the Gold Coast and the Southern Section with the southern peoples of the Colony.[26]

When a new Constitution for the Gold Coast was promulgated in 1954, the Legislative Assembly was transformed into a body consisting entirely of persons elected directly by universal suffrage from one hundred and four constituencies covering the Gold Coast and British Togoland as a whole. The Gold Coast Cabinet was thenceforth to be completely appointed by the Assembly. Togoland's place in this system is described in a later Report:

Togoland is treated in matters of representation and participation in the functioning of the political institutions as if it were part of the Gold Coast. The electoral boundaries, which are not related to the boundary between the two territories, determine the representation of its people in the Legislative Assembly; there are fourteen constituencies which lie wholly or partly within the Territory. The election results determine their participation in the government; two Togolanders were in fact chosen by the leader of the successful party to serve as Minister of Education and Ministerial Secretary to the Ministry of Local Government respectively.[27]

Thus when, following the submission of the memorandum to the Trusteeship Council, the British suggested to the ninth General Assembly that the time had come to consider the termination of the trusteeship for British Togoland, the history of the political development of the territory had been inextricably bound up with that of the Gold Coast, and it was perhaps something of a classic of understatement when the British delegate stated that in his government's view "the objectives of the Trusteeship System would best be fulfilled by the union of Togoland

[26] *General Assembly, Official Records: Ninth Session, Report of The Trusteeship Council covering the period from 22 July 1953 to 16 July 1954*, pp. 53-54.

[27] United Nations Document T/L.579, Annex. One qualification to this is that no Gold Coast legislation could be applied in Togoland if in conflict with the trusteeship agreement.

under United Kingdom administration with a fully self-governing and independent Gold Coast." [28]

After considerable discussion, during the course of which representatives of the indigenous population of both Togolands were heard, the Fourth Committee, and later the General Assembly, adopted a resolution calling for a special visiting mission appointed by the Trusteeship Council to visit the territories and "ascertain the wishes of the inhabitants as to their future, without prejudice to the eventual solution they may choose whether it be independence, unification of an independent Togoland under British administration with an independent Togoland under French administration, unification with an independent Gold Coast, or some other self-governing or independent status. . . ." [29]

The mission was appointed at the fifteenth session of the Council, and its detailed terms of reference adopted at the sixteenth session.[30] It was composed of representatives of India, Australia, Syria, and the United States, charged with carrying out the General Assembly's resolutions quoted above, and asked to report to the Trusteeship Council not later than November 1, 1956.

The mission spent six weeks in the territories during August-September, 1955.[31] During the course of its visit it received thousands of communications and consulted orally with the representatives of the various organized groups in both Togolands. In British Togoland two main views emerged: (1) federation with the Gold Coast, supported by the Convention Peoples' Party (which now forms the government in the Gold Coast) and the Northern Peoples' Party (backed by the traditional chiefs who exercise considerable influence in the northern section of the territory); (2) unification with an independent French Togoland, supported by the Togoland Congress Party, the All-Ewe Conference and a few southern chiefs. In geographic terms this meant that the northern Togolanders generally were in favor of joining the Gold Coast, while those in the south were split between the two views. All parties in the territory, as well as the administering authority, agreed on the desirability of a plebiscite to determine finally the wishes of the inhabitants.

[28] *Official Records of the General Assembly, Ninth Session, Fourth Committee, 1954*, p. 336.

[29] *Resolutions adopted by the General Assembly during its Ninth Session.* Resolution 860 (IX). The vote on the resolution was 44 in favor, 0 opposed, with 12 abstentions.

[30] *Official Records of the Fifteenth Session of the Trusteeship Council* (January-March, 1955), *Resolutions.* Resolution 1084 (XV). *Official Records of the Sixteenth Session of the Trusteeship Council* (June-July, 1955), *Resolutions.* Resolution 1252 (XVI).

[31] "Visiting Mission Recommends Plebiscite to Resolve Future of British Togoland," *United Nations Review*, Vol. 2, No. 6 (December, 1955), pp. 33-37, summarized the mission's work in the territory and its report.

In French Togoland, again two views emerged: (1) parties that at present provide most of the members of the Government Council "vehemently favored" continuing association with the French Union, while (2) the Ewe people and others in the south favored unification of the two Togolands. For its part, the French administration assured the visiting mission that, while the termination of trusteeship in the territory was not immediately envisaged, plans were under way to provide for consultation with the indigenous inhabitants as to their ultimate future.

After congratulating the French government on its proposals to consult with the inhabitants in the near future, the mission reported that the time had come for a plebiscite in British Togoland. Specifically, it was suggested that two alternatives—in the form of questions—be given the people of the territory: (1) Do you want the integration of Togoland under British administration with an independent Gold Coast? (2) Do you want the separation of Togoland under British administration from the Gold Coast and its continuance under trusteeship, pending the ultimate determination of its political future?

It might be argued that since a significant portion of the population in both Togolands favored a unified independent Togoland this should have been made an alternative in the proposed plebiscite. Two things argued against this, however. First, as long as the French were not as yet prepared to relinquish their trusteeship no final determination of this question could be made. Secondly, and more important, suppose the British Togolanders voted for a unified Togoland and in a few years the French Togolanders voted to remain associated with the French Union.[32] It is doubtful if the British Togolanders would then desire a unified Togoland. The only way to assure protection of the British Togolanders was to make continuance under trusteeship the alternative to incorporation by the Gold Coast.

Because of the conflicting views in various parts of the territory, the mission recommended, finally, that the plebiscite be held in four separate areas, each permitted to determine its own future.

The Trusteeship Council considered the report of the mission at its fifth special session (October-December, 1955) and, with little discussion, decided to transmit it to the General Assembly as a useful basis for further action.[33]

When the General Assembly considered the report at its tenth ses-

[32] The French Togoland Territorial Assembly recently voted in favor of this. *Ibid.*, p. 36.

[33] *Official Records of the Fifth Special Session of the Trusteeship Council* (October-December, 1955), *Resolutions.* Resolution 1368 (S-5). It will be recalled that under the Charter the administering authority and the General Assembly, not the Trusteeship Council, must agree to the change or termination of trusteeship agreements for nonstrategic territories.

sion,[34] while many of the delegates stated that they would have preferred to see a simultaneous plebiscite in both territories, all except the Soviet bloc agreed that the present proposal was the most feasible in consequence of the different political status of the two Togolands. One substantive change in the mission's recommendations which was adopted at the urging of the British and Indian delegates provided that the plebiscite be conducted in the territory as a whole, rather than in separate parts. The justification for this was that Article 76b of the Charter referred to the wishes of the inhabitants of the *territory*, not various segments of it. In its final form the proposal was adopted by large majorities in both the Fourth Committee and the General Assembly.[35] Eduardo Espinosa Prieto of Mexico was appointed to serve as the Plebiscite Commissioner.

The plebiscite was held on May 9, 1956. The chart below gives a breakdown of the official results by district:

District	*Union*	*Separation*	*Rejected*	*Total*
Ho	7,487	18,981	35	26,503
Kpandu	8,581	16,959	49	25,589
Buem-Krachi	28,178	18,775	57	47,010
Gonja	3,166	2,729	—	5,895
Dagomba	28,083	6,549	603	35,235
Mamprusi	17,870	3,429	351	21,650
	93,365	67,422	1,095	161,882[36]

At its eighteenth session in the summer of 1956 the Trusteeship Council, after being officially notified of the plebiscite results, adopted a resolution recommending to the General Assembly that "appropriate steps" be taken, in consultation with the British, to end the trusteeship agreement for the territory. The effective date would be the same day on which the Gold Coast attained its independence.[37]

At the same time however, the Council rejected by a tie vote a French proposal to send a United Nations team to French Togoland to observe

[34] See "Plebiscite Soon for Resolving Future of West African Trust Territory," *United Nations Review*, Vol. 2, No. 8 (February, 1956), pp. 14-25.

[35] The vote in the Fourth Committee was 40 in favor, 5 against, with 8 abstentions; in the General Assembly: 42 in favor, 7 against, with 11 abstentions.

[36] "People of British Togoland Vote on Their Country's Future," *United Nations Review*, Vol. 2, No. 12 (June, 1956), p. 9.

[37] "Togoland Trust Territories," *United Nations Review*, Vol. 3, No. 3 (September, 1956), pp. 20-22. In July of 1956 a five day election was held in the Gold Coast at which time one party (the Convention People's Party) won 71 of 104 Assembly seats, garnering about 57 per cent of the total popular votes cast. As a result the country, now called Ghana, became an independent state within the British Commonwealth of Nations in March, 1957. For the election returns see The New York *Times*, July 13, 16, 18, 19, and 20, 1956.

a referendum to be held in October, 1956. The primary argument against the proposal was that the upcoming referendum provided for a choice between association within the French Union and continued trusteeship. No opportunity was to be given for the voters to express a preference for complete independence from France. It was decided to send the proposal and the records of the debate concerning it to the eleventh session of the General Assembly.[38]

Other than its importance as the first termination of a trusteeship, perhaps the most significant aspect of the recent events in Togoland is that at the bottom of the final disposition of the territory lie the different colonial policies of France and the United Kingdom. As one of the mission members pointed out:

> owing to forty years' association with their respective Administering Authorities, their (the two Togolands) economic, social, educational, political and jurisdical institutions fell into divergent patterns. Those divergencies were to be seen particularly in connection with the integration of the two Togolands. In British Togoland there was no objection to union with the neighboring Territory provided that the whole Territory was joined with the Gold Coast. In French Togoland, which was about two and a half times the size of British Togoland both in area and population, there was no objection to the union of the two Togolands provided that such a unified Togoland remained in the French Union. These were . . . the popular conceptions held by the people in the two Territories, and they were not likely to be changed by any political arguments put forward in the Assembly's Fourth Committee.[39]

Summarizing with respect to the questions raised at the beginning of this chapter, the evolution of the trusteeship system to date has shown, in so far as political advancement is concerned, that incorporation by a politically independent state with democratic institutions constitutes adequate fulfillment of the goals of the Charter.

Further, it seems clear that while the final political status of neither Tanganyika or, especially, Ruanda-Urundi can be confidently predicted as yet, for the French and British West African territories the road to political maturity leads either to integration with an independent neighboring state or autonomy within the French Union. While theoretically the British Togolanders were given their choice as to their ultimate political destiny, British administration from the first looked toward incorporation by the Gold Coast, just as the administration of the British Cameroons implicitly assumes ultimate federation with an independent Nigeria, and French administration admittedly points the indigenous peo-

[38] "Togoland Trust Territories," *United Nations Review,* Vol. 3, No. 3 (September, 1956), pp. 23-24.

[39] "Plebiscite Soon for Resolving Future of West African Trust Territory," *United Nations Review,* Vol. 2, No. 8 (February, 1956), p. 20. The mission member was Robert R. Robbins of the United States.

ple in the direction of association. And, although ethnic patterns have been taken into account in the attempt to alleviate hardships caused by arbitrary political divisions, such considerations have not so far proved fundamental in the ultimate disposition of a territory—nor is there any evidence they they will in the future.

When the Fourth Committee was discussing the proposed plebiscite for British Togoland the Philippine delegate expressed the doubts of many representatives in the United Nations when he stated:

> the annexation or integration of Togoland under British administration with the Gold Coast would create a precedent which would have its repercussions on the whole system of administration of dependent peoples, whether in Trust or in Non-Self-Governing Territories. If the United Nations countenanced such annexation, there would be nothing to prevent the annexation of Togoland under French administration to Dahomey, of the Cameroons under British administration to Nigeria, of the Cameroons under French administration to the French Union, of Ruanda-Urundi to the Belgian Congo, of Tanganyika to Kenya . . . and so on. In that event even the International Trusteeship System as established by Chapters XII and XIII of the charter, the system in which 220 million people had placed their hopes, would be nothing but an empty mockery.[40]

Yet it is difficult for a citizen of a country whose motto is *E Pluribus Unum* to accept the contention that justice is done only when every identifiable dependent territory, regardless of size or condition, achieves separate independent status. It perhaps would be ideal if all the administering authorities had the same policies with respect to their various trust territories, but they do not, and there is nothing in the trusteeship provisions of the Charter which can compel them to. If, at the end of a period of trusteeship, a genuine plebiscite, overseen by United Nations officials, indicates that the people of the territory prefer to be incorporated by a neighboring colony about to become independent, or remain associated in a union with the administering state, it would seem just as logical to argue that this showed the success of the administration rather than to have demonstrated any coercion on the part of the administering authority. In short, there is more than one definition of political maturity, and if the people of a territory are assured adequate representation in the organs of an independent state or international union, and if, further, their choice is made freely under international supervision, who is to say that the requirements of trusteeship have not been met?

[40] *Official Records of the General Assembly, Ninth Session, Fourth Committee,* 1954, p. 434.

CHAPTER ELEVEN

Conclusions

A survey of the formation and functioning of the trusteeship system leaves the over-all impression that the system is functioning—and functioning well. All the provisions of the Charter concerning international supervision of the administration of trust territories have been carried out, and the Council has evolved procedures for performing its activities efficiently. Perhaps the most encouraging result of this study is the realization that this organ of the United Nations is functioning successfully. Certainly this functioning has not always been smooth—but the Council is, on the whole, doing the job it was designed to do.

Having completed the investigation of the trusteeship system, it is now possible to revert to the series of questions raised in the Introduction, and formulate answers based on the results of this investigation.

What are the significant differences between the mandates and trusteeship systems? At the very outset the latter differed from the former in that the mandates system was an integral part of the peace settlement following World War I, while the organization of the United Nations, of which the trusteeship system is a part, was not connected with the treaties of peace following the second World War. In part because of this, the trusteeship system is much broader in potential scope than its predecessor. Mandates were evolved primarily as a specific solution to the problem of the disposition of former enemy colonies, although there was, of course, nothing to prevent that system from developing into something more. From this point of view the trusteeship system can be viewed as the logical extension of mandates, in terms both of the kinds of areas placed within the system, and the degree of international supervision.

Another significant difference in connection with the formation of the two systems is that, while in both cases the major powers made the crucial decisions concerning their organization, the smaller states took a much more active part in drawing up the trusteeship provisions of the Charter than they had in drafting Article 22 of the Covenant. This is particularly significant with respect to those states recently emerged from colonial status, such as Iraq, Egypt, and the Philippines, which were able to introduce important modifications in the proposals of the Big Five concerning trusteeship—proposals designed to protect further the rights of trust peoples and to make clear that the goal of trusteeship was to prepare the peoples of all trust territories for self-government or independence. The latter had been envisaged specifically only for "A" mandates under the League.

In addition to providing for self-government or independence, there are other important differences between the trusteeship provisions of the Charter and Article 22 of the Covenant. First, while the Permanent Mandates Commission had entertained some petitions, and the Council had sent out missions to the mandates, these supervisory devices were not provided for in the Covenant and were not used to any considerable extent. The Charter, however, provides for both of these as well as for the consideration of annual reports, which had been the Commission's main activity. Second, where the attempt was made to neutralize the mandates by forbidding their fortification, the Charter recognizes that the trust territories may play an active role in the preservation of international peace and security, and permits both fortifications in the territories and the raising of volunteer units for the indigenous inhabitants. In connection with this point, the Charter makes a distinction between strategic and nonstrategic territories, the former under the aegis of the Security Council, the latter under the General Assembly. This distinction recognizes, in effect, that there may be some areas of such strategic importance, that the international supervision of these areas must take second place to security considerations. No such distinction, of course, was made with respect to mandates.

A third major difference as between Charter and Covenant on this subject concerns the composition of the Trusteeship Council and the Permanent Mandates Commission, and their respective positions in the United Nations and the League. The Permanent Mandates Commission was an advisory body to the Council, composed of private persons, expert in the field of colonial administration. The Trusteeship Council is the primary organ in the trusteeship system. Representation of states, rather than private individuals, lessens the degree of expertness on the Council as compared to the Commission, but this is mitigated by the fact that each delegation has its own experts, and that those members of the Council not as fully competent on colonial matters as might be wished have the opportunity to gain firsthand knowledge through membership on the visiting missions. Making the Trusteeship Council a major organ of the United Nations was, in essence, a recognition on the part of those who drafted the Charter that the problems of dependent areas had assumed an increased importance in the realm of international affairs over that accorded to those problems by the delegates who drafted the Covenant in 1919. Further, making states members of the Trusteeship Council gave that body an authority not enjoyed by the Permanent Mandates Commission.

In so far as the trusteeship agreements for former mandates are concerned, the major differences from the mandates agreements were implicit in the changes between Covenant and Charter. The agreement for former Italian Somaliland, however, represents a great deal more international supervision and much greater restriction of the rights of the administering authority than was demanded by the Charter. The time limit of ten years within which the territory was to become independent, the creation of an Advisory Council to operate within the territory, and the Annex of Constitutional Principles to the agreement were all innovations. Further, the administering authorities concerned had submitted, and the United Nations approved, the agreements for the first ten territories placed under trusteeship. This followed the same practice as had been used for the mandates agreements. With regard to the agreement for Somaliland, however, the United Nations not only approved the agreement, but the Trusteeship Council took an active part in its drafting. One robin does not make a spring, and the agreement for Somaliland may well prove an exception rather than a precedent should any more territories be placed under trusteeship. Nevertheless, in at least this instance, it was demonstrated that the trusteeship provisions of the Charter can be interpreted very broadly, and that they may have become more meaningful than perhaps the administering powers expected, in terms of actually bringing a territory from a status of dependence to independence.

The differences between the functions of the Trusteeship Council and of the Permanent Mandates Commission are, again, for the most part implicit in the terms of the Charter as contrasted with the Covenant. Two aspects of Council functioning have developed, however, which were not foreseen by the Charter. The first is that, whether for better or worse, the trusteeship system generally, and the Council in particular, have been caught up in the whirlpool of the East-West struggle. The decision to place Somaliland under trusteeship, with Italy as the administering authority, was definitely a part of this unfortunate state of affairs, and much of the debate in the Council is marked by charges and counter-charges between the Soviet Union and the administering authorities. It might be argued that this was inevitable once the decision had been made to make states, rather than private individuals, the members of the Council. This, however, is doubtful. Had the Trusteeship Council been organized in exactly the same manner as the Permanent Mandates Commission, most assuredly a national of the Soviet Union would, by prior arrangement, have been selected for its membership. And that member most assuredly would have acted in the same manner as the Soviet delegate on the present Council. All evidence points to the fact that Communism does not recognize the difference between public and private personality for its adherents.

The second development results from the ambiguity of the Charter as to the precise relationship of the Trusteeship Council to the General Assembly. This has resulted in disputes concerning the proper role of the latter within the trusteeship system. The respective jurisdictions of the Council and the Permanent Mandates Commission were much more clearly defined than in the case of the General Assembly and Trusteeship Council. The Fourth Committee has not hesitated to adopt resolutions recommending action in the trust territories, and the Trusteeship Council has likewise not hesitated to water down these resolutions, making it clear that in its opinion the Council, not the General Assembly, is primarily responsible for the international supervision of the trust territories. So far the precise relationship between the two bodies has not been worked out—all that can be said at present is that the relationship is by no means clearly defined.

To what extent are the administrative duties of the Trusteeship Council influenced by the vicissitudes of the world political situation? This question has already been touched upon, but a few further points should be noted. In the first place, the Soviet representative on the Council may be consistently counted on to criticize any and all aspects of the administration of any given territory. While this may be irritating to the administering authorities, it serves to needle them into improving conditions in their territories and in this way has a beneficial effect on the operation of the system. From another point of view, however, the Soviet delegate has the reverse effect on Council action. That is, representatives of many of the nonadministering states on the Council clearly do not like to side with the Soviet Union on all issues, with the result that on some matters they will either abstain or vote with the administering authorities even though their predilections may correspond to those of the Soviet Union. There are, of course, manifest dangers to the trusteeship system in this development. In so far as the positions of East and West become rigidly opposed, cooperation becomes that much more difficult. Complete rigidity might well lead to a withdrawal from the activities of the United Nations by one side or the other. This has occurred temporarily, already. Should the day come when such a withdrawal is permanent the potentialities of the United Nations, and the trusteeship system as part of the organization, will be acutely jeopardized.

The East-West issue is not the only matter of world politics which affects the trusteeship system. It has become increasingly apparent that nationalism, particularly in Africa, is one of the predominant forces presently at work in the world. The trusteeship system is, of course, designed to solve the problem by permitting legitimate nationalist aspirations to materialize in a peaceful and orderly process. The point is, however, that on the one hand not all the colonial powers are willing to recognize the national aspirations of all their territories, and, on the other, the colonial peoples are becoming more and more impatient with what they consider to be the slow rate of progress at which they are attaining self-government, if, indeed, there is any progress at all. The trusteeship system is thus torn from two directions. The trust peoples continually press for greater measures of self-government, while the administering powers are constantly fearful that too speedy realization of the goals of trusteeship may produce unfortunate effects in their territories not under trusteeship. There is a good deal of justice in the complaint that the people of Somaliland, obviously not as ready for self-government as some dependent peoples, will receive their independence in four years. This is precisely why the French, among others, have been reluctant to see the Council move rapidly in the direction of promoting self-government in the territories. As a consequence the Council must attempt to steer some kind of middle ground between the demands of the trust peoples and the natural reluctance of the administering authorities to grant these demands.

On what assumptions does the Council depend for its successful functioning? The underlying fact to be remembered about the trusteeship system is that it is a voluntary organization. That is, the successful functioning of the Council depends in the last analysis on the willingness of the administering authorities to cooperate in the international supervision of their territorial administration. The point has been made in this study that there has been an increased emphasis on supervision as opposed to cooperation in the trusteeship as compared to the mandates system. This is undoubtedly true. But it is also true that half the Council's membership is composed of administering authorities—and that body can reach no decision that is not concurred in by the administering authorities. Thus, while the Council does accent supervision more than did the Permanent Mandates Commission, this is possible only because the administering authorities have agreed. Should they not agree, there could be no supervision. These remarks do not refer to the position of Italy on the Council. In the case of Somaliland, the General Assembly gave, and the General Assembly could take away. But, as the situation with regard to South West Africa has shown, there is little the United Nations can do to prevent the other administering states from treating their trust territories as they desire. It was thus wise to provide that the Trusteeship Council could take no action not acquiesced in by at least one of the administering states. Council resolutions would become meaningless unless those states agreed to carry them out.

This consideration brings up the subject of what modifications have so far occurred in the functioning of the trusteeship system. One observable modification, or at least potential modification, is implicit in the tendency of the Fourth Committee to adopt resolutions more critical of the administering authorities than those passed by the Council, and the attitude on the part of some members of the United Nations, as well as residents of the trust territories, that if the Trusteeship Council will not act, then the General Assembly should. This tendency indicates that some persons have forgotten the voluntary nature of the trusteeship system. Some of the discussions in the Fourth Committee have taken on an Alice-in-Wonderland aspect, devoid of any appreciation of the position of the administering authorities in the system. It is perhaps very natural, and certainly understandable, that people in the trust territories and representatives of states recently emerged from colonial status should want to do all in their power to further the political development of the trust territories. Too often, however, it is apparently forgotten—if it was ever realized—that nothing can nor will be done in the trust territories without the consent of the administering states involved. It may be unfortunate that this is so; it may be unfortunate that the United Nations generally depends on a spirit of cooperation among its members for its successful functioning. This is not the question here. The real point is that unless and until there is an acceptance by the administering authorities of modifications of the trusteeship system in the direction of giving the General Assembly more genuinely supervisory powers, any attempt by the latter body to modify the basic voluntary nature of the trusteeship system can lead only to recalcitrance on the part of administering states, with a concomitant breakdown in the successful functioning of the system.

Another development which may be considered a modification of the original provisions for trusteeship concerns the role of the Security Council in respect to action taken within the nonstrategic territories for the preservation of international peace and security. The provisions of the Charter on this point leave room for two possible interpretations: (1) that the Security Council has no particular control over fortifications or the raising of troops in nonstrategic areas, or (2) that the Security Council, while not generally concerned with the nonstrategic territories, must be consulted with respect to all measures (such as fortifications or the raising of troops) taken in those territories for the maintenance of international peace and security. If the decision to confer on the Security Council "primary responsibility for the maintenance of international peace and security" was to be fully implemented, then a good case can be made for the second interpretation. In fact, however, it is the first interpretation that has so far been accepted for all nonstrategic areas. Thus the Security Council has no control over the means used in each territory by the administering authority to maintain peace and security.

What does the evolution of the system reveal concerning the attainment of self-government or independence for the trust territories? Essentially the answer to this question is that the colonial policies of the administering states are fundamental in determining the attainment of the political goals of trusteeship. To say this, however, is not to say that the system has no effect on the administration of the trust territories. In the case of British Togoland, for example, it was on the basis of a United Nations-administered plebiscite that the territory became a part of the Gold Coast.

More generally, the three main methods of international supervision—consideration of annual reports, petitions, and visiting missions—provide a method of throwing the constant light of publicity on the operation of the system so that at the very least pressure is put on those administering authorities whose territories are not as advanced politically as others to speed the development of self-government. For example, the fact that the United Kingdom has been willing to terminate its trust for British Togoland, and itself urged the holding of a plebiscite, undoubtedly had much to do with recent political advances made in French Togoland.

Further, the visiting missions have not been backward in suggesting stepped-up political advancement in the territories, even to the point of recommending time limits by which various territories should have reached a self-governing status. And it is certain that if the experiment in Somaliland succeeds, increased pressure will be put on the administering authorities to hasten the political development of their respective trusts.

In short, while it is impossible to measure the exact influence of the system, it is undeniable that under it political advances have been made in all territories. And if the system cannot itself change the colonial policies of any administering state it can and does subject those policies to international inspection, shed the light of publicity on them, and require justification for them in both the Council and the General Assembly.

On this basis it is not difficult to see that, while the administering authorities can prevent the adoption of resolutions by the Trusteeship Council either condemning delay or encouraging further development of political autonomy and the nonadministering states conversely hold the upper hand in the Fourth Committee, the effectiveness of the trusteeship system will doubtless not be measured by victory of either the Fourth Committee or the Council in any jurisdictional squabble. Victory for either side would almost certainly mean a setback for the trust peoples. Rather the success of the system will remain based on the ability of the Council and the Fourth Committee, or more precisely the administering and non-administering authorities, to cooperate one with another.

Finally, what has the study of trusteeship revealed as to the nature of the general international decision-making process? The first thing that appears to anyone examining the records of the Trusteeship Council is the importance of procedures in the activities of that body. As was mentioned in Chapter 5, much of the debate in the Council has to date been concerned with how to do something rather than what should be done. The reason for this is that procedural questions very often have what might be called substantive overtones. For example, even though all the members of the Council agreed that petitions could be submitted to the Secretary-General, for transmission to the Council, directly through the administering authorities, or via the visiting missions, the Council spent considerable time discussing what was to be the "normal" method of submission. On the surface, there would seem to be few questions of less importance, in view of the fact that all members of the Council receive copies of the petitions long before they are considered. Actually, however, this point meant a great deal to the administering authorities. They were particularly concerned with the authority of the local administration in each territory, which, they felt, might be jeopardized should the indigenous popuplation make a habit of by-passing it in submitting petitions. After all, it is the administering authorities who must actually administer the territories, and any derogations of the prestige of the local administration makes the task that much more difficult. The student of British and American government, whose institutions have evolved over a considerable period of time and whose procedures are now fairly well settled, may find it difficult to understand why so much time is devoted to procedural questions in the United Nations. If he pauses to reflect on the importance of procedure in these two governments, however, and remembers that the United Nations is but eleven years old, it should not be surprising to him that great attention is paid to these matters.

A second important factor in the decision-making process of the Council concerns the effect of the formal, as distinct from the ulterior, positions taken by Council members, the administering authorities in particular. That is, even though the latter are naturally reluctant to admit faults in the administration of their territories and consistently urge the Council to "go slow" in terms of passing resolutions calling for fundamental changes in the territories, they are nonetheless committed to the principles of trusteeship as stated in the Charter, and as such are similarly reluctant to appear backward about implementing the Charter's provisions. The point is that, even though many issues in the Council find the administering and nonadministering states divided, the situation is not one of reactionary imperialist powers forced into an organization with enlightened liberal states whose sole concern is the benefit of dependent peoples. *Both* administering and nonadministering states are committed to the principles of the Charter—the commitment on the part of the former acts as a continual pressure in the direction of having them accept measures for the improvement of conditions in the territories as well as their helping them along the road to self-government. The willingness of the administering authorities to cooperate with the nonadministering states on the Council toward those ends is a measure of the real success the Council and the system have so far enjoyed.

A third conclusion, based on the study of trusteeship, is that there is no such thing as an "objective" United Nations decision, as distinct from power politics. Many of the small states in the General Assembly are often highly critical of the so-called colonial powers, and defend the actions of the Fourth Committee on the grounds that, including as it does all members of the United Nations, it can be a more objective judge of conditions in the territories than can the Council, where the administering authorities have equal representation with nonadministering states. This argument, however, does not stand up in the light of what happens when one of the nonadministering states becomes directly involved in a territorial question. For example, Ethiopia is often looked to as the state which most forcefully pleaded the cause of supporting the League of Nations in its attempt to stop the imperialist designs of Fascism. Yet, when it came to the disposition of the Italian colonies, the state was not at all backward about presenting claims for territorial compensation from Eritrea and Somaliland, and bitterly opposed the General Assembly's resolution placing the latter territory under trusteeship with Italy as the administering authority. The point of this is not to accuse the Ethiopians of hypocrisy. Rather it is to illustrate that it cannot be expected that traditional national policies will change, just because they are pursued within rather than outside of the United Nations.

The United Nations is, after all, not a supranational, but an international, organization. It provides the machinery by which the resolution of international conflicts can be settled. But it depends ultimately—and the Trusteeship Council's functioning is illustrative of this—on the desire of member states to cooperate with one another in the solution of problems. It is idle, therefore, to expect solutions to world problems based on idealistic or humanitarian notions of what is "right" for the international community, any more than decisions of Congress are the result of disinterested consideration of national problems by our legislators. But it is perhaps more mistaken to view the United Nations as merely a propaganda platform whereon states rationalize their power politics behind high-sounding sentiments. Rather the United Nations, as exemplified by the Trusteeship Council, is an institution where the various national policies may be pursued with the assumed understanding that any clash of those policies will be peacefully resolved. The latter assumption depends ultimately on the desire of the member states to cooperate in the solution of problems. In the case of the members of the Trusteeship Council, this desire—despite all the charges and counter-charges made in the debates of that body—is real, and the trusteeship system functions successfully as a result.

Appendix

Part I

Article 22 of the Covenant

1. To those colonies and territories which as a consequence of the late war have ceased to be under the sovereignty of the States which formerly governed them and which are inhabited by peoples not yet able to stand by themselves under the strenuous conditions of the modern world, there should be applied the principle that the well-being and development of such peoples form a sacred trust of civilization and that securities for the performance of this trust should be embodied in this Covenant.

2. The best method of giving practical effect to this principle is that the tutelage of such peoples should be entrusted to advance nations who, by reason of their resources, their experience or their geographical position, can best undertake this responsibility, and who are willing to accept it, and that this tutelage should be exercised by them as Mandatories on behalf of the League.

3. The character of the mandate must differ according to the stage of the development of the people, the geographical situation of the territory, its economic conditions and other similar circumstances.

4. Certain communities formerly belonging to the Turkish Empire have reached a stage of development where their existence as independent nations can be provisionally recognised subject to the rendering of administrative advice and assistance by a Mandatory until such time as they are able to stand alone. The wishes of these communities must be a principal consideration in the selection of the Mandatory.

5. Other peoples, especially those of Central Africa, are at such a stage that the Mandatory must be responsible for the administration of the territory under conditons which will guarantee freedom of conscience and religion, subject only to the maintenance of public order and morals, the prohibition of abuses such as the slave trade, the arms traffic and the liquor traffic, and the prevention of the establishment of fortifications or military and naval bases and of military training of the natives for other than police purposes and the defence of territory, and will also secure equal opportunities for the trade and commerce of other Members of the League.

6. There are territories, such as South West Africa and certain of the South Pacific Islands, which, owing to the sparseness of their population, or their small size, or their remoteness from the centers of civilisation, or their geographical contiguity to the territory of the Mandatory, and other circumstances, can be best administered under the laws of the Mandatory as integral portions of its territory, subject to the safeguards above mentioned in the interests of the indigenous population.

7. In every case of mandate, the Mandatory shall render to the Council an annual report in reference to the territory committed to its charge.

8. The degree of authority, control or administration to be exercised by

the Mandatory shall, if not previously agreed upon by the Members of the League, be explicitly defined in each case by the Council.

9. A permanent Commission shall be constituted to receive and examine the annual reports of the Mandatories and to advise the Council on all matters relating to the observance of the mandates.

Chapters XII and XIII of the Charter

CHAPTER XII—INTERNATIONAL TRUSTEESHIP SYSTEM

Article 75. The United Nations shall establish under its authority an international trusteeship system for the administration and supervision of such territories as may be placed thereunder by subsequent individual agreements. These territories are hereinafter referred to as trust territories.

Article 76. The basic objectives of the trusteeship system, in accordance with the Purposes of the United Nations laid down in Article 1 of the present Charter, shall be:

a. to further international peace and security;

b. to promote the political, economic, social, and educational advancement of the inhabitants of the trust territories, and their progressive development towards self-government or independence as may be appropriate to the particular circumstances of each territory and its peoples and the freely expressed wishes of the peoples concerned, and as may be provided by the terms of each trusteeship agreement;

c. to encourage respect for human rights and for fundamental freedoms for all without distinction as to race, sex, language, or religion, and to encourage recognition of the interdependence of the peoples of the world; and

d. to ensure equal treatment in social, economic, and commercial matters for all Members of the United Nations and their nationals, and also equal treatment for the latter in the administration of justice, without prejudice to the attainment of the foregoing objectives and subject to the provisions of Article 80.

Article 77. 1. The trusteeship system shall apply to such territories in the following categories as may be placed thereunder by means of trusteeship agreements:

a. territories now held under mandates;

b. territories which may be detached from enemy states as a result of the Second World War; and

c. territories voluntarily placed under the system by states responsible for their administration.

2. It will be a matter for subsequent agreement as to which territories in the foregoing categories will be brought under the trusteeship system and upon what terms.

Article 78. The trusteeship system shall not apply to territories which have become Members of the United Nations, relationship among which shall be based on respect for the principle of sovereign equality.

Article 79. The terms of trusteeship for each territory to be placed under the trusteeship system, including any alteration or amendment, shall be agreed upon by the states directly concerned, including the mandatory power in the case of territories held under mandate by a Member of the United Nations, and shall be approved as provided for in Articles 83 and 85.

Article 80. 1. Except as may be agreed upon in individual trusteeship agreements, made under Articles 77, 79, and 81, placing each territory under the trusteeship system, and until such agreements have been concluded, nothing in this Chapter shall be construed in or of itself to alter in any manner the rights whatsoever of any states or any peoples or the terms of existing international instruments to which Members of the United Nations may respectively be parties.

2. Paragraph 1 of this Article shall not be interpreted as giving grounds for delay or postponement of the negotiation and conclusion of agreements for placing mandated and other territories under the trusteeship system as provided for in Article 77.

Article 81. The trusteeship agreement shall in each case include the terms under which the trust territory will be administered and designate the authority which will exercise the administration of the trust territory. Such authority, hereinafter called the administering authority, may be one or more states or the Organization itself.

Article 82. There may be designated, in any trusteeship agreement, a strategic area or areas which may include part or all of the trust territory to which the agreement applies, without prejudice to any special agreement or agreements made under Article 43.

Article 83. 1. All functions of the United Nations relating to strategic areas, including the approval of the terms of the trusteeship agreements and of their alteration or amendment, shall be exercised by the Security Council.

2. The basic objectives set forth in Article 76 shall be applicable to the people of each strategic area.

3. The Security Council shall, subject to the provisions of the trusteeship agreements and without prejudice to security considerations, avail itself of the assistance of the Trusteeship Council to perform those functions of the United Nations under the trusteeship system relating to political, economic, social, and educational matters in the strategic areas.

Article 84. It shall be the duty of the administering authority to ensure that the trust territory shall play its part in the maintenance of international peace and security. To this end the administering authority may make use of volunteer forces, facilities, and assistance from the trust territory in carrying out the obligations towards the Security Council undertaken in this regard by the administering authority, as well as for local defense and the maintenance of law and order within the trust territory.

Article 85. 1. The functions of the United Nations with regard to trusteeship agreements for all areas not designated as strategic, including the approval of the terms of the trusteeship agreements and of their alteration or amendment, shall be exercised by the General Assembly.

2. The Trusteeship Council, operating under the authority of the General Assembly, shall assist the General Assembly in carrying out these functions.

CHAPTER XIII—THE TRUSTEESHIP COUNCIL

COMPOSITION

Article 86. 1. The Trusteeship Council shall consist of the following Members of the United Nations:

a. those Members administering trust territories;

b. such of those Members mentioned by name in Article 23 as are not administering trust territories; and

c. as many other Members elected for three-year terms by the General

Assembly as may be necessary to ensure that the total number of members of the Trusteeship Council is equally divided between those Members of the United Nations which administer trust territories and those which do not.

2. Each member of the Trusteeship Council shall designate one specially qualified person to represent it therein.

FUNCTIONS AND POWERS

Article 87. The General Assembly and, under its authority, the Trusteeship Council, in carrying out their functions, may:

a. consider reports submitted by the administering authority;

b. accept petitions and examine them in consultation with the administering authority;

c. provide for periodic visits to the respective trust territories at times agreed upon with the administering authority; and

d. take these and other actions in conformity with the terms of the trusteeship agreements.

Article 88. The Trusteeship Council shall formulate a questionnaire on the political, economic, social, and educational advancement of the inhabitants of each trust territory, and the administering authority for each trust territory within the competence of the General Assembly shall make an annual report to the General Assembly upon the basis of such questionnaire.

VOTING

Article 89. 1. Each member of the Trusteeship Council shall have one vote.

2. Decisions of the Trusteeship Council shall be made by a majority of the members present and voting.

PROCEDURE

Article 90. 1. The Trusteeship Council shall adopt its own rules of procedure, including the method of selecting its President.

2. The Trusteeship Council shall meet as required in accordance with its rules which shall include provision for the convening of meetings on the request of a majority of its members.

Article 91. The Trusteeship Council shall, when appropriate, avail itself of the assistance of the Economic and Social Council and of the specialized agencies in regard to matters with which they are respectively concerned.

Part II

Text of a "B" Mandate, Ruanda-Urundi

The Council of the League of Nations:

Whereas, By Article 119 of the Treaty of Peace with Germany signed at Versailles on June 28, 1919, Germany renounced in favor of the Principal Allied and Associated Powers all her rights over her oversea possessions, including therein German East Africa; and

Whereas, The Principal Allied and Associated Powers agreed that, in accordance with Article 22, Part I (Covenant of the League of Nations), of the said treaty, a mandate should be conferred upon His Majesty the King of the Belgians to administer part of the former colony of German East Africa, and have proposed that the mandate should be formulated in the following terms; and

Whereas, His Majesty the King of the Belgians has agreed to accept the mandate in respect to the said territory, and has undertaken to exercise it on behalf of the League of Nations in accordance with the following provisions; and

Whereas, By the forementioned Article 22, paragraph 8, it is provided that the degree of authority, control or administration to be exercised by the Mandatory, not having been previously agreed upon by the members of the League, shall be explicitly defined by the Council of the League of Nations:

Confirming the said mandate, defines its terms as follows:

Article 1. The territory over which a mandate is conferred upon His Majesty the King of the Belgians (hereinafter called the Mandatory) comprises that part of the territory of the former colony of German East Africa situated to the west of the following line: [Clauses indicating frontier lines are omitted here].

Article 2. A boundary Commission shall be appointed by His Majesty the King of the Belgians and His Britannic Majesty to trace on the spot the line described in Article 1 above.

In case any dispute should arise in connection with the work of these commissioners, the question shall be referred to the Council of the League of Nations, whose decision shall be final.

The final report by the boundary commission shall give the precise description of this boundary as actually demarcated on the ground; the necessary maps shall be annexed thereto and signed by the commissioners. The report, with its annexes, shall be made in triplicate: one copy shall be deposited in the archives of the League of Nations, one shall be kept by the Government of His Majesty the King of the Belgians and one by the Government of His Britannic Majesty.

Article 3. The Mandatory shall be responsible for the peace, order and good government of the territory, and shall undertake to promote to the utmost the material and moral well-being and the social progress of its inhabitants.

Article 4. The Mandatory shall not establish any military or naval bases, nor erect any fortifications, nor organize any native military force in the territory except for local police purposes and for the defence of the territory.

Article 5. The Mandatory:

(1) shall provide for the eventual emancipation of all slaves and for as speedy an elimination of domestic and other slavery as social conditions will allow;

(2) shall suppress all forms of slave trade;

(3) shall prohibit all forms of forced or compulsory labor, except for essential public works and essential services, and then only in return for adequate remuneration;

(4) shall protect the natives from abuse and measures of fraud and force by the careful supervision of labor contracts and the recruiting of labor;

(5) shall exercise a strict control over the traffic in arms and ammunition and the sale of spirituous liquors.

Article 6. In the framing of laws relating to the holding or transfer of land, the Mandatory shall take into consideration native laws and customs, and shall respect the rights and safeguard the interests of the native population.

No native land may be transferred, except between natives, without the previous consent of the public authorities. No real rights over native land in favor of non-natives may be created except with the same consent.

The mandatory will promulgate strict regulations against usury.

Article 7. The Mandatory shall secure to all nationals of states members of the League of Nations the same rights as are enjoyed by his own nationals in respect to entry into and residence in the territory, the protection afforded to their person and property, the acquisition of property, movable and immovable, and the exercise of their profession or trade, subject only to the requirements of public order, and on condition of compliance with the local law.

Further, the Mandatory shall ensure to all nationals of states members of the League of Nations, on the same footing as to his own nationals, freedom of transit and navigation, and complete economic, commercial and industrial equality; provided that the Mandatory shall be free to organize essential public works and essential services on such terms and conditions as he thinks just.

Concessions for the development of the natural resources of the territory shall be granted by the Mandatory without distinction on grounds of nationality between nationals of all states members of the League of Nations, but on such conditions as will maintain intact the authority of the local government.

Concessions having the character of a general monopoly shall not be granted. This provision does not affect the right of the Mandatory to create monopolies of a purely fiscal character in the interest of the territory under mandate, and in order to provide the territory with fiscal resources which seem best suited to the local requirements; or, in certain cases, to carry out the development of natural resources for the benefit of the Mandatory or his nationals, directly or indirectly, nor any preferential advantages which shall be inconsistent with the economic, commercial and industrial equality hereinbefore guaranteed.

The rights conferred by this article extend equally to companies and associations organized in accordance with the law of any of the members of the League of Nations, subject only to the requirements of public order, and on condition of compliance with the local law.

Article 8. The Mandatory shall ensure in the territory complete freedom of conscience and the free exercise of all forms of worship which are consonant with public order and morality; missionaries who are nationals of states members of the League of Nations shall be free to enter the territory and to travel and reside therein, to acquire and possess property, to erect religious buildings and to open schools throughout the territory, it being understood, however, that the Mandatory shall have the right to exercise such control as may be necessary for the maintenance of public order and good government, and to take all measures required for such control.

Article 9. The Mandatory shall apply to the territory any general international conventions applicable to contiguous territories.

Article 10. The Mandatory shall have full powers of administration and legislation in the area subject to the mandate: this area shall be administered in accordance with the laws of the Mandatory as an integral part of the territory and subject to the preceding provisions.

The Mandatory shall therefore be at liberty to apply his laws to the territory under the mandate subject to the modifications required by local conditions, and to constitute the territory into a customs, fiscal or administrative union or federation with the adjacent possessions under his own sovereignty or control; provided always that the measures adopted to that end do not infringe the provisions of this mandate.

Article 11. The Mandatory shall make to the Council of the League of Nations an annual report to the satisfaction of the Council. This report shall contain full information concerning the measures taken to apply the provisions of the present mandate.

Article 12. The consent of the Council of the League of Nations is required for any modification of the terms of this mandate.

Article 13. The Mandatory agrees that if any dispute whatever should arise between the Mandatory and another member of the League of Nations relating to the interpretation or the application of the provisions of the mandate, such dispute, if it cannot be settled by negotiation, shall be submitted to the Permanent Court of International Justice provided for by Article 14 of the Covenant of the League of Nations.

The present instrument shall be deposited in original in the archives of the League of Nations. Certified copies shall be forwarded by the Secretary-General of the League of Nations to all members of the League.

Done at London, the twentieth day of July one thousand nine hundred and twenty-two.

Text of the Trusteeship Agreement for Ruanda-Urundi

Whereas the territory known as Ruanda-Urundi has been administered in accordance with Article 22 of the Covenant of the League of Nations under a Mandate conferred upon Belgium;

Whereas Article 75 of the United Nations Charter signed at San Francisco on 26 June 1945 provides for the establishment of an international trusteeship system for the administration and supervision of such territories as may be placed thereunder by subsequent agreements;

Whereas under Article 77 of the said Charter the international trusteeship system may be applied to territories now held under mandates;

Whereas the Belgian Government has indicated its desire to place Ruanda-Urundi under the international trusteeship system; and

Whereas under Articles 75 and 77 of the Charter the placing of a territory under the international trusteeship system is to be effected by means of a trusteeship agreement;

Now, therefore, the General Assembly of the United Nations hereby resolved to approve the following terms of trusteeship for Ruanda-Urundi.

Article 1. The present Trusteeship Agreement shall apply to the whole of the territory of Ruanda-Urundi as at present administered by Belgium and as defined by Article 1 of the Belgian Mandate and by the Treaty concluded in London on 22 November 1934 by Belgium and the United Kingdom.

Article 2. By the present Agreement, the Belgian Government is designated as Administering Authority for Ruanda-Urundi in accordance with Article 75 of the Charter. The said Government shall assume responsibility for the administration of the said Territory.

Article 3. The Administering Authority undertakes to administer Ruanda-Urundi in such a manner as to achieve the basic objectives of the international trusteeship system laid down in Article 76 of the United Nations Charter. The Administering Authority further undertakes to collaborate fully with the General Assembly of the United Nations and with the Trusteeship Council in the discharge of all their functions as defined in Article 87 of the United Nations Charter.

It likewise undertakes to facilitate such periodic visits to the Trust Territory as the General Assembly or the Trusteeship Council may decide to arrange, to decide jointly with these organs the dates on which such visits shall take place and also to agree jointly with them on all questions concerned with the organization and accomplishment of these visits.

Article 4. The Administering Authority shall ensure the maintenance of peace and order as well as the good government and defence of the Territory. The said Authority shall ensure that the Territory shall play its part in the maintenance of international peace and security.

Article 5. For the above-mentioned purposes, and in order to fulfill the obligations arising under the Charter and the present Agreement, the Administering Authority:

1. Shall have full powers of legislation, administration and jurisdiction in the territory of Ruanda-Urundi and shall administer it in accordance with Belgian law as an integral part of Belgian territory, subject to the provisions of the Charter and of this Agreement.
2. Shall be entitled to constitute Ruanda-Urundi into a customs, fiscal or administrative union or federation with adjacent territories under its sovereignty and to establish common services between such territories and Ruanda-Urundi, provided that such measures are not inconsistent with the objectives of the international trusteeship system and with the provisions of this Agreement.
3. May establish on the Trust Territory military bases, including air bases, erect fortifications, station its own armed forces and raise volunteer contingents therein.

The Administering Authority may likewise, within the limits laid down by the Charter, take all measures of organization and defence appropriate for ensuring:

The participation of the Territory in the maintenance of international peace and security.

The respect for obligations concerning the assistance and facilities to be given by the Administering Authority to the Security Council.

The respect for internal law and order.

The defence of the Territory within the framework of special agreements for the maintenance of international peace and security.

Article 6. The Administering Authority shall promote the development of free political institutions suited to Ruanda-Urundi. To this end the Administering Authority shall ensure to the inhabitants of Ruanda-Urundi an increasing share in the administration and services, both central and local, of the Territory: it shall further such participation of the inhabitants in the representative organs of the population as may be appropriate to the particular conditions of the Territory.

In short, the Administering Authority shall take all measures conducive to the political advancement of the population of Ruanda-Urundi in accordance with Article 76 (b) of the Charter of the United Nations.

Article 7. The Administering Authority undertakes to apply to Ruanda-Urundi the provisions of all present or future international conventions which may be appropriate to the particular conditions of the Territory and which would be conducive to the achievement of the basic objectives of the international trusteeship system.

Article 8. In framing laws relating to the ownership of land and the rights over natural resources, and to their transfer, the Administering Authority shall take into consideration native laws and customs and shall respect the rights and safeguard the interests, both present and future, of the native population. No native land or native-owned natural resources may be transferred, except between natives, save with the previous consent of the competent public authority. No real rights over native land or native-owned resources of the subsoil, in favor of non-natives, may be created except with the same consent.

Article 9. Subject to the provisions of the following article, the Administering Authority shall take all necessary steps to ensure equal treatment in social, economic, industrial and commercial matters for all States Members of the United Nations and their nationals and to this end:

1. Shall ensure to all nationals of Members of the United Nations the same rights as are enjoyed by its own nationals in respect of entry into and residence in Ruanda-Urundi, freedom of transit and navigation, including freedom of transit and navigation by air, the acquisition of property, both movable and immovable, the protection of person and property, and the exercise of professions and trades.

2. Shall not discriminate on grounds of nationality against nationals of any Member of the United Nations in matters relating to the grant of concessions for the development of natural resources of the Territory and shall not grant concessions having the character of a general monopoly.

3. Shall ensure equal treatment in the administration of justice to the nationals of all Members of the United Nations.

The rights conferred by this article on the nationals of States Members of the United Nations apply equally to companies or associations controlled by such nationals and formed in accordance with the law of any Member of the United Nations.

Article 10. Measures taken to give effect to the provisions of the preceding article shall be subject always to the overriding duty of the United Nations and of the Administering Authority to promote the political, economic, social and cultural advancement of the inhabitants of the Territory, and to pursue the other objectives of the trusteeship system as laid down in Article 76 of the Charter of the United Nations.

The Administering Authority shall, in particular, be free:

1. To organize essential public services and works on such terms and such conditions as it thinks just;

2. To create, in the interests of Ruanda-Urundi, monopolies of a purely fiscal character in order to provide the Territory with the resources which seem best suited to local requirements;

3. Where the interests of the economic advancement of the inhabitants of the Territory may require it, to establish or permit to be established, for specific purposes, other monopolies or undertakings having in them an element of monopoly, under conditions of proper public control provided that, in the selection of agencies to carry out the purposes of this paragraph, other than agencies controlled by the Government or those in which the Government participates, the Administering Authority shall not discriminate on grounds of nationality against Members of the United Nations or their nationals.

Article 11. Nothing in this Agreement shall entitle any Member of the United Nations to claim for itself or for its nationals, companies or associations the benefits of Article 9 of the Agreement in any respect in which it does not give to the inhabitants, companies and associations of Ruanda-Urundi equality of treatment with the nationals, companies and associations of the state which it treats most favourably.

Article 12. The Administering Authority shall develop the system of elementary education in the Trust Territory in order to reduce the number of illiterates, to train the inhabitants in manual skill, and to improve the education of the population. The Adminstering Authority shall, so far as possible, provide the necessary facilities to enable qualified students to receive higher education, more especially professional education.

Article 13. The Administering Authority shall ensure throughout the Trust Territory complete freedom of conscience, freedom of religious teaching and the free exercise of all forms of worship which are consistent with public order and morality; all missionaries who are nationals of any State Member of the United Nations shall be free to enter, travel and reside in the Trust Territory, to acquire and possess property, to erect religious buildings and to open schools and hospitals therein. The provisions of the present article shall not, however, affect the duty of the Administering Authority to exercise such control as may be necessary for the maintenance of public order and good government and also the quality and progress of education.

Article 14. Subject only to the requirements of public order, the Administering Authority shall guarantee to the inhabitants of the Trust Territory freedom of speech, of the press, of assembly, and of petition.

Article 15. The Administering Authority may, on behalf of the Trust Territory, accept membership in any advisory regional commission (regional authority), technical organization, or other voluntary association of States. It may co-operate with specialized agencies, whether public or private, and participate in other forms of international co-operation not inconsistent with the Charter.

Article 16. The Administering Authority shall make to the General Assembly of the United Nations an annual report on the basis of the questionnaire drawn up by the Trusteeship Council in accordance with Article 88 of the Charter of the United Nations.

Such reports shall include information regarding the measures taken in order to give effect to the suggestions and recommendations of the General Assembly and of the Trusteeship Council.

The Administering Authority shall appoint an accredited representative to attend the meetings of the Trusteeship Council at which the reports of the Administering Authority for Ruanda-Urundi will be examined.

Article 17. Nothing in this Agreement shall affect the right of the Administering Authority to propose at any future date the designation of the whole or part of the Territory as a strategic area in accordance with Articles 82 and 83 of the Charter.

Article 18. The terms of the present Trusteeship Agreement may not be altered or amended except as provided in Articles 79, 83 or 85 of the Charter.

Article 19. If any dispute whatever should arise between the Administering Authority and another Member of the United Nations relating to the interpretation or application of the provisions of the present Trusteeship Agreement, such dispute, if it cannot be settled by negotiation or other means, shall be submitted to the International Court of Justice provided for by Chapter XIV of the Charter of the United Nations.

Text of a Pacific Mandate, Western Samoa

The Council of the League of Nations:

Whereas, by Article 119 of the treaty of peace with Germany signed at Versailles on June 28, 1919, Germany renounced in favor of the Principal Allied and Associated Powers all her rights over her overseas possessions, including therein German Samoa; and

Whereas, The Principal Allied and Associated Powers agreed that, in accordance with Article 22, Part I (Covenant of the League of Nations), of the said treaty a mandate should be conferred upon His Britannic Majesty to be exercised on his behalf by the Government of the Dominion of New Zealand to administer German Samoa, and have proposed that the mandate should be formulated in the following terms; and

Whereas, His Britannic Majesty has agreed to accept a mandate for and on behalf of the Government of the Dominion of New Zealand and has undertaken to exercise it on behalf of the League of Nations in accordance with the following provisions: and in respect of the said territory.

Whereas, by the aforementioned Article 22, paragraph 8, it is provided that the degree of authority, control or administration to be exercised by the Mandatory not having been previously agreed upon by the members of the League, shall be explicitly defined by the Council of the League of Nations;

Confirming the said mandate, defines its terms as follows:

Article 1. The territory over which a mandate is conferred upon his Britannic Majesty for and on behalf of the Government of the Dominion of New Zealand (hereinafter called the mandatory) is the former German colony of Samoa.

Article 2. The Mandatory shall have full power of administration and legislation over the territory subject to the present mandate as an integral portion of the Dominion of New Zealand and may apply the laws of the Dominion of New Zealand.

The Mandatory shall promote to the utmost the material and moral wellbeing and the social progress of the inhabitants of the territory subject to the present mandate.

Article 3. The Mandatory shall see that the slave trade is prohibited, and that no forced labor is permitted, except for essential public works and services, and then only for adequate remuneration.

The Mandatory shall also see that the traffic in arms and ammunition is controlled in accordance with principles analogous to those laid down in the convention relating to the control of the arms traffic, signed on September 10, 1919, or in any convention amending the same.

The supply of intoxicating spirits and beverages to the natives shall be prohibited.

Article 4. The military training of the natives, otherwise than for purposes of internal police and the local defense of the territory, shall be prohibited. Furthermore, no military or naval bases shall be established or fortification erected in the territory.

Article 5. Subject to the provisions of any local law for the maintenance of public order and public morals, the Mandatory shall ensure in the territory freedom of conscience and the free exercise of all forms of worship, and shall allow all missionaries, nationals of any state member of the League of Nations, to enter into, travel and reside in the territory for the purpose of prosecuting their calling.

Article 6. The Mandatory shall make to the Council of the League of Nations an annual report to the satisfaction of the Council, containing full information with regard to the territory, and indicating the measures taken to carry out the obligations assumed under Articles 2, 3, 4, and 5.

Article 7. The consent of the Council of the League of Nations is required for any modification of the terms of the present mandate.

The Mandatory agrees that, if any dispute whatever should arise between the Mandatory and another member of the League of Nations relating to the interpretation or the application of the provisions of the mandate, such dispute, if it cannot be settled by negotiation, shall be submitted to the Permanent Court of International Justice provided for by Article 14 of the Covenant of the League of Nations.

The present declaration shall be deposited in the archives of the League of Nations. Certified copies shall be forwarded by the Secretary-General of the League of Nations to all Powers signatories of the treaty of peace with Germany.

Certified true copy.

Secretary-General

Made at Geneva the 17th day of December, 1920.

Text of the Trusteeship Agreement for a Pacific Territory, Western Samoa

Whereas the territory of Western Samoa has been administered in accordance with Article 22 of the Covenant of the League of Nations and pursuant to a mandate conferred upon His Britannic Majesty to be exercised on his behalf by the Government of New Zealand;

And whereas the Charter of the United Nations signed at San Francisco on 26 June 1945, provides for the establishment of an international trusteeship system for the administration and supervision of such territories as may be the subject of trusteeship agreements;

And whereas under the said Charter the international trusteeship system may be applied to territories now held under mandate;

And whereas the Government of New Zealand have indicated their willingness that the said international trusteeship system be applied to Western Samoa;

And whereas the said Charter provides further that the terms of trusteeship are to be approved by the United Nations;

Now, therefore, the General Assembly of the United Nations, hereby resolves to approve the following terms of trusteeship for Western Samoa, in substitution for the terms of the aforesaid mandate.

Article 1. The Territory to which this Agreement applies is the Territory known as Western Samoa comprising the islands of Upolu, Savai'i, Manone, and Apolissa, together with all other islands and rocks adjacent thereto.

Article 2. The Government of New Zealand are hereby designated as the Administering Authority for Western Samoa.

Article 3. The Administering Authority shall have full powers of administration, legislation and jurisdiction over the territory, subject to the provisions of the Agreement, and of the Charter of the United Nations, and may apply to the Territory, subject to any modifications which the Administering Authority may consider desirable, such of the laws of New Zealand as may seem appropriate to local conditions and requirements.

Article 4. The Administering Authority undertakes to administer Western Samoa in such a manner as to achieve in that Territory the basic objectives of the international trusteeship system, as expressed in Article 76 of the Charter of the United Nations, namely:

(a) to further international peace and security;

(b) to promote the political, economic, social and educational advancement of the inhabitants of the trust territories, and their progressive development towards self-government or independence as may be appropriate to the particular circumstances of each territory and its peoples and the freely expressed wishes of the peoples concerned, and as may be provided by the terms of each trusteeship agreement;

(c) to encourage respect for human rights and for fundamental freedoms for all without distinction as to race, sex, language or religion, and to encourage recognition of the inter-dependence of the peoples of the world; and

(d) to ensure equal treatment in social, economic, and commercial matters for all Members of the United Nations and their nationals, and also equal treatment for the latter in the administration of justice, without prejudice to the attainment of the foregoing objectives and subject to the provisions of Article 80.

Article 5. The Administering Authority shall promote the development of free political institutions suited to Western Samoa. To this end as may be appropriate to the particular circumstances of the Territory and its peoples, the Administering Authority shall assure to the inhabitants of Western Samoa a progressively increasing share in the administrative and other services of the Territory, shall develop the participation of the inhabitants of Western Samoa in advisory and legislative bodies and in the government of the Territory, and shall take all other appropriate measures with a view to the political advancement of the inhabitants of Western Samoa in accordance with Article 76 (b) of the Charter of the United Nations.

Article 6. In pursuance of its undertakings to promote the social advancement of the inhabitants of the Trust Territory, and without in any way limiting its obligations thereunder, the Administering Authority shall:

1. Prohibit all forms of slavery and slave-trading;
2. Prohibit all forms of forced or compulsory labour, except for essential public works and services as specifically authorized by the local administration and then only in times of public emergency, with adequate remuneration and adequate protection of the welfare of the workers;
3. Control the traffic in arms and ammunition;
4. Control, in the interest of the inhabitants, the manufacture, importation and distribution of intoxicating spirits and beverages; and
5. Control the production, importation, manufacture, and distribution of opium and narcotic drugs.

Article 7. The Administering Authority undertakes to apply in Western Samoa the provisions of any international conventions and recommendations as drawn up by the United Nations or its specialized agencies which are, in the opinion of the Administering Authority, appropriate to the needs and conditions of the Trust Territory, and conducive to the achievement of the basic objectives of the international trusteeship system.

Article 8. In framing the laws to be applied in Western Samoa, the Administering Authority shall take into consideration Samoan customs and usages and shall respect the rights and safeguard the interests both present and future of the Samoan population.

In particular, the laws relating to the holding or transfer of land shall ensure that no native land may be transferred save with the prior consent of the competent public authority and that no right over native land in favour of any person not a Samoan may be created except with the same consent.

Article 9. The Administering Authority shall ensure in the Territory freedom of conscience and the free exercise of all forms of worship, and shall allow missionaries, nationals of any State Member of the United Nations, to enter into, travel and reside in the Territory for the purpose of prosecuting their calling. The provisions of this Article shall not, however, affect the right and duty of the Administering Authority to exercise such control as it may consider necessary for the maintenance of peace, order and good government.

Article 10. The Administering Authority shall ensure that the Trust Territory of Western Samoa shall play its part, in accordance with the Charter of the United Nations, in the maintenance of international peace and security. To this end the Administering Authority shall be entitled:

1. To establish naval, military and air bases and to erect fortifications in the Trust Territory.
2. To station and employ armed forces in the Territory.
3. To make use of volunteer forces, facilities and assistance from the Trust Territory in carrying out the obligations toward the Security Council undertaken in this regard by the Administering Authority, as well as for local defence and the maintenance of law and order within the Trust Territory.
4. To take all such other measures in accordance with the Purposes and Principles of the Charter of the United Nations as are in the opinion of the Administering Authority necessary to the maintenance of international peace and security and the defence of Western Samoa.

Article 11. The Administering Authority shall as may be appropriate to the circumstances of the Trust Territory, continue and extend a general system of education, including post-primary education and professional training.

Article 12. Subject only to the requirements of public order, the Administering Authority shall guarantee to the inhabitants of the Trust Territory, freedom of speech, of the press, of assembly and of petition.

Article 13. The Administering Authority may arrange for the cooperation of Western Samoa in any regional advisory commission, regional technical organization or other voluntary association of states, any specialized international bodies, public or private, or other forms of international activity not inconsistent with the Charter of the United Nations.

Article 14. The Administering Authority shall make to the General Assembly of the United Nations an annual report on the basis of a questionnaire drawn up by the Trusteeship Council in accordance with the Charter of the United Nations and shall otherwise collaborate fully with the Trusteeship Council in the discharge of all the Council's functions in accordance with Articles 87 and 88 of the Charter. The Administering Authority shall arrange to be represented at the sessions of the Trusteeship Council at which the reports of the Administering Authority with regard to Western Samoa are considered.

Article 15. The terms of the Agreement shall not be altered or amended except as provided in Article 79 of the Charter of the United Nations.

Article 16. If any dispute should arise between the Administering Authority and another Member of the United Nations, relating to the interpretation or application of the provisions of this Agreement, such dispute, if it cannot be settled by negotiation or similar means, shall be submitted to the International Court of Justice.

Text of the Trusteeship Agreement for the Trust Territory of the Pacific Under United States Administration

PREAMBLE

Whereas Article 75 of the Charter of the United Nations provides for the establishment of an international trusteeship system for the administration and supervision of such territories as may be placed thereunder by subsequent agreements; and

Whereas under Article 77 of the said Charter the trusteeship system may be applied to territories now held under mandate; and

Whereas on 17 December 1920 the Council of the League of Nations confirmed a mandate for the former German islands north of the equator to Japan, to be administered in accordance with Article 22 of the Covenant of the League of Nations; and

Whereas Japan, as a result of the Second World War, has ceased to exercise any authority in these islands;

Now, therefore, the Security Council of the United Nations, having satisfied itself that the relevant articles of the Charter have been complied with, hereby resolves to approve the following terms of trusteeship for the Pacific Islands formerly under mandate to Japan.

Article 1. The Territory of the Pacific Islands, consisting of the islands formerly held by Japan under mandate in accordance with Article 22 of the Covenant of the League of Nations, is hereby designated as a strategic area and placed under the trusteeship system established in the Charter of the United Nations. The Territory of the Pacific Islands is hereinafter referred to as the trust territory.

Article 2. The United States of America is designated as the administering authority of the trust territory.

Article 3. The administering authority shall have full powers of administration, legislation, and jurisdiction over the territory subject to the provisions of this agreement, and may apply to the trust territory, subject to any modifications which the administering authority may consider desirable, such of the laws of the United States as it may deem appropriate to local conditions and requirements.

Article 4. The administering authority, in discharging the obligations of trusteeship in the trust territory, shall act in accordance with the Charter of the United Nations, and the provisions of this agreement, and shall, as specified in Article 83 (2) of the Charter, apply the objectives of the international trusteeship system, as set forth in Article 76 of the Charter, to the people of the trust territory.

Article 5. In discharging its obligations under Article 76 (a) and Article 84

of the Charter, the administering authority shall ensure that the trust territory shall play its part, in accordance with the Charter of the United Nations, in the maintenance of international peace and security. To this end the administering authority shall be entitled:

1. to establish naval, military and air bases and to erect fortifications in the trust territory;

2. to station and employ armed forces in the territory; and

3. to make use of volunteer forces, facilities and assistance from the trust territory in carrying out the obligations towards the Security Council undertaken in this regard by the administering authority, as well as for the local defense and the maintenance of law and order within the trust territory.

Article 6. In discharging its obligations under Article 76 (b) of the Charter, the administering authority shall:

1. foster the development of such political institutions as are suited to the trust territory and shall promote the development of the inhabitants of the trust territory toward self-government or independence as may be appropriate to the particular circumstances of the trust territory and its peoples and the freely expressed wishes of the peoples concerned; and to this end shall give to the inhabitants of the trust territory a progressively increasing share in the administrative services in the territory; shall develop their participation in government; shall give due recognition to the customs of the inhabitants in providing a system of law for the territory; and shall take other appropriate measures toward these ends;

2. promote the economic advancement and self-sufficiency of the inhabitants, and to this end shall regulate the use of natural resources; encourage the development of fisheries, agriculture, and industries; protect the inhabitants against the loss of their lands and resources; and improve the means of transportation and communication;

3. promote the social advancement of the inhabitants and to this end shall protect the rights and fundamental freedoms of all elements of the population without discrimination; protect the health of the inhabitants; control the traffic in arms and ammunition, opium and other dangerous drugs, and alcohol and other spirituous beverages; and to institute such other regulations as may be necessary to protect the inhabitants against social abuses; and

4. promote the educational advancement of the inhabitants, and to this end shall take steps toward the establishment of a general system of elementary education; facilitate the vocational and cultural advancement of the population; and shall encourage qualified students to pursue higher education, including training on the professional level.

Article 7. In discharging its obligations under Article 76 (a) of the Charter, the administering authority shall guarantee to the inhabitants of the trust territory freedom of conscience, and, subject only to the requirements of public order and security, freedom of speech, of the press, and of assembly; freedom of worship, and of religious teaching; and freedom of migration and movement.

Article 8. 1. In discharging its obligations under Article 76 (d) of the Charter, as defined by Article 83 (2) of the Charter, the administering authority, subject to the requirements of security, and the obligation to promote the advancement of the inhabitants, shall accord to nationals of each Member of the United Nations and to companies and associations organized in conformity with the laws of such Member, treatment in the trust territory no less favourable than that accorded therein to nationals, companies and associations of any other United Nation except the administering authority.

2. The administering authority shall ensure equal treatment to the Members of the United Nations and their nationals in the administration of justice.

3. Nothing in the Article shall be construed as to accord traffic rights to aircraft flying into and out of the trust territory. Such right shall be subject to agreement between the administering authority and the state whose nationality such aircraft possesses.

4. The administering authority may negotiate and conclude commercial and other treaties and agreements with Members of the United Nations and other states, designed to attain for the inhabitants of the trust territory treatment by the Members of the United Nations and other states no less favourable than that granted by them to the nationals of other states. The Security Council may recommend, or invite other organs of the United Nations to consider and recommend, what rights the inhabitants of the trust territory should acquire in consideration of the rights obtained by Members of the United Nations in the trust territory.

Article 9. The administering authority shall be entitled to constitute the trust territory into a customs, fiscal, or administrative union or federation with other territories under United States jurisdiction and to establish common services between such territories and the trust territory where such measures are not inconsistent with the basic objectives of the International Trusteeship System and with the terms of this agreement.

Article 10. The administering authority, acting under the provisions of Article 3 of this agreement, may accept membership in any regional advisory commission, regional authority, or technical organization, or other voluntary association of states, may co-operate with specialized international bodies, public or private, and may engage in other forms of international co-operation.

Article 11. 1. The administering authority shall take the necessary steps to provide the status of citizenship of the trust territory for the inhabitants of the trust territory.

2. The administering authority shall afford diplomatic and consular protection to the inhabitants of the trust territory when outside the territorial limits of the trust territory or of the territory of the administering authority.

Article 12. The administering authority shall enact such legislation as may be necessary to place the provisions of this agreement in effect in the trust territory.

Article 13. The provisions of Articles 87 and 88 of the Charter shall be applicable to the trust territory, provided that the administering authority may determine the extent of their applicability to any areas which may from time to time be specified by it as closed for security reasons.

Article 14. The administering authority undertakes to apply in the trust territory the provisions of any international conventions and recommendations which may be appropriate to the particular circumstances of the trust territory and which would be conducive to the achievement of the basic objectives of Article 6 of this agreement.

Article 15. The terms of the present agreement shall not be altered, amended or terminated without the consent of the administering authority.

Article 16. The present agreement shall come into force when approved by the Security Council of the United Nations and by the Government of the United States after due constitutional process.

Trusteeship Agreement for the Territory of Somaliland Under Italian Administration

PREAMBLE

Whereas Chapters XII and XIII of the Charter of the United Nations provide for an International Trusteeship System,

Whereas, by Article 23 of the Treaty of Peace between the Allied and Associated Powers and Italy, signed in Paris on 10 February 1947, Italy renounced all right and title to the Italian territorial possessions in Africa,

Whereas, under paragraph 3 of Annex XI of this Treaty, the General Assembly of the United Nations was requested to make recommendations regarding the future status of the territories referred to in Article 23 thereof,

Whereas, under paragraph 3 of Annex XI of this Treaty, the Governments of France, of the Union of Soviet Socialist Republics, of the United Kingdom of Great Britain and Northern Ireland, and of the United States of America agreed to accept the recommendations made by the General Assembly of the United Nations in this matter,

Whereas the General Assembly, after having examined the question at its third and fourth sessions, adopted, at its 250th plenary meeting on 21 November 1949, a resolution recommending, with respect to the territory formerly known as Italian Somaliland, that the Territory shall be an independent and sovereign State; that its independence shall become effective at the end of ten years from the date of approval of the Trusteeship Agreement by the General Assembly and that, during this period of ten years, the Territory shall be placed under the International Trusteeship System with Italy as the Administering Authority, aided and advised by an Advisory Council composed of representatives of Colombia, Egypt and the Philippines,

Whereas the Trusteeship Council, as requested by the General Assembly, has negotiated the draft of a Trusteeship Agreement with Italy and approved it at the eighth meeting of its sixth session on 27 January 1950,

Whereas the Government of Italy has accepted responsibility as the Administering Authority of this Territory,

Whereas the Governments of Colombia, Egypt and the Philippines have accepted the responsibility of aiding and advising the Administering Authority in their capacity as members of the Advisory Council,

Now, therefore, the General Assembly of the United Nations approves the following terms of trusteeship for the territory formerly known as Italian Somaliland:

Article 1. The territory to which this Agreement applies is the territory formerly known as Italian Somaliland, hereafter called the Territory, bounded by the Somaliland Protectorate, Ethiopia, Kenya, the Gulf of Aden and the Indian Ocean. Its boundaries shall be those fixed by international agreement and, in so far as they are not already delimited, shall be delimited in accordance with a procedure approved by the General Assembly.

Article 2. Italy shall be entrusted with the administration of the Territory, and the Government of Italy (designated in the Agreement as the Administering Authority) shall be represented therein by an Administrator. The Administering Authority shall be responsible to the United Nations for the peace, order, and good government of the Territory in accordance with the terms of this Agreement.

The Administering Authority shall be aided and advised by an Advisory

Council composed of representatives of Colombia, Egypt and the Philippines.

The headquarters of the Administrator and of the Advisory Council shall be in Mogadishu.

Article 3. The Administering Authority undertakes to administer the Territory in accordance with the provisions of the Charter of the United Nations relating to the International Trusteeship System as set out in Chapters XII and XIII thereof, the relevant parts of the resolution 269 (IV) of 21 November 1949 of the General Assembly, and this Agreement (which includes an annex containing a Declaration of Constitutional Principles), with a view to making the independence of the Territory effective at the end of ten years from the date of the approval of this Agreement by the General Assembly.

The Administering Authority shall:

1. Foster the development of free political institutions and promote the development of the inhabitants of the Territory towards independence; and to this end shall give to the inhabitants of the Territory a progressively increasing participation in the various organs of Government;

2. Promote the economic advancement and self-sufficiency of the inhabitants, and to this end shall regulate the use of natural resources; encourage the development of fisheries, agriculture, trade and industries; protect the inhabitants against the loss of their lands and resources; and improve the means of transportation and communication;

3. Promote the social advancement of the inhabitants, and to this end shall protect the rights and fundamental freedoms of all elements of the population without discrimination; protect and improve the health of the inhabitants by the development of adequate health and hospital services for all sections of the population; control the traffic in arms and ammunition, opium and other dangerous drugs, alcohol and other spirituous liquors; prohibit all forms of slavery, slave trade and child marriage; apply existing international conventions concerning prostitution; prohibit all forms of forced or compulsory labour, except for essential public works and services, and then only in time of public emergency with adequate remuneration and adequate protection of the welfare of the workers; and institute such other regulations as may be necessary to protect the inhabitants against any social abuses.

Article 4. The Administering Authority, recognizing the fact that education in its broadest sense is the only sure foundation on which any moral, social, political and economic advancement of the inhabitants of the Territory can be based, and believing that national independence with due respect for freedom and democracy can be established only on this basis, undertakes to establish a sound and effective system of education, with due regard for Islamic culture and religion.

The Administering Authority therefore undertakes to promote the educational advancement of the inhabitants, and to this end undertakes to establish as rapidly as possible a system of public education which shall include elementary, secondary, vocational (including institutions for the training of teachers) and technical schools, to provide free of charge at least elementary education, and to facilitate higher and professional education and cultural advancement in every possible way.

In particular, the Administering Authority shall take all appropriate steps:

(a) To provide that an adequate number of qualified students from among the indigenous population receive university or professional education outside the Territory, so as to ensure that sufficient qualified personnel will be available when the Territory becomes a sovereign independent state;

(b) To combat illiteracy by all possible means; and

(c) To ensure that instruction is given in schools and other educational institutions regarding the activities of the United Nations and its organs, the basic objectives of the International Trusteeship System and the Universal Declaration of Human Rights.

Article 5. The Administering Authority shall collaborate fully with the General Assembly of the United Nations and with the Trusteeship Council in the discharge of all their functions as defined in Articles 87 and 88 of the Charter of the United Nations.

Accordingly, the Administering Authority undertakes:

1. To make to the General Assembly of the United Nations an annual report on the basis of the questionnaire drawn up by the Trusteeship Council in accordance with Article 88 of the Charter of the United Nations, and to include in this report information relating to the measures taken to give effect to the suggestions and recommendations of the General Assembly and of the Trusteeship Council;
2. To designate an accredited representative to be present at the sessions of the Trusteeship Council at which the reports of the Administering Authority and petitions relating to conditions in the Territory are considered;
3. To facilitate periodic visits to the Territory as provided for in Article 87 of the Charter of the United Nations at time and in accordance with arrangements to be agreed upon with the Administering Authority;
4. To render assistance to the General Assembly or the Trusteeship Council in the application of these arrangements and of such other arrangements as those organs of the United Nations may make in accordance with the terms of this Agreement.

Article 6. The Administering Authority may maintain police forces and raise volunteer contingents for the maintenance of peace and good order in the Territory.

The Administering Authority, after consultation with the Advisory Council, may establish installations and take all measures in the Territory, including the progressive development of Somali defence forces, which may be necessary, within the limits laid down in the Charter of the United Nations, for the defence of the Territory and for the maintenance of international peace and security.

Article 7. The Administering Authority shall have full powers of legislation, administration and jurisdiction in the Territory, subject to the provisions of the Charter of the United Nations, of this Agreement and of the annex attached hereto, and shall have power to apply to the Territory, temporarily and with such modifications as are considered necessary, such Italian laws as are appropriate to the conditions and needs of the Territory and as are not incompatible with the attainment of its independence.

Article 8. The Advisory Council shall be fully informed by the Administering Authority on all matters relating to the political, economic, social and educational advancement of the inhabitants of the Territory, including legislation appertaining thereto, and may make to the Administering Authority such observations and recommendations as it may consider will be conducive to the attainment of the objectives of this Agreement.

The Administering Authority shall seek the advice of the Advisory Council on all measures envisaged for the inauguration, development and subsequent establishment of full self-government for the Territory; in particular, it shall consult the Advisory Council regarding plans for:

(a) The establishment and development of organs of self-government;

(b) Economic and financial development;

(c) Educational advancement;

(d) Labour and social advancement; and

(e) The transfer of the functions of government to a duly constituted independent Government of the Territory.

The Administering Authority shall seek the advice of the Advisory Council on ordinances which, in accordance with article 5 of the annex to this Agreement, the Administrator of the Territory may make and promulgate in exceptional circumstances.

Article 9. The Advisory Council shall be accorded such facilities and shall have free access to such sources of information as it may require for the performance of its functions.

Article 10. In the Territory, members of the Advisory Council shall enjoy full diplomatic privileges and immunities, and their staff shall enjoy the privileges and immunities which they would enjoy if the Convention on the Privileges and Immunities of the United Nations were applicable to the Territory.

Article 11. States members of the Advisory Council, if they are not members of the Trusteeship Council, shall be entitled to participate without vote in the debates of the Trusteeship Council on any questions specifically relating to the Territory.

In the course of such debates, members of the Advisory Council, or the majority of the members, acting in the name of the Advisory Council, or each of the members acting separately, may make to the Trusteeship Council such oral statements or may submit such written reports or memoranda as they may deem necessary for the Council's proper consideration of any question specifically relating to the Territory.

Article 12. The Administering Authority undertakes to maintain the application of the international agreements and conventions which are at present in force in the Territory, and to apply therein any conventions and recommendations made by the United Nations or by the specialized agencies referred to in Article 57 of the Charter of the United Nations, the application of which would be in the interests of the population and consistent with the basic objectives of the Trusteeship System, the provisions of resolution 269 (IV) of 21 November 1949 of the General Assembly, and the terms of this Agreement.

Article 13. The Administering Authority shall take all the necessary steps to enable the Territory to co-operate with the specialized agencies referred to in Article 57 of the Charter of the United Nations and with other international agencies and regional organizations, and to participate in their activities.

Article 14. In order to promote the economic and social advancement of the indigenous population, the Administering Authority shall, in framing laws relating to the holding or alienation of land or other natural resources, take into consideration the laws and customs of the indigenous population and respect their rights and safeguard their interests, both present and future.

The Administering Authority shall not, without the consent in each case of a two-thirds majority of the members of the Territorial Council (provided for in article 4 of the annex to this Agreement), permit the acquisition by non-indigenous persons or by companies or associations controlled by such persons of any rights over land in the Territory save on lease for a period to be determined by law. In cases involving the alienation to non-indigenous persons or to companies or associations controlled by such persons of areas of agricultural lands in excess of one thousand acres, the Administering Authority shall also request in advance the advice of the Advisory Council. The Administering Authority shall include in its annual report to the Trusteeship Council a detailed account of such alienations.

The Administering Authority shall prohibit the acquisition by non-indigenous persons or by companies or associations controlled by such persons of any rights over any other natural resources in the Territory, save on lease or grant of concession for a period to be determined by law.

Nothing in this article shall apply to building land within the municipal area of Mogadishu which may be disposed of in accordance with regulations prescribed by law.

Article 15. Subject to the provisions of articles 14, 16 and 17 of this Agreement, the Administering Authority shall take all necessary steps to ensure equal treatment in social, economic, industrial and commercial matters for all States Members of the United Nations and their nationals and for its own nationals, and to this end:

(a) Shall grant to all nationals of Members of the United Nations and to its own nationals freedom of transit and navigation, including freedom of transit and navigation by air, and the protection of person and property, subject to the requirements of public order and on condition of compliance with the local law;

(b) Shall ensure the same rights to all nationals of Members of the United Nations as to its own nationals in respect of entry into and residence in the Territory, acquisiton of property, both movable and immovable, and the exercise of professions and trades;

(c) Shall not discriminate on grounds of nationality against nationals of any Member of the United Nations or its own nationals in matters relating to the grant of concessions for the development of the natural resources of the Territory and shall not grant concessions having the character of a general monopoly; and

(d) Shall ensure equal treatment in the administration of justice to the nationals of all Members of the Untied Nations and to its own nationals.

The rights conferred by this article on nationals of Members of the United Nations or on the Administering Authority's own nationals apply equally to companies and associations controlled by such nationals and organized in accordance with the law of any Member of the United Nations or with the law of the Administering Authority.

Article 16. Measures taken to give effect to article 15 of this Agreement shall be subject always to the overriding duty of the Administering Authority, in accordance with Article 76 of the Charter of the United Nations, to promote the political, economic, social, and educational advancement of the inhabitants of the Territory, to carry out the other basic objectives of the International Trusteeship System and the provisions of resolution 289 (IV) of the General Assembly of 21 November 1949, and to maintain peace, order and good government. In particular, the Administering Authority shall be free:

(a) To organize essential public services and works on such terms and conditions as it thinks just;

(b) To create monopolies of a purely fiscal character in order to provide the Territory with the fiscal resources which seem best suited to local requirements, or otherwise to serve the interests of the inhabitants;

(c) Where the interests of the economic advancement of the inhabitants may require it, to establish, or permit to be established, for specific purposes, other monopolies or undertakings having in them an element of monopoly, under conditions of proper public control; provided that, in the selection of agencies to carry out the purposes of this paragraph, other than agencies controlled by the Government of the Territory or those in which Government participates, the Administering Authority shall not discriminate on grounds of nationality against Members of the United Nations or their nationals.

Article 17. Nothing in this Agreement shall entitle any Member of the United Nations to claim for itself or for its nationals, companies and associations the benefits of article 15 of this Agreement in any respect in which it does not give to the inhabitants, companies and associations of the Territory equality of treatment with the nationals, companies and associations of the State which it treats most favourably.

Article 18. The Administering Authority shall include in its first annual report to the Trusteeship Council a report on the position in the Territory of property belonging to nationals, associations and companies of Members of the United Nations.

Article 19. The Administering Authority shall, in a spirit of religious tolerance, ensure in the Territory complete freedom of conscience and religion and shall guarantee freedom of religous teaching and the free exercise of all forms of worship.

Missionaries of any faith shall be free to enter, travel and reside in the Territory; to acquire and possess property therein, subject to the conditions laid down in article 14 of the Agreement; to erect religious buildings and hospitals therein; and to open schools subject to such regulations as may be prescribed by law for the educational advancement of the inhabitants of the Territory.

The provisions of this article shall be subject only to such limitations as may be necessary for the maintenance of public order and morality.

Article 20. The Administering Authority shall guarantee to the inhabitants of the Territory complete freedom of speech, of the Press, of assembly and of petition, without distinction as to race, sex, language, political opinion or religion, subject only to the requirements of public order.

Article 21. Nothing in this Agreement shall affect the right of the Administering Authority or the Trusteeship Council to propose, at any future date, the alteration or amendment of this Agreement in the interests of the Territory or for reasons not inconsistent with the basic objectives of the International Trusteeship System.

The provisions of this Agreement shall not be altered or amended except as provided in Articles 79 and 85 of the Charter of the United Nations.

Article 22. If any dispute whatever should arise between the Administering Authority and a State Member of the United Nations relating to the interpretation or the application of the provisions of the Agreement, such dispute, if it cannot be settled by direct negotiation or other means, shall be submitted to the International Court of Justice.

Article 23. The present Agreement, of which the Declaration of Constitutional Principles attached hereto as an annex is an integral part, shall enter into force as soon as it is approved by the General Assembly of the United Nations and ratified by Italy.

Nevertheless, after the Trusteeship Council and Italy have agreed upon the terms of trusteeship and pending approval of this Agreement by the General Assembly, the Administering Authority shall provisionally administer the Territory in accordance with the provisions of the Charter of the United Nations and of this Agreement and shall assume this provisional administration at a time and pursuant to arrangements for the orderly transfer of administration agreed upon between Italy and the United Kingdom of Great Britain and Northern Ireland.

Article 24. The present Agreement shall cease to be in force ten years after the date of the approval of the Trusteeship Agreement by the General Assembly, at the conclusion of which the Territory shall become an independent sovereign State.

Article 25. The Administering Authority shall submit to the Trusteeship Council, at least eighteen months before the expiration of the present Agreement; a plan for the orderly transfer of all the functions of government to a duly constituted independent Government of the Territory.

Annex

Declaration of Constitutional Principles

PREAMBLE

In view of the recommendation made by the General Assembly of the United Nations at its fourth regular session with respect to placing the territory formerly known as Italian Somaliland under the International Trusteeship System with Italy as the Administering Authority,

Considering the provisions of the Charter of the United Nations which establish an International Trusteeship System, the terms of this Trusteeship Agreement, of which this Declaration is an integral part, and in accordance with the provision of resolution 289 (IV) of the General Assembly,

For the purpose of solemnly guaranteeing the rights of the inhabitants of the Territory and of providing, in accordance with democratic principles, for the gradual development of institutions designed to ensure the establishment of full self-government and independence, and the attainment of the basic objectives of the International Trusteeship System in conformity with the Charter of the United Nations,

It is hereby declared:

Article 1. The sovereignty of the Territory is vested in its people and shall be exercised by the Administering Authority on their behalf and in the manner prescribed herein by decision of the United Nations.

Article 2. The Administering Authority shall take the necessary steps to provide for the population of the Territory a status of citizenship of the Territory and to ensure their diplomatic and consular protection when outside the limits of the Territory and of the territory of the Administering Authority.

Article 3. The Administrator shall be the chief executive officer of the Territory.

Article 4. The Administrator shall appoint a Territorial Council, composed of inhabitants of the Territory and representative of its people.

In all other matters than defence and foreign affairs, the Administrator shall consult the Territorial Council.

The legislative authority shall normally be exercised by the Administrator, after consultation with the Territorial Council, until such time as an elective legislature has been established.

Article 5. In exceptional circumstances the Administrator may, after consultation with the Advisory Council, make and promulgate such ordinances as in his opinion the circumstances demand.

These ordinances shall be laid before the Territorial Council as soon as may be practicable and the Administering Authority shall include an account of all such ordinances in its annual report to the Trusteeship Council.

Article 6. In matters relating to defence and foreign affairs as in other matters, the Administering Authority shall be accountable to the Trusteeship Council, and shall take into account any recommendations which the Council may see fit to make.

Article 7. The Administering Authority shall establish a judicial system and shall ensure the absolute independence of the judiciary. The Administering Authority shall also ensure that representatives of the indigenous population be progressively entrusted with judicial functions and that the jurisdiction of courts of first instance be progressively increased.

As may be appropriate in each case, the Administering Authority shall apply territorial legislation, Islamic law and customary law.

Article 8. The Administering Authority, in accordance with the principles laid down in its own Constitution and legislation, shall guarantee to all inhabitants of the Territory human rights and fundamental freedoms, and full equality before the law without distinction as to race, sex, language, political opinion or religion.

Article 9. The Administering Authority shall guarantee to all the inhabitants of the Territory full civil rights, and also such political rights as are consistent with the progressive political, social, economic and educational development of the inhabitants and with the development of a democratic representative system, due regard being paid to traditional institutions.

In particular, it shall guarantee:

1. The preservation of their personal and successional status with due regard to its evolutionary development;
2. The inviolability of personal liberty, which may not be restricted except by warrant of judicial authority and only in cases and accordance with regulations prescribed by law;
3. The inviolability of domicile, to which the competent authority may have access only by due legal process and in a manner prescribed in accordance with local customs and subject to the guarantees prescribed by law;
4. The inviolability of freedom and secrecy of communication and correspondence, which may be limited only by means of a warrant of judicial authority stating the reasons and subject to the guarantees prescribed by law;
5. The rights of property, subject to expropriation carried out for a public purpose, after payment of fair compensation, and in accordance with regulations prescribed by law;
6. The free exercise of professions and occupations in accordance with local customs and with regulations prescribed by law;
7. The right to compete for public employment in accordance with regulations prescribed by law; and

8. The right to emigrate and to travel, subject to such regulations as may be prescribed by law for health and security reasons.

Article 10. The Administering Authority accepts as a standard of achievement for the Territory the Universal Declaration of Human Rights adopted by the General Assembly of the United Nations on 10 December 1948.

Bibliography

Books and Pamphlets

Adam, Thomas R. *Modern Colonialism.* Garden City, New York: Doubleday and Co. 1955.

Bentwich, Norman. *The Mandates System.* London: Longmans Green. 1930.

Byrnes, James F. *Speaking Frankly.* New York: Harper and Bros. 1947.

Goodrich, Leland S. and Edward Hambro. *Charter of the United Nations, Commentary and Documents* (Second Edition). Boston: World Peace Foundation. 1949.

Gunther, John. *Inside Africa.* New York: Harpers. 1955.

Haines, C. Grove (Ed.). *Africa Today.* Baltimore: The Johns Hopkins Press. 1955.

Hall, H. Duncan. *Mandates, Dependencies and Trusteeship.* Washington: Carnegie Endowment for International Peace. 1948.

Hertslet, E. *The Map of Africa By Treaty.* 3 vols. London: printed for His Majesty's Stationery Office by Harrison and Sons. 1909.

Hocking, W. E. *Colonies and Dependent Areas,* Problem IX. Boston: Universities Committee on Post-War International Problems. 1943.

Hull, Cordell. *Memoirs.* 2 vols. New York: Macmillan. 1948.

League of Nations. *The Mandates System, Origin—Principles—Application.* (League of Nations Publication 1945, VI. A. 1.)

Lugard, F. D. *The Dual Mandate in British Tropical Africa.* Edinburgh: W. Blackwood and Sons. 1922.

Margalith, A. H. *The International Mandates.* Baltimore: Johns Hopkins Press. 1930.

McDonald, A. H. *Trusteeship in the Pacific.* Sydney: Nagus and Robertson. 1949.

Miller, David Hunter. *The Drafting of the Covenant.* 2 vols. New York, London: G. P. Putnam's Sons. 1928.

———. *My Diary at the Conference at Paris.* 22 vols. New York: printed for the author by the Appeal Printing Co. 1924-26.

Schwebel, Stephen M. *The Secretary-General of the United Nations: His Political Powers and Practice.* Cambridge: Harvard University Press. 1950.

Sisco, Joseph John. "The Soviet Attitude Toward the Trusteeship System." Unpublished doctoral dissertation, University of Chicago, 1951.

Stettinius, Edward R., Jr. *Roosevelt and the Russians.* Garden City, New York: Doubleday and Co. 1949.

Stimson, Henry L. and McGeorge Bundy. *On Active Service in Peace and War.* New York: Harper and Bros. 1948.

Temperley, H. W. V. *A History of the Peace Conference at Paris.* 6 vols. London: H. Frewde and Hedder and Stoughton. 1920-24.

Walker, Eric A. *Colonies.* Cambridge: Cambridge University Press. 1944.

Wright, Quincy. *Mandates Under the League.* Chicago: University of Chicago Press. 1930.

Articles

Armstrong, Elizabeth and William T. Cargo. "The Inauguration of the Trusteeship System of the United Nations," *Department of State Bulletin*, Vol. XVI (January-June, 1947), pp. 511-21.

Bunche, Ralph. "The Trusteeship System and Non-Self-Governing Territories in the Charter of the United Nations," *Department of State Bulletin*, Vol. XII (July-December, 1945), pp. 1037-44.

Commission to Study the Organization of Peace. "Colonial Aspects of the Post War Settlement," by Benjamin Gerig and others. *International Conciliation*, No. 379 (April, 1942), pp. 195-217.

Finkelstein, L. S. "Trusteeship in Action: The United Nations Mission to Western Samoa," *International Organization*, Vol. 2 (1948), pp. 268-82.

Gerig, Benjamin and Vernon McKay. "The Ewe Problem: A Case Study in the Operation of the Trusteeship Council," *Department of State Bulletin*, Vol. XXIV (January-June, 1951), pp. 120-37.

Gilchrist, Huntington. "Colonial Questions at the San Francisco Conference," *American Political Science Review*, Vol. XXXIX (1945), pp. 982-92.

Haas, Ernst B. "The Attempt to Terminate Colonialism: Acceptance of the United Nations Trusteeship System," *International Organization*, Vol. VII, No. 1 (February, 1953), pp. 1-21.

———. "The Reconciliation of Conflicting Colonial Policy Aims: Acceptance of the League of Nations Mandate System," *International Organization*, Vol. VI, No. 4 (November, 1952), pp. 521-36.

Haines, C. Grove. "The Problem of the Italian Colonies," *Middle East Journal*, Vol. I (1947), pp. 417-31.

"Half Way to Independence," *United Nations Review*, Vol. 1, No. 1 (July, 1954), pp. 46-58.

"The International Interest in Colonies," *Round Table* (London), No. 137 (December, 1944).

Lugard, F. D. "A World Colonial Charter," *The Times* (London), January 10, 1945.

McKay, Vernon. "International Trusteeship—Role of the United Nations in the Colonial World," *Foreign Policy Reports*, Vol. XXII.

"Meeting the Deadline for Independence," *United Nations Review*, Vol. 1, No. 3 (September, 1954), pp. 20-24.

"Nauru and the 60-Year Deadline," *United Nations Review*, Vol. 2, No. 2 (August, 1955), pp. 46-51.

"New Deal in the French Union," *The Economist* (London), March 31, 1956, p. 683.

"Plebescite Soon for Resolving Future of West African Trust Territory," *United Nations Review*, Vol. 2, No. 8 (February, 1956), pp. 14-25.

"Report of the King-Crane Commission," *Editor and Publisher*, Vol. LV (December 2, 1922), pp. 4-26.

Rivlin, Benjamin. "The Italian Colonies and the General Assembly," *International Organization*, Vol. 3 (1949), pp. 459-70.

Sayre, Francis B. "Legal Problems Arising from the United Nations Trusteeship System," *American Journal of International Law*, Vol. XLII (1948), pp. 693-99.

Stafford, F. E. "The Ex-Italian Colonies," *International Affairs*, Vol. XXV (1949), pp. 47-55.

"Visiting Mission Recommends Plebiscite to Resolve Future of British Togoland," *United Nations Review*, Vol. 2, No. 6 (December, 1955), pp. 33-37.

Documents

League of Nations

(Unless otherwise noted all League of Nations and United Nations documents are available from the International Documents Service of the Columbia University Press, New York.)

Assembly. *Records of the First Assembly, Plenary Meetings* (November-December, 1920).

Council. *Proces—Verbal of Council Sessions.* Eighth Session (July-August, 1920). Eleventh Session (November-December, 1920).

Official Journal. Vols. 3-8 (1922-27). The minutes of the first fifteen sessions of the Council were published separately. Thereafter they were published in the *Official Journal.*

Permanent Mandates Commission. *Minutes.* Seventh, Ninth, and Twelfth Sessions (1925-27).

United Nations

General Assembly. *Official Records of the General Assembly, Plenary Meetings.* First through Sixth Sessions (1946-51).

———. *First Committee.* Third Session, Part II (April-May, 1949), Fourth Session (September-December, 1949).

———. *Fourth Committee.* First through Sixth Sessions (1946-51).

———. *Resolutions.* First through Sixth Sessions (1946-51).

———. *Reports of the Trusteeship Council,* covering its First through Eleventh Regular Sessions, First through Fourth Special Sessions (1947-52).

Economic and Social Council. *Official Records.* Fourth Session (February-March, 1947), Fifth Session (July-August, 1947), Eleventh Session (July-September, 1950).

———. *Resolutions.* Eleventh Session (July-September, 1950), Thirteenth Session (July-September, 1951).

Preparatory Commission. *Executive Committee of the Preparatory Commission. Sub-Committee IV, Summary Reports.* (September-October, 1945). London: The Commission. 1945.

———. *Committee 4: Trusteeship. Summary Records.* Meetings 1-15 (November-December, 1945). London: Church House, Westminster. 1945.

———. *Journal* (November-December, 1945). London: Church House, Westminster. 1945.

———. *Report of the Executive Committee of the Preparatory Commission.* London: The Commission. 1945.

———. *Report of the Preparatory Commission.* London: The Commission. 1945.

Secretariat. *Organization of the Secretariat* (1951).

———. *The Question of Fortification and Volunteer Forces in Trusteeship Territories. Article 84.* (November 3, 1946).

Security Council. *Official Records.* Nos. 1-593 (1946-52).

Trusteeship Council. *Official Records.* First through the Eleventh Sessions. First through the Fourth Special Sessions. (1947-52).

———. *Resolutions.* First through Eleventh Sessions (1947-52).

———. *Rules of Procedure.* Revised, 1952.

———. *Supplements.* Fourth Session, Supplements 2 and 3 (Reports of the

Visiting Mission to East Africa on Ruanda-Urundi and Tanganyika). Seventh Session, Supplement 2 (Reports of the Visiting Mission to West Africa). Eighth Session, Supplements 2-5 (Reports of the Visiting Mission to the Pacific on the Trust Territory of the Pacific under the administration of the United States, Nauru, New Guinea, and Western Samoa).

Yearbook of the United Nations. 1946-47, 1947-48, 1948-49, 1950, 1951.

United Nations Conference on International Organizatons, Documents. 15 vols. New York: United Nations Information Organization in cooperation with the Library of Congress. 1945.

United States

A Decade of Foreign Policy, Senate Document No. 123, 81st Congress, 1st Session, p. 53.

Interim Arrangements Concluded by the Governments Represented at the United Nations Conference on International Organization, San Francisco, California, June 26, 1945. (State Department Publication No. 2357, 1945.)

Japanese Peace Conference. (State Department Publication No. 4392, International Organization and Conference Series II, Far Eastern 3. 1951.)

Post-War Foreign Policy Preparation. (State Department Publication No. 3580, General Foreign Policy Series 15. 1950.)

Treaties of Peace with Italy, Bulgaria, Hungary, Roumania and Finland. (State Department Publication No. 2743, European Series 21. 1947.)

The Treaty of Versailles and After, Annotation of the Text of the Treaty. (State Department Publication No. 2724, Conference Series 92. 1946.)

Bibliographical Note on Sessional Papers of the Trusteeship Council

Much of the documentary material on trusteeship is contained in sessional papers which are mimeographed, but, for the most part, are neither printed nor bound. The numbering of documents follows a definite pattern which makes it relatively easy to locate desired information. The following general description of the documents, while specifically relating to the Trusteeship Council, is generally true for other United Nations organs, with the corresponding change in symbol.

T/—. (In this case and hereinafter the dash (—) refers to a number, i.e., T/243.) These are general documents relating to trusteeship. They include such things as the observations of administering authorities on petitions during the first ten sessions of the Council, comments by members of the Fourth Committee on Reports of the Trusteeship Council, and various comments, observations, or proposals that Council members desire to present in written form. Broadly, they include everything related to the Trusteeship Council not otherwise provided for. Beginning with the eleventh session the observations of the administering authorities on petitions are issued under the designation T/Obs.—/—. These correspond to the petition designations.

T/SR.—. These are the summary records of the Council meetings, which eventually find their way into publication in the form of the Council's *Official Records.* In some instances these records are issued under a T/PV.— designation. This means that the Council debates are produced verbatim, rather than summarized. Verbatim minutes are taken at all sessions, but are not available outside of United Nations Headquarters in all cases. To date the First, Second, and Eleventh Sessions have been published as verbatim minutes, the others as summary records.

T/L.—. This designation applies to restricted documents which are for the most part proposed resolutions or amendments to resolutions. There is some ambiguity concerning the listing of proposals as T/ or T/L. documents, although most resolutions are designated the latter.

T/AC.—. This designation is used for the documentation of the Council's *ad hoc* committees, of which there have so far been forty-three. These committees may have their own summary records or L. documents corresponding to those of the Council. Thus the Committee on Italian Somaliland was designated T/AC.18. The summary records of that committee are listed as T/AC.18/SR.—, while proposals made to that committee are labeled T/AC.18/L.—.

T/Agreement—.This, as the designation shows, refers to the agreements bringing the territories under the trusteeship system. The agreement for the American trust territory is not included in this designation; it has, instead, a Security Council designation (S/318).

T/Pet.—/—. All petitions received by the Secretary-General are classified according to the territory concerned, and given the appropriate document number. All petitions from each territory are given the same Pet. number, as the following list shows:

- T/Pet. General/—: refers to petitions raising questions concerning all territories generally.
- T/Pet. 1/—: refers to all petitions concerning Western Samoa.
- T/Pet. 2/—: refers to all petitions concerning Tanganyika.
- T/Pet. 3/—: refers to all petitions concerning Ruanda-Urundi.
- T/Pet. 4/—: refers to all petitions concerning the Cameroons under British administration.
- T/Pet. 5/—: refers to all petitions concerning the Cameroons under French administration.
- T/Pet. 6/—: refers to all petitions concerning Togoland under British administration.
- T/Pet. 7/—: refers to all petitions concerning Togoland under French administration.
- T/Pet. 8/—: refers to all petitions concerning New Guinea.
- T/Pet. 9/—: refers to all petitions concerning Nauru.
- T/Pet. 10/—: refers to all petitions concerning the Trust Territory of the Pacific under American administration.
- T/Pet. 11/—: refers to all petitions concerning Somaliland.

Since the creation of the Standing Committee on Petitions, those petitions raising general questions which the Council considers in the course of its examination of annual reports and the reports of visiting missions, as well as those submitted for information purposes only, are circulated under the designation T/Com.—/—.

T/C.— The designation applies to the standing committees of the Council of which there are two at present. T/C.1 refers to the Committee on Administrative Unions; T/C.2 refers to the Committee on Petitions. As with the *ad hoc* committees, each of the standing committees may have its own SR or L. documents.

Index